THE LEGAL AID LAWYER

Mel Eichelbaum

Copyright © 2019 by Mel Eichelbaum

All rights reserved

This book or any portion thereof may not be reproduced or used in any manner whatsoever without the express written permission of the author, Mel Eichelbaum, or his duly designated agent or representative, except for the use of brief quotations in a book review.

Printed in the United States of America

First Printing, 2019

Print ISBN: 978-1-54397-553-6

eBook ISBN: 978-1-54397-554-3

Published by: BookBaby, 7905 N. Crescent Blvd., Pennsauken, NJ 08110

DISCLAIMER:
Some names and identifying details have been changed to protect the privacy of individuals.

I have tried to recreate events, locales and conversations from my memories of them. In order to protect anonymity, I may have changed some identifying characteristics and details such as physical properties, occupations and places of residence.

CREDITS:

Many individuals have helped me in writing this book, and I owe a great deal of gratitude to all of them. I have attempted to name many of the individuals who have contributed and helped, and references to these individuals are contained in the "Acknowledgements and Sources of Information" at the end of this book.

For inquires or information, the author may be contacted at:
melneichelbaum@gmail.com

ENDORSEMENT:

As a former probate consultant to county judges and a retired Constitutional elected District Clerk, I have personal knowledge of the real stories written in this book. Mel writes from his personal experiences having been a Legal Aid lawyer being deeply involved in poverty law, as well as a prominent trial attorney. Mel is what I refer and call a legal crusader. A Don Quixote no, Mel is a real hero with a passion for the law. His approach to legal issues was dynamic when addressing the concerns of persons in financial despair and those who were disadvantaged. This book produces a powerful tool for those seeking the strength and inspiration to fight for justice.

David J. Garcia

FORWARD

This book was written by my father. I am incredibly proud of him for deciding to share with you this story, and I am happy that you are taking the opportunity to read about his experiences. There are several stories my father could have chosen to write. He could have shared his insight on being a father and that, by itself, would have been an insightful journey. When I was a young boy, my mother became gravely ill with double kidney failure and was given a terminal prognosis. My father managed to comfort and support my mom, while at the same time caring for myself and my younger brother, maintaining our home environment, and practicing law as a partner of one of the largest firms in San Antonio at that time. To this day I am not sure how he managed. I suspect there were moments of difficulty and doubt, challenging his strong ethical core and faith in God. Through nothing less than a medical miracle, my mother regained function in her kidneys, and eventually recovered.

As a father of two children, I have tried to emulate my Dad and serve in many roles at a time. I have learned that even though a person can have several titles and responsibilities, we each elect what level of participation and responsibility we accept. My father took each challenge with incredible energy and gusto. Early on, he was my Cub Scout leader, religious school teacher, and basketball coach. He was the artist that decorated my bedroom with pictures of sesame street characters and then later super heroes. He was a mediator between me and my brother and was also the authoritarian, when necessary. Later, he would drive me to camps and to play practices. He was there in middle school when I secured my first acting job as a puppeteer for the city public transportation system. He congratulated me, and I will always remember that moment. I will also always remember the moment just a few months later when I felt my first relationship heart break, and he was there with wisdom and then silence when I needed it. He was my tutor, editor, and spellchecker. He was my idea man and manager.

As I entered my teen years, he was an advisor. My dad would give advice, much of which I did not appreciate at the time it was given. Moreover, I was not hesitant to tell my father that I did not need his advice or that his opinion was not relevant or correct. However, he was still present and active in sharing his opinions. So many years later, I would tell him that he was right more often than not and that I would have had some easier times had I listened to his advice more often. Along the way, he too advised me that he was not perfect and that there were times that his advice was wrong and that he had made mistakes. Humility is probably one of my father's greatest gifts.

There is a defining moment where I can recall the transition from an adult and child relationship with my father to that of two adult men. This relationship is different. However, my admiration and respect for my father is the same. In fact, it may have become deeper with this second act in our combined lives. I chose to go to law school and then to work with my father at his firm. These decisions were independent of his direction, but certainly made with his astute insight and influence. Here is just one more life lesson shared by my father. It is easy to give advice, but it is much more challenging to be supportive. I am a deeply religious person and just as I thank God for the recovery of my mother mentioned above; I believe there was Divine intervention that directed my selection of law, which provided me the opportunity to work daily with my father for over a decade before his retirement. It was through the perspective of a law student and then a practicing attorney that I was reintroduced to my father. I had always known him only in the roles discussed above and perceived him through the tainted glasses of my dad. However, sitting in a Family Law class and reading cases which I had heard discussed informally at my living room table gave me a new and very different understanding of my father. As a young child, I had gone to work with my father on numerous occasions. I carried his briefcase in court and shook hands politely with several Judges, Attorneys, and people of influence. I sat underneath the Municipal Court bench during trials and drew pictures in my father's office. At the time,

I was not old enough to comprehend the work being done by my father and the influence he was having on our legal system. This wisdom came afterwards, as client upon client would walk into our office and share their appreciation for the work completed by my father. My father has changed the lives of so many individuals.

My father was a very hard worker and, as mentioned before, was very humble about his accomplishments. I recall a number of awards my father received throughout his legal career. He displayed two very prominently. The first was a school bell award given to him for an outstanding newspaper editorial supporting teachers in the state of Texas. The second was the inaugural award for Pro Bono services granted by the Bankruptcy section of the State Bar of Texas. From a practice comparison, the awards were very different. However, both awards acknowledged the need for community service and commitment to change the world in a way that not all people are willing to do. My father proudly, and often, put himself out on the line, took an unpopular position, and then worked hard to help others.

After my Father's retirement, he has continued to serve as an example and model to me in new and unexpected ways. He is an excellent grandfather. He has altered his physical life, quitting smoking and becoming a lifetime member of Weight Watchers. He has discovered new ways to fill his time and enjoy life and appreciate each day. He still gives great advice, and as I sit here revising this Foreword, I am already thinking about the introduction I will provide him when he comes to speak at my Family Law class at St. Mary's University School of Law next week.

There are still so many things I would like to say about my father and that I would like you to know as you begin this book. They don't fit neatly into any other portion of this introduction, so I will mention them here. My father likes movies and novels. He is a historian. He enjoys trivia and can identify over 100 Scottish plaids. He does not like to travel but puts up with it because it makes my mom happy. He gets frustrated when he gets interrupted but doesn't mind interrupting others when he has something he wants to say. This used to bother me greatly, but I have learned that he has so much he wants to share and to tell people, and the fact of the matter is that he is really good at it.

With everything that I have to say about my father and all of the roles he has played in my life, it is hard to deliver a summary statement, but I am going to try. The reason I love and respect my father so much and the reason you will enjoy this book is because my father is an amazing storyteller.

Being a good storyteller is not a simple task. Many people dedicate their entire lives to perfecting presentations and editing articles in order to attempt to share their lessons and experiences. Some people are blessed with good material to work with. Just like an athlete is born with natural ability, certain strength, or height, a good storyteller will have the natural advantage of pulling from many adventures to fill their narratives. However, an athlete is unable to reach success based solely on physical traits. They must work diligently on perfecting his or her sport, pouring tireless hours into making the difficult look ordinary. Similarly, a storyteller may have interesting experiences or sage advice, but it will not be entertaining if the storyteller does not deliver the information the correct way. A storyteller uses narration to bring the audience into the story and creates a deep and full environment for the story. With well-fleshed characters, both heroes and villains, a storyteller creates syntax, establishes the environment, and hopefully, provides entertainment with the precise combination of wit, irony, and suspense.

As a child my father would spend hours creating narratives, sometimes with the help of my action figures and other toys, and sometimes through his detailed imagery of characters and plots. My Father's stories were always entertaining. They also most often followed a formula that established an important lesson. The main characters would always find themselves with an opportunity for adventure. Early in the story, my father would often ask if the heroes should pursue these quests. I remember one time suggesting that the hero of a particular story should not accept the challenge and not go on an adventure. That was the shortest story my father ever told me, and I learned very early that declining a challenge was an option, but one that led to a short, predictable (and boring) conclusion.

The second part of my Father's stories always involved explanation as to why the hero would select a quest. Oftentimes his stories had people (or mystical animals) who were suffering hardships and difficulties. The story felt familiar, and I recall trying to guess where my Father was borrowing this storyline from. Could it be his interpretation of a science fiction movie where the Rebellion was in need of assistance, or was it him retelling the narrative of children passing through a closet to rescue a strange land enchanted with darkness and despair? Perhaps this was my Father sharing his favorite Holiday story; that of the rescue of the Israelites by a former Egyptian Prince. Much later I realized that these were all good guesses, but that in actuality, my Father's ongoing lesson of fighting for others came directly from his day to day experiences as a lawyer and from the stories you are about to read. My Father worked hard to help others. He selected to go on the adventure and to fight for the benefit of others. Sometimes, these challenges only impacted an individual or a single family; other times, his expedition would impact thousands now and in the future.

His goal is two-part. First, to show his audience that there is great benefit which comes from choosing the more difficult path and fighting for what is right on behalf of others. Of course, there are sacrifices that come from these challenges. My father spent many long hours working on cases that did not go his way. However, as you can see from this story you are about to read, his pride and his accomplishment is derived only through choosing to engage in these challenges. The second goal of this book is to serve as a role model and to lead by example. The heroes in the childhood stories told by my father found success by helping others, and, similarly, so did my father in his practice.

It is my hope that you enjoy this book and you get to see a glimpse of the inspiring man who is my father and hero. Additionally, I hope you, as a reader, learn from my father's stories and experiences. With this insight, I challenge you to take on the next task and decide to volunteer and help

{ V

others in your community. Most importantly, I hope you share that experience with someone else and then lead them by your example to assist even more people, the same way my father has done for most of his life. It is by not only working hard, but by sharing the inspiration with others that there is meaningful improvement to our neighborhoods and cities.

    Rob Eichelbaum

TABLE OF CONTENT

1 A Time of Tragedy and a Time of Hope 1
2 Our Journey South and Traveling the Texas Trail 13
3 The Alamo City 22
4 The Politics and the Peregrinus 33
5 What Were the Odds? 48
6 My Fort Dix Adventure 66
7 My Dream Job Begins 77
8 The Texas Welfare Wars 98
9 A Drive to the Top 124
10 Ten and a Half Months to Home 148
11 You're in the Book 169
12 So Why Can't Girls Wear Pants? 182
13 The Amicus Curiae 198
14 A Grandparent's Dilemma 214
15 Who Will Speak for the Disabled 227
16 Sometimes a Loss Becomes a Win 239
17 We're Going to New Orleans 249
18 Food for Thought 266
19 A Child's a Child, No Matter How Born 284
20 Transitions 316
21 My Last Hurrah 337
22 Acknowledgements and Sources of Information 370

CHAPTER 1

A Time of Tragedy and a Time of Hope

November, 1963

It was a typical, mild mid-November Thursday, as I sat at the dining table in my parent's apartment on Club Drive. Thanksgiving was just right around the corner, but before then I had a lot of work to do. Books and papers were strewn all over, as I nervously fidgeted with a pencil, trying to solve one of Brother John Malinchak's sample problems that I was pretty sure would be on the mid-term exam scheduled for tomorrow. It was the first semester of my senior year in college at St. Mary's University. I was majoring in accounting, with a double minor in business administration and economics. Brother Malinchak had a well-deserved reputation of being a really hard teacher, and the mid-term exam would count as a significant part of my final grade. So the pressure was on. I had no other choice but to study and study hard, if I was going to even have a chance at making it. I was in a rather glum mood, feeling a bit sorry for myself, as my mind temporarily drifted to the phone call that I received last night.

"Hey Mel, this is Henry." "Oh, hi Henry, what's up?" I replied. "Well you know President Kennedy will be landing in San Antonio tomorrow, and I thought we would get a small delegation of St. Mary's Young Democrats to be on hand to meet and greet him. Me, Tom and a couple of others are going, and we wanted you to be included, if you can make it." I paused, and

{ 1 }

boy was I tempted, but practicality got the better of me, as I responded. "Man I would really like to, but I got this tough accounting exam on Friday, and I'm afraid that I will be studying my ass off all day tomorrow, so I better pass." "Okay Mel, I understand. Good luck on your exam buddy, and we'll see you some other time", said Henry, as our phone conversation ended.

I first met Henry while I was attending San Antonio College (SAC), a junior college, during my freshman year (1960--1961). Professor John D. Brantley, our English Literary teacher had asked me to help tutor him, which I did. As "Gonzalez" is a rather common sur-name in San Antonio, I had no idea who he was. It wasn't until then that I discovered that this Henry, Jr. was the son of the Henry B. Gonzalez, then a Texas state Senator, serving at the Capitol in Austin. During that time, my Sociology professor emphasized that good grades, although most important, would not be enough. Major universities would be looking for well-rounded students when considering transfers from junior colleges like SAC. So he recommended that we consider joining at least one or two clubs or organizations and make an effort to engage in some extra-curricular college activity. At that time, Henry, Jr. was forming the SAC chapter of the Young Democrats, and he asked me to join. I agreed because I felt it would look good on my transcript. Henry ended up becoming the president, and somehow I managed to get elected as vice president. We worked well together and ended up building a fairly good organization.

In 1961, there was a vacancy for the 20th congressional district in San Antonio for the U.S. House of Representatives. Although no one of Mexican-American ancestry had ever been elected before in the state of Texas to a federal office, Henry B. decided he would try. After some discussion, he designated Henry, Jr., Tom Harrell, and me to head up the youth support organization for his campaign. We visited all of the colleges in San Antonio and met with various youth leaders in quite a few of the high schools, as well. We put together a rather enthusiastic group of volunteers, who helped pass out bumper stickers and campaign literature, and on Election Day, helped man the phones, worked the poles, and served as messengers, scurrying from headquarters to varying polling places and back. The vote count ended up being the highest ever recorded for that district up to that time. Despite a strong Republican opponent (John Gould) and being outspent, Henry B. won and made history, being the very first Mexican-American to be elected to national office from the state of Texas. Afterwards, Henry B. gratefully thanked us and stated what a fine job we had done in organizing the youth campaign for him. He said some day he would like for us to come to Washington D.C. for a visit. I congratulated him, thanked him for the kind invite, and then dismissed it out of hand, without any further thought.

By the end of May, 1962, I completed my first two years of college at SAC. That Fall I had transferred to St. Mary's to complete my undergraduate degree. While there, although I remained a member of the Young Democrats, I became less active. I was carrying a full academic load, and the courses had become harder and more time consuming. In addition, at times I was working as many as three jobs. My parents were not wealthy, and they were kind enough to let me continue to live at home, furnishing me with board and room. However, it was understood that the cost of college was my responsibility and solely on me. Working was no option. I had to work in order to earn enough to pay for tuition, books and fees, as well as to cover expenses so as to have at least some social life. After all, dating did cost money too. So two or three afternoons a week I worked as a staff accountant for the Fox Photofinishing Co. at their headquarters on Broadway. Then on Saturdays and also on special sale days, I worked as a ladies' shoe salesman at Bakers shoe store at Wonderland Mall. On occasion, I was also hired as a tutor to help students who were having trouble with some of the more difficult classes, like Professor George Costus' Statistics class, which was known as a "killer course".

My mind continued to drift, as I thought back to the early part of 1963, when I received a phone call from Henry. "Hey Mel, Henry here, how the hell are you?" It had been a while since I had heard from him, so I replied "I'm doing okay. It's been a while man, and so what's going on with you?" Henry's voice seemed to be getting excited as he said, "You know spring break is coming up pretty soon, and I've got a surprise for you buddy. You're going to Washington D.C." "What the hell…" I exclaimed, as Henry continued, "Yep, it's all been arranged. Dad wants me to drive his car up to D.C. for him, and he wants you and Tom Harrell to join me on the trip." Henry then proceeded to explain that we would use that first weekend to make the some 1400 mile drive up, spending the Monday through Friday of spring break week in D.C. We would then fly back the following Saturday, giving us Sunday to rest up and prepare for resuming classes on Monday. It sounded great, but then I got practical. This was the second semester of the school year, and my reserves were getting close, where I had to kind of watch every penny, until the summer hit. Then I could work full time in order to build up funds again that would be adequate for beginning the fall semester of the next school year. "It sounds great Henry, but you know figuring the cost of hotels, food, and airfare back, I just can't afford all of that right now." Henry went on to explain that there really wouldn't be any hotel cost as we would be staying in his Dad's apartment in D.C. As far as food expenses, he anticipated that there would be some minimum cost going up, but that once in D.C., if he knew his Dad, he figured most of the meals would be on him. "Oh and by the way," he continued, "Dad has decided that he will be paying for the flight back for all of us, out of his own pocket." "Oh come on. You've got to be kidding," I said in disbelief. "Nope," Henry stated, "Mel, you know Dad well enough that once he makes up his mind there is no arguing with him, and this is something he really wants to do. You're coming along buddy. Besides, I need you to help do the driving. Tom doesn't drive, you know." I graciously accepted and thanked him and told him to thank his Dad for me. Before our conversation ended, he reminded me to bring a coat and tie because we were scheduled to meet with President Kennedy and of course there would be pictures taken. I was excited, to say the least, as I explained all of this to my parents, and began to think of what to pack.

It never snows in San Antonio, well that March it did. So much that snow had actually stuck to the ground, and icy remnants were piled up along the sides of the roads. In fact snow flurries had been prevalent throughout the entire south, up to and including D.C. Undaunted, we stashed our luggage in the trunk and piled into the white Chevy to begin our journey. Henry and I shared the chore of driving, with each one of us doing several hours' worth, while the other one of us rested or slept in the back seat. Tom sat shotgun and played navigator, keeping whoever was driving company and furnishing coffee and chit-chat, as we proceeded along. We continued this way, stopping only for gas, meals, and bathroom breaks. Henry was anxious to get through the south—what he called "Klan country," and he voiced being a bit concerned about "a Mexican, a Jew, and a Yankee Irishman" being pulled over and stopped. With all that had been happening regarding the civil rights movement and vicious racist and reactionary responses to it, none of us thought his concerns were completely off the wall. However, our trip was without incident, except for the frightening experience of cautiously maneuvering through Lookout Mountain, Tennessee, in the dark and during what seemed like a mini blizzard. Somehow we made it, and the following morning, we were peaceably passing through the beautiful Shenandoah Valley in Virginia, where we stopped for a well-deserved, good old fashion southern breakfast. We finally arrived in Washington D.C. that afternoon, and after getting settled and grabbing a quick bite to eat, we crashed, sleeping through until late the following morning.

When we finally did wake up, we got dressed, ate a quick breakfast, and headed over to Henry B.'s congressional office. It was much smaller than what I had originally imagined it would be. We sat down in visitor chairs in front of a rather ordinary mahogany-colored office desk, behind which sat Henry B. He took the time to officially welcome us and tell us how happy he was that we came. He gave us a rough outline of our itinerary, and told us that his staff would furnish us with the details. Behind him were massive bookshelves, covering nearly the entire wall, just crammed full of books, some of which I recognized as literary works that we covered in Professor Brantley's English lit class at SAC. Tom asked Henry B. if he had actually read all of them. Henry B. just looked at Tom, and with a smile said, "As a matter of fact, I have, and most of them more than once." I could just sense that he really had, and I felt a strong feeling of admiration for him. We then met with his secretary, Gail Chapel, and his legislative assistant, Steve Newman, who I previously had met through his younger sister, Susan. She and I had been fellow members of the San Antonio Federation of Temple Youth (SAFTY) at Temple Beth-El. Both of our families belonged to that congregation. Gail and Steve detailed our schedule, which was chucked full of activities and interesting things to see. Needless to say, we were all excited with anticipation of all the neat things that we were going to get to do. That afternoon we saw the Declaration of Independence and the United States Constitution. Although I had seen replicas and pictures of them many times before, there was still that sense of patriotic pride in actually seeing the originals. That night Henry B. took us to see the movie, *Billy Budd*, which was adapted from a stage play version of Herman Melville's short novel by the same name. Terrance Stamp played the tragic role of the child-like natured seaman Billy, while Robert Ryan portrayed the abusive and cruel Master of Arms Claggart. Both gave outstanding performances, along with Peter Ustinov, who played the troubled Captain Vere, torn about what to do when Billy ended up unintendedly killing Claggart. Afterwards we went to a restaurant and ate Chinese food, while we discussed the moral dilemmas presented by the film. The following days we were up at the crack of dawn, so as to get a quick start in order to complete our busy daily schedule. But no matter how early we arose, Henry B. had already left for work. That week in D.C. taught me that he was a dedicated, well-educated, and very hard-working Congressman, but of course I already suspected that. San Antonio was indeed fortunate to have him, and I wondered if the people back home really knew just how lucky they were.

I think we saw every single Washington D.C. monument there was to see, and of course, we saw the changing of the guard at the tomb of the Unknown Soldier at the Arlington Cemetery. We saw a whole host of different museums, spending nearly an entire day at the Smithsonian. Naturally, we visited Congress, and while at the Senate, we saw Senator Strom Thurman actually giving a speech, while wearing a vest, depicting the confederate stars and bars, under his unbuttoned suit jacket. We also got to see the U.S. House of Representatives in session, and afterwards, we had a chance to eat lunch with Henry B., and several other Congressmen at the congressional cafeteria. We visited the U.S. Supreme Court, and little did I realize then that there would come a day when I would actually have some cases before that august body. When we visited the White House, we had a special appointment to meet with President Kennedy; however, at the last minute, something important came up for him, so that our meeting with him had to be cancelled. As a consolation prize, I suppose, we were scheduled to meet with Vice President, Lyndon B. Johnson, instead. When we met with him, he was extremely friendly and gracious. He actually took time to talk to us, and he appeared to be genuinely interested in hearing our views on a whole range of political issues. Afterwards, I was thankful that I had the opportunity to meet and spend some time with him. One of the highlights was when we accompanied Henry B. to the TV studio, where he filmed his weekly Washington D.C. news show, and we were going to be on it with him. It was aired on local television on Sunday mornings, so that the folks back home could be informed as to what was happening at the Capitol. Never having been on TV before, I was rather excited, as we briefly went over what we were going to discuss. Then "lights, camera, action," and it happened. It was over before I knew it. I was intrigued by the fact that my parents and I would get to see the interview and discussion on TV together on Sunday, after I got home. All in all, it was truly a fabulous trip.

Suddenly, my mind snapped back to reality. Enough already with the daydreaming and reminiscing, I thought. Okay, so I missed meeting President Kennedy once, and now this was twice. "Que sera, sera" I told myself, and it was time to get back to business. I stared intently at the paper in front of me, as I tried concentrating further on Brother Malinchak's problem, which I found to be more than difficult.

Finally, it was Friday, November 22, 1963. The date of the dreaded mid-term exam was upon me. A cold front must have come in the previous night, because temperatures had dipped below freezing. I found myself struggling to scrape the ice off the windows of my VW Beetle before driving to St. Mary's. As if that wasn't enough of a bad omen, on the way I got a speeding ticket, my very first one, while doing 33 miles per hour. I guess I was just oblivious to the school zone sign, which in truth was half covered by tree branches. No excuse, I thought, I had driven past there a hundred times, and I knew better. It was clearly my fault. By the time I got to St. Mary's I was a nervous wreck. I grabbed a quick cup of coffee, which curiously had the effect of calming me down. I reported to Brother Malinchak's class, took my seat, and settled down for the inevitable. Brother Malinchak arrived right on time. He passed out the exams, told us to get started, and took a seat at his desk in the front to monitor the test, as he always did. I started, and as I progressed, I wasn't feeling so bad about it. In fact, I felt I was doing reasonably well. Perhaps all of my studying had done some good after all. I think I was over half way through, when I heard a loud commotion outside. Suddenly the door of our classroom flew wide open, and a student excitedly yelled "They shot Kennedy." Everyone froze in shock, and someone muttered "that's nothing to kid around about." The student at the door emphatically repeated "Really, no fooling, they just shot the President." Brother Malinchak immediately took control. He was as white as a ghost, and I had never seen him so shaken. I vaguely recall him saying something like for those of you who want to continue, you can do so. For those of you who would rather not, you're excused, and there will be a makeup scheduled at a later date. Not a sole remained, as everyone quickly left and headed over to the student center. There we all stared at the news on TV, until Walter Cronkite, wiping a tear from his eye, announced that President Kennedy was dead. You could literally feel the amount of despondence and melancholy in the room. It was a miserable drive back home, as I contended with feelings that were a strange mixture of anger and sadness. For the next couple of days, like most Americans, I found myself transfixed to the TV watching, half way in disbelief, and mesmerized by the events unfolding.

During the next few days, several places of worship, including Temple Beth-El, opened their doors to the public so that people would have a place to go in order to seek solace, pray, or just to contemplate. In the midst of my depression, I found myself being drawn to Temple Beth-El. As I entered the sanctuary, I walked down the center aisle, toward the ark where the Torah scrolls are kept. When I reached about the seventh row, I spotted a prayer book that had been left in the pew. I took a seat there and started to restlessly thumb through the prayer book. I finally found the *Mourner's Kaddish*, a special prayer that is recited by the congregation in honor of those who have died. I wasn't even sure if it was appropriate for me to say it alone, because traditionally one needs a minion of ten people to recite the prayer. Regardless, I felt compelled, and I struggled through the Hebrew and said the prayer for President Kennedy anyhow. I then mumbled some prayers for Jackie, Caroline and John-John and hoped that God would grant them some comfort and peace. After that, I didn't know what else to do, so I just began staring at the eternal light, the ark, and the words carved above it: "Thou shalt love thy neighbor as thyself." Like in a hypnotic state those words and the words of our traditional Yom Kippur *Haftarah* reading (*Isaiah* 58; 1-14): "Is not this the fast I look for: to unlock the shackles of injustice, to undo the fetters of bondage…and to break every cruel chain?" kept swimming around in my head. These words went on to challenge us Jews to help the hungry, the homeless, and the poor. In my mind that then connected with the words of President Kennedy: "…ask not what your country can do for you, but rather what you can do for your country."

I don't know how long I sat there, but it seemed like forever. Finally, an idea began to formulate in my head. I would go to law school and become a lawyer, with the goal of helping the poor and oppressed. Almost in a dream-like state, my mind began to wander and my thoughts flew back to my days at Horace Mann Junior High School. I recalled how Mr. Brantley, who taught English Literature there, had covered the *Devil and Daniel Webster,* and how I was entranced with the concept of a lawyer. In fact, that is where I experienced my very first case. In Civics class a fellow student, Ann Eisenstein, was charged by our class Sergeant of Arms with talking out of turn. Our teacher thought it would be a good experience to have a class trial. A student was selected as Judge, and twelve classmates were picked to serve on the jury. Somehow, I got chosen to serve as her defense counsel, while Charles Woods, a much smarter kid than me, was selected as the prosecutor. I did my best "Perry Mason" job in questioning and cross-examining witnesses, but evidently it wasn't good enough. I lost, and Ann was found "guilty". However, she was given a rather light punishment, not because anything I had done, but because she was a very likeable and popular girl at school. After the trial, she thanked me, and gave me a kiss. It was the very first time ever that I had been kissed by a girl, who wasn't a family member or related to me.

During my high school years at Thomas Jefferson, my friend Louis Paletz, who always wanted to be a lawyer, lent me a book about the life story of Clarence Darrow. He was a famous attorney in the 1920s & 30s, who often represented the disadvantaged, underprivileged, downtrodden, and politically unpopular. Often he would represent labor folks against rich and powerful interests. I was especially inspired by the story of how in 1925 he partnered with the American Civil Liberties Union (ACLU) in representing John Thomas Scopes, a teacher, in *Tennessee v. Scopes,* commonly referred to as the "Scopes monkey trial." The case challenged the state's Butler Act, which banned the teaching of evolution in the public schools. It was probably one of the most significant cases of the 20th century. Although at trial the case was technically lost, the ultimate result was far reaching. The Butler Act was never again enforced, and similar laws prohibiting the teaching of evolution were defeated in 22 other states. The

ACLU gained a national reputation as a stalwart defender of civil liberties. This ended up being the basis of one of my English class reports, on which I made an "A". Later on the case became the theme for the famous movie *Inherit the Wind,* starring Spencer Tracey, a movie whose message would still be relevant today. So why didn't I think of becoming a lawyer before. Perhaps it was because I didn't have the confidence that I could do it, or maybe it was the fact that it would be another three and a half years of higher education and the additional costs that would involve, or both. But now I felt a compulsion that I needed to at least try. Yes indeed, I really wanted to become a lawyer, who could make a difference, and I was more resolved than ever to do so. Could it be that the tragedy of President Kennedy's death ended up in aiding to shape me by instilling hope in my heart and a firm commitment in my mind that I could actually accomplish this?

As I drove home, I began to think of how I was going to break the news to my parents about going to law school and explain to them about my new career goal. I just knew that I would be getting a ton of questions about why am I changing plans all of a sudden? And how in the world did I plan to handle all the extra expenses? And what makes me think that I could even get into law school, in the first place. This is not going to be easy I thought. When I arrived home, I told my father that we needed to have a talk. We sat on the steps at the back door, which was adjacent to the kitchen, each sipping a cup of coffee. I took a deep breath and then calmly explained how I wanted to go to law school to become a lawyer, and why. When I had finished, I anxiously awaited for his response. Dad looked me straight in the eyes, and said "Mel, I think you should go for it." Evidently, he clearly approved and that was all I needed to hear. To satisfy Mom, I did promise her that I would go ahead and finish up my accounting degree and graduate first, before starting law school. She was concerned about what if I couldn't get into law school or couldn't make it through. "Don't you think you need something to fall back on, just in case?" she asked. "Sure", I said

"You're right of course." But even when I said that, I felt a confident resolve that there would be no stopping me.

CHAPTER 2

Our Journey South and Traveling the Texas Trail

1942 – 1954

I was born in New York City, approximately nine months after Pearl Harbor and the U.S. entry into World War II. We lived in the Bronx borough in a small flat on the third floor of a brownstone apartment building, located near the intersection of Tremont and Vise Avenue. It was near a subway entrance and three blocks from the Bronx zoo. Although my father, Milton, had very little formal education, never having gone to high school; nevertheless, he seemed to possess a reservoir of wisdom, picked up through "the school of hard knocks" of the city streets and truly tough life experiences while growing up. Despite all of that, he was rather well read and fairly cultured, having a deep appreciation for classical music and opera. Dad was a cop in the New York City police force, whose beat was in the Harlem area of the city. My Mom, Pauline, had graduated from high school, but after marrying Dad, she sought to go no further in school and became a housewife and a mother, dedicated to hovering over me. I was a little, skinny kid, who tended to be somewhat sickly. My parents were always very concerned about my health. According to my Mom, the doctor had assured her that I would likely remain a rather small and frail person for the rest of my life. Boy did he turn out to be wrong.

In the same building lived my Uncle Oscar, who was a Taxi cab driver, and my Aunt Mary, a rather large woman, who was also a housewife. They had one child, my Cousin Marilyn, who was a young teenager then. She seemed to enjoy spending time with me, reading me fairy tales while babysitting, during evenings when our parents got together to play cards. In the building also lived my friend, Steve, who was my age, and my very first girlfriend, Sheila, who was a couple of years older than me and who had red hair that she typically wore in pigtails. On occasion, Cousin Marilyn would take the whole gang of us to the zoo, where we would spend most of the day. We weren't wealthy and times were simpler then, but it was a pleasant childhood. In the summer, our families would go to Jones Beach or Coney Island, and every once in a while, Dad would actually take me to see a baseball game at Yankee stadium. In the winter, I can recall seeing the giant Christmas tree at Rockefeller Center, and watching the graceful ice-skaters as they magically performed to perfection. One of my fondest childhood memories is when my Mom and Cousin Marilyn took me to the Macy's Thanksgiving Day parade. I remember marveling at the floats, the marching bands, the precision dancing Rockettes, and especially the giant balloons. And of course being a little kid, the anticipation and excitement built when Santa Claus and his sleigh arrived at the end. I recall standing in line to see Santa at Macy's, and how frightened I was to actually go up to talk with him. I was so scared; I don't think I had much to say. Although I was born Jewish, circumcised, and had a *bris*, during my childhood years I was raised in a rather secular fashion. I was probably more familiar with "Christianity", or at least the secular side of it, and Santa Claus and the Easter Bunny were very big deals.

Aside from playing games, the chief source of home entertainment was listening to the radio. Dad and Oscar enjoyed listening to baseball games and the opera; whereas, Mary was particularly keen about the boxing matches, on which I believe she wagered. She had a reputation of being a gambler and just loved going to the race track. According to everyone, she had a real knack for picking winning horses. Naturally, we all listened to the news and the fireside chats of Franklin Delano Roosevelt. Not that I understood anything he said, but I kind of remember his voice and the calm strength and reassuring nature that it seemed to have. As a kid of course, I was more interested in programs like *The Lone Ranger* and *The Shadow*. On rare occasion, Mom and Cousin Marilyn would take me to see a movie. My very first experience was seeing Walt Disney's *Bambi*, and I cried up a storm when Bambi's mother got shot and died. It really had an effect on me. The other movie I recollect seeing was *The Jazz Singer*, starring Al Jolson. This was my first experience of seeing a white man dressing up in black face in order to imitate being a black man, and my wondering why. I recall asking my Mom about it and being told that it was merely part of the costume and performance, and how some actors just did that type of thing. I was only a kid of course and was absolutely clueless as to any racial implication or significance, yet I seemed to have sensed a somewhat uncomfortable tenseness in her voice, which I didn't understand and which left me with a slight unsatisfied feeling that I couldn't quite explain.

Sometime afterwards there was an incident where Dad had successfully disarmed and arrested a knife-wielding man who was attempting to break into a business. During the scuffle, Dad was slightly wounded, with his arm being cut by the man's knife. Dad never thought it was all that significant, and he certainly healed up just fine, even though he carried a small scar where the knife had cut him. Even so, I think that began Mom's campaign that Dad should be doing something other than being a cop. The war had ended by then, and Dad thought that with all the veterans returning home, they were likely to be given preference as to employment and advancement. That situation, combined with the fact that he had never graduated from high school, made it very unlikely that he would ever be promoted and be able to achieve the rank of sergeant. As fine a cop as he was, it appeared as if this was going to be a "dead end" job, with him remaining frozen at his current level and pay status. At about that time, Dad was contacted by my Uncle Martin. He and his wife, Elizabeth, were operating a very popular and successful deli restaurant in Detroit called

"The Bagel". Evidently a nearby bakery had become available for sale, and there was an opportunity to acquire it. Martin figured that such a bakery could provide their restaurant with all the breads, bagels, and baked goods that were needed. Moreover, he felt that if ownership stayed in the family, it could assure him of a reliable and steady source of product at reasonable and controlled prices. He knew that Dad had experience and worked as a baker when he was younger. Meanwhile, My Uncle Irv had just gotten out of the military. He had served in the Army as a Major and was an accountant. Martin thought that with Dad's baking experience and being able to handle production and with Irv's accounting background and being able to handle the business aspect, it would make for a good partnership. The restaurant, itself, would provide enough of a demand for the baked goods produced, whereby Dad and Irv could make a fairly good living by operating the bakery. And anything else they sold over that would be gravy. It would be a win-win situation, all the way around. Dad and Irv agreed, and so a deal was cut. Martin funded the buying of the bakery. Dad and Irv went into partnership. And off to Detroit we went. But before we moved, my childhood took an abrupt change in that I was no longer the center of attention. My sister, Sandy, was born and joined our family. I was the "big brother" now, and it would take me into my young adult years to really learn how to properly play that role.

In Detroit Uncle Martin's scheme worked like a charm. The little, neighborhood bakery thrived, and "The Bagel" continued to be wonderfully successful. My parents bought a small, red brick house, which had a lovely, extensive flower garden, and which was located within a couple blocks from the elementary school that I would attend. I apprehensively began my school career and in the early years, became nothing more than a rather mediocre student. We had the first TV in the neighborhood, which was black and white and no bigger than a ship's porthole, but after school, the neighborhood kids often came over to watch *Howdy Doody*, while Mom provided treats of cookies and Ovaltine. I don't know whether it was foreshadowing or just a strange premonition, but for me back then everything was about being a cowboy and moving to Texas. I faithfully watched Red Ryder and his trusty companion Little Beaver on TV, and constantly nagged my parents until I got a Daisy Red Ryder BB gun for Christmas. Dad took me to my first rodeo, starring Tex Ritter, and Mom took me to Hudson's Department Store to personally meet William Boyd, who played Hopalong Cassidy and who was my favorite.

The Detroit winters were brutal with lots of snow. Although sledding and snowball fights were fun, the bitter, cold weather proved to be rather unhealthy for me. I was in the hospital far too frequently, with complex respiratory illnesses. Finally, the doctors diagnosed me as having chronic bronchial asthma. They advised my parents that the cold climate was poison for me and that they should consider relocating to a warmer part of the country. Somehow, Dad managed to get in touch with the owner of Pector's Bakery, a wholesale bakery located in Miami Beach, Florida, and which sold bread and baked goods to various retail establishments in the area. Mr. Pector was an elderly gentleman, who personally wanted to ease up, and he was looking for someone who could handle the hard work of production. He and Dad evidently came to terms, and it was announced that we were moving south. Our house was put up for sale. One evening, our neighbor from across the street knocked on our door and wanted to speak with Dad. He wanted to make sure that dad was not going to sell the house to a Negro family, because that would "ruin the neighborhood." Dad assured him everything would be fine, and he finally left. But I recall the look of disgust on my Dad's face, and from the look in his eyes, it was clear that this was not going to be a subject for conversation with us children. Dad had already received an initial offer from a white family, which ended up being confirmed, and the house was sold. Our furniture and goods were packed and would be shipped through Railway Express, and we would make the drive to Florida in our very first car, a maroon Chevy sedan. During our drive south, for the first time I was confronted with the concept of "separate but equal." It was in-your-face disparity between whites and blacks. There were different drinking fountains, bathrooms, eating areas, and motels, and it was anything but equal. When I asked Dad about it, he sternly said: "That's just the way they do things down here." From his voice, it was crystal clear that he didn't want to discuss the matter any further. However he did make a stern command that I was never to use the term "Nigger," and I never did.

When we reached Miami Beach, we moved into a modest, upstairs apartment in a small, white stucco apartment complex on a coconut palm tree lined street that was within a couple of blocks from the public beach. Within a block or two in the other direction was the elementary school where I would go, and just beyond there was Flamingo Park, with its swings, skating rink and baseball diamond. I tried baseball, but I was a flop. In school however, I started out on a positive note. My third grade teacher was a young, attractive blond with an angelic voice, who just loved teaching our age group. My grades actually improved. She was married to a military man, who got transferred, and she had to leave. She was replaced by an older grump, who seemed not to enjoy teaching at all, and I quickly reverted to mediocre student status. Sometimes after school Sammy, a neighborhood kid slightly older than me would sit at the round cabana table in the courtyard playing chess with his grandfather. I was allowed to quietly watch, and I became entranced with the chess pieces and the moves. Having expressed an interest, Dad bought me a small chess set and an instruction book. Even though he hadn't played chess before, he taught me how to play. On occasion, Sammy would allow me to play him, and along with continuing pronouncements "you're not much of a challenge", he would beat me consistently. Until one day I finally checkmated him, and that was the last time we would play chess together.

While in Florida, I experienced my first hurricane, after which I remember seeing a broomstick imbedded in a telephone pole. It left a lasting impression and a healthy respect for the power of those storms. The warmth of the Florida climate had helped my asthma some, but the humidity factor was not favorable for me, and the doctor had suggested that perhaps a dryer climate would be better. At about that time, Mr. Pector had decided to retire completely, and he sold his bakery to a large chain, which was going to bring in its own people. Dad was suddenly out of a job. He rationalized it as an omen, saying we needed to move to a dryer place like Arizona anyhow. So we packed up and left the Sunshine State. I was thrilled. We were moving west where the cowboys lived.

During our drive near Ocala, I experienced severe and painful stomach cramps that would not subside. When taken to the emergency room at the hospital, the doctor's diagnosis was acute appendicitis, and I was scheduled for immediate surgery to remove my appendix. The doctor informed my parents that they were just in time, that within another hour it would have likely burst, and that would have been a really bad situation. The operation was successful, but I must have been allergic or had a bad reaction to the anesthetics used, because afterwards I became very ill. I could not keep food down and became very weak. I was in the hospital for at least a week, and then we stayed at a nearby cottage, where I saw the doctor nearly every day. The cottage had a common back yard with an adjacent cottage, where an elderly couple lived. They owned a charcoal colored Scottie dog by the name of Peaches. The dog had a deformity in that one of its front legs was shorter than the other. Yet Peaches loved to play ball. You would throw a rubber ball at her, and despite her disability nine times out of ten, she would catch it in midair and bring it back to you so you could throw it again. Peaches became my heroine. I figured if she could do all of that, then I could get well, which I eventually did, and at last we were able to travel again.

We continued our trip west, and I was delighted when we crossed the border into Texas. It was like my childhood dream had come true. We had to stop when we got to Houston, as it was time for the clamps that fastened my appendix incision to be removed. Evidently, there were some healing issues involved that mandated medical attention, and the doctor advised my parents that we would not be able to travel for a while. School was going to start up soon anyhow, and it was decided that we would stay in Houston for the time being. We moved into a small apartment very close to an elementary school. Dad was able to find a job selling ladies' shoes at Foley's Department Store. The ladies' shoe department there was run by Wolff Shoe Company, which was a large wholesale shoe company, headquartered in St. Louis, having retail branches operated in various department stores throughout Texas and other parts of the south. Although Dad started as a salesman, he managed to advance to the position of Assistant Manager. On days off, Dad would take us to see interesting sites such as the San Jacinto Monument and the Battleship Texas. In the summer, we would take short vacation trips to Galveston, where we could go to the beach.

My school experience was rather mundane with me remaining as just a very average student. It was then that I incurred my very first anti-Semitic experiences. There were some neighborhood school kids, who obviously did not like Jews. From time to time I would be derogatorily referred to as a "kike" or "dirty Jew". I didn't see myself as being different, and I really didn't understand it, other than I was being picked on and insulted, and I didn't like it one bit. At times those incidences led to unpleasant scuffles.

Like Miami, the Houston climate tended to be humid, so my asthma remained relatively the same. I had pretty much resolved that it was just something that I would have to contend with for the rest of my life. For a chance at improvement, the doctor was still recommending a dryer environment. Meanwhile Dad had been notified by the Wolff Shoe Company higher ups of a promotion opportunity. There was an opening for a Manager's position of their shoe department in a small department store located in El Paso, and they wanted Dad to take it. It would mean more money for our family and a dryer climate for me. It was a no brainer, and the decision was that we would be moving west again.

When we arrived at El Paso, we moved into a nice, modern apartment, which had a small but attractive cactus and rock garden, located near an elementary school which my sister and I would attend. We were older and perfectly capable of staying home alone. So when Dad began his position as manager, Mom became a saleswoman working with him. Some evenings we would attend picnic symphony concerts at a nearby park, where we would sit on a blanket under the stars and listen to the orchestra's classical music. For special celebrations, we would go across the border and have a really fine multi course dinner at the Florida Café in Juarez. On Saturdays, I frequently joined my neighborhood playmate, Dennis, in our jaunt to the neighborhood movie theater for the afternoon matinee, where we would see, a newsreel, a cartoon, a Three Stooges short, and two whole feature films, all for the price of nineteen cents. The dryer climate proved to be effective, and my health situation improved to the point where I was bothered by my asthma only on very rare occasions. Although I first began to learn to swim when living in Houston, It was in El Paso where I really honed my swimming skills and became a rather proficient swimmer.

For the first time in my memory, we became members of a Jewish congregation, having joined a Conservative Synagogue, where I was entered into the religious school program in order for me to learn Hebrew. It was there I met Ezra, the religious school educator's son, who was my age and in my class. He was brilliant when it came to Hebrew; whereas, I was beyond deficient. We became good friends, however, having a common interest in art and scouting. It was Ezra who introduced me to Boy Scouts, and I took to it like a duck to water. Aside from swimming, I finally found an activity at which I seemed to excel and which rated some approval from my father. Those were happy days that came crashing down. Dad had been promised a much larger department branch, and finally the word came down from the top that there was a Manager's position opening at the Wolff & Marx Department Store, which was a major flagship store located on E. Houston Street in downtown San Antonio. I didn't want to leave El Paso, and my parents were somewhat concerned about the climate change, but this would mean a big promotion with a large salary increase. The decision was we would take a chance and go.

CHAPTER 3

The Alamo City

1954 – 1964

I was twelve years old when we came to San Antonio. Dad went downtown to check out Wolff & Marx and took us to see the Alamo as a reward. For a couple of weeks we stayed at the Lighthouse Motel which was located on Fredericksburg Road in the northwest side of the city, until Mom and Dad located an upstairs apartment on Donaldson Avenue, within a block from Thomas Jefferson High School. There I met my next door neighbor, Ronald Serber, who was my age and who happened to be Jewish, and we became good friends. The San Antonio climate seemed to work out for me, and although I had to take shots upon occasion, my asthma pretty much remained under control. A few years later Dad would leave the Wolff Shoe Company and venture into his own business, opening the New York Shoe Factory Outlet on Jefferson Street. After struggling for several years, it became apparent that the business was not going to make it. Dad eventually ended up working for the U.S. Post Office, while Mom became a saleswoman, selling lingerie at Frost Department Store.

But that year in 1954, I began school with some trepidation. I had completed elementary school, and I would be entering Horace Mann Junior High, and of course that was going to be a whole different matter. Fortunately, there I met John D. Brantley, an English teacher, who turned out to become a major influence in my life. Not only did he teach me language and writing skills, but he instilled within me a deep appreciation of literature and poetry. I even became a fan of classic novels and Shakespeare of all things. He was the first teacher to convince me that I was capable of making an "A" grade if I would try hard enough. And indeed, in his class I finally made my very first "A" in my school career. I had no idea then that later on I would have the privilege of being a student of his again when I attended college at SAC. My second "A" came from my general science teacher, Mr. Cobb, who ended up becoming the faculty sponsor of our brand new school chess club that we had formed. The club included some excellent players, like Morris Steen, who was our super star, and Carolyn Awalt and Tom Lee, who were no slouches either when it came to playing chess. In our first year of competition the club made a credibly good showing. Tom Lee and I were the movers behind forming the club. Tom was small in stature, wore glasses, had shortly cropped black hair, and was of Chinese-American extraction. He was very intelligent and a straight "A" honor student. Why he chose me to become his companion is beyond me. Perhaps it was our mutual interest in chess or just plain chemistry, but we became very good friends. We often would get together at each other's house to play chess or just talk. Frequently at recess, as neither one of us was that much into athletics, we would sit on a bench and play chess. One day a bully by the name of Charley, who disliked "Chinks" and "Kikes", and who wasn't shy about making his feelings known approached us. He purposely threw a ball at our chess board, disrupting our game and scattering the pieces all over. When I confronted him a scuffle ensued, which was promptly broken up by the P.E. teacher. We were both instructed to report to the gym the very next day, which we did. There we donned boxing gloves to settle our dispute. I was no fighter; whereas, Charley was, and there was no doubt that he clearly got the best of me that day. However, somehow I did manage to land a few blows. Afterwards Coach made us shake hands, and that was it. But after that Charley never bullied us again.

My parents joined Agudas Achim, the same congregation to which the Serber family belonged. It was a Conservative Synagogue located about six blocks further down Donaldson Avenue. It was convenient and clearly within walking distance, so in a situation when neither of my parents would be able to transport me by car, I could still manage and could get there and back. As I had to prepare for my Bar Mitzvah, I was enrolled in their Hebrew school which I went to twice a week, plus mandatory attendance of Saturday morning services. In Judaism, going through Bar Mitzvah is a very big deal. Supposedly that is when a boy becomes a man, and from a congregational religious standpoint, rather than a child he is treated as an adult. My linguistic inability evidently survived our move from El Paso, and I remained a horrible Hebrew student. I viewed the entire experience as an ordeal. I disliked the religious services there, as they were conducted nearly entirely in Hebrew, which I obviously did not understand, and so I found it to be boring and uninteresting, with the ceremonies and prayers being virtually meaningless to me. My only reprieve was if a conflicting Boy Scout event, such as a weekend campout, was scheduled, so then and only then, would Dad allow me to skip services. At that time between scouting and religion, I clearly viewed scouting as being more important and relevant to my life. Nevertheless, for the sake of my parents, I managed to mottle through my Bar Mitzvah ceremony.

I lucked out and found an excellent Boy Scout troop, which was sponsored by a Methodist Church, located on Donaldson Avenue, just a couple of blocks from us. That enabled me to attend all meetings, where I vigorously pursued my scouting education and training. I enthusiastically collected merit badges, and before I knew it I had achieved the rank of Eagle. Dad took me to the Court of Honor ceremony where my Eagle badge and certificate were presented, and I will never forget the look of pride on his face. Scouting led to my very first full-time summer job. I was fourteen, and there were four Trainee positions to be filled for the counseling staff at the Indian Creek Boy Scout Camp. Despite the fact that there were numerous applicants from all over the city, somehow I got selected. Indian Creek was outside of Ingram, some 73 miles west of San Antonio. It would mean that I would be working away from home for nearly the entire summer, a total of ten weeks in all. I was beyond excited to embark on this adventure. At camp, as Trainees we were circulated on a weekly basis to work in different areas, everything from the rifle range and archery to the demonstration area, dealing with first aid and camping skills. We even had turns of working KP in the mess hall. Since I was a strong swimmer, more often than not I found myself assigned to the swimming pool or the water front. Before long I had become certified as an instructor in swimming and water safety, and was also certified as a lifeguard to boot. I was out in the hot Texas sun continuously, usually without a shirt. I had become quite tan and color wise beyond bronze. By the end of the summer when my parents came to pick me up, I was positively brown. On the way home, we decided to stop at a restaurant In Kerrville to get something to eat before continuing our trip home to San Antonio. As we walked in and approached a table to sit down, we were suddenly approached by a man in a white apron, who I assumed to be the owner. He abruptly stated to my Dad: "I'm sorry Sir, but you're going to have to leave. We don't serve his kind here", pointing to me and then to a sign that made some reference to "Whites only". I had rarely seen Dad get so angry, and I thought he was going to deck the guy, but my Mom grabbed his arm, saying: "Come on, we're leaving," which we promptly did. It was obvious that my parents did not want to talk about the matter, and nothing further was said, but that incident left a lasting imprint on me, which I never forgot.

Overall my Indian Creek experience was a big plus. Somehow after that my asthma disappeared. I guess I must have outgrown it, and during the rest of my time at junior high, and all throughout my high school, college and law school years, I never had another asthma episode. The certifications I had achieved there enabled me to maintain full-time summer employment for several years, working at the Woodlawn public swimming pool with the city of San Antonio summer program. Every weekday in the morning I would teach beginners swimming, and then during the afternoon I would serve as a life guard. I managed to get a used bicycle which served as my transportation means from home to work and back. The pool was located about twelve blocks from the slightly bigger and more comfortable apartment to which we had moved and which was well within bike range. The apartment was a bottom floor, pale yellow brick duplex on Club Drive, nearly right across the street from Thomas Jefferson High School.

In 1957, with great anticipation, I began my high school career at Jefferson, the home of the "Mighty Mustangs." It was one of the most architecturally unique schools I had ever seen, and had a deep sense of tradition. While there I was fortunate enough to be in Ms. Longworth's Speech class. She put me on the debate team, and one year we actually beat Alamo Heights for the city championship. According to Ms. Longworth that was the first time Jeff ever beat Alamo Heights in debate. Of course we got wiped out in the next round of competition and never made it any further up the ladder toward State.

It was there that I also met Coach Pat Shannon, and little did I know that I would run into him again, under even more adverse circumstances. Coach Shannon rather obviously took to and liked the athletic guys, and I clearly wasn't one of them. He wasn't especially kind to the others. I hated gym and would just about do anything to get out of it. Subsequently I found out that an acceptable alternative to PE was ROTC. An upperclassman, David J. Garcia, who was a member of the Army National Guard and who on occasion worked with the cadet corps, encouraged me to join ROTC. As it would turn out, I would also have future dealings with him, as well. At any rate, I joined ROTC, which I found to be a lot more interesting and enjoyable, and it got me out of the arduous task of gym. I likened it to be much more like scouting, and I enthusiastically pursued my training. Before too long, I was selected for membership on the ROTC drill team, and we represented Jeff as one of the units performing in the famous Fiesta Flambeau Parade. Perhaps my biggest challenge was attending the mandatory Military Ball. Fortunately, Carolyn Awalt, my old school chum from Horace Mann, who I had gotten to know in the chess club there, came to my rescue and agreed to be my date. She was a cute, perky redhead, who was as charming and comfortably at ease, as I was clumsy and a nervous wreck. It was my very first date, and she managed to get me through that ordeal without a single miscue.

My English teacher, Ms. Saine, coaxed me into giving journalism a try, and while working on the school newspaper, I met Stuart Baum. He was tall, wore glasses and had short cropped dark hair. He was an honor student and happened to be Jewish, and we became close friends. One day he invited me to attend the Friday evening religious service at which he was going to be confirmed. It was at Temple Beth-El, a Reform Jewish congregation, located on Belknap, adjacent to SAC. As a favor to Stuart I went. The religious service there was a whole new experience for me, as most of it was in English, rather than Hebrew. For the first time in my life, I actually understood the prayers and was able to comprehend their meaning. Rabbi David Jacobson's sermon resonated with me. Though rooted in traditional biblical text, he was able to apply the message to current issues of our day. He pointed out that even though Confirmation was a milestone whereby the confirmation class would be ending its formal Jewish education classes at Temple that how it was of paramount importance for them and all Jews to continue their Jewish learning. After the service, I was invited to attend a party that was being thrown by the San Antonio Federation of Temple Youth (SAFTY) in honor of the confirmation class. All the kids were so friendly and extending I felt as if I was part of the group right away. Later that night, when my Mom asked how things went, I told her that I had found a new religious home, and that I was going to quit Agudas Achim and become a member of Temple Beth-El, which I promptly did. I became a very active member of SAFTY and eventually rose to the office of vice president. With the help of Stuart Baum, Louis Paletz and others, the organization grew from about 25 members to over 150 members, becoming the largest Jewish youth organization in San Antonio. During this time I had a chance to have numerous conversations with Rabbi Jacobson, who emphasized the concepts of loving thy neighbor as thyself and *Tikkun Olam* (making the world a better place). He also practiced what he preached. He actively worked with other prominent church leaders pushing to end discriminatory conditions and practices that existed in San Antonio at that time. We kids in our own miniscule way attempted to do our part, as well. When Stuart and I went to a movie at the Majestic, we purposely sat in the balcony, which was the area designated for black patrons. When we ate at the lunch counter at Woolworth's, we intentionally sat in the section set aside for black customers. It was our small way of indicating our displeasure with the discriminatory practice. I also had discussions with Reverend Milton Bendiner, who was the religious school educator there, and who took me under his wings. He provided me with volumes of books on Jewish history and philosophy, which I veraciously read. I felt I had a bunch of catching up to do, and in the process I began to discover my Jewish identity. One night, on a double date, Stuart and I had taken some SAFTY girls to a movie. Afterwards we were going to get a bite to eat at the Bun and Barrel, one of a few restaurants that were open late. On the way there we passed the San Antonio Country Club which I thought was a rather impressive building. I asked Stuart what it was, and he explained that it was a country club where no Jews were allowed. My response was, "Well then I might have to visit that place someday." Everyone in the car laughed, and I had no idea how prophetic my remarks would be.

"Suddenly its 1960" was our high school class moto, and suddenly it was, and I would be graduating from Jeff. While there, I had steadily improved my academic climb which I had begun in middle school. I had made mostly "B"s, with some "A"s and on occasion some "C"s. Clearly, I had not set the academic world on fire. In fact, one of my counselors had advised my parents not to waste their money sending me to college, and that I might be better off going to some kind of trade school. Fortunately, I did not follow her advice, and that fall I began my college career at SAC.

Although some of my more uppity acquaintances teased and derogatorily referred To SAC as "San Pedro High," I had done my research, and it was an excellent school. At that time, it had more PHDs on its faculty than any other college in San Antonio, and was ranked in the top ten Junior Colleges in the entire country. Besides by then I had formulated the belief that when it came to education, it was the quality of the student that was most important, and not necessarily the prestige of the school. For me SAC was the right choice to begin my college career. Not only was it more affordable, but it was accessible by bus, with the bus stop being only a couple of blocks from our home. I didn't own a car yet or have one readily available, and so transportation to the campus was of major importance. I got into a daily routine of taking an early morning bus to campus, attending all of my scheduled classes, and then planting myself in the library where I would study and prepare for the next day or so. My dogmatic goal was not only to keep absolutely current in all my courses, but also to stay slightly ahead. It was at SAC that I developed the disciplined study habits that lasted me a lifetime. Early into my first semester, I put my name and personal information on an index card and posted it on the bulletin board in the student center, seeking a possible ride sharing program. I really didn't expect anything to come from it, but I figured it was worth a try. One evening I got a call from a college co-ed by the name of Sharon Isaacs, and we arranged to meet for lunch at the student center the next day. She was petite, attractive, and had short stylish brown hair. As it turned out, she had a car and lived only six blocks away from me, and it would not be inconvenient for her to pick me up in the morning and drive to SAC together and then to give me a ride back home later in the afternoon, when our schedules matched. Even though it was not every single day, it usually turned out to be several times a week. So just driving back and forth and seeing each other on campus from time to time, we really got to know each other and became close friends. Even though we never dated, we developed a comfort zone between us whereby we could just talk about anything—our goals, classes, relationships, and troubles. We became true confidants with one another.

  I took to college like I was destined for it. My first semester, I made pretty high grades. That emboldened me, and despite working two part-time jobs, I went ahead and registered for twenty-one hours of courses. Shortly thereafter I got a message to come to the Assistant Dean's office. He advised me that I needed his approval to carry that many hours during the semester and under my particular circumstances, working and all, that he did not think it would be prudent for me to attempt this. I explained that I only had limited funds for college, and I had no time to waste. My endeavor was to complete my first two years at SAC, and while there accumulate the maximum number of college hours that I could transfer to a senior university. After some discussion, he finally granted me permission, but wrote "Approved Reluctantly," on my permanent student record form, which he had me initial. Well, I just took that as an additional challenge, and by the end of that semester, I made the Dean's Honor Role List and was inducted into the Sigma Tau Sigma honorary fraternity. I had finally achieved the academic standard that Mr. Brantley said I could, and I was determined to maintain it from then on out. My only academic hiatus was of a physical nature. At that time, SAC required completion of twelve hours of PE in order to earn an Associate's Degree. Although lousy at gym, I was a strong swimmer, and swimming was a PE option. Naturally, I took it, and before too long, I was placed on the varsity swim team, swimming first place in the breaststroke, and second slot in the four man relay medley. In the first few competitive meets, our team did pretty good, and then along came trouble. I contracted an ugly foot rash, which simply would not clear up. After several visits with a dermatologist, it was determined that what I had was way more than a case of athlete's foot, but rather it was a severe skin eczema that would take time to heal. In the meantime, I was no longer allowed to go into the swimming pool. Needless to say, my swimming career came to a screeching halt. I had to quit the swim team, drop swimming for PE, and I was not looking forward to the dreaded transfer to gym that was likely to take place. Thank goodness Sharon came to my rescue. In speaking with her about my problem, she suggested that I talk with her dancing instructor. Sharon was taking Folk Dancing as her PE option, and she thought that their class could use a few more boys anyhow. She introduced me to her instructor, and since my condition was "medical," the school authorities approved the transfer. My PE problem was solved.

Dancing embodied a healthy physical activity; moreover, it was fun, and as a bonus, it offered an opportunity to meet a lot of new girls.

Not only did I blossom academically at SAC, but I developed socially, as well. Whereas in High School I dated only sporadically, while at SAC I dated frequently and seldom did a weekend go by without my being in the social company of one or more females. The fact that I didn't own a car didn't stop me. When I couldn't borrow Dad's car, I either double dated with guys who owned cars, or dated girls who had cars and didn't mind driving on a date. I suppose I became an early believer in equal rights for females. Regarding equality, one of my proudest moments at SAC was being one of the main instigators and charter members of the Lambda Epsilon Phi fraternity. At that time SAC had a social fraternity, which included only all white Anglo students. Wayne Parker, one of my ROTC companions from Jefferson who eventually married Sharon, John Libertus, several others, and I wanted to change that. Our idea was to establish a multi-ethnic and multi-racial social fraternity at SAC. In order to gain official school approval and authorization, we ended up having to go to the same Assistant Dean who had put "Approved Reluctantly" on my school record when I had insisted in carrying more hours during a semester than what was normal. By then, I'm pretty sure he probably viewed me as "a trouble maker." After some rather tense discussion, during which he professed that this would not be a good idea because potentially it could lead to friction and conflict, he finally relented, and the Lambda Epsilon Phi fraternity was officially established with a charter that clearly prohibited any discrimination on ethnic or racial grounds. Our group picked the fraternity colors of blue and gold. John Libertus and I designed the frat pin, which was an elongated six pointed blue star, with the Greek letters of the fraternity being emblazoned in gold vertically thereon. By the end of my time at SAC that fraternity had become the largest and most prominent on campus. Some eighteen years later when I was teaching an evening real estate law class at SAC, I noticed several students wearing the same frat pin that we had initially designed. It made me feel good to see that we had started something back then that evidently had continued, at least up until that point in time.

By the end of my SAC career, I received an Associate's Degree, and every one of the sixty-six hours that I had accumulated there was accepted for transfer to St. Mary's, a major university in San Antonio, where I had chosen to complete my undergraduate college degree. In the fall of 1962, I began my first semester at St. Mary's. Since the tuition there was much more than it was at SAC, It became abundantly clear that selling shoes on Saturdays was just not going to provide enough income. I would need another job. Through a contact at St. Mary's, Wilfred Haberman, I was able to land a job as a staff accountant at Fox Company, which provided me two to three afternoons of work every week, as well as a full time summer job over the next few years (1963—1966). However, in order to be able to maintain this job, I would finally need my own car. Keeping gas economy in mind, with my parent's help, we bought a white VW Beetle that had orange seats, and interior trim. It was simple and relatively inexpensive, but it was my very first car, and it suited me just fine. While at St. Mary's I maintained a high grade point average and was inducted into the Kappa Pi Sigma honorary fraternity. At the end of my senior year I graduated *cum laude*, receiving a Bachelor of Business Administration Degree. A good part of that year, I had concentrated on my next big endeavor, getting into law school.

CHAPTER 4

The Politics and the Peregrinus

1964 – 1967

Louis Paletz and I chatted with anticipation as we made the early morning drive downtown to the old St. Mary's law school to take the LSAT. The LSAT is a very comprehensive examination that is an absolute prerequisite for entrance into law school. As we settled in at our table, we munched the tacos and gulped the coffee that we had picked up on the way, while waiting for the exam proctors to arrive. When they appeared, I attentively listened to the instructions as the exams were passed out. Finally I heard the fateful announcement: "You may begin", and I started to take the dreaded exam which was just as onerous as I had imagined, yet somehow I managed to get through it. Eventually we got our test scores. Louis had scored well within the high range, but my score was far less, disappointedly sitting slightly in the lower mid-range. I was worried about how that would affect my law school applications. I sure as hell didn't want to have to take that exam over again. I had only applied to two law schools: St Mary's, a private school where I had completed my undergraduate degree, and the University of Texas (UT) which was a state supported school in Austin. Both schools had solid reputations, and fortunately for me did not judge applicants strictly on the LSAT scores alone. Although they certainly considered the LSAT score, they factored the applicant's undergraduate record, as well, and also viewed how well-rounded the applicant was. Evidently my high grade point average at the undergraduate level saved me, and I was really relieved when I received acceptance letters from both law schools. Now the problem was in choosing which one. Each had advantages and disadvantages. With UT clearly tuition would be less and there would be the new adventure of going to school away from home. On the other hand, I would have the seemingly impossible task of having to finance board and room, which would be rather expensive, as well as having to find new employment in Austin. With St. Mary's even though the tuition was much higher, I could continue living at home, without any board or room charge. My steady income stream from Fox Co. and Bakers would continue without a hitch, and my comfortable social life could remain relatively unchanged. For the most part, it looked like things were definitely breaking in St. Mary's favor, but then almost fatalistically a course of events began to unfold the summer of 1964.

Leonard Schwartz, who was seriously dating my sister, Sandy, and my old friend, Ronald Serber, would be attending their senior undergraduate year at UT in the fall. They had hooked up and found a modern, comfortable apartment located on Riverside Drive with its back adjacent to Towne Lake. It had two bedrooms and two bathrooms, with an adequate living area, dining space and kitchen. It was a perfect school residence which could easily be shared by four men. They had located a third undergraduate, Ed Stein, who was willing to go in with them, but they needed a fourth and invited me to take that slot. When considering splitting the rent four ways it wasn't near as bad economically as what I thought it would be. Meanwhile because of our involvement in the Young Democrats, Leonard and I had met George Rigely, and he and Leonard had become really good friends. The three of us had been invited to a meeting at the law office of Vale, Torres, Gonzales and Alaniz, which was located downtown in the old Tower Life building. The lawyers in that firm were very active politically, with three of them being considered as real players in the local Democratic Party. R.L. (Bob) Vale and Johnny Alaniz had been elected as members of the Texas State House of Representatives. Pete Torres would eventually be elected as a Member of the San Antonio City Council, and only

Gil Gonzales chose not to run for office and remained in the background. There we met another State Representative, Jake Johnson. Although not a lawyer, Jake tended to be extremely knowledgeable concerning legal and political matters. He was quick-witted, blunt and outspoken, but all served up with a congenial and charming Texas drawl. Jake was of moderate build, had wavy brown hair, and was inflicted with a rather visible hunch back condition on the left side of his back. He seemed somewhat pleased when he saw my reaction was absent of any feelings of defensive recoil. All of them tended to be liberal, and they were familiar with our past activity in political campaigns. After some discussion, it was made known that they would need Legislative Assistants for the up-coming regular session of the 59th Legislature, which would start in Austin next winter on January 12, 1965. In Texas, the legislature meets once every other year, with its regular session beginning on the second Tuesday of every odd numbered year. The position of Legislative Assistant paid way more than what I was making at my current job in San Antonio. During the five months of the session (January--May) I would earn as much if not more than I could working during the entire nine month school year at Fox Co. and Bakers. It seemed that Austin might work out really well for me after all. I wouldn't have to work at all during my initial fall semester, giving me unencumbered time to adjust to law school, and my first semester would be all but over by the time the legislative session began. As a plus, they all expressed how they could be really flexible with us concerning our work schedules. It was decided that Leonard would work for Johnny, George would work for Bob, and I would work for Jake, if I wanted it. I had one more obstacle that I needed to clear. I did not want to jeopardize my full-time summer job at Fox Co. My strategy of working all summer, saving the bulk of the money earned, and then using those savings to fund the ensuing school year had gotten me through four years of college without any student loans. If possible, I wanted to accomplish the same result regarding law school. I spoke to Bill Maddox, my immediate supervisor, who took me to see Harvey Erben, the Secretary-Treasurer of Fox Co. They felt that I had achieved a depth of understanding of their various accounts and systems, and that I had sufficiently familiarized myself with their practices. They both felt very comfortable that my absence during the school year would not detract from my value as a worker for them during the summer, when I would be needed most to fill in for those on vacation. They assured me that my job position would be firmly secure. Well that just about did it. Now things really tended to be bending in favor of UT. Could it be that my white VW with orange interior was some kind of an omen. Because I had never had an away from home school experience, to sweeten the pot my parents said they would contribute $50.00 a month during the school year. Then the clincher came. I had applied for scholarships to both schools. I was pretty sure nothing would come of it but that it wouldn't hurt to try. I had received a letter from St. Mary's apologetically but politely rejecting any scholarship help. Then I received the letter from UT, and when I opened it up I couldn't believe it. I excitedly showed it to my parents. UT had granted me a full tuition and books scholarship for my first year of law school. That did it. I was going to become a "Longhorn"—"Orange and White, Texas Fight."

So at the end of the summer of 1964, I moved into our Austin apartment and got ready to begin the fall semester of law school at Texas. The law school was located at the extreme northeast corner of the enormous UT complex, and was somewhat separate and distant from the hectic main center of the campus. It was a distinguished cream-white masonry building with an orange tile roof, and it just looked like the very nature of a law school. On the portal above the entrance doorway, the words "Equal Justice Under Law" were distinctively carved. Passing through almost daily, those words were like a subliminal advertisement implanting that paramount principle deep within my psyche. At the Texas law school, it seemed that the emphasis was that the law must bring about justice and that concept was embodied in the *Peregrinus*, which was the law school's mascot and which symbolically served as a constant reminder of that message. "Perry", as it was affectionately called, was a strange looking mythical beast. It was a quadruped having fur, which in texture and design kind of resembled that of a pinto horse, but which was colored in orange and white, of course. Its arched back represented the law's readiness to spring into action in order to do justice. It had a large, bushy tail so it could brush aside all technicalities in favor of justice. It had a beaked head, which on top was a white crown. With its beak it could delve into the mass of relevant and irrelevant facts and fancies, separating the wheat from the chaff, in order to get to the truth, which was symbolized by the white crown atop its head.

At our initial orientation assembly, our first year class piled into the law school auditorium. There we were addressed by Dean W. Page Keeton. He was a highly respected and almost legendary figure, having been Dean of the Texas law school since 1949. With his thinning dark hair, studious looking glasses, and lawyer-like appearance, he reminded me of Atticus Finch in the novel *"To Kill a Mockingbird"*. He instructed us to look to our right and then to our left, and then sternly announced that only one of the three would make it through law school. I got the idea that this was going to be extremely competitive and rather difficult and work intensified. I was right. Law school was like college on steroids. Although it took some getting used to, especially the Socratic Method, whereby professors would ask questions rather than just give lectures, I found myself beginning to adjust and even preferring it. My first semester, I had the usual standard classes of Contracts, Property, Torts, Legal Research, and the really tough course of Civil Procedure taught by the infamous Gus M. Hodges. Professor Hodges had balding grey hair and a prominent matching handlebar moustache. He was considered "the expert" in the area and almost an icon. His mannerism tended to be brittle and imposing, and in retrospect he reminded me of the austere Professor Charles W. Kingsfield at Harvard in *The Paper Chase* novel. Like Kingsfield if a student was unprepared when called upon, Professor Hodges with a dramatic wave of both hands would toss him out of class, and it would take nearly an act of Congress for that student to be allowed to come back. The lesson was clear and brought back to mind the old Boy Scout motto: "Be Prepared".

My other nemesis course was Legal Research. We all packed into the Tarlton law library and amidst the myriad volumes of law books we learned how to find the pertinent case, statute, regulation, or article from a legal periodical that would tend to answer the particular legal question being asked. The problem was that when I tried to find the correct book, at times it was gone, as some other student had already pulled it. So this was going to require some team work. A group of us got together and formed a research team, which we named the "Legal Beagles", in order to handle the research and share the results. The strategy worked, and although research was not necessarily my "strong suit", thanks to my teammates, I managed to get through it. Having endured the pressure of my first law school final exams, by the end of the semester, I was both physically and mentally exhausted. Somehow I survived and was able to achieve a solid, respectable grade point average. However, Dean Keeton's words proved true in that some of my classmates failed to make it, and this was just the first semester. In fact by semester's end, our apartment roommate, Ed Stein, had decided to cash it in and leave. He was replaced by George Rigely, who came up from San Antonio to join us. George and Leonard were a year behind me and would start law school the following fall.

It was now January, 1965. John Connally was Governor, Ben Barnes was Lt. Governor, and George, Leonard, and I would begin working for the Texas legislature. I reported to the Capitol and sought out Jake Johnson's office. He sat me down and explained that my duties would consist of: Going through his mail and sorting it into categories of type and importance. Dealing with and handling constituents and visitors, including lobbyists that either he was too busy to see or just didn't want to see. Keeping his calendar and making sure that I reminded him of all floor votes, committee meetings, and other important appointments. I would also be consulting with the Legislative Counsel regarding Bill drafting and assisting in marshalling his Bills through the complex legislative process. Jake was particularly concerned about his pet "Liquor by the Drink" Bill. Although at that time in certain counties, restaurants, taverns, and other places of public gathering could serve beer, and in some cases wine, but cocktail drinks that contained hard liquor, such as a Martini or Margarita, were strictly prohibited. If you wanted the "hard stuff", you had to belong to a private club. These clubs were often referred to as "Bottle Clubs". There you could bring in your own bottle or flask of liquor; they would furnish soft drink set-ups; and then using your own liquor, you could mix your own cocktail and consume it. Jake felt that this led to more drinking with an increased risk of DWI, and he wanted to change this with his "Liquor by the Drink" Bill, which he was bound and determined to get passed. The Bill was generally favored by the big cities, such as Houston, Dallas, and San Antonio, as it was felt it would be a boon to conventions and tourism. But the rural areas, the beer lobby, and those religiously indoctrinated against drinking alcoholic beverages were vehemently opposed to it. It was going to be a real challenge in trying to get his Bill passed. In the House of Representatives, members shared an office, and so our suitemate was Joe Bernal, who was also from San Antonio and was newly elected. Joe and I got to know each other and since we were both freshman, we resolved to help one another as much as possible. I learned a great deal while working as a Legislative Assistant. My skills in administratively managing an office and in politically dealing with people increased immeasurably. I had the opportunity to see the inner workings of politics that most people never get to see, and I was able to meet other individuals, like Representative Tom Lee, another member of our Bexar County delegation, who would have a later impact on my life.

By the end of the spring of 1965, I had made it through my first year of law school and my first year at the Texas legislature. I was about to lose two roommates but gain a brother-in-law. Ronald Serber got married to his sweetheart, Marilyn, and eventually they moved to Tyler, where as a CPA, Ronald set up a successful accounting practice. Later that summer on July 4, Leonard married my sister, Sandy. From the standpoint of maintaining our Austin apartment, this kind of left George and I in the lurch for the ensuing fall semester, and the search to find two replacements began in earnest. The problem was partially solved when Miles Appleberry, a Young Democrats contact from SAC, agreed to join us. He was starting law school that year and would be in the same first year class as George and Leonard. The solution was complete when we were able to add a fourth, another law student, James Broussard, who hailed from Lafayette, Louisiana. He referred to himself as the "Crazy Cajun" and was a fabulous cook. His Louisiana gumbo was superb, and his famous fried pies were absolutely delectable. The girls next door would always want to come over for dessert when James had those pies available. Also that fall, my old friend, Louis Paletz, who had always wanted to be a lawyer since I knew him at Jefferson High School, was beginning law school at UT, as well. I felt like the senior guy as I had already completed one year, and they were all just starting. Although 1966 was an off year for the Texas legislature, Governor Connally had called for a special session. So at least for the month of February, I had a job at the Texas legislature working for the Bexar County delegation, as a whole. This gave me at least some income, which when added to my savings from my summer job at the Fox Co. enabled me to financially get by. The second year of law school, which is supposed to be easier than the first, ended up being just as hard. I had opted to take the International Law class, even though I had little or no interest in that legal field, and I was certainly not inclined to practice in that area. However, it was a course that would count toward my law degree, and time wise, it just so happened to fit nicely into my overall class schedule. Even though I had some good study partners, it was of no avail, and I ended up making one of my worst grades in law school in that class. Things just did not get any easier; nevertheless, I had gotten more accustomed to the rigors of law school and had become pretty darn good when it came to personal efficiency and time management. By the end of the school year, I had managed to make it through two years of law school, while having maintained a decent, respectable grade point average. But not everyone survived. Despite my having given him some encouragement and guidance, my old friend, Louis Paletz, fell by the wayside and did not make it. He eventually ended up becoming a civil servant contract officer working with the military. Another casualty was our roommate, James Broussard, who dropped out at the end of the school year and never returned. So for my senior year (1966-1967), from an apartment standpoint that left George, Miles, and me, and again we were one guy short. With a little hunting, we were able to find Hugh Stanton Parker, a fellow law student who was in my senior class, and who we convinced to join us. "Stan", as we called him, came from Arlington, where his father owned a substantial funeral home. He had no interest in ever practicing law, but rather he intended to go into the mortuary business with his father. However, they both strongly felt that an academic background in law would be of benefit to their business, so Stan definitely planned on finishing law school.

Meanwhile back in San Antonio, the 1966 election year was a disaster for the Democrats. Johnny Alaniz and Tom Lee both lost their re-election bids, and even the veteran, Jake Johnson, lost and went down in flames. A slew of Republicans swept into office, including an attorney by the name of Don Hand. I desperately needed a job for the 60th legislative session, and so somehow I managed to get up the courage to call Don Hand's office and arrange an appointment with him. When the day came, I managed to shake off my nervous feeling, and I felt uncannily calm. I put on my dark suit, white shirt, and a conservative tie, and arrived at his office a little early to demonstrate my promptness. When ushered into his office, Don greeted me from behind his desk, gestured to one of the chairs in front, and asked me to be seated. He was a somewhat young attorney with thinning brown hair, and wearing half-spec reading glasses. As he leaned back in his chair, he glanced at what I recognized as my resume, which I had mailed to him previously, along with my letter thanking him for granting me an interview. After some polite conversation and routine questions about the schools I had attended and grades I had earned, then came the one question that I had feared but anticipated. Don looked straight at me and said: "You know Mel, I am a conservative Republican, and you are a liberal Democrat. So why in the world should I hire you as my Legislative Assistant?" I smiled, leaned forward slightly, and staring straight back at him, replied: "Well, Mr. Hand, to be quite honest, if you are looking for someone who will be politically agreeing with you all the time, then you really shouldn't. On the other hand, if you want someone who will be able to present and explain the other point of view, while at the same time able to effectively run your office, handle your constituents and correspondence, manage your calendar, and shepherd any of your Bills through the committee system, then I'm your man, and you won't find anyone more dedicated, loyal, and better able to do the job." Don paused for a moment, then stood up, extended his hand and said: "Mel, you're hired." As we shook hands, I thanked him and told him how I looked forward to working with him that coming January.

In September of 1966, I began my senior year of law school with anticipation, knowing that I was almost through. One day I was sitting in the student lounge, sipping coffee, while going over some class notes, when I was approached by Jack Gatewood, a fellow classmate, who had been in some of my previous classes. Jack and I were friendly, and on occasion had coffee together, while discussing politics and law school happenings. He was an active member of the International Law Society, and he informed me of an important meeting which some of the guys were having and which he invited me to attend. He advised me that it could be advantageous for me and that it could put me in, on the ground floor, with a legal publication that would be akin to Law Review. I checked my schedule and told him I'd go. At the meeting, I met about half a dozen top notch students, who had a common interest in the field of international law. This small inside group were keenly desirous of starting a student edited and published periodical that would be devoted to the study of public and private international law. The journal would contain major articles written by renowned authorities, as well as casenotes, comments, and book reviews written by students. They came up with the name of the *Texas International Law Forum*. I was literally shocked, when Earl Bentley, the Editor-in-Chief, asked me to join them and become a member of the editorial board. I explained that I really wasn't interested in international law and how that class and legal research were my lowest grades in law school. So, why in hell would they ever want me? Earl responded, indicating that he was aware that I had an accounting background and had some actual experience in running an office at the legislature. "Look Mel, we've got the legal writing and skilled research positions covered. Jack is going to be our articles editor, Jay [Kaplan] will be in charge of book reviews, Otto [Kitzinger] is going to handle casenotes, and Jim [Coats] is a crack wiz when it comes to research. What we need is your accounting and business skills. We want you to be our Administrative Editor. If we are going to put the Texas brand on this thing, then for sure it has to be first rate, and we could really use your help." By that time Jack and some of the others chimed in. I promised I would think about it and give them an answer, and after some further coaxing by Jack and some of the other guys, I finally said okay.

This was in the days before personal computers, and so I invested in some accounting pads and put together a simplistic but adequate accounting program designed for a publishing enterprise, which would keep track of income and expenses, and a more detailed process to maintain up to date information on prospective and actual subscribers. My thoughts were to put out an absolute outstanding journal for our first issue, which we would then distribute "for free" and without charge to a wide ranging list of potential subscribers. The idea was to first show them the product and ask them to review it, and then if they liked it to consider subscribing to it. In order to accomplish this, we would need some seed money, so we went to Professor Carl H. Fulda, who was the bigshot on international law at UT, and who was to become our faculty advisor. He managed to get us a small grant, which with some frugality, would cover the costs of publication and distribution of our first issue. But he made it clear that from then on the journal would have to be financially self-sustaining. Despite the cramped conditions of our little dedicated office space and hard to meet deadlines, the guys worked hard and put together an extraordinary, first rate journal. In the meantime, we had developed a list of law schools, both in the US and abroad, which had international law classes and study programs. To the list we added private law firms and governmental agencies, which might also have an interest in this type of journal and would likely find it to be beneficial and useful. Finally, the very first issue of the *Texas International Law Forum* was published, and rightly so, we all had this feeling of pride. Off it went, and now came the waiting game to see what the subscription response would be. Typically on a first attempt, I had conservatively anticipated that a five percent positive response would be acceptable. Everyone was joyously ecstatic when the initial subscription rate came in at over ten percent, and eventually would climb to near twenty percent. Before the end of the school year, the *Texas International Law Forum* had become a huge success. In fact at that time, it was one of only three student edited international law journals that were listed in the *Index to Legal Periodicals*.

Shortly after New Year's, I began to prepare for the 60th legislative session, which officially started on January 10, 1967. I met Don Hand at the Capitol. As a freshman Representative he had been assigned to one of the smaller and less convenient offices. Already having had two years' experience there, I gave him a basic orientation, showing him where the nearest restroom was and explaining how the voting system worked in the House. At the front of the House chamber, on the wall behind the Speaker's podium, there was a giant board with the name of each member printed on it. To the right of each name there were three Christmas-like lights: one green for a "Yes" vote, one red for a "No" vote, and one white, signifying an abstention. Then on the right side of each member's desk in the chamber there was a keyed panel, having three buttons corresponding to the big lighted board, allowing members to vote either "Yes," "No," or abstain. Each member was provided a key that only worked on his own desk panel, assuring for example that only Don, and no one else, could cast a vote in Don Hand's name. When a vote was called the members were given a certain amount of time in which to cast their votes, which they could change, as long as they did so within the voting time limit. What was interesting was that sometimes during the voting, the big board initially would light up mostly green so that one would think that the particular Bill up for consideration was going to pass. Then out came the "Lobbyists" and "Legislative Handlers", who would buzz around and circulate amongst various members, and all of a sudden, the lights began changing from green to red, until it was apparent that the measure had failed. Of course at times this phenomenon happened vice versa, as well. It was politics up front and ugly, and one could only imagine the last minute deals and trade-offs that were struck.

As Don was a newcomer, I had rightly figured that he hadn't thought of making arrangements for the usual photos, which could be used for press coverage and constituent brochures back home, and so I brought with me my trusty Canon 35 mm camera. I had gotten the camera on sale at the Fox Co., and although it wasn't a "professional camera," it was most serviceable and took pretty good pictures. And it was affordable because I was able to get the employee's discount on top of the sales price. Even though I worked in the accounting side at Fox Co., I had been there long enough to get to know people who worked in production and retail, as well. So I couldn't help learning a little bit about photography, and I had become a fairly good photographer. I went ahead and took the standard pictures of Don: standing on the Capitol steps, sitting at his House chamber desk, standing on the floor at the center of the Capitol dome, and sitting at his office desk. Naturally, I got the photos developed at Fox Co., using my employee's discount, of course. Don was very pleased with the pictures. Before I knew it, the word had spread about my picture taking ability, and I was doing the same type of photo lay outs for some of Don's member friends.

At his office, Don and I worked hard in establishing the parameters, procedures and processes that would be used in running his office in a most efficient manner. After that everything ran like clockwork. Don was a straight-up, honest guy, who was extremely ethical. He would not tolerate even the appearance of impropriety or conflict of interest. Because of this he tended to avoid the lobbyists altogether, and I was frequently used as a shield in that regard. When lobbyists came to our office, I would typically inform them that Don was not available, but that I would be happy to take their message and printed material and would pass it on. Usually their stuff would wind up in the trash. Sometimes they would leave tickets to shows or events and invitations to rather festive parties. Don seldom went to these, and at times he would just pass the tickets and invites on to me. And when my studies permitted, I would attend, as it was a free source of social entertainment. At a couple of those parties, where liquor was always served, I met Charlie Wilson, who was a newly elected member of the Texas Senate. Charlie was a most amiable and cordial guy, who really enjoyed drinking. He had a reputation of being a real party animal, yet I never saw him drunk or do anything embarrassing. Who knew that later he would be elected to the U.S. Congress, where as a Congressman he would become famous for his prominent role in securing weapons, munitions, and funding for the Afghanistan rebels in their ultimate successful struggle against the Soviet Union? Indeed, later a movie would be made about him entitled *Charlie Wilson's War*, starring Tom Hanks as the irrepressible Charlie.

While at the Capitol, I met another famous Texas Senator, who also had been recently elected. Barbara Jordan was the first woman ever to be elected to the Texas Senate. Given it was the state of Texas, the fact that she happened to be black made that feat even more amazing. She was well educated and was a dynamic and driven lady. I was fortunate to have discussed and worked with her on various issues concerning voting rights in the state of Texas. She also would eventually be elected to the U.S. House of Representatives, where she would become one of the most respected members of that body politic.

That spring one of the most interesting courses I had in law school was the Family Law class taught by Father Robert F. Drinan. He was the Dean of the Boston College law school, but was then teaching as a visiting professor at Texas. He was an energetic and enthusiastic teacher, who had a special knack of making the class enjoyable and fun. Father Drinan would likewise later get elected as a Congressman; thus, completing my triumvirate of contacts that year who would all end up serving in the U.S. Congress. But in the spring of 1967, as a mere law student, I would have never guessed that only three years later a famous American lawyer, Father Drinan and I would be locked up in an intense three way competition to see which of our law articles that we had each written for publication would receive the most prominent placement in a nationally syndicated legal periodical that was distributed throughout the United States.

CHAPTER 5

⚖

What Were the Odds?

1966 – 1967

It was a balmy, hot evening in July, 1966, typical for San Antonio, and I was about to receive the most fateful telephone call of my life. My parents and I had just finished dinner, when the telephone rang, and it was Sharon Lemson on the line. Sharon was on the verge of getting married soon. We had known each other from the old SAFTY days, as we had been friends in that youth group together. Since my parents and her parents were friends, as well, we had been invited to her wedding. Sharon also went to Jefferson High School, but since graduating from there, I kind of lost track of her and hadn't really communicated with her since. Evidently Sharon wanted to have an away from home college experience, so she decided to go to school in Omaha, Nebraska, where she could stay with her Aunt and Uncle, who resided there. While attending the University of Nebraska at Omaha (UNO), she met Marlene Sherman, a college co-ed, who was also attending there, and they became best friends. After her freshman year, Sharon decided to transfer to the University of Houston (UH) to complete her undergraduate degree, but she and Marlene continued to stay in touch with one another. While at UH, Sharon met Joey Kammerling. They began dating, fell in love, and became engaged. Since Sharon was an Alamo City girl, the wedding was scheduled to be held at Temple Beth-El in San Antonio. Having been good friends over the years, Sharon had asked Marlene to be her maid of honor, and Marlene accepted. Never having been to Texas, she had come in by bus from Omaha somewhat early in order to see some sights, and was staying with Sharon and her parents. After we exchanged pleasantries, and I congratulated her on her up-coming wedding, Sharon said that she would appreciate it if I could do her a big favor. I don't know whether she needed some private time with her parents to handle some final wedding details, or whether she just wanted to provide Marlene with some social entertainment while she was here in S.A. At any rate, she asked me if I would be willing to take Marlene out on a blind date, and I said as a favor to her that I would.

The night of the blind date arrived. I put on some dress slacks, a nice looking shirt, and a light weight sports jacket that had an inside pocket in which I could carry a small flask, which I had filled with some Bacardi rum. My plan was to take Marlene dancing where we could have some mixed drinks. First of all, having taken dancing at SAC, I was a fairly good dancer, and I thought that might impress her. Second, coming from Nebraska, I figured that girls at her age likely were used to socially consuming a cocktail on a date and probably even expected it. I didn't want her to be disappointed with our Texas provincial no "liquor by the drink" culture. Finally, the place that I knew would provide an opportunity for both dancing and drinking was the notorious Eastwood Country Club. Eastwood was a private "bottle club", located on the eastside of town, right in the heart of the area heavily inhabited by the Black community. Although chiefly attended by Afro-Americans, it was also a popular hangout for the hip, Anglo college crowd, who liked and appreciated the "Motown" sound. Quite frankly, I wanted to see what Marlene's reaction to this would be. So I hopped into my VW and proceeded to drive over to the residence of Sharon's parents. Sharon's father operated a small retail liquor store on Bandera Road, and they lived in a modest wood-frame house, located behind the store. On the way there, I had a strange premonition about this blind date and that somehow it was going to be special.

When I arrived, I was invited into the house, and there I was introduced to Marlene. She was 5' 4", had a shapely figure, and was dressed in a sharp-looking outfit. She had stylish short brown hair with blond highlights, flashing green eyes, and a cute coquettish smile. I was absolutely impressed. After engaging in some small talk with Sharon and her parents, we took off on our date. I learned that like me, she did not come from a wealthy family. From the time she was a young girl, she worked as a salesperson at the front counter of her father's small family bakery. Although neither of her parents had encouraged her to go to college, she adopted an independent attitude and insisted on doing so and did. Like me she worked and paid her own way through college, clerking in the office of her Uncle Jerry. He was a very reputable doctor who owned and operated a medical clinic, located in south Omaha. Marlene had graduated from University of Nebraska at Omaha, having obtained her Bachelor of Science Degree, with a double major in mathematics and education. She was a math teacher at a middle school back in Omaha. As this was her summer vacation, she was able to come to Sharon's wedding and spend a little time in San Antonio. We each had one sibling, and we chatted about them and our families. It had been a while since I had been to Eastwood, and I got a little lost but finally managed to find it. When we got there the parking lot was empty, and the sign on the door said it was closed for remodeling. It was too late for a movie, and I felt that Marlene would feel like this date was a bust. But being a good sport, she graciously said that she wouldn't mind just riding around and seeing some of the town. So I drove by various sites of downtown: the Tower Life Building, the Bexar County Courthouse, and the Alamo, of course. As we rode up Broadway, I showed her the Fox Co. headquarters where I worked. While riding around, we continued to talk. We spoke about our hopes, dreams, and cares; our beliefs and philosophy; and our outlook on life in general. And the more we talked, it seemed the more we had in common. In truth we both felt very comfortable in just talking with one another, and we were enjoying just doing that. I finally found a small hole-in-the-wall "bottle club" on the Old Austin Highway, where they charged a "cover charge," the supposed membership fee, and provided outrageously priced Coca-Cola set-ups, but we were able to mix in the Bacardi rum that I had brought in the flask and enjoyed a cocktail together, as we continued to chat. Marlene demurely disclosed it was the most time she had ever spent talking with a boy. The Jukebox played the Righteous Brothers' song of (*You're* my) *Soul and my Heart's Inspiration*, and on the extremely small dance floor, we romantically danced to it. When I finally dropped her off at Sharon's, we kissed goodnight and agreed to see each other again.

On the way home, I realized I was absolutely smitten. I had never felt so completely overwhelmingly enchanted by a girl before. When I reached my parent's apartment, I parked my car in the garage in back and walked in the back door, entering through the kitchen. For some reason my Mom was still up and was sipping a cup of hot tea that she had just made. She inquisitively asked: "So, how did the date go?" I looked at her and said: "Mom, you're not going to believe this, but I think I just met the girl I'm going to marry." In absolute shock, Mom dropped her tea cup and the liquid spattered all over the floor.

A couple of days later, I called and arranged for my second date with Marlene. I told her to dress casual and comfortable, as we would be going to a drive-in movie to see *Torn Curtain*, an Alfred Hitchcock suspense thriller. That evening I threw on some Docker type pants, a golf-type polo shirt and drove to Sharon's house. When I arrived I was ushered in and introduced to Mr. and Mrs. Kammerling, Joey's parents. They had come into town for the wedding and were visiting with Sharon's parents that evening. Marlene was wearing a short sleeve blouse and some pedal pushers. We all sat and visited a while, when someone asked what our plans were for that night. I caught the impulse look from Marlene that she preferred I not disclose that we were going to a drive-in, so I said: "That we didn't really know, but we would put our heads together and figure something out." At which time Mr. Kammerling, who had the reputation of being a bit of a jokester, quipped: "Just be sure not to put anything else together." Marlene blushed and was obviously embarrassed, so I politely replied: "Yes Sir" and we said our goodbyes and departed. We drove to the drive-in on Fredericksburg

Road, which was a popular social haunt for the older teen and young adult crowd. We picked up some goodies at the snack stand, and then snuggled in to watch the movie, while sipping our Cokes, eating popcorn, and kissing on occasion. After the movie we stopped at Jim's Frontier, a frequented burger joint also located on Fredericksburg Road, where we got an after-the- movie bite to eat. Marlene by that time had changed her mind about returning to Omaha by bus and had decided to fly back instead. She asked if I would be able to take her to the airport right after the wedding reception, and I, of course, said that I would be happy to do so. Before I took her back to Sharon's, we ended up on Inspiration Drive, which was a high place that overlooked the city. It was kind of a notorious lovers' lane, and it wasn't that far from Sharon's house. When I finally dropped her off, we kissed goodnight, and I said I would see her at the wedding.

The day of the wedding came, and I wore my light grey-taupe suit, a white dress shirt, and a dark striped tie. I arrived early as promised so I could load all of Marlene's suitcases into my VW. It was a beautiful wedding, and Marlene looked like a princess in her light blue bride's maid dress. After the ceremony, the wedding reception was held at Temple Beth-El, as well. We spent most of the time dancing with each other. Towards the end, it was Marlene who caught the bridal bouquet, and I managed to catch the bride's garter. So, I thought, was this some kind of an omen? After the reception, Marlene changed into her travel outfit, she packed her bride's maid dress into a hanging bag, which I loaded into my VW, and as promised drove her to the airport. By then it had become apparent that we kind of really liked one another. At the airport, I helped her check in her luggage, escorted her to her flight, and we kissed goodbye. As we departed, we promised that we would write one another.

These were the days before "I phones," and immediately upon her leaving, I commenced my letter writing campaign. Typically, I would write her twice a week, inquiring about what was going on in her life, detailing my happenings, and of course, always professing my love. Indeed, I was so in love with her, I stopped dating all the other girls that I had been seeing.

In the beginning, I had no idea that she would even write me back, but when she did, I was encouraged. We continued writing one another, and about once a week, we would talk on the telephone. Since she was a teacher, she got a Christmas / winter break, and as a law student, I was off that time, as well. Somehow I managed to convince her to come back to San Antonio, stay with us, in separate bedrooms of course, and spend her Christmas vacation with me. Despite the counsel from Margie, her sister-in-law, who advised her not to go, fortunately my luck prevailed, and Marlene agreed to come. So on December 17th I picked her up at the S.A. airport, and I felt as if I was the happiest guy in the world. We spent the next several days visiting many of the interesting sites in San Antonio: the Wonderland Mall, the Circus library, the Mexican market, the Buckhorn Hall of Horns, and the Alamo, of course.

I introduced her to Richard G. Santos and his wife, Sylvia. Richard was the Bexar County Archivist, and given my interest in history, we had become good friends. He took us to visit all of the old missions here, and with his knowledge, it was like having a private documented tour. Years' later Marlene and I would become the Godparents of their daughter, Cindy. That was some feat considering they were Roman Catholic, and we were Jewish. It took special permission from the Archbishop, who after meeting us, was convinced of our sincerity that should the occasion ever arise where we would have to care for and raise Cindy that we could bring her up as a Roman Catholic, despite our belief in Judaism. He granted his permission, blessed us, and we officially became Cindy's Godparents.

On December 24th I took Marlene to the Brackenridge Park area, where we rode the miniature railroad, saw the Sunken Gardens, and visited the San Antonio Zoo. San Antonio has one of the best zoos in the country, and it was at the zoo, in front of "Monkey Island" that I took her hand, dropped to one knee, and asked her to marry me. She smiled, said yes, and we hugged and kissed. Although I did not have an engagement ring yet, I pinned her using my Kappa Pi Sigma honorary fraternity pin. Marlene graciously accepted it, realizing how meaningful it was, and it was

{ 53

understood that a full-scale engagement ring would be forthcoming. That evening we announced our engagement to my parents and telephoned her parents and told them the news. So was it fate from the start? I've often wondered what the mathematical odds were for me to have met a girl on a blind date, arranged by an old mutual SAFTY friend, who I had not seen in years; and while at that mutual friend's wedding, for that girl to have caught that bridal bouquet and for me to have caught the bride's garter; and for the two of us to have spent a total of perhaps twelve hours with one another before we departed; then to be separated by over 900 miles during around a six month period of time, where the only communication was by mail and telephone; and finally after being reunited, within just a few days to become engaged. I would bet that the odds would be astronomical, but that is how I met my wife and soulmate.

My sister, Sandy, and Leonard had invited us to come up to Austin and go to a New Year's Eve party with them, which we did. While in Austin I showed Marlene the apartment where I resided, the law school where I attended, and the Capitol where I worked. As mementos I took pictures of her at the different places, and I think she felt like a photo model. We got dressed and ready for the gala New Year's Eve party, at which we had a blast. Shortly after midnight, we jumped into my VW and headed back to San Antonio. We reached my parent's apartment in the wee hours of the morning and crashed, sleeping late. When we woke, it was almost time for Marlene's New Year's Day flight back to Omaha. I took her to the airport, and once again we departed, but we knew that the time would come when we would be together.

After New Year's, in January, 1967, it was back to the grind of law school and working at the Texas Legislature. Marlene and I stayed in touch with each other, talking about my parents and I coming up for spring break and our wedding plans for that summer. As it turned out at the end of the spring semester, I would still need twelve more hours to graduate. Checking the law school summer schedule, I figured I could take two courses during the first summer semester, which would give me six hours of credit, and then take another two courses during the second summer semester, which would give me the final six hours of credit that I needed. Between the two summer semesters there was only a small window, which was the week over the July 4th holiday period. So the only Sunday that would be possible for our wedding would be Sunday, July 2nd. That then would give us barely enough time for an abbreviated honeymoon for a few days over the July 4th week, with our using that following weekend to settle in at Austin, as I would have to begin the second summer semester at the law school on Monday, July 10th. Obviously, the first problem was could Marlene secure the Synagogue in Omaha for our wedding and get the Rabbi there to officiate our ceremony on that Sunday evening. Otherwise our wedding would have to be delayed until sometime in the fall, and neither of us was in favor of that. So with only one single date possible, and the odds against us, undauntedly Marlene went to work on it. I was overjoyed when she called and told me she got it—both the Synagogue and the Rabbi had been secured for Sunday, July 2nd. The second part of the problem was up to me. Because of the compression of time, it meant summer courses moved at a much faster pace. The reading and homework requirements would be about three times harder and heavier than what it would be for the same courses during the fall or spring semester. To boot the courses offered that summer that I could take and which would count toward my degree were no slouch classes either. It meant I would have to work my ass off if I was going to make it, so I could graduate that September and take the Bar Exam that October. But I was very determined and assured Marlene not to worry and that I could do it.

Spring break finally came, and that Saturday Mom and Dad drove to Austin to pick me up. I was already packed, and I jumped into Dad's car to begin our trip to Omaha. I was anxious to see Marlene and to finally get to meet her parents. It would be an opportunity for Mom and Dad to meet them, as well. After all, arrangements had to be made concerning the rehearsal dinner and our wedding. Dad and I shared the driving, and we got to Omaha Sunday afternoon. A picnic dinner had been prepared at her parent's house, and we got to meet some of Marlene's family. Her mother, Rose, was a housewife, who had two older brothers: Morris, who was a Jewish War Veteran, and Irvin, who was a lawyer, and kind of the titular head of the family. Her father, Max, had gotten out of the bakery business some time ago, and now owned and operated a small Pawn shop in south Omaha. He came from a larger family, having five brothers and one sister, who had married the Uncle Jerry, who was a doctor and at whose clinic Marlene had worked her way through college. Some of her aunts and uncles, as well as some cousins, had come to meet us. I also met her brother, Stanley, who operated a kosher bakery, and who along with the help of her father, kindly agreed to provide the wedding cake and the groom's cake for us. Likewise, I also met his wife, Margie, the one who had tried to convince Marlene not to come to San Antonio for her Christmas break. After meeting me, I hoped she had finally changed her mind about that.

While in Omaha, Marlene took me to see her brother's bakery, the UNO campus where she had gone to college, her uncle's clinic, and her father's pawn shop. There she showed me the diamond that she wanted for her engagement ring. Although not overly large, it was of decent size and excellent quality. Set in the right mounting, it would look gorgeous. Her father had a contact in the jewelry business, where we were able to select a mounting and wedding bands. Finally, Marlene was going to get her engagement ring that I had promised her. But as a poor law student how was I going to be able to pay for it? Well fortunately, when I first went to work for Fox Co., some four years ago, I had a hunch that the company would grow. I took a chance and invested some of my savings in Fox Co. stock. During that time the stock had split and quadrupled in value. I would sell my stock, and the limited investment I had made would give me enough to cover the cost of the rings, with some left over to pay for our honeymoon.

There was still a lot to do. Marlene and I dropped by the Indian Hills Lodge, an upscale motel, located on the west part of Dodge Street, where we reserved one of the bridal suite rooms for our night's stay after the wedding. We accompanied our parents out to dinner at Marlene's favorite Italian restaurant, Caniglia's Venice Inn. They had a private room available that was of sufficient size, and my parents agreed that the price was reasonable. So arrangements were made for our rehearsal dinner. Marlene and I visited Brandeis Department Store where we worked on our gift registry selections. She also took me to her favorite shopping haunt, the Crossroads Mall, where I was introduced to the tasty Runza, a light dough bread roll, stuffed with grilled ground meat and onions, and baked to perfection. One afternoon, we met her Uncle Irvin at the Blackstone for lunch, where he treated us to Rueben sandwiches. Like me, he was into photography, and he advised us that he would be taking care of the wedding photographer and pictures as part of his wedding gift to us. And before spring break ended, he had arranged for a gala dinner party at the Highland Country Club, where he was a member, and which he and his wife were going to host in honor of our engagement. The dinner party was a splendid affair, which nearly all of Marlene's family attended. There were many toasts, most of which made tribute to Marlene and what a wonderful girl she was, of which I was already thoroughly convinced.

The week had gone by fast, but we had accomplished a lot. We all said our goodbyes, and my parents and I headed back to Texas. Once back in Austin, I buckled down to my law school classes and returned to work at the Capitol. In between though, I managed to find time to make arrangements for our honeymoon, which was going to be a three day--four night package at Six Flags over Texas in Arlington, located between Dallas and Ft. Worth. I also began in earnest hunting for an apartment where Marlene and I could live. We certainly didn't need the four-man type apartment where I currently resided, nor could we afford it. I finally found a little efficiency unit consisting of one bedroom, one bathroom, a small den, and the tiniest kitchen imaginable, but it would do. It was located on the Southside of Austin, where rents were considerably less as compared to the pricier Northside.

It was the end of May, and the spring semester and the 60th legislative session were finally over. I had only a few days to catch my breath before I began the two courses for which I had registered for the first summer semester. The work was difficult and intense, but the time went by fast. Before I knew it, the first summer session was over, and I had aced both classes. Immediately, I caught a flight back to Omaha, arriving a few days before our wedding. Marlene had seen to all the last minute details, and everything was ready to go. We had to meet with Rabbi Myer S. Kripke, who would over-see and perform the ceremony at the Beth-El Conservative Synagogue. I felt it was rather whimsical that it had the exact same name as my Temple back in San Antonio. On Saturday evening, July 1, we joined our parents, wedding party, and out of town guests for the rehearsal dinner at Caniglia's. Marlene's suggested choice for the restaurant was perfect. The meal was delectable and the service impeccable. Everyone had a great time. As we parted, under Jewish tradition I knew that I would not see Marlene during the next day until the following evening when she would walk down the aisle as a bride to become my wife.

Sunday, July 2, 1967, was the big day, and I spent it alone in anxious anticipation with my mind racing with thoughts that with all the obstacles and waiting this was finally going to happen—the beginning of our lives together. Our wedding was scheduled for that evening and was a typical Jewish wedding, with a reception to follow. Marlene looked like an angel as her parents accompanied her down the aisle. We exchanged vows and rings, and at the end, I kissed my bride and broke the traditional glass amongst shouts of Mazel Tov. The reception with dinner and dancing followed and moved along at a rapid pace. Toward the end, Marlene changed into her going away outfit, and amidst applause and cheers, we jumped into Marlene's car and drove away to Indian Hills for our night's stay. I thought how unusual for the bride to be driving the groom away rather than vice versa, but considering our meeting, courtship, and engagement, as a couple not very much had been all that "usual" about us yet.

The following morning we reported to the home of Marlene's parents for a family goodbye brunch. After eating, socializing, and saying adieu, we were taken to the Omaha airport to catch our flight to Dallas Love Field. From there we took a shuttle to the Inn of the Six Flags in Arlington for our honeymoon. We spent Tuesday through Thursday at the Six Flags Park, which was divided into sections, with each one portraying a flag under which Texas was governed and dedicated to the theme and culture represented by that flag, to wit: Spain, France, Mexico, the Republic of Texas, the Confederacy, and the United States. Perhaps Tuesday, July 4th, was the most exciting day, because it being Independence Day, in the U.S. section of the park, all kinds of special parades, shows, and celebrations were scheduled. During our three days there, we ambled through all of the sections, and I think we rode on every ride and saw every show. Marlene's favorite was the water ride through the Spelunkers' Cave, which was a much miniaturized version and more simplistically designed ride roughly copied after Disney's *It's a Small world*. On Friday, July 7th, we left Six Flags, flew back to Austin, and moved into our little apartment. The weekend was spent getting settled, acquainting Marlene with where the grocery, drug store, and laundry mat were located, and teaching her to drive my VW, which was a standard stick shift. She had only driven automatic shift vehicles before, so she was not used to it, nor did she like it. But like a good sport she learned to drive it. The plan was to sell her car that she left back in Omaha, and we would become a one car family, with both of us sharing my VW, which was clearly the more economical of the two vehicles. By Monday, July 10th, I was back at school beginning the second summer session, taking the last two courses which encompassed the remaining six hours that I needed to graduate. The session went by quickly, and I managed to ace those two classes, as well.

So by the end of August, 1967, I found myself graduating from UT law school in the upper 25 percent of my class. As it turned out Dean Keeton was pretty much on target with his prediction. Of the nearly 1,000 students who had started law school with me, only 377 made it through and comprised the 1967 graduating class. Of that number only twelve were girls, and all of them and most of the rest of my fellow classmates had already graduated at the end of the spring semester. So there was only the remnant of about forty of us that were scheduled to attend the formal graduation ceremony set for September 24, 1967. It was the strangest and most unique graduation ceremony in which I had ever been involved. There were no cap and gowns, and none of us were called up to the stage to receive our degree. Rather we sat in rows in the audience, dressed in coat and tie-business attire, where we were each presented with a sunflower that was pinned to our lapel. There were the customary brief speeches of congratulations, and about the significance of becoming a lawyer and the importance of upholding the ethical standard of the legal profession. Then the spouse of every married graduate was called up to the stage, was honored, and presented with a very official looking document that said:

The University of Texas School of Law
In recognition of the distinguished service and in grateful acknowledgement
Of the outstanding contribution made by
Marlene G. Eichelbaum
To the support, well-being, and furtherance of the Profession of Law
Hereby confers on her this
P H T Degree
As our symbol of appreciation for Putting her Husband Through the School of Law

It was dated and signed by Dean W. Page Keeton, and I was absolutely gleeful, as Marlene blushingly walked across the stage to receive this Degree; whereas, on the other hand, I unceremoniously received my actual Law Degree afterwards through the mail.

Even before the enchanting sunflower graduation, I had already enrolled in a Bar Review class to help me prepare for the October Bar Exam. It was like cramming three and a half years of law school into just several weeks. Every weekday I would get up at 6:30 AM, and after having breakfast with Marlene, by 7:30 AM I would begin studying the course outlines that were scheduled for review that evening. With minor breaks, my studying would continue until 5:30 PM, when I would pause, to eat dinner with Marlene. After that I would attend the Bar Review class, which usually started at 7:00 PM and continued until about 11:00 PM. This grueling routine was day after day for several weeks. Saturdays, I would use for a general weekly review and study all day. On Saturday nights, Marlene and I would have a date night, or we would socially get together with another couple or two for a party. Sunday was a day of rest, and then it would start all over again.

  Finally, the Bar Review class was over, and the dreaded Bar Exam was upon me. Even though I had graduated from law school, in order to be considered an actual lawyer and able to practice law in Texas, I would have to pass the Texas Bar Exam. The exam had a reputation of being really hard, and so the pressure was really on. The exam was broken up into different sections, which were taken over a four day period of time. In those days, it was all or nothing. If you failed to pass even just one part, then that was considered failing the entire exam, no matter how well you did on all of the other parts. In essence then you would have to take the whole exam all over again. The night before the first day of the exam, fearing that I was getting too up-tight, I decided to close the books. As I was a big James Bond fan in those days, in order to relax, I took Marlene to see the James Bond movie *You Only Live Twice* starring Sean Connery. The movie seemed to curb my escalating nervous attitude. Afterwards Marlene surprised me by presenting me with a model ship kit of the Santa Maria. She knew how much I liked models of the old sailing ships. The next day I began the Bar Exam, which was a real endurance contest over the next four days. But that little model ship saved my life. Each night after dinner, rather than fret and worry about the test sections I had already taken that day or frantically trying to cram for the next day's portions, we worked on the model ship together and just rested. Somehow this scheme worked and kept me relatively calm and relaxed. And by the end of the Exam, although exhausted, I felt pretty good about it, and we went out to the Night Hawk Steakhouse to celebrate.

I had given our landlord notice for October 31st, and so by the end of the month, we left our little efficiency apartment in Austin, went back to San Antonio, and temporarily moved in with my parents at their two bedroom apartment in the Fleetwood complex on Vance Jackson, which was close to the U.S. Post Office sub-station that Dad would eventually end up managing. Even though it was later in the school year, Marlene applied for a teacher's position at the San Antonio Independent School District (SAISD). They were desperate for math teachers, and because of her double major in mathematics and education and the fact that she already had some teaching experience; she was hired, and ended up teaching math at Edison High School. With me it was a different situation. No one was going to hire me in any kind of law position, knowing that in the near future, I was subject to being called up for active military duty. In order to avoid just sitting around, I called up my old political connections at the Vale, Torres, Gonzales, and Alaniz law firm and visited them at their office in the Tower Life Building. Pete Torres was willing to take me on as his law clerk for the salary of $25.00 per week. Clearly it wasn't much, but it was better than just remaining idle, and it would give me a chance to continue learning about being a lawyer and giving me some practical experience, as well. Pete had me preparing various legal papers, and mainly drafting pre-trial discovery documents, such as Interrogatories and Requests for Admission. These had to be answered in a sworn to manner by the other side. At that time, these were unlimited in number, and so in one case I had drafted some 150 very specific and detailed questions as our Interrogatory package. According to Pete, it pushed the other side into settling, because they didn't want to have to answer all of those questions under oath. When the case settled he paid me a $150.00 bonus as a reward for the "extraordinary job" that I did. Amongst his colleagues, he began referring to me as his "Duke of Discovery." I also did nearly all of his court filings, making periodic trips to the Bexar County Courthouse. One day while filing some pleadings, I was in the Courthouse elevator, when one of the girls who worked as a clerk in Jimmy Knight's County Clerk's office spotted me and said: "Congratulations." I gave her a rather puzzled look and replied: "For what?" She smiled and said: "For passing the Bar Exam. Your name was in the newspaper." I was shocked and surprised, but felt unbelievably happy, and I thanked her for the very good news. On the way back to the office, I picked up a newspaper and anxiously turned through the pages. And there it was. A small box column that said: "New San Antonio Lawyers." It listed those from S.A. who had passed the October Texas Bar Exam. There were seven names listed, and mine was one of them. At the office, the whole gang congratulated me. When I got home, I told the news to Marlene and my parents, and we all went out to eat to celebrate. I got the official word from the State Bar of Texas in the mail a few days later. It was an interesting experience about how the press knew about me even before I did. In the next few days, Pete arranged to formally introduce me before the State Presiding Court Judge in Bexar County, Solomon Casseb, Jr., who administered my oath of office and swore me in. I was now officially a Texas lawyer.

One day while filing some pleadings for Pete, I ran into an old college acquaintance, Harry B. Adams, III. I first met Harry at SAC, and I would see him from time to time on campus and at various socials. At a fraternity off campus party, I spotted him seated alone at a table in the corner drinking a beer. I approached him, and it appeared that he was pretty smashed. I sat down and talked with him, and it was evident that he was rather sullen and despondent. He had a severe crush on a cute red-haired girl named Beverly. According to Harry, she came from a fine upper-class family; whereas, like me, he came from a family that was not exactly wealthy. He was absolutely "in love with her," but he didn't think that "she would ever give him the time of day," because he felt he was not good enough. I must have spent the better part of an hour with him, trying to dispel his inferior feelings and negative attitude in that regard. I made every effort to convince him not to give up and for him to truly express his feelings toward her. I finally was able to convince him to stop drinking, and most important, to allow me to drive him home. After SAC, I had kind of lost contact with him. Although right about a year younger than me, he had already become a lawyer. Upon graduating from SAC, he had opted for a combined program, whereby he attended St. Mary's for only one more year, and then went straight into their law school at the downtown campus. In that way he was able to obtain his Law Degree in a total of six years; whereas, it had taken me seven plus years to do so. Harry ended up graduating from St. Mary's in the spring of 1967, took the summer Bar Exam, and was a new lawyer working for the Bexar County Legal Aid Association. We made a date to have lunch together and to get reacquainted.

The following week I met Harry for lunch at the Mexican Manhattan restaurant. While waiting for our lunch, we chomped on tortilla chips and salsa, and I learned that in 1966, Legal Aid operated out of a small, two-room office in the Bexar County Courthouse. The organization consisted of an elderly lawyer, Hilmer Schmidt, and some top notch law clerks, who were attending St. Mary's law school. Jimmy Lytton and Mike Moriarty came on aboard first, and Harry joined them slightly thereafter. They were known as the "Three Musketeers," and according to Harry, pretty much ran the show. In fact it was Jimmy Lytton who had, in large part, drafted the funding grant proposal to the National Legal Services, which was then part of the War on Poverty Program. Jimmy was the one who was primarily responsible for overseeing and shepherding the process of actually getting the grant money. The three had worked very close together and had become really good friends. In fact Jimmy was Mike's best man when he got married in 1966. After graduation in 1967, Mike left Legal Aid and went to work for Helm, Jones & Pletcher, which was a prominent trial law firm in Houston. Eventually he would become a very successful personal injury attorney. Jimmy Lytton remained as a Legal Aid lawyer, but regrettably during the following year, he died in a glider plane accident in California, cutting short which what undoubtedly would have been a most brilliant legal career. Harry ended up marrying that girl named Beverly and stayed as a lawyer with Legal Aid. When our lunch came, we enjoyed our chalupes compuesta, as Harry extolled the attributes of working for Legal Aid. "You know Mel, the salary isn't the best, but it's roughly equivalent to what a starting lawyer would make in most places in San Antonio. And for right now it's okay." He went on to explain: "They pay all of your Bar dues and malpractice insurance, but most of all, you get a ton of legal experience—more than you would ever get in the private sector. Hell, I bet in just a few years, I'm going to get to do things that most lawyers would never get to do in a lifetime." Harry concluded: "And the neat thing is that you get to legally help folks who really need it, but who could never afford it. It leaves you with a pretty damn good feeling inside. I'm telling you Mel, you ought to join us." I told Harry that he was preaching to the choir and as a starting lawyer, this is exactly the kind of job position that I envisioned for myself. In fact, this would be "my dream job." I explained to him that first I had a military commitment that I would have to satisfy, but as soon as that was done, I would definitely be in touch with him. As we parted, I had a strange feeling that our paths would cross again.

CHAPTER 6

My Fort Dix Adventure

1967 – 1968

It was October, 1967, and having graduated from UT law school the month before and having just completed taking the Texas Bar Exam, I was acutely aware of the fact that my higher education military deferment was over. The Vietnam War was in full bloom. I, along with a number of my classmates, did not think that the U.S. involvement in that war was such a wise decision, but clearly that was not going to be my call. I was classified 1-A, and fully subject to the draft. Being married was no exemption. They were drafting married guys all the time. Several of my law school contacts and I felt that just waiting around to be drafted in the near future really wasn't conducive to any kind of planning. So after talking it over with Marlene, who agreed, I and some of my law school buddies decided to enlist in the Army National Guard at Camp Mabry in Austin. While there I became reacquainted with Johnny Tafolla, who was an officer with the Guard Unit. Johnny was a lawyer from San Antonio, who I had previously met through my political involvement with the Democratic Party. He explained that the National Guard Unit at Camp Mabry was an administrative unit, filled with accountants, lawyers, and all sorts of admin types. That basically their duty was to help the Army with all kinds of paperwork, and how it would be a great way for a guy like me to serve. He also assured me that I wouldn't be scheduled for active duty call up until after the first of the year. I thought that would work, as I would get my Bar Exam results before I got called up, and it would give Marlene and I time to move back to San Antonio, get settled and situated, and be able to spend some time together before my reporting for active duty. I thanked Johnny for his consultation, and I went ahead and signed up. Marlene and I spent the rest of the year together, and then after New Year's, in January, 1968, I received the official notice that the following month I was to report for active duty.

It was right around the time of the Tet Offensive in Vietnam, when on February 13, 1968; Marlene took me to the San Antonio airport, where we said a tearful goodbye as we parted. On my flight to New York City I reflected that we were separated through nearly all of our year-long courtship, and since our marriage we had been together for only slightly more than six months, and now we were going to be separated again, for at least six months, and maybe longer. Oh well, I mused: whoever said that true love would be easy? Upon arrival, I oriented myself, caught a cab to Grand Central Station, where I found the proper bus going to Fort Dix, New Jersey and hopped aboard it. I had travelled very light, literally with the clothes on my back and carrying just a few personal items. From the letter I had received from the U.S. Army, it was made clear that they would be providing everything. So far it had been true, as the flight, cab, and bus fare were all paid with military vouchers sent to me with my call up letter.

When the bus pulled in at Fort Dix, it dropped me off at what was evidently the Induction Center, which consisted of several old wooden, barn-like looking buildings that housed the processing center, the medical exam and shot stations, the quartermasters, and a mess hall for the new arrivals. It all appeared rather dismal. To add to the dreary setting, the weather was absolutely abysmal. It was a totally overcast, cloudy sky, which was colored a deep, dark grey. I would not see a speck of sun light for days. The temperature was a bitter cold, and it was damp, with frequent intermittent sleet and snow flurries. The trip had pretty much taken all day, so it was fairly late when I arrived. A number of us were gathered together, pushed through the mess hall for a quick meal, and then shoved into crowded barracks for the night. The barracks were old dilapidated, rectangular wood buildings, with rotting wooden floors. They were lined with rows of very Spartan-type army cots, crammed in rather close together on each of the longer sided walls, with an aisle in the center. At the far end were the lavatory facilities, having old rusty shower heads and toilets that would likely fail a city inspection. There was no central heat or air, but rather space heaters were "strategically" placed throughout the barracks. If your cot was near one, you sweated profusely, and if your cot was far away from one, you froze to death. Either way it was most uncomfortable.

The following morning we woke up at the crack of dawn, and our mundane processing continued. More paperwork was filled out, and we were issued dog tags, bearing our individual name and serial number, which we were instructed never to take off. We were herded through the barber station, where everyone received the infamous GI haircut. Next we were lined up and shoveled past doctors, where I received the quickest medical exam I had ever experienced. From there we were funneled through the shot center where we received a multitude of injections, which were all very expeditiously done with "shot guns," devices designed for rapidly giving vaccinations to a large number of people. Several of the guys fainted going through this ordeal. We then moved through the quartermasters, where we were issued a giant duffel bag and all of our clothing and gear. Everything, including your boots, had to be labeled with your military I.D. on it. So labels had to be done, brass shined, and boots polished, and in between there was plenty of PE and marching. Everywhere we went it was always double-time. We rushed from place to place, and then after we got there, spent time just waiting until they were ready for us. This was the military concept of "hurry up and wait," and I guess it was the Army's way of teaching us patience. Those were hellish days, but my previous scouting background and ROTC training definitely helped me endure. Finally after several days at the horrible Induction Center, a large group of us were loaded onto trucks and taken to our Basic Training Unit facility. We were a motley-looking bunch of all sizes and shapes; racially, ethnically, religiously, and culturally diverse; and coming from many divergent parts of the U.S. It was the Army's job to turn us all into soldiers, and it was clear they intended to do just that. I was assigned to Company A, 1st Battalion of the 3rd Basic Combat Training Brigade. There was a small headquarters building with a larger adjacent quartermaster center, where our weapons and equipment were stored. We were each issued a rifle, which we had the responsibility to maintain and keep it highly proficient. In the days to come we would learn to quickly disassemble and then reassemble the weapon, and even do so blindfolded. These buildings were located on one side of a large, open field that was used for marching and training. On the other side of the field were the barracks where we were housed. These were much more modern. They were three story brick buildings, with tile floors. They had central heat and air, where temperatures were kept within a reasonably comfortable range. The lavatory facilities had much more contemporary showers and toilets, similar to what one would find in a health club. Each floor would contain rows of dorm-like suite rooms, which although in somewhat close confines, each one would adequately house about a dozen or so men. Although still very basic, compared to the Induction Center, it was like a luxury hotel. The mess hall, located a few blocks away, was within walking distance. In those days, we all took rotated turns in doing KP duty, which was an all-day duty from very early in the morning until late in the evening.

At the Basic Training Unit we met the officers and non-com cadre who would be in charge of training us. It seemed like their greatest pleasure was to terrorize us. Our concepts of individuality and privacy were consciously assaulted, as we were constantly told how useless we were, and how we'd better shape up, or else. We were continuously yelled at for everything, and for nothing. Those who made it learned not to take it too personally, and that it was all part of the game. We also learned surviving meant hanging in there together. If one guy's bunk was not made up properly, or if his shoes weren't shined or brass polished, then not only did he get punished, but the whole squad got penalized right along with him. We quickly learned the concept of teamwork and helping one another. I guess that was the Army's way of teaching unit cohesiveness.

The moment we arrived at the Basic Training Unit our training began in earnest. From a military prospective it was multifaceted and all encompassing, as we were rushed from one station to the next. We had daily classes where we learned about military conduct, a soldier's duty, the chain of command, unit logistics, and a plethora of other pertinent subjects. At the conclusion of all the classes, a comprehensive exam was given that we were required to pass. I ended up not missing a single question and making a perfect score. Later on our Company Commander, Captain Braun, complimented me on that achievement, stating it was only the second time he had ever seen that happen.

Everyone had to qualify as to being able to proficiently shoot with the rifle, at least to the minimal level of "marksman." The intermediate level was "sharpshooter," and the highest level was "expert." We had been issued the M-14, which was the standard rifle that the Army had been using for quite some time. It was a very reliable weapon, and we spent many practice sessions at the rifle range shooting pop-up targets with it. Finally, it was qualification day for our Company, and everyone wanted to do the very best they could. As an extra incentive, for those who qualified "expert," as a special reward they would receive a 48 hour furlough weekend pass, and also they would get the opportunity to shoot with the Army's M-16, which was the newer, more modern rifle that would eventually be replacing the M-14. Most of the Company qualified at the "marksman" or "sharpshooter" level, which was plenty respectable, but somehow I managed to qualify as "expert." For those dozen or so of us who did, one night we were taken to the "night range." There we were given the M-16 rifles, which at that time, when compared to our M-14s, looked like they came out of some kind of science fiction movie. They were lighter, easy to handle, and fired rather nicely. We were able to shoot with them using tracer bullets, and it was quite an experience.

As our training continued, I held my own in hand to hand combat, utilized the bayonet with proficiency, and made it through the various and sundry obstacle courses. And then there was drill, drill, and more drill. Here again my past ROTC experience really came in handy. But when it came to the onerous PT run, I simply could not do it, no matter how hard I tried. Roughly about half way to two thirds the way through the run I would find myself helplessly out of breath and would end up collapsing and passing out. I continued to make the effort, but to no avail. Evidently, I simply just did not have the wind capacity to do it.

I do not know whether it was the icy cold, damp climate, the physical rigors of training, or both, but around the latter part of March, I had contracted a severe respiratory infection that put me in the military hospital for over a week. The doctors there diagnosed me as having chronic bronchial asthma. Apparently a condition that I had outgrown and of which I had absolutely no episodes over the past twelve years had decided to revisit me with a vengeance. By early April the doctors put me on a PT waiver, specifying no running or extensive marching. Thereafter, I was put into the headquarters detachment of the Company, with the official specialty designation as "general clerk." Here I was in my element of doing paperwork, for which I had a ton of experience and was very good at.

Right about that time the "scuttlebutt" was that our Company's old First Sergeant, who nobody was going to miss, was being transferred, and we were scheduled to get a brand new First Sergeant. Then late one afternoon, I was summoned into the Company Commander's office. As I entered, I snapped to attention, saluted, and said: "Private Eichelbaum reporting as ordered, Sir." Captain Braun, who was seated at his desk, returned my salute, told me to stand at ease and be seated, and then said that he wanted to talk with me. "First of all", he began, "because of your PE situation, it is very likely that eventually you will be receiving an honorable medical discharge, but that will probably take quite some time," he said. "But have you heard that we are getting a new First Sergeant?" he asked. "Yes Sir", I responded. Captain Braun went on to disclose that his name was

Sergeant Lowery. He had twice served in Vietnam, was a family man, and just happened to be Black. Captain Braun pointed out that although the Army had a good representation of Sergeants who were Black, at that time, there were not that many who were serving as First Sergeants. Captain Braun emphasized: "He is an exemplary individual, and I want him to make it. But his weakness is paperwork, which happens to be your strength." The Captain paused and glanced at an armband that was lying on his desk. He then stated: "It won't make any difference in your actual rank or pay status. You'll officially remain a PFC and continue to be paid accordingly. But for all other purposes, and especially those of command, we would like to promote you to the rank of Acting Sergeant E-7, and designate you as our Company's Operations Sergeant." Captain Braun continued to explain how he wanted me to back up Sergeant Lowery and be his right hand, coach him through the paperwork, and assist him in reforming and streamlining our Company's training schedule. "Now you don't have to do this," he stated. "You can just remain a clerk and continue your routine duty until your discharge arrives, because doing this will mean a lot more work for you, but you would be doing us a big service. So soldier, what do you say?" he asked. I looked at Captain Braun and with a slight smile and nod of my head, said: "Captain, it will be my privilege to be of service to the Company, and I will be more than happy to do it, Sir." Captain Braun handed me the armband, bearing the rank of Sergeant E-7, and said: "Welcome aboard Sergeant." I snapped on my new rank, and except for the First Sergeant, this made me the highest ranking non-com in our Company. I now outranked all of the Platoon Sergeants and the rest of the non-com cadre that trained me. Politically, I felt this could be rather difficult, as I could easily foresee how jealousies might very well arise. I decided to "low key" the issue. I made sure that I did not portray an attitude of "lording it over" any of my fellow non-coms. Rather I acted humble, treated everyone with respect, and adopted the concept of a "team" approach, often asking for the advice, suggestions, and help of my fellow non-coms.

In the following weeks I assisted Sergeant Lowery with all of the paperwork, and everything passed through my desk before it went to his. It was kind of like when I was working as a Legislative Assistant at the Texas legislature all over again, except this was military style instead. I reviewed our Company's training program and looked for ways to make it more efficient and streamlined. For example, under the current schedule, trucks would come to our Company area, and pick up the men and transport them to the rifle range for shooting practice. When finished, the trucks would arrive and carry them back to the Company area for hand to hand combat and bayonet training. Once done, the trucks would return and transport them to an area that was right next to the rifle range for grenade throwing practice, and then afterwards, would again return them to our Company area. This meant four separate truck trips. I thought that we should switch things by first doing the rifle range, followed by the grenade throwing practice, and then engaging in the hand to hand combat and bayonet training. This would reduce the truck trips to only two; thereby, cutting them in half. Another situation was that with our present schedule we had chemical defense and gas mask training right after breakfast, and too many guys got sick and puked, which wasted time in allowing for them to recover. My idea was to move it to later on in the day, which would lessen the chances and frequency of this happening. Of course all of this required coordination with the various training sites, but everyone proved cooperative for the most part. And so it went on and on, until Sergeant Lowery had developed a training schedule format that was a significant improvement. I guess we did a fairly good job, because after submitting our final version, we were visited by the major, who was our Brigade Commander. He said that we had created such an exemplary model that they were planning to adopt it for the entire Battalion. In fact, he said that he wouldn't be surprised if the entire Brigade followed suit. He commended us for our excellent work. By the end of June, it was clear that my discharge would be coming down the pike soon. Captain Braun called me into his office and gave me a letter which read as follows:

Subject: Letter of Appreciation 21 June 1968
PVT Melvin N. Eichelbaum NG25871639
Company A, 1st Battalion, 3rd BCT Brigade
Fort Dix, New Jersey 08640

On the occasion of your departure from this unit, I wish to express my appreciation for your outstanding performance of duty as Acting Operations Sergeant.

Your constant review and analysis of training programs and your preparation of training schedules insured maximum utilization of available cadre and time.

The establishment of an exemplary training program is indicative of your loyalty, concern for subordinates, and leadership ability. I bid you continued success in all future undertakings. Working with you has been my distinct pleasure. I wish you the best of luck.

Thank you again for a job well done.

Conrad D. Braun
CPT, INF
Commanding

Marlene had come up to join me for my trip home and stayed at the Fort Dix Visitors Center. On July 1, 1968, the day before our first wedding anniversary, I was effectively discharged from the Army. I said my goodbyes to Captain Braun, Sergeant Lowery, and the rest of the cadre. Marlene and I spent our anniversary in New York City, and after a brief trip to visit the Dutch Country Pennsylvania area over the July 4th holiday, we then caught a flight back to San Antonio and retuned home. Already having been released from active duty, I reported to Camp Mabry in Austin on July 7, 1968, when I received my official honorable discharge from the Army and the National Guard, and thus ended my military service obligation.

To celebrate my homecoming and transition back to civilian life, Marlene had picked up a two day ticket package to Hemisfair. It was the 1968 World's Fair, hosted by San Antonio, which had opened April 6th and was scheduled to run for six months, until October 6th. The international exposition was located in the heart of downtown and sprawled over nearly a 96 acre park, which included a man-made lake. Its espoused theme was the confluence of the civilizations of the Americas, and its featured centerpiece, called the Tower of the Americas, was a huge, circular revolving restaurant that sat atop a giant 750' column, and which overlooked the entire city. Over thirty nations and more than a dozen major corporations had chosen to participate in this international extravaganza, which up to that time had been the most expensive exposition in the history of world's fairs. Tracing nearly all the way around the circumference was the mini monorail, and traversing a large segment of the park from a perpendicular perspective was the Swiss sky ride. Both rides offered excellent bird's-eye views of the fair grounds. The most popular attraction was the famous Aztec Flying Indians, which was part of the exposition of Mexico. It was an amazing spectacle to see. The chief and four braves would ascend a large pole, extending about 100' up into the air, high above the fairground below. The chief would position himself in the center, with each brave on one side, of a small, square platform that sat atop the pole. At the signal, and without any safety net below, the four braves would drop from the platform and with each one being tethered only by a rope, they would execute a dramatic descent, head first and with arms extended, whirling around the pole, as they made their way back to the ground. Once at the bottom, the braves would take one of the ropes, extend it, and the chief from the top of the pole, would quickly slide down it. At night each of the braves would hold a lighted flare in each hand as they flew to the ground, making it a sparkling wonderment to watch.

In the two days there, we visited all the expositions, rode on nearly all the rides, and saw most of the shows. There was a romantic dinner atop the Tower of the Americas, and it was just a marvelous time. The last night, Marlene and I sat at a pub that was part of the Lone Star Beer pavilion, and which overlooked the man-made lake. We were listening to the music of "Him, He, and Me", a group that performed many of the songs of the Kingston Trio, while enjoying our nightcap cocktails. I reminiscently thought how proud Jake Johnson would be to know that his pet Bill of "Liquor by the Drink" had finally passed the Texas Legislature and became the law, even though it was after he departed. I made a sentimental toast in honor of "Good Old Jake."

CHAPTER 7

My Dream Job Begins

1968

Having completed my military obligation and after celebrating a couple days at Hemisfair, it was now time for me to get to work. Marlene had already locked in her teaching position from the previous year at Edison, and she would resume teaching math there right after Labor Day. But in my case, I really needed to find myself a job. The first thing I did was to re-contact Harry Adams and make a lunch date with him. He was still working as an attorney with Bexar County Legal Aid (BCLA), which was now under the auspices of the federal Office of Economic Opportunity (OEO).

In 1964, President Lyndon B. Johnson pushed through the Civil Rights Act. That same year, as part and parcel of his "War on Poverty," the Economics Opportunities Act was passed, as well. Amazingly, I had met with LBJ just the year before and had the opportunity to discuss with him current issues that college age folks were concerned about, civil rights and poverty being among them. Johnson designated Sargent Shriver to head up the OEO. That very year Edgar and Jean Cahn wrote an article in the Yale Law Journal, entitled: *The War on Poverty: A Civilian Perspective.* In it they espoused the concept that providing civil legal assistance to low income people was an important element in striving for equal justice. They forcefully argued that neighborhood law offices with neighborhood lawyers should be part of an anti-poverty effort. Later Edgar became Shriver's

Executive Assistant, and Jean joined him from the State Department as an OEO consultant. The push for legal services for the poor was well on its way. They sought and got approval from the American Bar Association (ABA), which at that time was led by Lewis F. Powell, Jr., who later became a Justice on the U.S. Supreme Court. By 1965, OEO had launched its Legal Services Program, which funded legal aid organizations throughout the United States.

During our cordial lunch Harry and I got reacquainted, and I learned that the funding grant that Jim Lytton had initially worked on evidently went through. Bexar County Legal Aid (BCLA) was no longer a small time operation with just a few lawyers working out of a hole-in-the-wall office at the Bexar County Courthouse. Rather it had become adequately funded, fully staffed, and operated out of a decently sized, modern law office that took up most of the third floor of an office building at 203 W. Nueva Street, which was conveniently located only a couple blocks from the Bexar County Courthouse. The BCLA program had obtained co-operation and support from the local San Antonio Bar Association (SABA), under the leadership of its President, Richard Tinsman, who was a prominent San Antonio trial lawyer, and under the guidance of its Executive Director, Jimmy Allison. Meanwhile the elderly, semi-retired Hilmer Schmidt was no longer the program's director, but had been moved down the rung of the ladder and was nominally named as assistant director. The organization had received a new, dynamic director, who had supervised Legal Aid's growth and expansion. His name was Frank P. Christian. Locally he was a well-respected attorney, who had significant connections with the Good Government League (GGL) business and civic leaders, who pretty much ran the city of San Antonio. He was independently wealthy and resided in the more affluent Alamo Heights area, located on the Northside. According to Harry, Christian didn't have to work at all but had "beaucoup" money coming in from family holdings and interests in Virginia, from where he originally hailed. Harry said that he came from an old, distinguished Virginia family going all the way back to colonial times. Mr. Christian was a rather cultured individual, who had a passionate interest in the arts and the San Antonio Little Theater (SALT), of which he was a patron and one of their top actors. With all his complexities, he had a deep devotion to the law and an absolute dedication to the concept of equal justice. Aside from its central downtown office, and being mindful of the neighborhood law office concept, the BCLA association had opened up four satellite offices to service low income individuals throughout the city. The Guadalupe Street office was near the public housing sites of Alazan Apache Courts and Cassiano Homes, where large numbers of poor people lived. Likewise the Zarzamora Street office was near the San Juan Homes public housing project. Both were Westside offices, where significant numbers of the Hispanic community resided. The General McMullen office serviced the deep Southside; whereas, the E. Houston Street office was located on the Eastside, where large numbers of the Black community lived.

After lunch I accompanied Harry to the downtown legal aid office, which is where he worked, and he gave me a guided tour of the place. The office had an ample size reception area where clientele could be seated. From there, down the hall there were a bevy of small kiosk-type spaces, where law clerks, typically students from St. Mary's law school, would initially interview potential clients in order to see if they met Legal Aid's eligibility criteria and to determine what the basic nature of their legal problems or questions were. Further down the hall, there were a number of small, but rather functional attorney offices, where the clients could visit privately with a lawyer and confidentially discuss their particular legal situation. In one part of the large center area was a conference room, which contained a large conference table with seats all around it. Its walls were lined with shelves of law books that comprised a basic law library. For any legal research that required more sophistication, the extensive SABA law library at the Courthouse was just a couple blocks away. The other part of the center area was the secretarial pool, which contained several legal secretary L-desks, on which sat modern electronic IBM "Selectric" typewriters that were kept plenty busy by the skilled secretary pool. At one side of the secretary area was a workspace for copying and collating, and where a modern, state-of-the-art Xerox copying machine was placed. On the other side were a row of file cabinets, where the clients' case files were kept. At the very back end, a more secluded secretary office existed that was occupied by Patsy Neyland, who was Mr. Christian's private secretary. And that area led into Mr. Christian's office. All in all, I was most impressed with the entire set up. As far as I was concerned working there would be my dream job. Harry introduced me to Patsy, who was a young, shapely woman with short blond hair. She graciously allowed me to fill out an application for employment and accepted my resume, even though she pointedly told me that they were already fully staffed, and there were no openings. As I handed her my papers, she smiled and commented, "I'll keep these on file because you can never tell what will happen." I thanked her, said goodbye to Harry, and left.

That evening I excitedly related my Legal Aid experience to Marlene. She realized that was where I really wanted to work, but from our personal economic standpoint, I could not just wait around for them, and I would have to apply elsewhere. So in the ensuing days I made the rounds. I tendered applications at the Internal Revenue Service (IRS), the Bexar County District Attorney's Office—Child Support Section, the City of San Antonio—Municipal Court Division, as well as several private practice law firms. But the answer was always the same. No one seemed to be hiring. I was getting somewhat discouraged, to say the least, and out of concern I finally contacted Pete Torres. Of course his firm could not provide me with any salary, but they were comfortable enough with me to let me come in as a suitemate. They could let me have the same little room that I had when I was clerking there and to utilize that as my office. I would be expected to pay my fair share of rent and expenses, but Pete felt the guys would agree to give me a pass on those obligations for a couple of months so I could have some time to get started. I knew that they might throw me some bones every now and then, but these were more likely to be what most lawyers called "garbage cases"—high risk and with very little chance of earning any real money. In short, I would be "hanging up my own shingle," and I would be very much on my own. Of course at this stage of the game, I felt that I would be better off having a job that would bring in a steady salary, and I knew it, but so far nothing was seeming to pan out in that direction.

It was the very end of August, 1968, and Marlene and I were still living with my parents in their two bedroom apartment on Vance Jackson while my job search was underway. It was a hot, humid day with the weather threatening rain but not quite seeming to get there. Out of desperation, I had called Pete the day before and made an appointment with him for this afternoon to come down and talk about making final arrangements on a deal. I was half way down the apartment complex's stairway, heading to my car to drive to Pete's office, when all of a sudden I heard Marlene's voice. "Mel, Mel, you better hold up," she yelled. "What's up?" I asked. "It's Legal Aid on the phone, and they want to talk to you," Marlene excitedly replied. I quickly shot back up the stairs, followed Marlene into the apartment, and grabbed the phone. It was Patsy Neyland on the line. "Hi Mr. Eichelbaum," she said. "Are you still interested in a job with Legal Aid?" she asked. "Yes Mam," I enthusiastically responded. Patsy continued, "Well, we've had an unexpected opening, and Mr. Christian said he would like to talk to you. When do you think you could come here to see him?" she asked. "Right away," I stated. "I can be there within the hour." "That would be fine, Mr. Eichelbaum, and we will look forward to seeing you," Patsy said. As I hung up the phone, I could barely contain my excitement. While I hurriedly put on a coat and tie, I instructed Marlene to call Pete's office and advise them that something had come up, and I would not be keeping the appointment, but I would be back in touch with them later. As Marlene wished me luck, I kissed her goodbye, dashed out of the apartment, jumped into my VW, and headed downtown. I already knew where Legal Aid's main office was, as Harry had given me a grand tour of the place weeks ago.

I parked at a familiar parking lot near the Courthouse and walked the couple of blocks to Legal Aid. Once there I was taken into Patsy Neyland's office, where she greeted me and promptly buzzed me in to see

{ 81

Frank Christian. His office was well-apportioned and much larger than the other attorney offices there, yet it was not grandiose. Mr. Christian was a tall, bald, middle-aged looking gentleman, who wore dark-framed glasses. He introduced himself as the Director of Legal Aid, which of course I already knew, and gestured me to take one of the seats in front of his desk, behind which he sat. After exchanging pleasantries and engaging in a little bit of small talk, he got right down to business. He said he had already reviewed my resume and stated he was rather impressed with it, for which I thanked him. He said he only had a couple of questions, the first of which I anticipated. He wanted to be sure as to what my military status was. It was a fair question. After all they did not want to spend the time and make the effort in training me, only to have me suddenly yanked and forced to leave because of a military obligation. I explained that I had already served and completely satisfied my military commitment, that I had received an honorable discharge, and that I was no longer subject to the draft. The second question came as a complete surprise. "How do you feel about Black people?" he asked. "I mean do you have any feelings of prejudice towards them?" he inquired. My response was immediate as I declared: "Mr. Christian, I don't have a prejudice bone in my body." Christian seemed satisfied and went on to explain that it was his intention to place me in the E. Houston Street satellite office, which was located on the Eastside, in the heart of the Black community. He pointed out that likely most of my clients would be Black and wanted to know if I felt I could handle that. I assured him that I could and that it would not be a problem for me. After advising me of the starting salary, which I thought was adequate; he offered me the job of Staff Attorney, which I readily accepted. "Alright," he said, "I would like you to start this Monday and report here for initial orientation and training." I told him that would be great, we shook hands, and I departed. On the way out I looked for Harry to inform him that I had gotten the job, but he wasn't in his office. He's probably in court I thought, and I left. As I briskly walked back to my car, the sky opened up, and the rain came in a downpour. I had no umbrella, of course, and I got completely soaked, but it didn't matter as I had just landed my dream job.

When I got back to the apartment I excitedly told Marlene the good news. I called Pete Torres and informed him that I had accepted an attorney's position with Legal Aid. He congratulated me, and said he was sure that we would see each other at the Courthouse on occasion. Later that evening I enthusiastically related all the details to my parents. I was on a real high. My Mom had a saying that she often repeated: "When it rains, it pours." And I suppose that at times that is true. Given the fact that for nearly two months I had received nary a nibble as to employment, within the next two weeks, I was contacted by the Child Support Section of the Bexar County District Attorney offering me a job that would pay me $50.00 a month more than my starting salary at Legal Aid. Two weeks later the IRS called offering me a job that would pay me $100.00 a month more than what I was making at Legal Aid. I turned them both down, as I was dead set on being a Legal Aid Lawyer. Marlene understood and was fully supportive. I'm not sure how many wives would have not pushed their husbands toward taking the position with the higher salary. But between her salary and mine, it was enough for us to get started. Within the next month, we had purchased a vehicle and became a two car family. Since we were both employed now, we each needed a car to handle job related transportation. Marlene got a brand new Chevy Malibu, which she nicknamed "Molly." She was so happy that she no longer had to drive our VW. By the following month we located an affordable, small but comfortable one-bedroom apartment on Blanco Road that wasn't too far from the North Star and Central Park Malls, which comprised the "shopping mecca" on the Northside. And to boot, the apartment was within a reasonable drive distance to our respective places of employment. At Jorries and Stowers furniture stores we found basic but suitable furniture for our new apartment. We finally had our own place.

That following Monday after my interview with Mr. Christian, I reported to work. The first part of the morning I spent in Patsy Neyland's

{ 83

office filling out a bunch of employment papers: the IRS W-2, OEO payroll information, various insurance forms, and both State and local Bar Association documents. In Texas, in order to be a practicing lawyer you had to belong to and maintain your membership in the State Bar Association. It was absolutely mandatory. On the other hand, belonging to the local Bar Association was strictly optional. Patsy explained, however, that Mr. Christian insisted that all Legal Aid lawyers belong to the San Antonio Bar Association (SABA). It was comforting to note that Legal Aid picked up the tab with respect to paying the membership dues for both, and so there would be no out-of-pocket costs on my part. Later that morning, Patsy ushered me into Mr. Christian's office where I was officially welcomed on board. He gave me some documentation regarding Legal Aid's client eligibility criteria and briefly went over it. He then informed me that there were a few concerns that he wanted to discuss with me. First of all, he advised me that the attorney at the E. Houston Street office, who I would be replacing, was in a hurry to leave, and so he apologized that my initial training would have to be somewhat abbreviated. Second, he explained that currently the client caseload at E. Houston Street was only around 50 to 60 service cases, and how that was really too low of a case volume to justify keeping that office open. Yet he personally was very reluctant to shut it down, as he recognized it was the only satellite office that was well situated to service low income individuals within the Black community. Although he really preferred not shutting down that office, he made it clear that somehow the caseload numbers would have to come up. Finally, he mentioned that the secretary there, Thelma Jerkins, was a young Black girl, who perhaps was not as well trained or skilled as the other secretaries at Legal Aid. The attorney there had complained about her constant miss-spellings, typos, and general lack of competence. Yet at that time, she was the only Black employee within the organization. Christian stated he would fire her if necessary, but that he would rather not do so. From our discussion, it was evident to me that bringing up the caseload numbers and getting the secretary up to par would be challenges that would be squarely on my shoulders.

Upon concluding my conference with Christian, it was just about lunch time. I dropped down the hall, and Harry was in his office. He was just finishing up a phone call, and he motioned me in. It was evident that he already knew I had gotten the job, and he was obviously pleased about it. He invited me to come to lunch with him and some of the other Legal Aid lawyers. At lunch I met John Sanders, who was the organization's juvenile specialist. Legal Aid handled only civil cases and no criminal cases whatsoever. At that time the State's Juvenile Code was completely distinct and separate from the State's Criminal Code, and so even if juvenile cases could very well be kind of criminal in nature, they were not considered as criminal cases per se, and so under the guidelines Legal Aid was permitted to handle those cases if the clients met the agency's economic criteria. I also met Al Alonzo, who was the lawyer in charge of the Guadalupe Street satellite office. During lunch I listened intently to their stories about their cases, and their tales about Legal Aid in general. I particularly focused on Al's special slant on the circumstances regarding running a neighborhood law office. I learned in the Army that listening to "scuttlebutt" could prove helpful at times.

After lunch I continued my training, and for the next few days I immersed myself in doing client intake forms with the law clerks. Here I learned that Mr. Christian was a real stickler on eligibility. The client definitely had to be a low income individual, whose income fell under OEO's poverty guidelines. And even if this qualification was met, there were asset qualifications, as well. For example if a person had low income but had assets available which could be utilized to hire a private attorney, then Legal Aid would not take the case. Assuming the client met the income and asset criteria, there was still one more hurdle to jump. If the case was a personal injury case or other similar types of cases, whereby a private attorney would likely be willing to accept the case on a contingent fee basis, without the client having to front any out-of-pocket costs, then Legal Aid still would not take the case, but rather would suggest that the client seek the assistance of a private attorney instead. So only if the client met all of the criteria and circumstances would Legal Aid agree to handle the case. But once accepted that client would receive the most dedicated, highest quality legal service, as if he or she were the most important millionaire type client of a high-end private law firm.

After a few days of training, I was shipped out to the E. Houston Street satellite office. It was a converted old, small wood framed house. Much of the front had been replaced with a large, smoke glass window, which bore a painted sign designating the address and that this was a Bexar County Legal Aid office. Adjacent was the front door, which had also been revamped into a business looking metal frame, smoke glass door, having signage stating "welcome" and detailing the hours the office was open. As I entered the office, I saw that the living room had been converted into a client reception area together with a secretary work station furnished with an L-desk, atop which sat a "Selectric" typewriter and other secretarial accouterments. Along one side wall were two metal file cabinets, where the case files were kept. Along a portion of the back wall, where the burglar alarm box was mounted, was a small work table on which sat the coffee maker and an old style, barely working "Thermofax" copier. Next to the table was a door that led to a very short hallway. On one side was the bathroom. On the other side was the main bedroom, which had been made over into a work area adequate to encompass two law clerk work stations. On the right side of the client reception and secretary area was a door that led into a smaller bedroom, which had been transformed into a small but workable attorney's office, which would become my inner sanctum.

At the office I met Thelma Jerkins, the secretary who worked there. She was a young, attractive Black woman with a pleasant personality. I also met Jerry Gonzales, who was the attorney that was leaving Legal Aid. He had opted out for a legal position in the South Texas Valley. He was rather anxious to go and had only one day to give me. We spent the time going over office procedures and reviewing the current case files so I could get a handle on where each client's case stood. He was rather negative on Thelma and suggested that I lobby Christian to get rid of her and to get me someone else. At the close of the day, Jerry turned over the office door and burglar alarm keys to me. I would not see him again. As I set the alarm for the night and locked up, I realized that it was now on me, and that the E. Houston Street office was going to be my baby from here on out. During the weekend I constantly chattered to Marlene about how I had my own office. I packed my briefcase with my personal attorney's desk items, along with two identical copies of the Webster's spelling dictionary that I had bought, one for me and one which I planned to give to Thelma.

That Monday I got to the office early and opened up, deactivated the alarm, and set up my desk. When Thelma came in, I greeted her and said that I would like to have a heart to heart talk with her. During our conversation, I carefully listened, and it became evident that Thelma felt intimidated by Jerry. She explained how she felt unappreciated and under constant pressure. She admitted that she had become discouraged and how she had already started looking for another job. In a calm manner and with an understanding smile, I said: "Look here Thelma, I'm not Jerry, and I very much would like for you to give me a chance." I then explained how I operated under a concept of teamwork, how it was my goal to make the E. Houston Street office the very best neighborhood office at Legal Aid, and how I felt we could do this by working together. "But I need you to do me one big favor," I pleaded. "What is it?" she asked, as she looked somewhat puzzled. "Let me tell you," I said, "I am the world's worse speller, and I can't proof read worth a crap, so I'm going to need you to utilize your skills in that regard to protect me." As I handed her a copy of the Webster's spelling dictionary, I said: "Here, I bought this for you. Now seriously, I'm going to really need your help here." I found that not only was Thelma receptive, but also she proved to be very responsive, as well. In the weeks to come, even Mr. Christian commented that he had noticed a positive improvement in the inter-office memos coming to him from our office.

Thelma and I immediately put in place some new management systems. Neither one of us liked the pressure of last minute work, right before a deadline. So the idea was to stay ahead and to get the work done well in advance of any deadline. A double calendar system was implemented; whereby, all appointments, court appearances, deadlines, diaries, and other important matters were placed on each calendar as a double check. If something accidently did not get scheduled on one, it would be very unlikely that it would be skipped on the other, as well. All of the case files were divided and placed into two broad categories. First were the "hot cases." These were ones that required some fairly quick action, and those files were placed in racks in my office, so that I could give them more immediate attention. Second were the "regular cases." These were the ones that were moving through the legal system in a more routine and sedate manner. We installed a diary system whereby the "hot cases" would be reviewed daily, and at least twenty percent of the "regular cases" also would be reviewed each day, insuring that all of those cases would be reviewed at least weekly. I also took some time to introduce myself to our immediate neighbors, simply to make them aware of our presence and our availability to be of service to the community.

Meanwhile, Christian sent out two new law clerks to compliment and round out our office staff. Both were law students at St. Mary's law school. First there was Ben Samples. He was a young, Black man, who was very calm in nature, soft spoken, and tended to choose his words rather cautiously. His rather ultra-traditional dress, which typically entailed a dark suit, white shirt, and complimentary dark tie, matched his rather reserved and conservative personality. Then there was Tom Rickhoff, a young, White-Anglo man, who linguistically was much more expressive. His dress customarily consisted of boots, jeans, a sport shirt or sweater, along with a black motorcycle jacket, all of which went along with his colorful and flamboyant personality. I thought that it was rather ironic that Ben was a liberal Democrat and Tom was a conservative Republican. At that time, just given their dress and mannerisms, likely most people would have called it the other way around. During break time it was interesting listening to them energetically debate various issues, yet when it came to work it was amazing to see how well the two of them worked together. In time both of them would become judges, serving as part of the Bexar County Judiciary. My apparent ability in training law clerks would end up being recognized by Christian, and I ended up becoming the law clerk trainer in chief.

One morning Thelma buzzed me and excitedly announced that Rev. Claude Black was here and would like to speak with me. I welcomed him into my office, and we sat down. He was a distinguished looking Black gentleman, who was in his early 50s, with slightly greying hair. He wore a black suit, white shirt, and matching solid black tie. I was acutely aware of the fact that he was a veritable icon within the Black community. Rev. Black introduced himself as the Pastor of the Mount Zion First Baptist Church. He apologized for not having an appointment but explained that he was in the area, and he just wanted to drop by in order to become acquainted and to welcome me to the neighborhood. I thanked him for coming in, and we began to chat. I learned that aside from being a highly respected minister, he had been active in the civil rights movement since the 1950s, when he began challenging the establishment for the fair treatment of minorities and to end discriminatory practices in San Antonio and throughout the South. He worked with some noted movers, such as Martin Luther King, Thurgood Marshall, and many local leaders, like Rabbi Jacobson, who was from Temple Beth-El and who inspired me on the subject of civil rights when I was a teenager there and a member of SAFTY. "Small world," I thought. Back on March 13, 1960, Rev. Black addressed a large anti-discrimination rally, along with the President of the S.A. chapter of the NAACP, and gave the City of San Antonio an ultimatum: To integrate the lunch counters in the city by the 17th or prepare for "sit down" protests. With the help of a group of local civic, business, and religious leaders, of which Rabbi Jacobson was among them, the lunch counters throughout the city were integrated by the 16th, and San Antonio became the first major city in the South to achieve integration in that regard without demonstrations.

Rev. Black continued his work in the civil rights movement, and he was named by President Lyndon B. Johnson as a member of, and participated in, the Whitehouse Conference on Civil Rights in 1966. During the 1960s he twice ran unsuccessfully for a position on the San Antonio City Council. However, later on in the 1970s, after gaining Good Government League (GGL) backing, he got elected and served as a City Councilman. He eventually became the first Black Mayor Pro-Tem in the State of Texas. After a rather pleasant talk, he could see that I was very much in tune with his civil rights concepts, and he seemed impressed with my background and dedication to Legal Aid. He invited me to visit his church on Sunday and asked if after services I would be willing to speak to his congregation about Legal Aid and answer some questions concerning it. I replied that I would be more than happy to do so, and of course I did. It was an interesting experience in talking to nearly an entire Black congregation at Rev. Black's church, and I really felt honored to have been invited to address them. Mr. Christian had always encouraged Legal Aid lawyers to go out in the community and speak to groups about Legal Aid's mission, and I certainly agreed that doing so was a worthwhile endeavor.

Before too long our office at E. Houston Street was operating very efficiently, and the word began to spread that: "there was a new sheriff in town." Our service case numbers had already began to increase, and after having spoken at Rev. Black's church, our numbers steadily climbed. Before Thanksgiving, which had only been about three months, our case numbers more than doubled. From then on out there was never any further mention from Christian about possibly having to close the E. Houston Street office.

Then one afternoon we received a visit from another important person in the Black community. It was Hattie Mae Briscoe, who was a well-known female, Afro-American attorney, indeed at that time the only one in town. She was a slightly portly woman in her early 50s, and she wore a navy pin-striped suit with a matching pillbox hat. Although I had seen her around the Courthouse before, we had never actually met. As I welcomed her into my office, she brashly announced: "I came here to meet you and check out my competition." I smiled, and as we sat down, I had a hunch I was about to be engaged in a rather interesting conversation. I learned that like me, she had worked her way through school, earning a Bachelor's Degree from Wiley College and a Master's Degree from Prairie View A & M. Her background was that of being a teacher and a cosmetologist. It wasn't until her mid-30s that she decided to go to law school, and in 1952, she began attending night classes at St. Mary's, while still working a full-time job during the daytime. In 1956, she not only graduated first in her class, but also, she was the very first Afro-American to ever graduate from St. Mary's University law school. Hattie was an active member of the NAACP and an outspoken person on civil rights issues. She had a successful practice, handling both civil and criminal cases out of her office at 1416 E. Commerce Street, which wasn't that far from our Legal Aid office. "So I suppose we're neighbors," I said, "but I don't think that we are really competitors." After briefly detailing my background, I went on to explain the Legal Aid concept, emphasizing how we would not be taking any profitable cases away from her. "By your reputation, my guess would be that within the community, you do some *pro bono* work for folks who can't afford a lawyer," I said. Hattie proudly acknowledged that she did. "Well, you can still do that to the extent you want," I asserted. "But I would think there will be situations where the case might be too demanding for you time wise or too expensive for you economically, and when that happens, you can send those cases here," I continued. "In that way not only would those clients receive first rate legal services, but you would be the hero for sending them here," I maintained. Hattie thought about it and then nodded, as I exclaimed: "Heck, it's a win-win situation. We're not competitors; we're compatriots." She seemed pleased, and we parted as friends. From then on out, when we saw one another in the Courthouse, we always acknowledged and greeted each other. And even when we had cases against one another, which were bound to happen, there was always the utmost respect and professionalism between us.

Harry was right when he said that Legal Aid was a place where a young attorney was going to get a lot of experience at a rapid pace. I had been with Pete Torres for about three months before the Army. While I definitely appreciated the valuable experience I received there, I had spent just about all my time in doing research, preparing papers, and drafting discovery, but I never actually got to try a case. Here I had been with Legal Aid for only a month, and I was faced with having to try my first contested case. I was representing Ms. H., a poor, widow-woman, whose husband had died some years ago, and she had no other relatives. All she had left was her pet pony, which she considered to be her family. She lived in a poor neighborhood, residing in a shack of a house on a small piece of land that wasn't worth a pittance. She received Aid for the Aged (AA), which was a small, monthly subsistence grant from the State of Texas, and occasionally some food stamps, when she could get them. And that had been her total income. Then about six months ago she leant out her pony to an individual, who owned a small stable, where he kept a few of his own ponies. He would contract, for a charge of course, to provide pony rides for children at birthday parties and at various fairs and events. After deducting for the feed and care of the animals, he would pocket the remaining money as profit. When it came to Ms. H.'s pet pony, he would pay her $10.00 per month for the use of the animal. Although it wasn't much, it acted as a small supplement to her meager income and helped her barely get by. Also by harboring her pony at his stable, he picked up the cost of feed, saving her the expense in that regard, and when the pony wasn't working, she could visit it any time she wanted. All in all, it was a rather symbiotic deal, and naturally with these folks there was no written contract, but rather everything was verbal.

At any rate, one day Ms. H. came to our office in tears. Evidently her pony had been injured and could no longer give rides. Not only did the $10.00 per month rental income stop, but also, she had received a bill from the stable owner for the board and room for her pony, which of course she could not afford to pay. When she tried to get her pony back, she was told there would be no way until the bill had been paid in full. And naturally, with each passing month the bill increased, making it even more impossible for her to pay. It was like the pony was being held as hostage for payment. The clincher came when she was served with a lawsuit. The stable owner was suing her to be awarded her pony in partial payment of his bill, to receive a monetary judgement against her for the remainder of his bill, and for her to have to pay his attorney fees and court cost, as well.

It was clear that from both an income and asset standpoint, Ms. H. was well within Legal Aid's eligibility guidelines, and I told her we would accept her case. "What are my chances? Are you going to be able to get my pony back?" she asked. "I don't know Ms. H.," I replied, "but we're sure as heck going to try." The stable owner was being represented by Joe Cumpian, who was an experienced attorney. When I called him to see if there was any chance of working out some kind of a settlement, he succinctly told me that he had no intention of negotiating with me and that he would see me in court. Later on I found out that he was no fan of the Legal Aid program. I quickly drafted a General Denial in answer to the stable owner's Petition, and then prepared a Cross-Action, whereby Ms. H. was seeking damages for the negligent injury to her pony and for the wrongful retention of the animal by the stable owner, and I had those papers served on him.

The case was in the Justice of the Peace Court, which in Texas was the jurisdictional court designated for the lowest amount of monetary controversy. The trial was before the Judge, without a jury, and it lasted all morning. At the end, the Judge awarded Ms. H. her pony back, as well as $150.00 in damages for the injury to her pony and the wrongful retention of the animal. To that amount he offset $100.00 as what he found to be a reasonable amount for the board and room of the animal, and so he ordered the stable owner to pay Ms. H. $50.00. The judge also denied the stable owner's request for attorney's fees and court costs. After hearing the judgement, Mr. Cumpian stormed out of the courtroom, stating that he had a luncheon date. Meanwhile Ms. H. gave me a big hug and thanked me. Surprisingly, the stable owner then approached me, shook my hand and congratulated me, stating that I had done a very good job. He wrote

{ 93

a $50.00 check to Ms. H. on the spot and gave it to me, which I in turn handed to her. That evening I told Marlene about my very first court trial.

It was December, and Marlene was looking forward to her up-coming Christmas school break. She was busily working on her end of the first semester papers, while I was reviewing some case notes in preparing for trial. I had been with Legal Aid for only slightly more than three months, and I found myself embroiled in a bitterly contested divorce case, involving the custody of a ten year old boy. It was a nasty case with a lot of "he said-she said" accusations going both ways. It involved everything from alleged lesbian sexual affairs on the wife's part to contentions of alcoholism and abusive conduct on the part of the husband. This was the type of case that most lawyers hated handling, and in fact, quite a few would refuse to do so. I was representing the wife, and Ed DeWeese, an experienced trial lawyer, was representing the husband. And about the only thing we agreed upon was that this couple really needed to get divorced.

The trial took place before Judge Robert Murray in the District Court, which in Texas was the highest jurisdictional trial court in the state court system. The trial had gone on all morning, going back and forth, with both sides presenting witnesses, who testified regarding rather vicious charges and counter-charges, and with respect to emphatic defensive denials, as well. Up to that point, I felt like it was almost a toss-up, when Judge Murray adjourned the court for lunch. Afterward, when we started up again, Ed DeWeese called the ten year old boy to the witness stand. Under direct questioning by Ed, the boy testified that it would be his preference to live with his Dad. I could see the look of disappointment and hurt on my client's face, and I was beginning to have some bad vibes about how things were going. But then it was my turn to question the boy on cross-examination. Somehow I managed to bring out that it was Mom who made him do his chores; whereas, Dad hardly bothered about that. It was also Mom who made and packed his school lunches and got him off to school each day. And she was the one who helped him with his homework, and made sure that he got it all done. Dad didn't have time for that either. The clincher was when I was able to bring out that he had just received a brand new bicycle that his father had bought for him as a "reward" for his promising to testify that he would prefer to live with his Dad. I spotted the shocked look on Ed's face when that came out. At the conclusion, each of us made passionate arguments on behalf of our clients. Fortunately, Judge Murray held in our favor, granting the divorce and awarding custody of the boy to my client. That evening I reported to Marlene that I had won my first contested custody case.

It was early Saturday morning around 3:30 AM, and I was fast asleep, when suddenly the telephone rang. Somewhat startled, I glanced at the alarm clock sitting on the nightstand and quickly reached for the phone right next to it. "Hello, who is this?" I asked. It was Mr. Christian on the line, who apologized for the late hour and calling me at home. "There has been an incident at E. Houston Street," he announced. "The burglar alarm went off, and it's making a racket. I need you to get down there to turn the alarm off and silence it." Mr. Christian went on to explain that he had been notified by the police, who had already done a drive by. No suspicious persons were there, and it did not appear to be a break in, but the alarm did have to be silenced. I was to take care of that, check the place out, and wait for the police who would return later that morning to talk with me and make a report. He added after that I was to give him a call and let him know what's happening. "Okay, I got it," I said. "Let me throw some clothes on, and I'm on my way." By that time, Marlene, who tends to wake up more slowly, was fully aroused. "What's going on?" she inquired. I repeated the content of Mr. Christian's phone call, stating that I had to leave right away, and I would see her later. "No way," she exclaimed. "You're not going to that part of town this time of night all by yourself. I'm coming with you," she declared. I knew that it was useless to argue with her, so I agreed. We quickly got dressed, dashed down the stairs from our apartment, jumped into my VW, and took off.

The roadways were pretty deserted then, and so we got to the office in record time. As I pulled into the driveway, I noticed a crowd of about ten people who were standing in front of the office. I grabbed the flashlight from my glove compartment, turned it on, and approached the group. I quickly recognized some of them as being the neighbors from next door and some of my clients from the surrounding area. "Hey Mable, what's going on? What are you all doing here?" I asked. "Well, Mr. Mel, we heard the alarm and got here as fast as we could. We wanted to make sure nothing bad was happening to the office," she replied. "Yeah," Ms. Brown chimed in. "We wanted to protect the office till the cops came. After all, it's our law office too, isn't it?" I saw many of the people nod their heads, and that moved me to the very core of my essence. I smiled and emphatically said: "yes. It is." I excused myself, unlocked the door which was still intact, turned on the lights, and turned off the alarm. The silence was a stark relief after its constant sounding. I quickly glanced around, and nothing appeared to be out of order. I asked Marlene to make some coffee, as I stepped back outside and addressed the group. I told them that it looked like everything was okay, sincerely thanked them for showing up, and suggested that they all return to their homes. After saying farewell to the people, I went back inside the office. My main concern was the client case files, but all of those were fine. I next turned my attention to the petty cash, the postage, the supplies, and equipment, and there were no problems there either. I did notice that in the reception area, on the floor, under the left corner of the window, laid a broken brick. At that point in the window was a hole about six inches in circumference with some spider web like cracks radiating therefrom. Ah, that's what tripped the burglar alarm, I thought. It appeared to me that it wasn't an attempted burglary at all, but rather an act of pure vandalism. I had a sneaky suspicion that it might have even been done by the irate husband from my recent divorce and contested custody case. It was just an eerie feeling, but of course I realized there was no proof in that regard, and that it could have been anyone. As Marlene and I drank our coffee, I commented: "Well, it could have been much worse." She saw that I was relieved and agreed. "But how about those folks who came out to guard the office—wasn't that really something?" I exclaimed.

As long as we were there anyhow, I gathered up some case files and began working on them. Might as well get a head start, I thought. Actually without the interruptions of telephone calls and client conferences, I accomplished quite a bit. It was about 7:30 AM by the time two police officers showed up. They interviewed me in order to make their official incident report. I showed them the chunk of brick, and one of them remarked that it wasn't a good candidate for fingerprints. They weren't interested in taking it and said that I could just throw it away. I reported that there was nothing missing and nothing was damaged, except for the window, of course. They agreed that it was a case of vandalism and wrote it up accordingly. They did say that they would increase their patrols in the area for a while, for which I thanked them. Following the police suggestion to cover up the hole with cardboard, I took the back of a legal pad, and using some office tape, sealed up the hole. By that time, it was after 8:00 AM, and I called Christian and brought him up to date. He seemed relieved that there wasn't anything more to it. Marlene and I then locked up and went to breakfast. The following Monday when I came to work I was surprised that the window had already been completely repaired. How Christian managed to get that done so quickly was beyond me, but that was Frank.

CHAPTER 8

The Texas Welfare Wars

1968 – 1970

Alvarez v. Hackney; Machado v. Hackney; Davila v. Hackney; and Felder v. Hackney

The U.S. Constitution begins by stating: "We the People of the United States in Order to form a more perfect union...." While our founders implicitly recognized that we had not yet achieved political perfection – far from it; nevertheless, the Preamble sets forth and enumerates the essential elements that establish the roadmap of rationale behind our very national existence in the first place. Two of those important ingredients that are specifically listed are: to establish justice and promote the general welfare.

From my Reform Jewish background came the conceptual influence of the Torah's Commandment: "Justice, justice shall you pursue" (Deuteronomy 16:20), and the Prophetic writings concerning helping the poor and disadvantaged. From my feelings of patriotic Americanism came the sense of a national brotherhood and an American creed that espoused: "One nation...indivisible, with liberty and justice for all." This all seemed to merge together into a powerful, philosophical force that provided me with a motivational drive and tended to serve as a guidance for my actions.

So historically as our country continued to evolve, and hopefully striving for perfection, from an idealistic attorney's perspective the central question was: should the poor have real and meaningful equal rights? For me the answer was a resounding "yes." Interestingly enough, coming from a completely opposite economic and political background, Frank Christian had reached the same conclusion.

It was late in 1968, when Christian called an attorneys' staff meeting to discuss an increased involvement in a law reform agenda. The idea was to bring major class action cases on behalf of the poverty community or significant segments thereof. While it was understood that he would never condone nor tolerate any slacking off regarding our handling the individual service cases for our clientele, he wanted us to know that he would be in favor and supportive of our engaging in a law reform approach in appropriate instances. Not only could this have a significant positive effect on large numbers of the poverty community, but also it would tend to put the Bexar County Legal Aid Association's name on the national legal services' map. "I believe with the right cases, OEO [Office of Economic Opportunity] will back us to the hilt," he declared. "Gentlemen, the time is right, and we must strike while the iron is hot," he asserted. At the same time he cautioned us to select law reform cases with great care. Christian insisted that these cases be well thought out, well planned, and well executed. "I want successes, not failures, and so gentlemen, I have every confidence that we can do this."

Momentarily my mind slipped back to my childhood days when I was enamored by the legendary tales of King Arthur and his Knights of the Round Table. Gathered around the conference table and hearing Christian push for law reform, it felt almost as if he was acting in the role of King Arthur, extoling us, as his good knights, to go forth and proceed down that virtuous path. I felt like I had been transported to a special time zone which was kind of tantamount to a legalized version of Camelot.

After listening to Christian's law reform sermon, I felt that in some ways he was preaching to the choir. For those of us who were in the trenches, fighting in the courts for the rights of poor people on a daily basis, it didn't take very long for us to realize that it wasn't only the sleazy businessman or slum landlord who preyed upon the poor. Rather it became readily apparent that there was such a thing as institutionalized discrimination against poor people. In some cases there were statutes, regulations, and procedures that if not overtly designed to discriminate against the poor; nevertheless, operated in such a way as to overburden those in poverty or to put them at an even greater disadvantage. So for many of us who were more philosophically oriented toward civil rights, the concept of law reform was no stranger. The challenge of course was to find a creative way to attack these discriminatory patterns and practices in the courts and administrative agencies by utilizing class action lawsuits and like measures, so as to help and benefit large numbers of poor people all at the same time. Little did I realize then that in about six months, having less than a year's notch in my belt as a practicing lawyer, I would be enmeshed in a major class action case that would affect the lives of thousands of poor people.

At that time, the Texas state welfare program presented a rather fertile field for law reform, and there likely existed a historical perspective that made that so. From the beginning, it seemed as if Texas was more interested in benefiting its big ranchers and wealthy oil industry owners rather than helping poor people. Indeed, its original state constitution, Article III, Section 5, in effect provided that the state could not utilize any public revenues whatsoever to help poor people.

Then shortly after the stock market crash in October of 1929, the United States (Texas included) found itself stuck in the midst of the Great Depression (1929—1939). This was the longest lasting and deepest economic downturn in the history of the country. The unemployment rate hit 25%, and in some parts of the nation effectively it ran even higher. The economic tailspin caused massive poverty and a very widespread misery index, which not only adversely affected blacks and other minorities, but also large numbers of white Americans, as well. In an attempt to pull out of this calamity, under the guidance of President Franklin D. Roosevelt, amongst other measures, Congress passed the Social Security Act in August, 1935, as part of the "New Deal." Aside from providing at least a basic retirement program for seniors, it generated an array of other programs to assist the needy: Aid to the Aged (AA), Aid to the Blind (AB), Aid to the Permanently and Totally Disabled (APTD), and Aid for Families with Dependent Children (AFDC). All these programs were designed to be administered by the various states, who would contribute only about 25% of the money necessary to help care for the needy individuals under such programs. Whereas, the federal government would take up the lion's share of the responsibility, by providing matching funds of around 75% of the monies to help meet the needs of those who required assistance under these programs.

With so many Texans finding themselves squarely inside the poverty boat, Texas politicians thought it wise to amend the onerous state constitutional prohibition so that Texas could participate in the "New Deal" and take advantage of the influx of federal funds the state would receive by doing so. But even then, rather than eliminating the prohibition entirely, a constitutional cap of $52 million on the amount of funds that the state would be allowed to spend on these programs was put in place.

Things pretty much stayed that way for decades, until in 1963, when the $52 million cap was raised to $60 million as part of President Lyndon B. Johnson's "War on Poverty" program, which allowed Texas even greater participation and of course even a larger increase of federal funds coming into the state to help fight poverty. Having some concern that for many years there had been no adjustment for inflation with regard to the standard of need for those in poverty, Congress passed the 1967 amendments to the Social Security Act, which was then signed into law by President Johnson. In doing so it implemented a directive in 42 U.S.C. Sec. 601 that required: "By July 2, 1968, the amounts used by states to determine needs of individuals will have been adjusted to reflect fully changes in living costs since the amounts were established, and any maximums the state imposes on the amount of aid paid to families will have been proportionally adjusted." Although the law took effect on January 2, 1968, the implementation requirement was delayed and not scheduled to go into effect until

July 1, 1969; thus giving the various states slightly more than one and a half years to consider their situation with respect to their welfare programs and come up with a way to update needs and payments and secure adequate state appropriations to comply. As stated before, this mandate was considered necessary because a number of states, including Texas, had totally ignored the situation for many years, failing to adjust the standard of need for food, clothing, housing, and other basic living expenses.

In 1968, even though Texas was doing rather well economically due to the demand for oil and gas, the political climate had definitely changed. Exceedingly large numbers of white Americans no longer found themselves in the poverty boat, which was now more inhabited by minority members. Vicious urban legends and mean-spirited lies about how welfare recipients were all driving Cadillacs and living the "Life of Riley," permeated talk radio and tended to be a prevalent topic of discussion at middle class social events. Welfare, particularly the AFDC program, had become unpopular. Far too many smug businessmen types pontificated about how all welfare recipients were lazy and just didn't want to work. Never mind the fact that they were unwilling to pay them a living wage in the first place, let alone consider covering their transportation and child care costs, which would possibly enable them to work. Perhaps the philosophy of human nature as espoused by the character of Alfred P. Doolittle, who was Eliza's father in *My Fair Lady*, rang truer than fiction. He was an impoverished dustman, who viewed the middle class with scorn and disdain, claiming that they were blindly infected with "middle class morality;" whereby, they contemptuously viewed the poor as lesser human beings, who had inferior intelligence and a lower standard of morality. So given that type of pervasive thinking, it was no wonder that an attempt to further raise the constitutional cap from $60 million to $75 million failed at the polls. Even the conservative Texas legislature recognized the absolute necessity for an increase, so it passed another proposal to raise the cap to $80 million and scheduled it to be submitted to the voters for approval at an election scheduled for August 5, 1969, and this time, some Texas politicians and prominent business people and civic leaders were going to get behind it and advocate its passage.

In 1968, the federal poverty level for a family of four people living in the state of Texas was considered to be $3,944.00 per year. Yet the state's standard of need for a family of that size was a paltry $2,184.00 per year. Even then that sum was further limited by DPW's deemed maximum family payment, which was only $1,368.00 per year, in other words, $114.00 a month. And that is what a family of four was expected to live on in the state of Texas—so much for the mythological falsehood that welfare recipients received such an opulent amount as to enable them to live in "a grand life style."

In the meantime, the DPW was being managed by Burton G. Hackney, an old curmudgeon of a man, who ran the agency with an iron fist. By that time, DPW was feeling the squeeze. With the welfare rolls having expanded, but the amount of money the state could spend on the assistance programs being frozen by the constitutional cap, something had to give. So the word went forth, and far too many welfare case workers, whose duty had been to traditionally try to help poor families, instead became much more like the "Gestapo," whose prime function was to prevent as many people as possible from getting welfare assistance, and for those persons who were already receiving benefits, to find ways of throwing them off the welfare rolls. One began to see the proliferation of arbitrary and unreasonable regulations. The one year residency requirement, the "man-in-the-house" rule, and others, were crafted and designed to artificially keep needy people from getting welfare and kicking those who were already recipients off the rolls. The agency had become thoroughly infected with institutionalized discrimination against the poor.

By 1968, the welfare rolls in Texas had risen to nearly 389,000. The AA program had about 230,000 needy old people. The AB and APTD programs for the blind and disabled had around 4,000 and 16,000, respectively. But the biggest growth had occurred in the AFDC program, which by then included approximately 139,000 families. In order to comply with the federal mandate Texas had to upwardly adjust its standard of need, and it minimally did so. Given the $60 million constitutional cap, DPW devised a rather diabolical scheme as to how to allocate the funds. About $48 million would be designated for the AA program, giving the elderly just about 100% of their standard of need. As for the AB and APTD programs, the blind and disabled would be allocated $1.4 million and $4.25 million, respectively, giving those recipients about 95% of their standard of need. The remnant of $6.15 million would be apportioned to the least favored AFDC program. Then in order to make the left over funds fit, DPW decreed that a 50% ratable reduction was to be applied to a poor family's standard of need, and so at best a family would receive only 50% of what its minimal designated need was. Rather than getting a cost of living increase in benefits as Congress had envisioned by passing the 1967 amendments to the Social Security Act, for many families the effect was an out-and-out reduction of their grant as compared to what they were receiving before. Mathematically the way the formula worked, it was estimated that roughly 25,000 families would have their grants lowered or be thrown off the rolls entirely. Even more economic devastation faced such families because once terminated from the AFDC program, they would also lose their Medicaid, social services, and job training benefits, as well. Texas had found a way to make the unpopular AFDC program almost unilaterally shoulder the burden for the state's neglect and failure to secure adequate funding for these programs. This scheme was scheduled to go into effect on May 1, 1969. Thus, that was the status of welfare in Texas at that time, and so the stage had been set for the welfare wars that were to come.

Even before Christian's big speech on the subject, some of the younger and more ambitious attorneys at Legal Aid had heard the clarion call and already had embarked down the arduous path, pursuing the quest for law reform. One of these stalwart warriors was Lonnie W. Duke. Before he became a lawyer, Lonnie was living in Houston, Texas, working for Tenneco Oil Company. He was already married and had three children when he decided to enter law school at the South Texas College of Law

(STCL). He had to attend classes at night while working a full-time job during the day – no easy task. Upon graduation, he accepted a job working with an older lawyer, who was a former county judge, in the small Texas town of Post, located in the Texas panhandle, southeast of Lubbock, and having a population of less than ten thousand. Although he became a partner almost immediately, after only eight months, his elder partner decided to retire and quit working altogether. That left Lonnie in a small town practice where he had limited connections. Added to the equation, his wife, Gloria, had been lobbying to move to San Antonio, where her sister lived. Gloria felt that in that way their two families could be closer together. Lonnie recognizing that there was really no future for him in Post, the Duke family moved to S.A. As fate would have it, Lonnie landed a job with the Bexar County Legal Aid Association, being hired by Hilmer Schmidt, the Pre-Mr. Christian director of the organization. He officially began as a staff attorney on November 1, 1967, right before his 31st birthday.

Right from the first, Lonnie became a champion for welfare justice. Within the course of a couple of months after his arrival, he hooked up with Jimmy Lytton, a young attorney at Legal Aid, who had just graduated from law school in the spring of 1967, and they filed *Alvarez v. Hackney*, a class action federal lawsuit, which constitutionally attacked the arbitrary one year residency requirement of the Texas Department of Public Welfare (DPW). Since neither Lonnie nor Jimmy were federally licensed yet, they got Andre Hernandez, one of the older Legal Aid attorneys to sign the pleadings and briefs pro forma, in order that the case could go forward in the federal court system. Later in 1968, Jimmy would be tragically killed in a freak glider plane accident, leaving Lonnie left to pursue that case on his own.

Early in 1968, Lonnie became aware of the plight of Margarita Machado, who he had met at the Guadalupe Street neighborhood office. She was a somewhat portly, Hispanic woman, who was the mother of several children, and who was receiving welfare payments under the state's program for Aid to Families with Dependent Children (AFDC). During

January and February of 1968, Ms. Machado and her children were summarily removed from the welfare rolls on the grounds that there was ostensibly a "substitute father" in the home, and therefore the children were "no longer dependent." Lonnie felt that this was patently unfair. First of all, to have desperately needed welfare benefits automatically withheld and denied without first having a meaningful hearing on the facts of the matter just didn't seem right. Secondly, the assumption of a man in the house, be it a visiting relative or boyfriend, who had no legal obligation to support the children, would somehow then render the children to be no longer dependent; thereby, making the family ineligible, was equally unreasonable in Lonnie's mind. After explaining his idea for a constitutional challenge and carefully detailing what her responsibilities would be as a class representative, Ms. Machado agreed to sign on as his client, and hence the case of *Machado v. Hackney* was filed in federal court. So by early 1968, Bexar County Legal Aid (BCLA) had two major class action cases pending against the Texas Department of Public Welfare (DPW).

It was a hot and humid Wednesday on June 18, 1969. It was mid-afternoon, and I was at the E. Houston Street office and had finished all of my client appointments for the day. I was looking forward to working with the law clerks on several cases, when the phone call came through. It was Patsy Neyland. "Mr. Eichelbaum, an emergency situation has developed and Mr. Christian would like to speak to you about it. He wants to see you right away. How soon can you get here?" She asked. "I'm on my way," I replied. I told Thelma and the law clerks to carry on, lock up at the end of the day as I didn't know whether I would be back, and I took off for the downtown location. Upon my arrival, I headed straight for Christian's office. Patsy greeted me at the office antechamber, and directed me to be seated. She immediately buzzed Lonnie Duke, saying: "Mr. Duke, Mr. Eichelbaum is here now, and Mr. Christian is ready to see both of you." Within a minute Lonnie came forth, and we were ushered into Christian's office.

As usual Christian got right down to business. He advised us that there was a protest demonstration going on at the main downtown DPW office. Apparently some welfare mothers had taken over the building, and some of them had their children with them. Christian informed us that the police had been called, and he was concerned about matters escalating out of control. "Gentlemen, I want you to get down there right away and observe what's going on", he directed. "See what you can do to get a handle on the situation and calm things down."

On our way, Lonnie and I discussed the matter, and we were acutely aware that a potential confrontation could be fraught with danger. The last thing we needed would be an altercation between the police and some welfare mothers, especially with children on the scene. In addition to the obvious, the press would have a field day. Not only could that have a chilling effect on the welfare law reform cases we already had filed, but also it could be a real spoiler with respect to the special election to raise the constitutional cap on welfare expenditures that was slated for August 5, 1969, which was just about two months away.

When we reached DPW's main office on S. Santa Rosa Street, there was a crowd of about fifty women and small children gathered near the front steps of the building and on the adjacent grounds. Some of them were carrying signs stating: "WELFARE UNFAIR" and a number of those signs were taped to the front of the building, as well. Above the archway of the two big double doors at the front of the building, a large sign had been posted that read: "ARE YOU PROUD SAN ANTONIO? (HUNGER)." Among the group, Lonnie spotted Ms. Machado, who already was his client and had been the named plaintiff in a class action welfare law reform case he had previously filed. Lonnie approached her, and we learned that there were more women inside the building. After talking with one of the policemen, we finally got permission to enter the building. Once inside, we saw another half a dozen women, some with children, occupying the reception area and hallways. Jo Ann Gutierrez, who had a somewhat peppery personality and was rather assertive, had seemed to assume the leadership role of the group. She said she was the head of the Welfare Rights Organization at the Alazan Apache Courts, and that the demonstration had been organized in order to bring attention to their plight in light of the recent welfare cuts, and to force DPW officials to consider demands regarding a number of grievances they had. After listening to some of their complaints, we convinced Jo Ann and some of the women to meet with us in order to discuss their problems. It took some persistent pleading, with Raymond Cheves, DPW's S.A. Regional Director, to finally convince him to let us use one of the administrative offices so that we could meet privately with some of the leadership of the welfare mothers.

So it was late in the afternoon when Jo Ann Gutierrez with about half a dozen women piled into an office with Lonnie and I in order to have a parley. Of course the main bone of contention was the insidious welfare cuts. It took quite a bit of persuasion, but we finally were able to convince them that this was a state-wide problem that would not be resolved by negotiating with local or even regional DPW officials, but rather it would likely take a lawsuit. Lonnie called Christian right then and there. He gave him the low down and got the go ahead to do a class action law reform case against DPW. That convinced the woman we were serious, and they agreed to co-operate and become our clients. We took detailed fact statements from several of the women, including Jo Ann Gutierrez and Maria T. Davila. From that point forward we made a list of principles. First, it was resolved that the demonstration would continue peaceably. There was to be no harm done to the building or any of its contents. Any confrontations or altercations with the police were to be absolutely avoided, at all cost. Second, we would get started on the lawsuit right away so we could file it as soon as possible. In the meantime, we would see what we could do within the community to get some temporary assistance for the families. Third, we would see if we could negotiate with DPW to try to resolve some of the grievances, such as the unfair hearing procedures that the agency utilized in far too many occasions. Finally, everyone realized the importance of getting "good press," and so we would issue out press releases, which would emphasize: the real crises of need, the legitimate complaints regarding the unfairness of the DPW hearing procedures, the fact that the demonstration had been totally peaceful and that no harm had been done by the protesters, and a request to S.A. Police Chief, George Bichsel, asking for a continued police presence in order to insure tranquility.

In order to defuse the situation and to allow time for things to cool off, and after some rather intense mediated discussions with DPW officials, it was decided to let the women remain in the building that night, provided everything stayed peaceful, no damage occurred, and there would be police monitoring of the situation. As we left, Lonnie and I promised Jo Ann and the women that we would see them the next day. Meanwhile our press releases evidently had some effect, and that evening, the press coverage was rather extensive, and for the most part, the press had been fair and even somewhat favorable in covering the story.

On Thursday, June 19, 1969, I met with Lonnie at the downtown BCLA office, and we began to outline the parameters of the lawsuit we intended to bring. Later that morning we had a conference with Christian. Evidently, the welfare demonstration had shaken up some of the civic leaders. Some city councilmen, prominent businessmen, and religious leaders were becoming involved. Things were beginning to happen to see if emergency assistance funds could be raised and a meeting could be scheduled in order to discuss matters. Later that afternoon, Lonnie and I returned to the demonstration. While Lonnie spoke with Jo Ann, I conversed with one of the monitoring policeman, and I was pleased to hear that everything remained calm and peaceful. After a short while, we were advised by Enrique Salinas, the DPW Assistant Regional Director that word had come down from Austin to close down the Welfare Office entirely and the protestors would have to vacate the building. In order to avoid any confrontation, it took everything we had to convince Jo Ann and some of the real die hards to leave. "Look, Jo Ann," I said. "You all can still continue your protest, but do it outside—kind of like a campout. The weather is mild, and actually the conditions outside will be healthier for you and the kids than the stifling atmosphere in the damn building." At that time, except for a few of the executive and administrative offices, the rest of the building had no air conditioning, and in the heat of the Texas summer it was not exactly comfortable inside. Jo Ann and the inside bunch finally agreed and moved their bedding and food to join with the women outside, and they resolved to maintain their vigil. Before we left, I spoke with Patrolman Jack Weaver, who informed me that there would be a police presence throughout the night, and that the order was to leave the women alone as long as they remained outside the building and were orderly. These were his orders from Police Chief Bichsel, but suspicion was they originated from Councilman Dr. D. Ford Nielsen.

It was Friday, June 20, 1969, and Bill Sinkin, a prominent businessman and noted civic leader showed up at the demonstration and commented on the Welfare office closure. "I can't pass judgement on why they closed," he said, "but hunger and need don't take a holiday, and I don't know how they (welfare officials) can." Bill was one of the leaders that were pushing for a resolution meeting. County Commissioner Albert Pena also turned up at the demonstration and addressed the protesters. "We help people all over the world and can't help our own people," he rejoined. "All the people who claim that people on welfare don't want to work are damn liars," he declared. "People on welfare can't work." He added, "Where is our mayor when we need him?" He was referring to San Antonio's Mayor, Walter W. McAllister, and the two of them were perennial political enemies. "I think we ought to insist that our governor and lieutenant governor, instead of fighting among each other, address themselves to this problem. The only way to do this is to declare this city very definitely and absolutely as a disaster area," he continued. Of course that wouldn't make Mayor McAllister look very good, and the last thing we needed was to lose focus and for this thing to become a political football between them. But meanwhile things were beginning to come together. Christian informed us that a meeting had finally been agreed upon between DPW officials; various civic, business, and religious leaders; and representatives of the welfare mothers with us as their attorneys. It was scheduled for Monday morning, June 23rd at the office of the Economic Opportunity Development Corporation (EODC).

In the meantime a commitment for an assistance fund of $50,000 had been cobbled together between the city, county, Council of Churches, and the Family Services Association, and there was indication that EODC would match that with an additional $40,000--$50,000.

Lonnie and I felt it was time to end the demonstration. Thus far the press had been relatively favorable, but to subject the children to a prolonged protest over the weekend, attitudes might begin to sour. Fortunately we were able to convince Jo Ann and the women to bring things to a conclusion, and so we announced to the press that: "Our point had been made," and informed them of our up-coming meeting at EODC on Monday. So Friday, late afternoon, saw the women taking down their signs, packing up, and returning to their homes, although Jo Ann vowed that they would be back on Monday if their demands were ignored.

That Monday negotiations were successful. Nearly $100,000 in supplemental funds would be made available to assist those families adversely affected by the welfare cuts in May. DPW agreed to aid city welfare in the distribution of the funds, which could be utilized to purchase food stamps. Another bone of contention was that DPW's welfare hearings were held only at their downtown office and were conducted only in English. In many instances, it was patently unfair in cases where a woman spoke primarily Spanish. Also it was unnecessarily burdensome and costly for welfare mothers to make it downtown when DPW just as easily could hold the hearings at their neighborhood offices. After some discussion, DPW agreed it would also conduct hearings in their neighborhood locations and even in the recipient's home, if necessary. Furthermore, if the recipient preferred, the hearing would be conducted in Spanish, or an interpreter would be furnished.

That afternoon, the front page newspaper headline read: "PROTESTERS WIN WELFARE ROUND," as Clay Robison, a news journalist detailed the story about how the three day welfare protest had brought some positive results. But of course we weren't done yet. Lonnie and I had put together a lawsuit challenging DPW's novel percentage reduction scheme in calculating the unmet budgetary needs of AFDC recipients as being unconstitutional under the due process and equal protection clauses and asserting that it violated the Social Security Act, as well. Of our two named plaintiffs, Maria T. Davila and Jo Ann Gutierrez, we decided to list Maria first. She was more demure than Jo Ann and actually presented a slightly stronger fact situation. So before the week was out, the class action case of *Davila v. Hackney* was filed in federal court, seeking a hearing before a three judge panel.

Unbeknown to us at the time we filed the *Davila* case in San Antonio, two attorneys with the Dallas Legal services Project, Ed J. Polk and Douglas Larson, had already filed *Jefferson v. Hackney*, which was a similar case in Dallas. As the cases were very much alike in nature, the federal courts decided to consolidate the two cases, and because the Dallas case was filed first, it was determined that the cases would be heard by a three judge federal court in Dallas. At first I was disappointed until I heard who the composition of our panel was going to be. It would consist of Judge Irving L. Goldberg from the 5th Circuit Court in New Orleans, and two Texas Northern District Judges, William M. Taylor and Sarah T. Hughes. Of course I immediately recognized Judge Hughes as the one who swore in Lyndon B. Johnson as President on Air Force One, after the assassination of President Kennedy. The thought of my trying a case before her made me feel kind of privileged.

We didn't have much time as the cases had been fast tracked, and our hearing was scheduled for Tuesday morning, July 1, 1969. We needed to get together with Ed and Doug to figure out how we were going to present the cases. Lonnie had already called them and made arrangements to meet with them the day before the trial. That evening I told Marlene how excited I was to get to argue before Judge Sarah T. Hughes. As our second anniversary would be on Wednesday, July 2nd, we came up with the idea of her joining me in Dallas, and we could spend a four day vacation celebrating our anniversary at Six Flags, where we had spent our honeymoon. How nostalgically romantic I thought. So the plan was that I would take my VW, and Lonnie and I would drive to Dallas together. The following day Gloria would drive up in her car with Marlene, and they would meet us after the trial. It would give us some time together. Then Gloria and Lonnie could drive home, and Marlene and I could spend our anniversary vacation at Six Flags.

So on Monday, June 30th, Lonnie and I left early in the morning. On the drive up we had plenty of time to discuss the case. Lonnie didn't know anything about Taylor, but we felt with Goldberg and Hughes we would have a fair shot. The facts had been stipulated, and so the oral argument on the law would be the whole deal. In this particular case between the constitutional and statutory contentions, we both agreed that the statutory argument was the stronger of the two and likely had a better chance of convincing the court to go with us. So naturally, in dividing up the argument, we preferred to handle the statutory part of it, and we were concerned about Ed and Doug agreeing to that.

It was early afternoon when we hit Dallas, and we went straight to the Dallas Legal Services Project office, which was located in an old, red brick building on N. Market Street. We introduced ourselves and went into Ed's office for a conference. Between him and Doug, it was obvious that he was the senior and would be calling the shots. Before we could say anything, Ed said that they wanted to go first and aggressively push the constitutional argument. He felt very strong about what he believed to be racial discrimination. It was no secret that the more favorably treated elderly, blind, and disabled programs happened to be more predominantly Anglo; whereas, the un-favored AFDC program was much more minority oriented in composition, being about 85% black and Hispanic. Ed proposed that we could then follow them and present what they viewed as the "secondary statutory argument." Well, that's just what we wanted, and so we agreed. It was a done deal, and we then adjourned for a casual lunch. Afterward Lonnie and I checked into our hotel room. Although we felt Ed might have a point with his racially motivated attack, but whether there was strong enough evidentiary linkage to convince the court, well that was another story. At any rate, we had gotten the statutory part of the argument, which is what we wanted. We went through several practice sessions, with each of us alternatively playing the court and interrupting with questions that we thought the judges might ask. After dinner we relaxed some, and then turned in early so we would be fresh in the morning. However, it was a restless night for me, as my mind kept on mulling over my part of the argument, and it was rather late before I finally fell asleep.

The next morning, I nervously awoke, got ready, and we met Ed and Doug at the Dallas federal courthouse. Inside the courtroom, we all sat at the right side counsel table and opposite us sat the lawyer from the Texas Attorney General's office with another lawyer from DPW. "All rise," called the bailiff, as the three judges paraded out and took their seats behind the judicial bench. As planned, the Dallas Legal Services lawyers went first. Ed set forth a passionate plea that DPW's scheme and categorical different treatment between the welfare programs was constitutionally defective on racial grounds. Instinctively, I had a hunch from the court's questions that they weren't exactly buying it. Next it was our turn. Lonnie began by summarizing the facts, emphasizing the devastating effects upon AFDC recipients, and outlining the statutory history. At last it was my turn, and I closed by arguing that DPW's regulations and practices violated the Social Security Act. I did not believe that DPW could just make a mere bookkeeping entry by increasing the family's needs on paper, only to immediately nullify it by applying a severe percentage reduction, so that in effect the family would receive less than what it was getting before, rather than more. That this cipher scam dodged the concept of a cost of living raise and clearly did not comply with the 1967 amendment to the Social Security Act and what Congress had intended by passing it. My final point was that even the "great state of Texas" still had to obey the law. From the questions we were getting from the court, I felt that they were more responsive to our part of the argument. Before I knew it, the trial was over. The judges would consider the matter and let us know.

The four of us went for coffee and had a "postmortem" session. We had no illusions, and we all realized it was a difficult case from the start. Plus going up against the powerful state of Texas, certainly was no easy task either. All and all, everyone felt like we had done our best. We took our leave of Ed and Doug and departed to meet the girls at a designated restaurant near Six Flags. We had a pleasant, relaxing lunch together, as we related our trial experience to them. Afterwards Gloria and Lonnie drove back to San Antonio, and Marlene and I spent the rest of a wonderful week at Six Flags.

It was Thursday, July 31, 1969, and I was at the E. Houston Street office when the phone call came in. It was Lonnie Duke. "Are you sitting down?" he said. "Yeah," I responded. "You know the *Davila* case, well the court just decided it unanimously, and we won it on the statutory grounds that we argued," Lonnie exclaimed. "Wow, no kidding," I replied. "Yeah, it's a big win," Lonnie continued. "I'm going to notify the clients, and Christian wants to meet with us tomorrow morning. See you then." Needless to say, I was on a high for the rest of the day. On my way home, I picked up the newspaper, and the headline blared: "Texas Told Pay Welfare," the news article went on to say: "Citing the Bexar County Legal Aid Association for its excellent work in preparing its part of a consolidated case, the court… said the state's plan put into effect May, 1, violates the requirements established by Congress and therefore is void." "Holy crap, they totally bought our statutory argument. Christian is going to go bonkers when he sees this," I excitedly exclaimed, as I showed the article to Marlene. And the fact that the court complimented us made me feel even better.

The morning of August 1, 1969, I met Lonnie at the downtown Legal Aid Office. Not only did the court declare the DPW scheme illegal and barred it from further use, but also it mandated that Texas incorporate a cost of living increase in its welfare grants as Congress had envisioned. It put Texas under an injunction, denying the state use of any further federal matching funds until compliance had been achieved, but then gave the state a 60 day probation period in which to straighten out its welfare mess.

Lonnie had already been on the phone with Ed Polk from Dallas, and unbelievably, he was livid. He wanted the court to favorably decide the case, but on the constitutional grounds, which the court declined to do, and so he wanted to appeal and wanted us to join him. "But we won," I said. "Why the hell does he want to do that?" "Don't know," said Lonnie, "he just seems totally fixated on the racial thing and just won't let it go. He definitely wants to appeal, and Christian wants to talk to us about it." About that time Patsy buzzed us, and we went in to see Christian. He greeted us with a big smile, and said: "Gentlemen, congratulations – splendid work, just splendid." We chatted about the case and trial for a while, and Lonnie related how pleased our clients were. When Christian asked about Polk wanting to appeal, Lonnie explained that he was dissatisfied about not prevailing on the constitutional grounds. I finally chirped in: "Mr. Christian, regardless of the grounds, we won, and I just don't think it's wise to jeopardize our victory on an appeal, and besides we've got other things we can be doing." Christian agreed, and he instructed Lonnie to inform Mr. Polk that we would not be joining him in an appeal, and the message was so related.

Welfare-wise, it seemed like indeed things were happening. Earlier that year, in April of 1969, the U.S. Supreme Court decided *Shapiro v. Thompson*. In that case, a nineteen year old mother moved from Massachusetts to Connecticut. When she applied for AFDC there, she was denied because of Connecticut's one year residency requirement. The Supreme Court held that the welfare regulation was illegal, as it unreasonably restricted the fundamental rights of Americans to travel from state to state. Poor citizens should be able to move inside the country just like anyone else. Lonnie had actually filed an Amicus Curiae brief in that case, as it was so similar to our *Alvarez* case. And it was fairly obvious that when the dust settled the *Shapiro* case was going to have an impact on our *Alvarez* case.

Then the next month, in May, 1969, the very month before the welfare demonstration, Lonnie had won the *Machado* case. The three-judge federal court in San Antonio, headed by Judge Adrian A. Spears, issued a ruling declaring the DPW "man-in-the-house" rule illegal, stating it violated the Social Security Act. In doing so the court cited the U.S. Supreme Court case of *King v. Smith*, which had been decided a year earlier; and whereby, a similar Alabama "man-in-the-house" rule had been declared illegal. Accordingly, the Texas DPW was ordered to reinstate Ms. Machado's AFDC grant and to pay her all the back benefits that were due her.

And now we had won the *Davila* case too. It seemed like we were on a real role. Just days after, on August 5, 1969, the Texas constitutional amendment to raise the welfare cap from $60 million to $80 million passed. That would have the effect of pushing enough additional funds into the system whereby DPW could comply with the court's decision in the *Davila* case. Many AFDC families would be getting an increase in benefits, as opposed to having their assistance grants cut or completely eliminated, and I felt pretty darn good about that.

With the big three welfare class actions fairly wrapped up, Lonnie felt it was time to move on, and so in August, 1969, he left legal Aid for a better paying position with Rivera & Ritter, a very reputable local law firm. I couldn't really blame him, but I was sad to see him leave. With Lonnie gone, Andre Hernandez was the only lawyer officially left on the *Alvarez* case, and in his words: "He didn't know squat about welfare law." A final agreement and stipulation had to be done to implement the court's ruling in the *Alvarez* case due to the implication of the U.S. Supreme Court's decision in the *Shapiro* case. So when Andy asked me to help him, of course, I obliged. My goal was to make sure that not only would our three named plaintiffs receive all the benefits they should have been paid when they were illegally denied, but also, that the whole class would receive full retroactive benefits, as well. And we did just that – making sure that DPW had to fulfill its obligation to the entire class, which included: 321 families, 68 elderly people, 18 disabled individuals, and 1 blind person. In October, 1969, the court approved the final draft, and the newspaper column headline read: "Effect on welfare law court ruling expanded." At this point, I felt the welfare battles were over. I should have known better.

In August, 1969, with Lonnie's departure from Legal Aid, just after my 27th birthday, and before Harry Adams' 26th birthday, Christian tapped us and put us in charge of all law reform cases at the BCLA. We had already partnered-up and were involved in several ongoing matters, so the last thing I expected was to have another one suddenly drop into our laps. It was sometime before Thanksgiving in 1969, when Geraldine Felder walked into the E. Houston Street office. She was a middle-aged, black woman, who was the mother of six children, ranging in age from 11 to 18. She and the children were receiving an AFDC grant of $209.00 per month. Earlier that year she had met Mr. Felder, who was employed as a janitor and earned $316.00 per month. They fell in love, and he moved into the household, where they all lived together as a family unit. But then in September, 1969, they decided to make it "legal," and they got formally married. That triggered DPW's infamous Code 82, which stated: "Your children are no longer deprived of parental support due to marriage." Hence the entire AFDC grant was terminated, and the family was thrown off the welfare rolls. There was no further assessment or examination of the family's needs, rather it was just an automatic termination resulting solely from Geraldine's marriage. I quickly ascertained that Mr. Felder was not the biological father of any of the children, nor had he legally adopted any of them. There wasn't even an implication of any "equitable adoption." Geraldine verified that although he played an adult male role within the family, the children never viewed him as their father. Indeed, rather than call him "Dad," he was always referred to as Mr. Felder. Under our *Machado* case, the Texas "man-in-the-house" rule already had been put into the legal dustbin, having been declared illegal. So it was rather difficult explaining to Geraldine that if they had just continued living together there would have been no adverse consequences regarding her AFDC assistance benefits, but just because they formally got married, DPW thought it justifiable to totally terminate the welfare grant. Geraldine didn't think that was fair, and quite frankly, neither did I. "Ms. Felder, sometimes the law doesn't seem to be fair," I said. "But maybe, just maybe, we might have a chance to change that." After some explanation, I told her we would consider taking her case as a class action against DPW. I saw her mood change from despondency to hope and even pride, as she agreed to act as the class representative.

I called Harry Adams. He was a veritable walking legal encyclopedia and a legal researcher extraordinaire. "I think I have a real whopper of a new law reform case," I exclaimed, as I detailed the fact synopsis in the Felder matter to him. "Hey Harry, do you know of any state law of general applicability which requires stepfathers to support the children in the household to the same extent that natural fathers are required to do?" I asked. "I don't think it exists," I declared. "I think you're right, but we can research it," said Harry. "What about this Code 82?" Harry asked. "Do you think that that computer code was ever properly filed with the Secretary of State as required by law? If not filed, it could be null and void," Harry surmised. Leave it to Harry to come up with such a nit-picking attack, I thought, as we both resolved to thoroughly look into the matter.

The more research we did, the more we were convinced that we had a very viable case. Further refining the theories used in the *Alvarez, Machado,* and *Davila* cases, we put together a "kitchen sink" pleading and brief, which put forth a very potent constitutional and statutory attack. We were able to paint Ms. Felder in a good light, as one fighting for marriage and family values, while portraying DPW's policy as aimed at discouraging morality, encouraging the breaking up of a family, and depriving children of a "father image." Before the end of the year, the class action law reform case of *Felder v. Hackney* was filed in federal court. Through painstaking and very detailed discovery we forced James C. Parker, the hapless welfare hearing officer, to admit that it was the formal marriage alone that caused the termination of the grant. Our goal was to put DPW in a box from which they couldn't squirm out. We wanted to make it clear that their action was arbitrary, capricious, and unreasonable. That it was only the formal marriage that was considered, and nothing else. That it was indeed an automatic result and that there was absolutely no further inquiry or consideration of the family's needs. The old "Duke of Discovery" had returned with a vengeance.

The newspaper reports and editorials were rather favorable stating: "As a result of a civil suit filed here, thousands of Texas poor families will have their day in court." Even one of the court officials characterized the case as: "This will be an important case to watch, involving the future of Texas' poor families." Several church groups started to come forward and speak out in favor of our position. I had the distinct feeling that DPW was beginning to feel the heat, and they didn't like it one bit. Moreover, we lucked out, as we felt we had drawn a good three-judge panel, consisting of Judge Homer Thornberry, from the 5th Circuit, and Texas Western District Judges, Adrian A. Spears from San Antonio, and Jack Roberts from Austin. Harry and I continued developing the *Felder* case and moving it toward trial, which we anticipated would likely take place in April or May of 1970.

Then sometimes fortuitous things just happen, and all of a sudden it just did. A New York welfare law case entitled *Goldberg v. Kelly* had been working its way up the appellate ladder, until it reached the U.S. Supreme Court and was argued there in October, 1969. It was a Monday afternoon on March 23, 1970, when I received a phone call from Deborah Weser, a reporter with the San Antonio newspaper. She had called me because she was familiar with me as we had conversed during the welfare demonstration and during the filing and outcome of the *Davila* case. "Did you hear about the new Supreme Court case on welfare?" she asked. "No, what's the deal?" I responded. Deborah continued by informing me that the U.S. Supreme Court had ruled 5 to 3 that day that people have a right to a formal evidentiary hearing before officials may decide to reduce or end their assistance benefits. She further stated that the Supreme Court had specifically referenced the San Antonio *Machado* case and even used it as an example, and she wanted to know if there would be any further implications with respect to that case. I told her that there very well might be, but that I didn't know. I promised her that I would look into it and get back to her, which I did.

Deborah's instincts were right, and her news story with its headlines: "High court ruling bears on S.A. case" and "Supreme Court refers to S.A. case" were dead on point, as well. In deciding *Goldberg v. Kelly*, the Supreme Court had held that the 14th amendment to the constitution requires "due process" before benefits were cut off. Indeed, the court was requiring a full due process proceeding, whereby the hearing must provide an opportunity for the welfare recipient to appear in person, to present evidence to support her claim for continued assistance, and to confront and cross-examine witnesses against her. In writing for the majority, Justice William J. Brennan, Jr. went on to say: "The interest of the eligible recipient in uninterrupted receipt of public assistance coupled with the state's interest that [her] payment not be erroneously terminated, clearly outweighs the state's competing concern to prevent any increase in its fiscal and administrative burdens." Oh my God, I thought, that was indeed the constitutional argument that we used in the *Machado* case. There the three judge federal court held that DPW's termination without a full and proper prior hearing was in violation of the Social Security Act. We had won the *Machado* case, but on the narrower statutory grounds; whereas, the *Goldberg* case had clearly broadened this to the constitutional grounds, as well. In fact the decision in that New York case would have implications regarding the law in California, Iowa, Georgia, Florida, and Texas. No doubt about it, I thought, the San Antonio three judge court will likely have to modify the *Machado* decision so as to incorporate the constitutional aspect of the *Goldberg* decision; thereby, making the *Machado* case ruling even stronger. I guessed right, and eventually I was contacted by Judge Adrian A. Spears' office and asked to work with the Texas Attorney General's office and DPW and come up with some suggested language that would indeed modify the judgement in the *Machado* case so as to fully incorporate the Supreme Court's ruling in the *Goldberg* case, which I of course enthusiastically did, and the matter was successfully accomplished without much further hassle from the other side.

In speaking with Harry, we both felt that although not right on point, the *Goldberg* case could have a tangential effect on our *Felder* case. Besides I felt that by this point DPW was getting tired of us and somewhat spooked by our streak of victories. So Harry and I thought that we just might have a chance at settling the case. In a strange coincidence, recently I had been dispatched to Austin to meet with Mr. Hackney and some of the top DPW officials in order to discuss a separate and unrelated matter. At that time Harry and I were working on another major case dealing with a rather revolutionary unique idea concerning the Texas child support law. We were seeking DPW's help in developing statistics on how many unwed mothers were on the state's AFDC rolls. If by chance we were successful in that case, it could have the effect of saving Texas millions of dollars in welfare costs, and I believe DPW began to see the potential of that. After having been in a state of enmity for so long, it was kind of refreshing to find an area where our two organizations could be co-operative for a change. I don't know for a fact if that had an effect, but I felt that our relations began to thaw.

At any rate with the *Felder* case moving towards trial, I believe that DPW and the Texas Attorney General's office began to see the handwriting on the wall. I think it was fairly apparent that we were going to win that case, and it was just a question of how much effort and state money did they want to waste in fighting us any further, and pushing the case all the way up to the U.S. Supreme Court, only to likely lose there in the end. Finally, practicality and sensibility overruled pride, and they decided to run up the white flag and agreed to completely capitulate. The onerous computer Code 82 was to be entirely eliminated and done away with forever. Ms. Felder's AFDC grant was to be restored, and also she was to receive full retroactive benefits. Accurate and complete information was compiled on the class, and full benefits were to be paid to them, as well. When I called Ms. Felder and informed her of the resolution, she could hardly believe it and cried tears of joy. The *Felder v. Hackney* case was over. And so in the spring of 1970, with the onset of baseball season beginning, if you were keeping score, it was the Bexar County Legal Aid Association—4, and the Texas Department of Public Welfare—0.

CHAPTER 9

A Drive to the Top

1969 –1971

Gaytan v. Cassidy, 403 U.S. 902 (1971)

Sometimes, life can be surprisingly strange, and so began a tale of how two seemingly unrelated events, in two different cities, separated by about nine months in time; nevertheless, somehow through fortuitous circumstances, became inextricably connected so as to have a wholly unpredictable outcome, which would result in changing the law in the state of Texas, and about forty other states, as well.

It was springtime in 1967, and I was in my senior year of law school at UT in Austin. At the end of spring break, it was time to get back into the routine grind of attending classes and working as a Legislative Assistant at the Capitol. My parents and I had just returned from a wonderful trip to Omaha, visiting my fiancée, Marlene, and her family. She and I were going to get married on July 2nd later that year. I had brought back with me a small, portable black and white TV, a vacuum cleaner, and some miscellaneous household items that Marlene's father had given us from his pawn shop. After returning to Austin, I had located a small, affordable apartment on the Southside of the city and signed a six month lease beginning May 1, and running through October 31. Even though it wasn't May 1st yet, the landlords, who were a nice, elderly couple, had graciously given me permission to move some of our stuff into the apartment, which was not being otherwise occupied.

So it was a balmy, moonlit evening in April when I loaded the stuff that I had brought back from Omaha into my VW to take over to our new apartment. I was driving west on Barton Springs Road and had slowed down to a near stop in order to allow the car ahead of me to complete making a left-hand turn. Just about the time he did so, and I began to accelerate and continue on my way, suddenly there was a loud "bang." I had been rear ended by a young lady, driving a much larger vehicle than mine, who obviously had become distracted and wasn't paying attention. She was pretty shook up, and as I tried to calm her down, she apologized profusely. Fortunately, neither one of us were injured, although our vehicles had sustained some damage. The front bumper of her car was scratched and dented, but my VW got it much worse. The rear bumper was completely smashed in, and on the driver's side, the back panel had been dented and the tail light broken. We exchanged information, and the police were called. When they showed up they interviewed both of us. The young lady admitted the accident was entirely her fault, but said that she had insurance that would take care of things. When the patrolman asked about my insurance, I informed him that I was insured through my father and that the Tommy Powell Agency in San Antonio handled our family's insurance. He also asked me if I estimated that the property damage was in excess of $100.00, and I told him that I assumed it was. Both vehicles were drivable, and so we went about our business.

The following day, I took my car to the VW dealership to be repaired. It was going to take a little more than a week. Although it was inconvenient, thanks to my suitemates who played chauffeur, I didn't miss any classes or work. Finally, my VW was repaired, and I thought this episode was over, and things would get back to normal. As it turned out, I was mistaken. Within the following week, I received a very official letter from the Texas Department of Public Safety (DPS). Except for routine periodic license renewals, I hadn't had any dealings with them since I originally got my driver's license when I was a teenager. The letter was signed by T.G. Ferguson, Manager of the Safety Responsibility Division, and notified me that because of the automobile accident in which I was involved, where property damage exceeded $100.00, pursuant to the Texas Safety Responsibility Act, Article 6701(h), my driver's license was hereby suspended. In order to get it reinstated, I would have to get a release from the other driver involved in the accident, or I would have to post a bond with the DPS in the amount of $500.00 and give proof of future financial responsibility. Upon failure to do so within the next twenty days, then I would be required to surrender my driver's license and motor vehicle registrations to DPS, and my suspension would last for a minimum period of two years. I was in absolute shock. The accident was in no way my fault, so why in the hell was DPS messing around with me? I called the young lady who was involved in the accident with me and politely asked her if she would be willing to sign a release for me. She apologized again but advised me that her insurance company had instructed her not to sign any release. Okay, I thought, but I believed that I also had liability insurance at the time of the accident, so why was this law being applied against me? The next thing I did was to call Dad to verify my insurance status. I learned that indeed I was fully covered under his policy, which specified both of our cars and listed him and two other designated drivers, Mom and me. I asked him to send me a copy of the policy and just to make it absolutely clear, to have Tommy Powell write a letter verifying the fact that I was covered. I told Dad to send the whole package via special delivery and direct it to me at Representative Don Hand's office at the Capitol. I figured that would enhance the chance of my getting it quickly. When Dad's package arrived it contained a copy of the insurance policy plus a notarized letter from Tommy Powell stating that the copy was true and correct and verifying that I was fully insured at the time of the accident. I surmised that because the policy was in Dad's name, and not mine, DPS had somehow picked me up as being uninsured; thereby, triggering this bureaucratic nightmare.

Now the problem was how to get this evidence before the right people at DPS who could straighten out this mess. Initially I tried telephoning them, but after frustrating hours of busy signals, being placed on hold, and hang-ups, I finally gave up. The DPS headquarter building was on N. Lamar Avenue, not far from the Capitol, so I decided that I would pay them a personal visit. Once there, and after making several inquiries, I located the offices of the Safety Responsibility Division. I announced to the receptionist there that I was the Legislative Assistant for Representative Don Hand and that I needed to speak with Mr. Ferguson, the Manager, on a rather urgent and important matter. Although I was being totally truthful in what I said, I realized it was a bit of a subterfuge, but it was successful in getting me in to see the man. Once inside, I introduced myself and related my problematic situation. Although I sensed that he was slightly miffed at the ruse used to get in to see him, he did advise me that an "aggrieved person" could request a DPS administrative hearing, a detail which the DPS notice letter I received totally failed to mention. Well, I certainly considered myself to be an "aggrieved person" and so advised him I wanted a hearing. I was ushered out of his office and turned over to a secretary, who furnished me with a booklet of information and a hearing request form, which I promptly filled out and signed. After checking the scheduling calendar, my hearing was set. Later that evening I appealed to one of my suitemates, George Rigely, to accompany me to my hearing and kind of serve as my counsel, and he kindly obliged.

On the day of the hearing, George and I reported to the Safety Responsibility Division offices at the DPS headquarter building. We were put into a small meeting room and sat together on one side of a conference table. Shortly after, two DPS officers entered. The senior of the two announced that he was the hearing officer, and he sat at the head of the table. The other one would be representing DPS, and he sat at the opposite side of the table from us. He began by presenting information from the DPS digest, which was an internal agency document, prepared from the police accident report and the agency's own follow-up notations. According to the DPS digest with regard to the accident in question, it appeared that the damages were in excess of $100.00, and the records indicated that at the time the other party was insured, but that I wasn't. I was asked to verify that I was a driver in the accident and that the damages were over $100.00, which I did. I was then asked how I got to the hearing today. That was a "gotcha" question. My driver's license was technically under suspension by DPS, and my testimony about driving to the hearing would be an admission under oath that I was driving while under "suspension" and that would not be good. Fortunately, I anticipated the situation, which is why George drove us to the hearing that day, and I so testified. Then it was my turn. When I tried to explain how the accident happened and that the other driver had admitted all fault, I barely got started, and I was summarily cut off by the hearing officer. I was told that the question of fault was completely immaterial and would not be considered. According to him, the only relevant issue was one of safety responsibility, i.e. did I have insurance at the time of the accident. After that I introduced the papers that I had received from Dad. The hearing officer reviewed them and seemed very impressed with the notarized letter from Tommy Powell. After a bit more testimony, he declared that it was his opinion that I was indeed covered by insurance at the time of the accident and that my driver's license suspension should be lifted. I was informed that the paper processing time could take a couple of weeks. On the other hand, if I was willing to pay a $10.00 reinstatement fee, the corrective action could take place immediately, and that everything could be concluded that day. I consulted with George, who said: "pay the damn fee," and I agreed. But it left a bitter memory. I felt like I was kind of treated as an offender, subjected to legalized blackmail, and that the whole power of the state had been used as a force against me, as an innocent victim of an auto accident, with no concern at all with respect to the individual who caused it. The whole system just didn't seem fair to me. At that time, I would have never guessed that fate would select me to be a key component in bringing about the entire downfall of DPS' Safety

Responsibility house of cards, which eventually would lead to the adoption of compulsory automobile liability insurance in the state of Texas.

It was a cool, crisp Monday morning in San Antonio on January 1, 1968. It was New Year's Day, and Antonio R. Gaytan, a 46 year old Mexican-American man was driving home after having picked up some Pan Dulce to bring back to his wife. He was headed south on Zarzamora Street and had stopped for a red light where that street intersected with Hazel Street. When the light turned green, he proceeded across the intersection. Then suddenly and without warning, a vehicle driven by Mr. Montoya crossed over the median on Zarzamora, and driving on the wrong side of the street, came speeding right toward Mr. Gaytan's car. A head on collision ensued. When the San Antonio police arrived, they made a complete accident report of the incident. Mr. Montoya was charged with unsafe speeding, improper lookout, negligent collision, and operating a vehicle without a driver's license. Mr. Gaytan was not given any traffic citation whatsoever. Fortunately no one was injured, but the damages to the vehicles definitely exceeded $100.00. After the accident Mr. Gaytan drove home and informed his wife as to what had occurred. Subsequently he tried to contact Mr. Montoya about the accident, but all his attempts were to no avail. It was like Mr. Montoya had disappeared off the face of the earth. After several months Mr. Gaytan was finally able to save up enough money to at least in part repair his car, and in the end, he chalked up the whole incident as to just being bad luck.

As things turned out, it wasn't the end, and his lousy luck continued. On May 4, 1968, Mr. Gaytan received a letter from the DPS, which was a notice of suspension. It advised him that due to the accident that had taken place on January 1st, and pursuant to the Texas Safety Responsibility Act, his driver's license was hereby suspended, and in order to get it reinstated he would have to get a release from the other driver, or he would have to post a bond with the DPS in the amount of $750.00 and give proof of future financial responsibility. Upon his failure to do so within the next twenty days, then he would be required to surrender to DPS his driver's license and motor vehicle registration, and his suspension would last for a minimum period of two years. The letter was signed by T.G. Ferguson, Manager of the Safety Responsibility Division. Getting a release wasn't an option, as Mr. Montoya had disappeared. As Mr. Gaytan was an indigent individual, he clearly couldn't afford to pay $750.00, nor was he capable of raising that sum in the requisite period of time. He did not have any auto liability coverage at the time of the accident as he could not afford the insurance premium payments. But he hadn't done anything wrong. At that time the state neither mandated nor required an operator of a motor vehicle to carry and maintain auto liability insurance as a condition precedent for being able to legally drive in Texas. So on May 24, 1968, not having any other known options, Mr. Gaytan's driver's license was officially suspended by DPS for the duration of a minimum two year period of time. Subsequently, on July 26, 1968, ostensibly for continual non-compliance, his driver's license was revoked.

It was February, 1969, and it had been slightly over a year since his accident. Mr. Gaytan wanted to undo his suspension and revocation status so he could get his driver's license back. Even though he lived closer to the Zarzamora Street neighborhood Legal Aid office, something told him that he should come and visit me. Somehow he managed to make it all the way across town to the E. Houston Street office, and so it was a fateful February day when Thelma showed him into my office. After cordially greeting him, we sat down to chat. Mr. Gaytan related his tale of woe regarding the accident and the subsequent DPS action against him. It was a story with which I was at least somewhat familiar due to my own prior experience with that agency. I quickly determined that there had been no releases of liability executed by either party, which was understandable, as Mr. Montoya couldn't even be contacted after the accident. I further learned that there had been no court litigation concerning the accident, as it was most likely that Mr. Montoya did not have any auto liability insurance either. Under such circumstances, a private attorney, acting on a contingent fee basis, would be unlikely to take a civil suit seeking damages on behalf of Mr.

Gaytan where there was no insurance, and regardless Mr. Montoya was long gone. So for a poor person like Mr. Gaytan there was no viable out from under the Safety Responsibility Act.

"But I didn't do anything to break the law, did I?" asked Mr. Gaytan. "No Sir, you didn't," I replied. I continued to explain that some states like Massachusetts require a person to have mandated auto liability insurance as a prerequisite in order to be able to drive. Actually that's better and even more protective of the driving public. But Texas doesn't do that. It leaves the choice as to whether to carry liability insurance up to each person. Of course most rich and middle class people would choose to carry it so as to be in a more protective status, but for a poor person, I could certainly understand the difficult choice in trying to decide between paying for insurance on the one hand or food or medicine on the other. At any rate, I pointed out that Texas never legally required him to have insurance in order to drive, and as long as he wasn't in an accident, he could have continued driving without ever being bothered. But once involved in an accident, however, then the full force of the Safety Responsibility Act comes into play against him. That's the way it works in this state. "But how could that be fair?" asked Mr. Gaytan. "I didn't do anything bad to cause the accident. It was entirely the other guy's fault," he exclaimed. "Well, you do have a point there," I replied. "I'll tell you what, Mr. Gaytan, let me research this and look into it further. Although it's going to take some time, I promise I'll get back to you. Would that be okay? I asked." "Yes Sir," he responded. "Oh by the way," I said, "I think I want to get our private investigator involved in this. I would like for him to verify the facts and to find out any pertinent additional information. His name is Joe Padilla, and he will be working for us. When he contacts you, and he will, I need you to be 100% truthful and co-operative with him. Do you agree?" I asked. Mr. Gaytan nodded his head affirmatively, and we shook hands and parted.

As I drove home, I kept on mulling over Gaytan's situation. The thought had already crossed my mind of possibly using Gaytan as a test case, but in that regard the facts would have to be absolutely solid. I wondered from a fault standpoint was the accident as completely one-sided as he had painted it? I'd been a lawyer long enough to realize that sometimes clients' statements will be colored by their own perspective and related in such a way as to slant things in their favor. I guess it was just human nature, and so at times things just had to be verified and checked out. But I felt that Joe Padilla would ferret out all of the details, and assuming Gaytan's story was accurate, then I couldn't think of a more overwhelming fact situation. Gaytan's words about how he hadn't broken the law or done anything bad kept ringing in my ears. I thought about the welfare law cases we were doing. Arguably if the state shouldn't be allowed to take a welfare recipient's grant away without due process, then why shouldn't that apply to a driver's license as well? Gaytan had not done anything illegal by driving without insurance. Just because he was unlucky and involved in an accident, which was not at all his fault, and then along comes the state of Texas and takes away his driver's license, essentially punishing him for driving without insurance, which was not against the law in the first place. The more I thought about it, the more I thought we just might have a constitutional case here.

The next morning I called Harry Adams. After detailing the Gaytan fact scenario to him, I advised him of my thoughts on the matter. "So where are you going with this? You're not thinking of a constitutional challenge, are you?" Harry inquired. "Hell, we'd be going up against the state's police power, and nothing is more of a sacred cow when it comes to state's rights," he declared. "Yeah, I know the federal courts tend to give states a lot of leeway in this area, but I think due process under the Fourteenth Amendment would still have to be applicable," I replied. "What about the notice letter? Was there any mention of an administrative hearing?" asked Harry. "Don't know, but I doubt it," thinking back to my own experience, "but at any rate, I promised Mr. Gaytan that we would look into the matter, I said." Harry agreed and thought that getting Joe Padilla involved was "a damn good idea." Since Joe worked out of the downtown office, Harry would contact him and get him started. We wanted a complete workup and to verify everything. In the meantime as the Vernon's Annotated Texas Statutes (VATS) statute books were in our law library at the downtown office, Harry would get a copy of the Safety Responsibility Act and the notations on the main cases dealing with it.

Joe Padilla was a short, middle-aged Hispanic man, with slicked-back, steel-gray hair and a matching moustache. He was an exemplary investigator with a natural knack for getting to the bottom of things. Weeks had passed and then one morning I got a call from Harry. He wanted to meet me for lunch to go over Joe's investigative file, which he just received. When we met Harry was smiling with excitement. Not only had Joe picked up a certified copy of the original police accident report, but also he got sworn statements from the two on-the-scene investigating police officers. In addition, he obtained sworn statements from three civilian eye-witnesses, who actually saw the accident happen. The facts Gaytan related bore out. There was absolutely no doubt that Gaytan was in any way the cause of this accident. We had one heck of an overwhelming, powerful fact situation.

It was time to do some in-depth legal research. We decided to divide it. I would take the Texas statute, make a detailed analysis of it, and research its history and the main Texas cases dealing with it. Harry would look at the other states with similar statutes, pick up the key state court cases about them, and check for any federal cases on the subject. The research was time consuming and painstaking but necessary. After we were done it was time to meet and compare notes.

"Well, what do you got?" asked Harry. I explained that the Texas Safety Responsibility Act had been around since 1951. That it operated and was administered pretty much as we had envisioned it. The supposed stated purpose was to protect the public from reckless and financially irresponsible drivers. But rather than make carrying auto liability insurance compulsory, as a requisite condition to being able to drive like was done in Massachusetts, the state of Texas instead decided to adopt an ass-backward approach, which dealt with the situation in a post-facto manner, after an accident had already happened and damages exceeded $100.00. That although administrative hearings were available, they weren't advertised and could only be held at DPS headquarters in Austin. The constitutionality of the statute had been challenged before in the case of *Gillaspie v. Department of Public Safety*, which made it up to the Texas Supreme Court in 1953. After much verbiage about the state's police power, driving being a privilege as opposed to a right, and the laudable goal about denying that privilege to financially irresponsible persons, the Texas Supreme Court held the statute to be constitutional. When that decision was appealed to the U.S. Supreme Court in 1954, certiorari was denied, and the U.S. Supreme Court refused to hear it. Although in *Gillaspie* the Texas Supreme Court did not say outright that fault could never be considered, it did kind of intimate it, and that's certainly the way DPS interpreted it. In addition relatively recently there had been two different state Court of Appeal decisions, citing *Gillaspie* and holding that fault didn't have to be considered. On appeal, the Texas Supreme Court refused to hear either of those two cases further. "Well," said Harry, "it looks like *Gillaspie* is the key Texas case, and the state law is kind of against us." "Right," I replied, "and that's putting it mildly. So what did you find?" Harry went on to explain that there were about forty other states that had selected this statutory scheme and had similar laws. In the last decade there had been constitutional challenges in several of those states, and with one possible exception, all of them had upheld their statutes. Only in California, did its Supreme Court intimate that perhaps fault possibly could be considered in a Gaytan-like situation, but the rest pretty much interpreted their statutes the way Texas did. Harry was able to find only one federal case, *Pollion v. Powell*, out of Illinois, which kind of supported us and said that there could be a possible constitutional question in these circumstances, but it wasn't litigated to finality, and so its authoritative strength was weak. On the other hand, the federal case of *Perez v. Tynan* was dead against us. There a federal district court interpreting a Connecticut statute that was very similar to our Texas one, had indicated that the statute there was constitutional and that there were no due processes or equal protection issues. Unfortunately *Perez* presented a stronger federal case authority position than *Pollion*. "Just wonderful," I sarcastically said, "so except for maybe California, all the rest of the state law is pretty much against us, and although we have a split in federal case authority, the stronger one is against us too." "Yeah, and unlike the welfare Law Reform cases where there was a Social Security Act statutory argument to bolster and back up the constitutional attack, we won't have that here," commented Harry. "You're right," I agreed, "and so this will have to be a direct flat-out, head-on constitutional assault."

It was late in the day, and Harry suggested that we adjourn to one of his favorite watering holes to continue our conference. At the bar we sat at a secluded corner table where we wouldn't be too distracted. Harry ordered us two Tecate beers, with sliced limes. That was his favorite. While sipping our beverages and munching on tortilla chips and salsa, we continued to commiserate and discuss the case. On the pro-side, we had a great fact situation and a half-way decent due process and equal protection argument under the Fourteenth Amendment. Against us stood the state's police power, the law of the state of Texas, and the law in about forty other states, as well. "Okay, so for argument's sake, let's say we take this—jurisdictionally, how do you think we should go? Harry inquired. "Hell, federal of course, and we ask for a three judge court," I replied. "Realistically, with *Gillaspie* sitting out there against us, I don't think we have any other choice." "I agree", said Harry, and so let's say we take it into federal district court, what do you think our odds would be?" he asked. "Well, of course it would depend on the three judge panel we drew, but at best I would say 50%-50%, and given the state of the law against us, we would likely lose, but we might be able to get a dissent," I replied. "Okay, so we would then have to appeal it to the U.S. Supreme Court," Harry surmised. "Right," I Responded, "I think that's where this case is going anyhow." Harry pointed out that the U.S. Supreme Court decides only about 2% of all the cases presented to it. Combine that with the fact that once before it had denied certiorari in *Gillaspie*, and one would have to conclude that the odds would be very much against us. "You're right of course," I admitted, "but let's say we could jump that hurdle, then I feel we would have a decent chance at winning this." I continued my analysis and explained that the Supreme Court had changed since 1954. Looking at the nine Justices, I figured Harlan and Stewart would likely be against us. Probably, we couldn't count on Burger either, and however he goes, Blackman tends to follow. So that would be four against us. On the other hand, I felt we had a real good shot at getting Brennan, Black, Douglass, and Marshall to go with us, and then if we could sway White our way, which I felt was very possible, we could win this five to four. So I believed if we could get this case up there, we would have a real good fighting chance. "So what's the final verdict?" asked Harry. I kind of shrugged my shoulders, but he read my mind. "You kind of really want to do it, don't you?" he asked. "Yeah, I do—I really do," I responded. "Oh, what the hell," he said, let's go with it." I ordered two more Tecate beers, and we resolved to talk to Christian about the matter.

The very next day we were in Christian's office. We related Gaytan's fact situation, summarized our legal research, and detailed our analysis. We didn't white-wash the matter, but rather disclosed that the vast bulk of state case law was against us; nevertheless, we wanted to proceed with the case. "Well gentlemen, it sounds like you're going to have a real uphill climb on your hands," Christian remarked. "Well Sir," I exclaimed, its way beyond uphill. Legally speaking, it will be more like climbing Mount Everest." "Okay gentlemen, I'll leave it strictly up to you, Christian stated," and so we obtained his approval.

The next thing was to inform Mr. Gaytan. I made an appointment to meet with him at the downtown office, which was actually more convenient for him than E. Houston Street. When we met, I introduced him to Harry and advised him that we would take his case and would like to push it forward as a class action. We went over the parameters of class action litigation, pointing out that this wouldn't only be just for him, but also for all others in his situation, as well. I further explained that the case would take some time and that he would need to have faith and be patient.

I cautioned him that the odds were against us, and we would likely lose at first, but not to become discouraged. "Mr. Gaytan, I think we're going to have to take this case all the way to the top, and so what do you think? Do you want us to go ahead?" I asked. He smiled and answered affirmatively, and we shook hands.

In the next couple of weeks Harry and I prepared our initial petition and brief, and in May, 1969, the case of *Gaytan v. Cassidy*, SA 69 CA 153, was filed in federal court. We served all of the Texas Commissioners of Public Safety: Clifton W. Cassidy, Jr., W. Blakemore, and Marion T. Key. We also served Wilson E. Speir, Public safety Director, and T.G. Ferguson, the Safety Responsibility Manager. We already guessed what their response would be: that all of our factual allegations were generally denied, that all our constitutional claims were all without merit, and that all of our requested relief should be denied and our case dismissed. We guessed right. Their official answer, signed by Jay Floyd, the Texas Assistant Attorney General, was just as we thought it would be.

We didn't delay and launched an aggressive discovery campaign, hitting them with a vicious set of interrogatories and cleverly crafted requests for admission designed to force them to concede and admit every single fact allegation we made. We had a real strong fact situation, and we wanted to nail it down so they couldn't attack it. In addition we contacted Eddie Morris, a local court reporter, and had him accompany us to DPS headquarters in Austin, where we took the deposition of T.G. Ferguson, Safety Responsibility Manager. I don't think he recognized me from my prior encounter with him a couple of years ago. At any rate, we wanted to establish that their administrative hearing procedures were basically a sham and that they never took fault into consideration even in the most one-sided cases. We learned that in the past three years the DPS had issued out 468,000 notices of suspension, and yet apparently held only 21 hearings. We wanted to paint a picture of just how arbitrary and unreasonable the statute and how DPS administered it really was. The idea was to push for the most overwhelming stipulation of facts we could possibly get. I think we were successful in that goal, and on February 25, 1970, a good pretrial order with a very favorable stipulation of facts had been filed with the court. Meanwhile, we had drawn our three judge panel, consisting of Judge Joe Ingraham from the 5th Circuit, and Texas Western District Judges, Adriane A. Spears from San Antonio, and Jack Roberts from Austin. Spears was somewhat liberal, but the other two were kind of conservative. Our trial date was set for April 3, 1970.

In preparing for trial, Harry and I were under no illusion. Given our panel, we felt we were likely to lose, but we would give it our best shot and try to make a strong record. With luck we might be able to sway Spears to go with us and get a dissent from him. We decided to divide our argument. Harry would start with the recitation of the facts and cover the narrower procedural due process issues, concentrating on the notice and hearing deficiencies. I would close and handle the broader and more complex substantive due process and equal protection argument. I would have to show how the statute and the way it was administered by DPS unreasonably discriminated against a vulnerable group. I figured a direct attack of "rich versus poor" would not work with this panel. Rather, I would have to subtly sneak in that concept. It was going to be a challenge. Then we had a piece of good news. On March 23, 1970, just eleven days before our trial, the U.S. Supreme Court came out with the *Goldberg v. Kelly* decision. This was the case where they held that a state couldn't take away a person's welfare grant without first affording the individual a full and meaningful due process hearing. Of course we were indeed familiar with *Goldberg* as it specifically referenced our *Machado* Law Reform case and which it would clearly impact. More important Judge Spears would be acutely aware of it too, as he was likely the one who was going to have to modify the district court's previous decision on *Machado* to incorporate the Supreme Court's constitutional ruling in *Goldberg*. "Listen Harry," I said, "I know the right to receive welfare isn't exactly the same as the right to have a driver's license, but they're both important, and if the state can't take one away without due process, then damn it that should apply to the other as well. We should be able to jump on the *Goldberg* horse and ride it all the way." Since all our facts were stipulated, in Harry's words our legal argument was going to be "the whole ball of wax."

Finally, it was April 3, 1970, the morning of the *Gaytan* hearing, and Harry and I reported to the federal courthouse, which at that time was across the street from the Alamo complex. It is where the bankruptcy courts are located today. Judge Spears' courtroom was famous for its uniquely stylized gothic and majestic appearance and had been used by Hollywood as a setting for several movies. When the three judges came forth and took their seats, Harry and I glanced at one another. We were ready, and Harry began. After summarizing the facts and emphasizing *Goldberg*, he argued that the very rudiments of due process would require notice and the opportunity to be heard. He pointed out that the DPS notice letter did not adequately appraise an "aggrieved person" of his opportunity for a hearing, nor did the DPS hearing process fairly satisfy due process requirements. When challenged by Judge Ingraham about how a driver's license was more like a privilege than a right; that it was different than a welfare grant; and that wasn't this really a matter for legislative policy rather than for the courts, Harry stuck to his guns. Then it was my turn. I immediately launched into an attack stating that regardless of whether a driver's license was a right or a privilege, it would be subject to constitutional protections. I hammered away at the fact that the DPS hearings could only be held in Austin, and how it was discriminatory, unfair, and unreasonable to expect an individual from El Paso to effectively be able to troop nearly 575 miles to Austin for an administrative hearing, especially if he had only limited resources. I contended that for the statute and the regulations thereunder to pass constitutional muster, the contemplated administrative hearings must be reasonably appropriate and meaningful, and in that regard would necessarily have to substantively deal with the issue of fault. I reminded the court that the Safety Responsibility Act did not require auto liability insurance as a prerequisite to getting a driver's license or maintaining one. Hence, I submitted the statute created a division between two classes of non-culpable, uninsured drivers, i.e. those who were involved in an accident versus those who weren't. With respect to those who weren't involved in an accident, they could continue to drive merrily on their uninsured way, without any consequences. How that satisfied the stated statutory aim of protecting the driving public from "financially irresponsible" individuals was questionable, to say the least. On the other hand, the unfortunate non-culpable driver, like Mr. Gaytan, who was involved in an accident, through no fault of his own, was required to either post a bond or lose his license. So here the state was requiring him in essence to effectually guarantee a "financial responsibility" for which the legal obligation had yet to be determined, and in Mr. Gaytan's case in our opinion would be non-existent. No court under the sun would hold him responsible for damages to Mr. Montoya, when clearly it was Montoya who was entirely responsible for the accident, and not Gaytan. And so here we have a sub-class of relatively rich unlucky non-culpable uninsured drivers versus those in that group who are poor. The former can afford to post a bond, thereby saving their licenses while going to court to resolve the damage liability issues. The latter can't afford to do that, and so end up losing their licenses by default due to their economic status, despite the fact they weren't at fault. I concluded that without a consideration of fault the whole process ran afoul of due process and equal protection. At the end, I was encouraged when Judge Spears asked me: "…what kind of judgment would you ask this court to write?" I responded by saying the court should write a triple-fold judgment: first, require DPS to give notice of an administrative hearing; second, that the hearing should be held in the town where the driver resided; and third, that DPS be directed to consider fault at least to the extent as to whether or not there is a "reasonable probability" that a judgment might be taken against the individual subject to the Act.

After the hearing Harry and I went to lunch. "So how do you think we did?" I asked. "I don't think I did all that well," commented Harry, "but you did great. I think you might have even swayed Spears to go with us." "Oh B.S.," I responded, "You did just fine. I think we made a great record and that was our goal." We finished our lunch and went back to work. All and all, I had a pretty good feeling about the argument that we presented, and now we would just wait for the court to decide. We didn't have long to wait. On April 10, 1970, the three judge court rendered a unanimous decision against us. We had lost, and as I suspected they heavily relied on *Gillaspie*, the key Texas case adverse to us, and *Perez*, the federal case against us. I was a little disappointed that we couldn't get a dissent from Judge Spears, because I felt that in his heart, he really wanted to go with us. But I certainly understood his finally deciding to bow to the more conservative "steri decisis" approach of the other two judges. I viewed this as only the first round. We had intended to push this all the way to the top from the beginning and so nothing had really changed in that regard.

Although Harry may have been a bit reticent when we first took the case, now he was in his words: "pissed off." And I learned the one thing you do not want to do is to get Harry B. Adams, III pissed off at you. It was like he caught his second wind, and he was completely re-energized and ready to go after DPS. "You notify Gaytan, and I'll start working on our notice of appeal," he exclaimed. I called Mr. Gaytan and informed him of our loss but assured him we were going to appeal. I reminded him of our initial discussion when we first began this journey, and I asked that he remain patient and not get discouraged. He told me that he remembered our talk, that he had faith in us and trusted us, and that he was committed to hang in there to the end.

We filed our notice of appeal, ordered a complete record and transcript, and began drafting our jurisdictional statement and brief to the U.S. Supreme Court. At that time, I wasn't even licensed to practice before the U.S. Supreme Court yet (that wouldn't happen until January 11, 1971) and neither was Harry. So Mr. Christian's name was added to the brief pro forma, despite the fact that he didn't write any of it, and he had zero input regarding it. Our brief had to convince at least four of the Court's Justices that the constitutional questions presented by the *Gaytan* case were sufficiently important and substantially worthy of being selected by the High- Court for its consideration. Harry and I put together a brief that was concise, hit the issues directly on point, and incorporated a powerful and effectively persuasive argument. When we completed writing it, we were pleased with the result.

During the drafting phase, I had the opportunity to work with Anita L. Herrera, who was one of the secretaries at the downtown Legal Aid office, and one that Harry frequently chose to utilize in handling a lot of his work. Anita went to high school at G.W. Brackenridge, and she was in the 1959 graduation class there. I didn't know it at the time, but Anita turned out to be one of the most loyal, trustworthy, and devoted employees that I had ever met. Later on when I left Legal Aid to go into private practice, she chose to come with me, becoming my secretary and following me throughout the many phases of my legal career. She continued working for me for some 32 years, very rarely missing a day of work, until she retired.

Now we had to get the final draft of the *Gaytan* jurisdictional statement and brief printed. Leave it to Harry to have found the Dixie Printing Company, which was a little hole-in-the-wall downtown printing outfit that just so happened to be very experienced in printing U.S. Supreme Court documents. The owner was totally familiar with all the rules and detailed printing requirements. We were notified by Dixie Printing when it had produced the printed preliminary proof draft, and Harry and I picked it up. We spent the next several days reading and re-reading it multiple times. We made the few necessary corrections, and returned the corrected version to Dixie, personally discussing the corrections with the owner to make absolutely sure he understood them. We knew that everything had to be perfect. Within the next couple of days Dixie had done its final print run, and all the requisite copies plus some extras were delivered to the downtown Legal Aid office. Finally on June 4, 1970, our appeal to the U.S. Supreme Court was filed, and the case of *Gaytan v. Cassidy* was officially docketed as Case No. 495 in the Supreme Court of the United States for the October Term, 1970. Now we would have to wait and see whether the

Supreme Court would accept our appeal and agree to consider the constitutional issues presented by the *Gaytan* case.

It was an autumn day, and I was busily working on a number of matters at the E. Houston Street office, when the phone rang. The secretary announced it was Mr. Adams on the line. "Go ahead and put him through," I said. "Hi Harry, what's up?" I asked. "Hey Mel, guess what? The Supreme Court accepted the *Gaytan* case appeal," Harry declared. "No kidding, that's fantastic," I responded. We chatted for a while, as Harry noted that this was the very first time that a Bexar County Legal Aid case had been accepted for consideration by the U.S. Supreme Court. We agreed to meet after work for a celebratory drink at one of Harry's favorite bars. I notified Mr. Gaytan, who was very pleased about the good news. Later at the bar Harry and I commented about how two young lawyers, just a few years out of law school might get a chance to argue a case before the U.S. Supreme Court. As much as I was excited about the possibility of that, I realized that not all cases accepted for consideration by the High-Court were scheduled for oral argument, rather only a percentage of those cases were selected to be actually heard by the nine Justices of the Court.

It was only later that we learned that another case out of the state of Georgia, entitled *Bell v. Burson*, had also been accepted for consideration by the U.S. Supreme Court. That case challenged the constitutionality of a Georgia statute that was similar to the Texas Safety Responsibility Act. Indeed, the statutory scheme and operation of the Georgia and Texas legislation were very much alike. The High-Court had accepted both cases, *Bell* and *Gaytan*, for review regarding the constitutionality of the respective statutes of Georgia and Texas. Although Harry and I were still hopeful of getting a chance to argue before the U.S. Supreme Court, we realistically knew that it was unlikely that the Court would schedule both *Bell* and *Gaytan* for oral argument. More than likely they would pick only one to be heard by the nine Justices, with the other then to be determined based on the briefs. So it was now up to the Court to decide which one they might hear.

As fate would have it, the Supreme Court selected *Bell* on which to hear oral argument, rather than *Gaytan*. The *Bell* case oral argument was set for March 23, 1971. Of course I was somewhat disappointed, but I didn't lose sight of our over-all goal in that the High-Court was going to substantially review the constitutional issues presented by these two cases. I thought it was good that the Court had selected both cases, as it might be an indication that the Court recognized what a prevalent problem this was nationally. I personally felt that our chances of getting a favorable decision were good.

Finally, on Monday, May 24, 1971, the U.S. Supreme Court decided *Bell V. Burson*, 402 U.S. 535 (1971), declaring the Georgia statute and its operation as unconstitutional. Even though the Texas Legislature was still in session at the time, there was no discussion or effort in trying to modify the Texas Safety Responsibility Act. Indeed, it was as if the Texas leadership, politicians, and the DPS were in a state of oblivious self-denial—somehow assuming that Texas would still be victorious and win *Gaytan*. For me, after the decision on *Bell*, I felt the handwriting was on the wall. Even though the Court hadn't mentioned *Gaytan* yet, I felt it was just a matter of time, and I fully expected a victory. We really didn't have long to wait. Just two weeks later, on Monday, June 7, 1971, the U.S. Supreme Court decided *Gaytan v. Cassidy*, 403 U.S. 902, (1971), unanimously ruling in our favor and declaring the Texas Safety Responsibility Act and the DPS operation thereunder as unconstitutional. It was a monumental win, and I felt pretty darn good about it.

By the following day, Tuesday, June 8, 1971, the media had gotten a hold of the matter, and the press went absolutely viral. Both local newspapers featured headline, front page stories, with the San Antonio Express proclaiming: "**Texas License Law Voided S.A. Motorist Wins Ruling**," and the San Antonio Light echoing: "**COURT KOs TEX. DRIVER LAW**." The news articles profiled Mr. Gaytan, traced the history of the case, reported the ruling by the U.S. Supreme Court, and reported on commentary from various individuals. The Texas Assistant Attorney General, Jay Floyd, who opposed us at the trial hearing on April 3rd could not be reached for comment. Wilson E. Speir, the DPS Public Safety Director, had earlier indicated that the Texas law had not been affected by the Georgia ruling on the *Bell* case, but evidently that was before the High-Court's ruling on the *Gaytan* case itself. Norman Suarez, the Legal Counsel for DPS, said Monday evening that he was not aware of the ruling against Texas, and he had no further comment. Governor Preston Smith's office late Monday said the Governor had not been informed of the Court's decision and would have no comment, until he had an opportunity to be briefed on the opinion. According to the press, in general the officials in Austin were "tight lipped" about the High-Court ruling. I think that they were so smugly over-confident that they were caught flat-footed. Judge Adriane A. Spears, one of the three trial hearing judges, said that the Supreme Court had instructed them to modify their decision in conformity with the High-Court's ruling. He cautioned that if the Texas Legislature chooses to amend the present law that it would have to provide for a hearing on the question of fault. He further noted that the fault hearing required by the Fourteenth Amendment must be "meaningful" and "appropriate" to the nature of the case.

Eventually, Judge Spears and the other judges would re-write their opinion and judgment to comply with the U.S. Supreme Court's decision. Their ultimate draft was remarkably similar to my "triple-fold" formula that I had advocated in my oral argument before that court back on April 3rd in responding to Judge Spears' inquiry, when he asked me: "…what kind of judgment would you ask this court to write?"

The newspaper editorial columns were positive and complimentary stating: "Court properly strikes down bad Texas driver's law" and "S.A. Case Made Legal History." According to the press, aside from Mr. Gaytan, there were approximately 40,000 other Texas drivers who were adversely affected by the "bad Texas law," and whose licenses would have to be reinstated. In time, the *Bell* and *Gaytan* decisions would end up changing the law in about forty states. Eventually, I would be called upon to testify before a Texas Legislative committee, at which time I suggested the adoption of a compulsory automobile liability statute that would be similar in nature to the Massachusetts system. Although it took a while, the Texas Legislature finally did act, and ultimately the *Gaytan* case paved the way toward the compulsory auto liability insurance law that Texas has today.

By the time the *Gaytan* decision had finally come down, Mr. Gaytan and his wife had left San Antonio and had moved to Houston. I wrote him to let him know about the final outcome of his case, and I thanked him for being so patient and such a cooperating client. In response, I received the following letter:

> July 23, 1971
> Dear Mr. Eichelbaum,
>
> I wish to thank you kindly for writing to me concerning my driver's license. I got my license without any trouble. I again wish to thank you for your effort in helping me regain my license. Mr. Eichelbaum I hope that in the near future I will get to come to San Antonio and thank you and Mr. Adams in person and maybe have a cup of coffee. I wish to congratulate you, both of you, in winning my case.
>
> Thank you kindly,
> Mr. and Mrs. Antonio R. Gaytan

As I read the Gaytan letter, my mind slipped back to that April evening in Austin in 1967, when that young lady rear ended me. As a result of that happenstantial accident and my personal experience with DPS, would I have been as aware of the shortcomings of that agency's suspension procedures under a flawed Texas Safety Responsibility Act, and would I have been as sensitive toward Mr. Gaytan's situation and as understanding of his plight, when he first came to see me? Although as a lawyer, I would like to think that I would have been, but I really don't know the answer to that. It is likely that my own experience did play an influencing role in my perspective of Mr. Gaytan's dilemma. I guess sometimes things seem to work out in rather mysterious ways.

CHAPTER 10

⚖️

Ten and a Half Months to Home

1969 – 1970

The Concerned Tenants Union (CTU) v. The San Antonio Housing Authority (SAHA)

It was early in the morning on October 14, 1969, and I was just on my first cup of coffee. I didn't have any court that day so I was in my office at E. Houston Street reviewing some files, when the phone rang. It was Al Alonzo, who was the attorney in charge of the Guadalupe Street neighborhood office. "Hey Mel," he said, "I've got two ladies here who have some complaints about the San Antonio Housing Authority (SAHA). There is no court case pending—I mean there's no eviction going on, or anything like that. It appears to be more like an administrative law matter, which would be more up your alley. I'd like to refer them to you." "Sure Al, go ahead and send them over," I replied. At that time I had no idea that I would become involved in a rather complex case, spanning ten and a half months, and where I would be representing over 250 tenants and going up against one of the most powerful and politically connected local agencies, the San Antonio Housing Authority (SAHA).

It was later that day when Ruth Borregos and her sidekick appeared at my office. They were public housing tenants from the Alazan Apache

Courts, which was located on the Westside of town, not too far from the Guadalupe Street office, and was one of the seventeen public housing facilities operated by the SAHA. Ruth was a middle-aged Hispanic woman. She was a single mother, who was of average height and a bit on the stocky side, yet she was muscular and showed strength, which definitely matched her personality. Her sidekick, who was also a Hispanic woman and a single mother, was somewhat younger, smaller, and slimmer.

"What can I do for you ladies," I asked, and Ruth, who was obviously the leader of the two, launched into a series of complaints about her unit. She grumbled about how only one of the two burners on her stove worked, how there were serious cracks and missing tiles on the floor of her bathroom, and how the window screens had rips and holes in them or were missing altogether. That was a big deal, given that during San Antonio summers the temperature could easily rise to 100 degrees. This was in the days before these units had air conditioning and so windows had to be left open or you could bake to death. Having defective screens, or no screens at all, meant that mosquitos could get in and that could be a real health problem. After a little prodding from Ruth, the sidekick griped about how an electrical plug didn't work, how there was a major crack and gap in her sheetrock, and she also echoed the same complaint about the window screens. Both ladies insisted that the walls looked dingy and that a fresh paint job was way overdue. "Did these damages occur while you were residing there?" I asked. Both of the ladies almost in unison answered: "no" and informed me that these conditions existed at the time they moved in. "Really," I remarked. "Well, have you requested management to make repairs regarding these matters?" I inquired. "Oh yes, frequently," declared Ruth, answering for both. "They say they'll do it and get around to it, but somehow they never do." I nodded, as I continued to make notes. "It's not just us," Ruth added. "There are other tenants with similar problems, and I'm speaking for them too." She went on to say that it wasn't just the damage matters that needed to be addressed, but that her group was discontented about other things as well. "Like what?" I asked. Aside from not making timely repairs, she claimed that management would charge tenants extra assessments for damages that they didn't even cause. If a tenant hassled too much or became too demanding, then likely that person would get a mid-year increase in rent—almost as if it were a punishment. Ruth continued to say that sometimes management would conduct surprise inspections, and without the tenant even being present. She disclosed how management disapproved of guests or even family relatives visiting and staying with them for a short period of time, and how sometimes tenants were charged "extra rent" when this happened. "There just doesn't appear to be a solution to all this," Ruth sorrowfully said. "It seems as if we're living in something that is more like a prison than a home," she decried, as the sidekick shook her head in complete agreement. "One more thing," Ruth emphatically stated, and she pointed out how much her group was dissatisfied with the current tenants' union, the Resident Association (RA). She explained that it was dominated by self-seeking, "company shop" types of tenants, who were more interested in pleasing management than seeking needed reforms. Indeed, its president even sat on SAHA's board of directors. "They're totally worthless and completely ineffective when it comes to representing the tenants' interests," asserted Ruth. "Look here Mr. Mel, we tenants want a better deal, and so is there anything you can do to help us?" she asked. "Well, I really don't know," I responded. "But if you'll give me some time, I'll look into it, and get back to you," I promised.

That evening I was telling Marlene about my day and mentioned the two ladies from Alazan Apache courts. "So what the hell do I know about public housing law?" I commented. "Not much," I admitted, and indeed, I was clueless and didn't really know in which direction to go. Fortunately, I recalled seeing an article dealing with the subject of public housing in *Clearinghouse Review*, which was a nationally published legal periodical that was widely circulated among Legal Aid organizations throughout the country. It was a great source of valuable information concerning the civil rights and poverty law areas. It kind of reminded me of the *Texas International Law Forum*, in which I was involved while attending law school at UT in Austin. Just as that publication dealt with the current and cutting-edge subjects in the field of international law, the *Clearinghouse Review* achieved the same purpose, and did so in an excellent fashion, except in the areas of civil rights and poverty law instead. Each issue featured in-depth articles, up to date news, and pertinent casenotes regarding current Law Reform cases, which were on-going throughout the nation.

On the following day, at the office, I asked my law clerk, Barry Snell, to do some research. Since the *Clearinghouse Review* was such a treasure trove of good information, I didn't discard past issues. Rather, I kept them in a large notebook binder that was kept in our office library. I directed him to get the notebook and search for an article on public housing, advising him that I thought I had seen one there several months ago. In a little while, Barry brought the *Clearinghouse Review* issue dated July, 1969, entitled *A Voice for Public Housing Tenants: The Modernization Program*. "Is this it?" he asked. "Man, you got it and thank you" I replied. The article was written by Alvin Hirshen, who was a leading lawyer with the National Housing and Economic Development Law Project. By this time several national back-up centers had been established concerning several legal areas, such as consumer law, welfare rights, and housing and economic development, for example, and which were staffed by lawyers having a high degree of skill and experience in these fields. Their goal was to provide research, technical assistance, and guidance to local Legal Aid lawyers throughout the country. Well, this time I read the Hirshen article with a great deal more intensity, rather than just the casual glance that I gave it when I first saw it. In his commentary, Hirshen explained that the U.S. Department of Housing and Urban Development (HUD) had embarked on its Modernization Program, in which numerous local housing authorities (LHAs) were involved. Simply stated, the program was designed for HUD to make available significant additional funds to assist LHAs in upgrading their projects with respect to both physical facilities and what it termed as "social objectives," which seemed to touch on many of the issues about which Ruth complained, such as unreasonable mid-year rental increases, unwarranted assessments, and unresponsiveness in dealing with repairs and improvements, etc. In order to obtain such funds, however, an LHA had to submit to HUD a detailed local Modernization proposal, which would call for not only the updating of its physical facilities, but also would include certain changes in management procedures, as well "[and] these two aspects of the program <u>cannot be separated</u>" (emphasis added). The "management changes" referred to were primarily in the "social objectives" area and were directed toward further achievement of "The Social Goals for Public Housing," which previously had been enunciated in HUD Circulars. This really sounded like the kind of stuff Ruth was talking about, I thought. According to Hirshen, a possible strategy could be devised whereby if the LHA's specific Modernization proposal had evaded the "social objectives" and if such proposal had not yet received HUD's approval, then the Legal Aid lawyer could file an administrative complaint with the agency and effectively block the funds coming from HUD, until the social issues were resolved through tenant-management negotiations. Wow, could I have found gold here, I wondered. I might have just discovered "our ticket to ride" in handling Ruth and her groups' problems.

Having completed my perusal of the Hirshen article, I thought the next best thing to do was to personally contact Alvin Hirshen. I was able to get in touch with him, and I was grateful that he took the time to thoroughly go over things and to answer all my questions. Through our conversation, I learned that SAHA was indeed involved and participating in the HUD Modernization Program, but as Hirshen informed me, our particular local situation was rather unique and distinctively more difficult. First of all, SAHA had already submitted its local Modernization proposal to HUD, and even though it might have merely glossed over the social issues, without any strong contravening stance from a tenants' union, HUD had just routinely approved it. Perhaps the only saving's grace was that the actual funds from HUD had not yet been released. Second, Hirshen pointed out that in all other instances where his strategy had successfully worked, the tenant clients had controlled the local tenants' union, and thus were able to present a united front vis a vi management. Clearly, that was not the case here. In no way did Ruth and her group control the RA, and given her description of that organization that wasn't likely to happen. Although Hirshen cautioned me against a competing tenants' union situation, he realized we might not have any other way to go. He graciously placed himself and his staff at my disposal, and in no time the back-up center supplied me with a wealth of information, including: the HUD Circulars, particularly the ones dealing with the social issues; sample administrative complaints; and model leases and grievance procedures. Without a doubt the aid and support received from Hirshen and his staff was indispensable. After having carefully reviewed the information, although I didn't consider myself as being an expert in public housing law yet, I felt that I was rapidly "getting up to speed" in that area.

It was time to contact my usual trustworthy and reliable co-counsel, Harry Adams. We had already hooked up and partnered on several major matters, and we seemed to work exceedingly well together. Christian referred to us as "his most potent Law Reform team." During our conference, I quickly brought Harry up to date, and it didn't take him long to get to the gist of things. "Well, they [SAHA] haven't gotten their HUD money yet," Harry commented. "Right, you hit the nail on its head," I replied, "and that means there's no time to waste, and we're going to have to act pretty fast." Harry agreed and suggested we meet with Ruth and her group. I contacted Ruth and arranged for a meeting at her unit at Alazan Apache Courts. She was flattered and pleased that we were going to meet on her turf. I advised her that I planned to bring my camera along. I wanted to obtain photographic evidence as to their damage complaints.

On November 1, 1969, Harry and I met Ruth at her place. She was joined by about ten women, who were all tenants at Alazan Apache Courts, save one. The exception introduced herself as Marcie and said she was a social worker and a friend of Ruth and some of the other women, and she was there just to lend her support. We then proceeded to visit around half a dozen units in the general vicinity. At each unit, Harry noted the specific damage and deficiency problems, while I photographed them as we went along. The entire process took about an hour, and when we were done, we ended up back at Ruth's place. Similar to the other units, hers was small and Spartan-like, and how we managed to fit everyone in the postage-stamp sized living area was beyond me, but somehow we managed to do so. A conversation regarding the social issues ensued, with many of the women repeating the same complaints that Ruth and her sidekick voiced when they first came to see me. A discussion followed as to the aspect of taking over the RA, the existing tenants' union versus just forming a new one instead. The group concluded that the former would be utterly impossible; whereas, the latter, although challenging, would be at least doable. Harry and I drafted a statement of the new organization's over-all goal, which the ladies then voted on and adopted. Thus the Concerned Tenant's Union (CTU) was born with the following avowed purposes: "To improve the environment of public housing; to represent and protect common tenant interests; to achieve social and economic goals beneficial to all tenants; to educate management, tenants, and others as to the current conditions in public housing and inform them of <u>constructive improvements</u> which can be made; and to negotiate with management and others to attain the above stated purposes." The tenants then elected officers, and it was no surprise that Ruth was unanimously selected as president. We emphasized that it was important to get additional members and grow the union. Everyone understood and pledged to work hard in that endeavor. It was late by the time we got out of there.

 I still had some contacts at Fox Company and got a rush on the photo processing of my pictures. My skills as a photographer hadn't failed me, and the photos were matched up with Harry's notations, resulting in a presentation that dramatically documented the physical damage and deficiency complaints of the tenants. Through several contacts we had obtained a copy of SAHA's standard "lease" agreement and existing appeal procedures. The so called "lease" was way overly management-oriented, unilaterally binding only the tenant, and wholly lacking necessary provisions that would fairly protect the tenants' interests. Likewise, the existing hearing procedures were ineffective and insufficient to ensure impartiality and preserve individual rights. Arguably, there were indeed some short-comings with respect to HUD's directives and goals. Using some of my statistical training that I learned in Professor George Costus' class at St. Mary's, I was able to analyze the tenants' various complaints on a causal basis, and by utilizing that criteria, we found that the problems could be attributable to and statistically categorized into the following proportions: (1) inadequate lease, 57%; (2) insufficient appeal procedures, 35%; and (3) inept tenant's union, 8%. Our case was beginning to come together. Harry and I knew that the membership base of the CTU would have to be broadened beyond just the Alazan Apache Courts. By using staff personnel at the Guadalupe Street and Zarzamora Street Legal Aid offices, we were able to develop additional tenant contacts from Casiano Homes and San Juan Homes, which were two more Westside public housing projects. Likewise, client information from my office at E. Houston Street yielded additional tenant contacts from Victoria Courts, a downtown facility, and Wheatly Courts, a project located on the Eastside of town.

  I felt the next step was to prepare a formal statement to Richard (Dick) Jones, who was the Executive Director of SAHA. Dick was politically well-connected. He had deep inside associations within the Good Government League (GGL), which pretty much ran San Antonio local government. He had a myriad of contacts with the local Republican Party infrastructure, while at the same time, having significant relationships with the Democratic Party establishment, as well. For example, he was a friend and supporter of Henry B. Gonzalez, who was the same San Antonio Democratic Congressman I helped to get elected when I was a student at SAC. Likewise, I believed that John Daniels, who was the Bexar County Democratic Party Chairman, was also the attorney for SAHA. At any rate, I titled the formal statement: "Problems in Public Housing and Objectives of the CTU." It had a five-fold platform: (1) to announce the CTU's formation and purposes; (2) to point out the various and existing problems; (3) to list the tenant demands, most of which were supported by several HUD requirements; (4) to offer some suggestions for constructive improvements; and (5) to call for negotiations. I intended this to be our important "first contact" with management and hoped it would set a positive stage. I was just about to wrap up my final draft of that document, when Ruth's phone call came through. She was rather excited and angry and informed me of a flyer put out by the RA, in which it deemed itself to be the "Authorized Voice of the Residents." The flyer announced an important meeting at which John Daniels, SAHA's attorney, was to be a speaker, and its text read: "…learn about the consequences that a rent strike may cause. Our tranquility and yours is being threatened. Be ready to avoid being implicated in a rent strike that is now being planned by professional organizers." According to Ruth, several RA officers were spreading the rumor that the "professional organizers" referred to were us and the CTU, and of course this would not be helpful in gaining new members. I was in absolute shock, because we certainly never suggested the tactic of a rent strike, nor had it ever been raised at any CTU meeting or advocated by any CTU member of which I was aware. Ruth advised me that this was the first she had heard of it, and she requested us to attend the meeting.

So on November 11, 1969, Harry and I attended the RA meeting held at the assembly room at the Alazan Apache Courts. A good crowd had showed up, and the room was fairly filled. It was there we met Dick Jones and John Daniels, and the ensuing preliminary discussion, although somewhat strained, was nevertheless cordial. Daniels delivered a brief and rather low-key speech about the consequences of a rent strike. He pointed out that the individuals that would end up being harmed would be those residents who participated in a rent strike, as they would likely be evicted for non-payment of rent. He continued to explain that SAHA had a waiting list of people who wanted to get into public housing, and so there would be an abundance of prospective tenants to occupy their vacant facilities. I felt his talk was professional and that under current Texas landlord-tenant law, I didn't find anything really objectionable as to what he said. After his speech, Malicio Sanchez, who was a tenant and the president of the RA took the stand. He proceeded to make several caustic and unwarranted remarks that were obviously aimed at our clients. When I tried to question him about his statements, he advised me that the RA bylaws specified that only tenants could speak at meetings and that I was out of order. Having previously procured and read a copy of their bylaws, I knew Sanchez was wrong. However, when I tried to make a point of order regarding the matter, I was gaveled down and the meeting was hastily adjourned amidst angry vocal exchanges between various tenants.

The very next day the newspaper headlines read: "Legal Aid Lawyer Disrupts Meeting" and "Point of order kills meeting on rent strike." Unknown to me and Ruth at the time of the meeting, evidently it was Marcie who had loosely mentioned rent strikes and who had arranged for the press to be there in the first place. The next couple of weeks were an absolute nightmare as emotion, rather than reason, prevailed. With the most wild and unfounded accusations hurled about, there was an almost constant barrage of belligerence from all directions. A few local politicians, not knowing the first thing about public housing and its problems, saw their chance to grab some free publicity. And, of course, we received criticism from certain members of the local bar association who were perineal antagonists of Legal Aid anyhow. Christian was not a happy camper, and this is not how I envisioned starting a negotiating phase with SAHA management. Something had to be done, and quickly, to cool the passion-packed atmosphere. Hoping that we might succeed in bringing about a rational approach to the substantive issues, I completed the draft of the formal statement introducing the CTU and calling for negotiations, which I had all but wrapped up before, and on November 20, 1969, it was sent to both Dick Jones and John Daniels. In the meantime and as a precaution, Harry and I began to prepare an official administrative complaint, along the lines of a modified "Hirshen theory," for contingent filing with HUD, in case SAHA would stonewall us or Daniels would try to play a stalling game.

My relationship with John Daniels went way back to when I was a Young Democrat in college and relatively active in politics. Once after the Democratic Primary election day, I had gone to the Precinct Meeting that evening, and somehow managed to get selected as a precinct delegate to the Bexar County Convention. At that convention, this was the year when the "Connallycrats," those who supported John Connally, actually walked out of the County Convention to form a "Rump Convention" of their own. As my precinct was rather a conservative one, all of the rest of the precinct delegates implored me to join them in the walkout, but I steadfastly refused. So when it came time to vote for the Convention's Chairman, and since I was the only one left in our delegation, I proudly announced and cast all of our precinct's votes for John Daniels, who was running for that position, and he ended up winning. Afterwards I introduced myself and explained what had happened, and he thanked me for my support.

So I was pleased when on December 1, 1969, Daniels contacted me and acknowledged receipt of our correspondence. After an exchange of mutual regrets for past occurrences, he stated that SAHA was seriously studying our letter and would make a formal response in the near future. In the meantime, he suggested a meeting to discuss some of the more urgent individual cases. I considered this a healthy start, for if SAHA would recognize the valid existence of some of the tenants' individual problems and deal with them in a positive manner, then maybe the process could be expanded to include the group complaints, as well. On December 5, 1969, Harry and I met with Daniels at Alazan Apache Courts. The discussion was calm and productive, and we were able to actually resolve a few of the critical cases in a satisfactory manner. However, our meeting was abruptly terminated by the appearance of Marcie, who was creating a commotion in the outer office by loudly instructing tenants not to pay their rent. Before leaving the premises, I loudly announced to the tenants in the chamber that I was one of the attorneys representing the CTU and that that organization was not advocating a rent strike nor suggesting that any tenant participate in one. On the way back to the downtown Legal Aid office, Harry was livid. "What the hell is the matter with her?" He asked, referring to Marcie, of course. "I'm telling you now, I won't even be remotely involved with a tenant group that is seeking a rent strike," he declared. "Hell, it would be a clear case of legal malpractice to advise these tenants not to pay their rent," he continued. "I couldn't agree with you more," I replied. "Well, that's it—I think it's time for a 'come to Jesus' meeting," Harry declared, and I understood exactly what he meant and concurred.

I arranged for Ruth and the CTU officers to meet with Harry and I at the downtown Legal Aid office. We settled the women in the conference room, and then still being a bit in his "miffed mood," Harry proceeded to address them. "Look," he said, "you don't have to be a lawyer to be an advisor or consultant to a union. If you want Marcie to serve in that capacity, it's quite alright with us, and we can withdraw and not legally represent you all." Harry paused and then sternly continued. "If you want us to continue to be your attorneys, we'll be happy to do it; however, we can't be your lawyers representing you with Marcie acting as your 'lawyer' too, undercutting our instructions and countering what we're trying to do. You'll have to choose," he insisted. "You can have her or us, but not both, so make a choice," he demanded, as he walked out leaving the room. Knowing that some of the ladies had a good relationship with Marcie, I stayed behind in the room and calmly tried to answer any questions the women had. Although more empathetic and sedate in my manner, I sturdily supported Harry's position and confirmed that he was right. "Look Ruth," I concluded, "it all boils down to either you trust us, or you don't." I gave them about fifteen minutes to confer, and I left the room and joined Harry in his office. "Well," he said, "do you think our 'good cop-bad cop' routine worked?" "I don't know, but I guess we'll see," I replied. After the expiration of time, we both returned to the conference room, and Ruth announced that they had conferred and that they wanted us to continue to represent them.

Later on just the two of us conferred. "Okay, where do we go from here?' asked Harry. In order to avoid a recurrence of the emotion-charged climate, I felt that some conciliatory expression toward SAHA was appropriate, yet on the other hand, I thought it was important to show our intent to proceed until our clients' claims were resolved. Harry and I both felt that any further delay in filing a complaint with HUD wouldn't be a good idea. Finally, after some discussion, we decided to use a combination approach. By this time we had all but completed our final draft of the 22 page agency complaint, together with all the supporting documentation we had gathered. After making our final corrections, on December 12, 1969, the formal administrative complaint entitled: *The Concerned Tenants' Union (CTU) v. The San Antonio Housing Authority (SAHA)* was sent to HUD for official filing with that agency. At that time the Secretary of the U.S. Department of Housing and Urban Development (HUD) was George Romney, and the complaint was directed to his attention. It asked for HUD to send a federal investigative team to San Antonio and to hold hearings here with regard to the tenants' issues concerning public housing. It also requested a delay of payment of more than $7 million ostensibly due SAHA for the first stage under its local Modernization program, which we claimed was inadequate and in violation of various HUD regulations. Shortly after, HUD acknowledged receipt of our complaint, advised us that it had been referred over to its regional office in Ft. Worth, and promised to review it and further investigate the matter.

At about the same time, I drafted and sent a letter to Daniels, expressing my regrets for the unfortunate incident that terminated our last meeting. I explained that Marcie was not my client and while I could not control the personal associations of every CTU member, I would not tolerate further interference with respect to the representation of my clients. I concluded by calling for negotiations. I can only speculate as to whether it was our HUD complaint, my conciliatory letter to Daniels, or management's self-realization that some reforms were really needed that triggered a response. Regardless, shortly after New Year's John Daniels called me. "Hey Mel, I got your letter," he acknowledged, "and I want you to know that Dick Jones and I have had some serious conversations regarding this. I think Dick would be in favor of a meeting to further discuss the matter, but he's rather concerned about all this rent strike talk." "Damn it John, you know me—we go way back," I said, and I reminded him of our shared experience at the Bexar County Democratic Convention several years ago. I'm not sure whether he recalled the incident, but regardless I felt it helped build a feeling of commonality. "This rent strike crap is a bunch of nonsense, and at least in part, were rumors spread by the RA to foster its propaganda campaign against the CTU," I asserted. "Tell Dick that the CTU is not advocating a rent strike, and he has my word on that," I stated. That seemed to do the trick, and a meeting was set for Thursday afternoon at Daniel's office. I called Harry to advise him of the meeting and to set up a get together for us to prep for it.

When I got to Harry's, I grabbed a quick cup of coffee before we sat down in his office to discuss the meeting with Daniels. Although we were both gratified with the response we had received from HUD thus far, now our focus shifted as to what would be the consequences if HUD proceeded to investigate right away. "Don't you think that might likely cause some antagonism on management's part and have a chilling effect on negotiations?" I posed. "Yeah, no doubt it would," Harry agreed. "Not to mention the press would pick it up and that entire "Hula-palooza" publicity circus would start all over again," he predicted. "Your right," I replied, "and that's the last thing we need." After some discussion, we came up with the idea of possibly writing HUD and requesting a stay of action on their part in order to allow an opportunity for the matter to be resolved through local negotiations. Of course, likely HUD wouldn't mind putting the matter on a back burner, but would it be a risk on our part. If it had been the pressure of the HUD complaint that had been the impetus which prompted management's favorable response and agreement to talk, then by seeking a stay and removing the heat, we could be undercutting the strength of our own bargaining position. On the other hand, arguably negotiations might tend to be more fruitful if all parties, including management, came to the bargaining table without feeling unduly coerced. "So, what do you think?" asked Harry. "Should we take the calculated risk?" "Yeah, let's go with it," I responded, and we drafted a letter to HUD and sent it off that day. A copy was made to hand-carry to Daniels and present to him right at the start of our scheduled meeting. After some further discussion I felt we were ready. I proposed that on Thursday we could first meet for lunch to go over any last minute things before going to the meeting with Daniels. "Well, we can go to lunch if you want," said Harry, "but I'm not going to the meeting with you." "What?" I exclaimed in a rather surprised manner. "Yeah, I've been thinking about it," Harry explained. "You're the one with the background and better rapport with Daniels, and we don't need both of us there for him to get the feeling that we're ganging up on him, two against one," Harry continued. "You take the lead, and I'll just stay in the background, and it will work better that way." Although I was a little disappointed, I didn't argue with him. I knew he was right.

On that Thursday, I headed over to Daniel's office, which was located in the Tower Life Building. This was my old haunt, and I recalled the many days I spent there clerking for Pete Torres before I went into the Army. I was thoroughly familiar with the building and had no trouble finding Daniel's office. We met in his conference room, and I immediately handed him a copy of our letter to HUD requesting a stay. He seemed pleased and said he would definitely show it to Dick Jones. I felt he took it as an indication of our good will. We began by working on the roughly dozen or so individual tenants' complaints. Without outright confessing any existing deficiencies of present management policies and practices, Daniels clearly agreed there was room for definite improvement. As far as I was concerned that was good enough. I wasn't interested in securing an admission of past guilt, but rather was more focused on achieving meaningful reforms. The personal cases were well documented, and under the HUD guidelines, I felt that our positions were rather strong. Before the afternoon was over, we had successfully settled all of the individual documented cases, with solutions that were favorable to the tenants and which were acceptable to management, as well. We felt our efforts had been productive and resolved to meet again. Before concluding we talked some about the union situation. By that time the CTU had expanded to over 250 members and had grown into a viable tenants' organization seeking bona fide reforms. Clearly, it had become a player, challenging the RA for supremacy and being the more dynamic representative force with respect to the tenants. On the contrary, due to ineffective leadership, myopic goals, and a fear of losing their monopolistic power, the RA had adopted a totally irrational and reactionary posture. Even Daniels admitted that unfortunately management had unwittingly allowed itself to be drawn into the predicament of exhibiting a de facto preference for the RA and disapproval of the CTU. Daniels indicated how Dick Jones already had regrets about this, and that he would speak to Dick further about it. In the meantime, he suggested that perhaps it might be a good idea to get the two groups together for a peace conference. There was a mutual feeling of accomplishment as we shook hands and parted.

In order to avoid the return of the over-heated, emotionally packed atmospherics dominated by mischievous personalities and trouble-making politicians, I had resolved to steer clear of the press. That resolution went by the wayside when the phone rang, and it was Deborah Weser on the line. She was one of the best newspaper reporting columnists in San Antonio and an excellent investigative journalist. I was familiar with her, having had past dealings on occasions regarding some of my other cases. She wanted to know what was going on with the HUD complaint, and I knew with her a "no comment" response wouldn't do at all. I calmly related that things had simmered down, that Daniels and I were engaged in negotiations, and that I felt we were headed in the right direction. I knew she would check things out, and I proved to be correct. The next day the newspaper headline read: "Parley seeking end to housing dispute." Deborah's story not only included parts of our conversation, but she also interviewed Daniels, who fortunately echoed my sentiments. Evidently, she also spoke with Merle Warren in the HUD regional office in Ft. Worth. He confirmed that our complaint was "still active," but currently on hold and that his office had taken no steps to initiate on-the-scene investigations of alleged SAHA irregularities. "So far as I know, they are working towards some settlement," Warren was quoted. He did reveal that if no "satisfactory settlement" is reached in San Antonio "there is a possibility that funds might be withheld." Deborah's story succeeded in piecing together where everything stood. She managed to verbalize and convey our formula of a combination approach, which was pressure from the top, but being held at bay by meaningful negotiations at the bottom in an attempt to secure a collective solution acceptable to all.

During February, 1970, at Daniel's suggestion, we had two meetings between the CTU and the RA. The idea in Daniels' words was to have a "clearing of the air" between the two groups, while we tried to broker a peace between them. Unfortunately, feelings of embitterment and jealousy ruled, and the meetings were disastrous. I began to fear that the "Hirshen warning" about competing tenants' unions might be the unwanted plague that had come to pass and for whose visitation upon us I had yet to find an answer. However, two good things emerged from the negotiations. First, Dick Jones finally had his craw full of the jealous and reactionary attitude of the RA. He now saw the CTU, which he initially viewed as a challenging threat, to be more of a co-operative partner with management in seeking needed reforms that HUD wanted to see put in place anyhow. Accordingly, shortly after the meetings, Jones issued a directive stating that SAHA would recognize the legitimacy of any tenant organization whose goals were to peaceably strive to improve public housing and the lives of the tenants therein, and that included the CTU. So we finally gained recognition. Second, Daniels was convinced that future meetings between the two groups would not be helpful. Perhaps more time needed to pass for a healing process to take place, and the best thing for us would be to continue conferring, meeting lawyer-to-lawyer. I wholeheartedly agreed.

Since most of the tenants' complaints relating to the social issues stemmed from the lease, we decided to tackle that matter first. This commenced a period of months of bargaining, where the basic method utilized was a process of reconciliation. Daniels and I took turns in drafting lease forms. After each draft we met and discussed the proposed lease, point by point. Remaining in the background, Harry would occasionally put in his "two cents worth." With each successive draft, more and more points were satisfactorily resolved, and our respective positions became more reconciled until we finally reached agreement. Virtually all of the CTU's tenant demands had been met and incorporated into the new lease, such as: (1) annual redetermination of rent, and no mid-year increases; (2) immediate rent reduction in hardship cases; (3) return of security deposit upon the tenant vacating, less rent owed or cost of damage repairs; (4) tenant's right to provide reasonable accommodation to visitors and guests; (5) extra assessments for damages only when caused by the tenant; (6) management's obligation to make repairs and improvements with reasonable promptness; (7) inspections on advance notice and with tenant present; (8) specification of grounds for eviction; and (9) tenant's right to utilize appeal procedures. We then utilized essentially the same process in developing specific appeal procedures, with my insisting that they would have to effectively protect the tenants and ensure their rights. It wasn't too much longer before we had come up with an agreed upon set of appeal procedures with conjunctive notice forms. The final product liberally allowed a tenant to gain a hearing on virtually any problem arising under the lease. Daniels and I were pleased with the final package, and even Dick Jones referred to it as a masterpiece. Now the only remaining stumbling block was the composition of the hearing panel. Daniels and I had already agreed that the panel would consist of three management representatives and four tenants. The problem was how to select the tenant members of the panel. If they were all selected from the CTU, then the RA would be up in arms and vice versa. Given the amount of contentious feelings remaining between the two groups, trying to artificially split the tenant members with two selected from each group would not be exactly ideal in our minds. We had been negotiating for five months, and we felt we were at an impasse on this final point. Finally, it was Dick Jones who came up with a novel solution. We would rely on neither group. Rather, once a year a letter would be sent to every tenant in public housing requesting them to serve on a hearing panel. All those tenants willing to do so would merely place their name on the enclosed post card and return it. The names then would be placed on a panel list, and the cards would be placed in a receptacle. Then with each case, four tenants would be selected by random drawing. It would be very similar as to how the county jury system worked. It was a brilliant concept, because all tenants would be represented by this endeavor, regardless of whether they belonged to the CTU, the RA, or remained unaffiliated with respect to either tenant's union.

On July 7, 1970, the CTU notified management of their approval of the settlement package, and finally on July 25, 1970, the RA did the same. A formal press conference was arranged, and on August 25, 1970, the agreement was signed and the new lease and appeal procedures went into effect. At the signing ceremony, I approached Ruth Borregos and mentioned that it had been a long ten and a half month journey, but that she and her group were patient and had stuck it out. She gave me a big hug and thanked me, saying: "Now I feel like I have a real home." When asked by the press if she was satisfied she responded by stating: "I think this is what we wanted. The thing is we didn't have a big fight. We are glad. And I'm talking for the people." It was Ruth's way of extolling the negotiating process and putting her stamp of approval on it and the results it achieved. On that day a copy of the settlement package, including the new lease, appeal procedures, and conjunctive forms were sent to HUD, together with our letter officially withdrawing our administrative complaint, stating that all matters had been successfully resolved. The next day the newspaper headlines proclaimed: "SAHA and Tenants Sign Agreement." The news story, including a picture of the agreement signing that reminded me of a depiction of the signing of a treaty in a history book, told the tale of the successful negotiating process and the excellent results achieved.

On September 8, 1970, HUD notified us that they received our letter and that as per our request the administrative complaint had been withdrawn. In his letter Secretary Romney expressed his appreciation and commendation of our efforts in resolving tenant-management problems to the mutual satisfaction of both. He further stated that in his belief, our efforts and the fruits therefrom were meaningful strides in an exemplary solution and in opening new avenues of communication and understanding, and this was the kind of attitude and example HUD would like to see in all locations. Christian was thrilled when I showed him the letter and asked if he could keep it as a keepsake memento. Of course, I couldn't refuse him. Later I learned that the lease and hearing procedures we created became model documents that HUD disseminated to various local housing authorities (LHAs) throughout the U.S. Locally, not only did the new lease and appeal procedures prove to be satisfactory beyond all expectation, but also the friction between tenants and management markedly dwindled to mere occasional minor incidents. The improved relationship and attitude of mutual understanding was a positive byproduct which fostered even further beneficial effects. For example, Legal Aid had printed a bilingual leaflet entitled: *What You Should Know About Public Housing*, which was aimed at the tenants with the purpose of explaining their rights and duties under the new lease and appeal procedures. With the cooperation and active participation of management, thousands of these were distributed to tenants in all seventeen projects of SAHA.

Subsequently, I was invited to be a presenter at a continuing legal education seminar that was going to be widely attended by a large number of Legal Aid attorneys. The subject on which I was asked to speak was negotiating tenant-management problems in public housing. I began by explaining that negotiation was a process of problem solving that involved conferring with others with the goal of reaching an agreeable settlement. I cautioned them not to become discouraged or overwhelmed if they encountered "bureaucratic backlash" – a phenomenon representing an initial resistance to change, especially when the impetus for that change comes from outside the agency's own structure. Since most agency employees regard themselves as "professionals" in their field, they may exhibit an initial hostility toward an outsider confronting them with a quest for reform, and even more so when it involves some criticism of their present operations. Here is where the advocate must be patient. The ills he is attempting to remedy are often complex and have existed for some time, and so there is no reason to expect that a cure can be concocted overnight. It is imperative to avoid factual exaggerations and unfounded, emotional appeals. Rather it is important to stay objective and to keep an open mind with respect to the proposals from the other side. He should realize that pre-conceived solutions utilized elsewhere are just "models" to be used as guides, and are not intended to be used as a packaged panacea solution in all cases. Each locality presents a slightly different situation, and imagination and creativity are often called upon to come up with a "tailored made solution." After all it should be remembered that the overall objective is to resolve the problem in such a way that the solution will be equitable, practicable, and acceptable to all.

CHAPTER 11

You're in the Book

1969 –1970

Case & Comment; **Volume 75, No. 2; March – April, 1970**

Economic Development in Poverty Areas

It was 1969, and I was working on some cases at the E. Houston Street office, when I was visited by a group of young African-American students from St. Philip's, which was a two-year community college on the eastside of town. They all professed to have an interest in the theater arts, which they were studying as part of their curriculum. Some of them were also members of a theater guild that was sponsored by the Second Baptist Church, which had been newly established to service the eastside community, which happened to have a predominantly black populace. According to the students, several community organizations had gotten together and had secured funding to restore the old Cameo Theater at 1123 E. Commerce Street. It had been originally built in the 1940s, with the goal of serving the eastside of San Antonio. The theater had both a vaudeville stage and movie screen and was designed as a multi-functional cultural facility, having the capabilities to handle events, ranging from premier film debuts to live theatrical performances, and from musical concerts to fabulous theme parties. In its heyday, for many inhabitants of the eastside community, it was the place to go and the place to be seen. It often hosted such renowned performers such as Louis Armstrong, B.B. King, and Fats Domino. However later, the theater fell into a state of disrepair and deterioration. The students enthusiastically described how the restoration project was going to keep and maintain much of the original 1940's historic and dramatic Egyptian art deco motif, featuring imperial-looking burgundy walls, glitz columns, and polychrome accents. They then informed me that they were interested in revitalizing live theater in the black community. Their idea was to form a repertory company for youths who were interested in theater and who would be capable of putting on plays at the restored Cameo Theater that would be relative to the black community. As a lawyer, they wanted me to assist them in forming a non-profit corporation for that purpose. When I asked them what was the need of a formal corporation, and why couldn't they do this through a school drama club or as part of the church theater guild, their answer was rather direct. They said they had talked about that, but they wanted something that would be run by the students rather than by the school or church. In addition, they wanted something not just for themselves, but also something that would be lasting and permanent and could be available for black youths interested in theater that would come after them. As one of the young ladies explained it: "…this would be a win-win situation in that not only would it obviously benefit the Cameo Theater and aid it in bringing live theater back to the black community, but also it would provide a place for black youths to enhance their thespian talents, as well as developing skills in running their own theatrical company. Their goals seemed both altruistic and sensible, and so I agreed to help them. It was the very first corporation I did, and before too long the students were operating an official Texas non-profit corporation. Later on that year, I read a drama critic's column in the newspaper, extolling how live theater was "exploding" in the eastside and giving rave reviews as to some of the recent performances. I was pleased to learn that the student group had been successful, and I felt a sense of real accomplishment in having been able to assist them. Little did I know then that I had made my first dabbling in the infancy of what was to become a major movement in helping poor communities—the concept of economic development in poverty areas.

Later on that year, I got a call from Genaro Cano, Jr. He was an Employee Training and Family Service Officer with the Economic Opportunity Development Corporation (EODC) Migrant Project. Christian had referred him to me and suggested that he give me a call. He wanted me to come visit their training center and speak to some of the migrant workers about Legal Aid and its availability to assist them with legal matters. Christian was always keen on the concept of community outreach and spreading the word as to Legal Aid's mission—an idea with which I wholeheartedly agreed. I told Mr. Cano that I would be happy to come out and see him, and we made arrangements for me to do so.

It was a long drive from my office at E. Houston Street to their place, which was located on the deep Westside. It seemed like once I got all the way across town that I was driving west on Culebra Road forever, until I finally arrived at a modest white, wooden frame and stucco building, which bore a sign denoting EODC Migrant Project. As I walked in Mr. Cano welcomed me and showed me around. The building had several compact offices and counseling rooms, a small but functional library, and a larger assembly room, which could accommodate about fifty people. A simplistic southwest décor was featured throughout, and it was furnished in a rather inexpensive fashion. In the assembly room were gathered a dozen or so individuals, who were migrant workers that the program served. Mr. Cano introduced me to the group, and I gave my typical Legal Aid informational speech. After my talk, there was a pleasant, homey social with punch and cookies, and I met some of the migrant workers, who were plain, unpretentious hard-working folks. I felt humbled because in those days, before all the lawyer jokes and when the legal profession had an overall positive reputation amongst the public, working-class people felt honored to meet a lawyer, and some of them just wanted to greet me and shake my hand.

Afterwards, Mr. Cano took me into his office for some coffee and a chat. I learned more about their wide-ranging program in trying to assist migrant workers and their families. He explained that during the crop harvesting periods the migrants would move from job to job, but that during the "off season," when crops weren't being harvested, a significant number of them had settled in a community on the far Westside. Their program would try to train them for employment and place them in other jobs, such as construction, hotel room service, general labor, etc. But the problem was that it was rather impossible for them to be able to get to job sites. The municipal bus line simply didn't run out that far to their community. There was no practical way for them to catch a bus downtown, where they could then get transfers to various buses that could carry them to different parts of the entire city. He asked if there was anything that I thought could be done to help the situation. I told him I didn't know, but I would look into it.

During the next several weeks, I discovered that the U.S. Department of Transportation (DOT) had funds available for "pilot programs" dealing with mass transit, which I felt just might possibly be appropriate in the migrants' situation. I contacted Mr. Cano and proceeded to work with him in drafting a proposal for a grant of funds under a "pilot program" that would in essence extend the bus line further out so it would reach the migrant community. We had to secure the co-operation of the San Antonio Transit Authority, which at that time ran the city bus system, and after discussing the matter with them, we were successful in getting them to concur with the idea. In due time, we were notified that the DOT grant of funds had been authorized, and then it only took the final step of getting the approval of the San Antonio City Council. Mr. Cano and I appeared before that body, and they voted their final approval. Mr. Cano thanked me, and bus service was extended to the migrant community. Unknown to me at the time, evidently Mr. Cano wrote a letter to the National Legal Aid and Defender Association, which in part read:

> Please know that the Legal Aid Association in San Antonio has certainly been very efficient and constructive in assisting the local migrant workers that have had legal problems.

Mr. Melvin Eichelbaum, Attorney with the San Antonio Legal Aid, I feel has been very efficient and affective and has certainly been a great asset to help not only our migrant program, but other war on poverty agencies to reach and defend the rights of the under privileged. Mr. Eichelbaum has gone beyond the call of duty and because of men like him, Legal Aid has been successful, he believes in what is just and true.

Respectfully, Genaro Cano, Jr.

Apparently, that letter got circuitously forwarded to the national headquarters of the Office of Economic Opportunity (OEO) and from there was re-routed to Mr. Christian in San Antonio.

It was November, 1969, right before Thanksgiving, and we had a surprise visitor. It was Mr. Christian, and he very rarely came out to the E. Houston Street office. As I grabbed a quick refill of coffee and invited him into my office, I was curious as to what his motivation was for coming by. "So what do you know about the subject of economic development in poverty areas? " Christian asked. "Not very much," I admitted. "Well, recently I've been in touch with National OEO and that appears to be the latest rage. It seems that they want Legal Aid lawyers to be more oriented toward working with community groups involved in that area," he continued. He went on to explain that National thought that a treatise on the subject, written by a Legal Aid lawyer with some background in the area and published in a widely circulated legal periodical, could give massive publicity concerning the matter. I sat quietly, passively nodding in concurrence and feeling nervously puzzled as to why I was the recipient of this news, and then it came out. "You know it will be a big coup for the Legal Aid program whose attorney writes such an article," Christian added, "so I volunteered you for the project." "But hold on Mr. Christian," I protested. "I have absolutely no experience in this area—none whatsoever." Christian smiled, as he handed me a copy of Gene Cano's letter that he said he received from National, which I immediately glanced at and quickly read its glowing, complimentary content. "Look here," said Christian, "you've worked with a black theater contingent, a migrant worker group, and now you're representing a public housing tenants' union, we felt that your breadth in working with community groups was more than adequate. Quite frankly, we believe you would be the perfect candidate for this endeavor." I felt positively trapped and finally consented to doing the task. As our conversation continued, I learned that Christian's idea for the target for publication of this "would be article" was none other than *Case & Comment*, just the most well-known legal periodical there was. Oh great, I sarcastically thought. Was there any way to add more pressure to my attempt at becoming an author?

In those days, the law book and legal publishing industry was dominated by two giants: West Publishing Company and Bancroft-Whitney Publishing Company. It was the latter that sponsored *Case & Comment*, which was a lawyers' magazine that had been in existence since 1894, and published at least quarterly. Bancroft-Whitney made it freely available to every lawyer in the United States who wanted it, and many did as every issue was chuck full of useful, informative articles on various legal topics. Over time, it had become one of the most renowned and widely circulated legal periodicals in all America. I made the necessary telephonic contact with the Editor, Sidney Bernstein, who advised me that the over-all subject matter of my prospective article would be something they would consider, but he made it clear that there was no promise of publication. It would strictly depend on the article and that the competition was pretty stiff. After outlining for me their length constraints and deadline requirements, he wished me luck.

That evening Marlene sensed my despondency and put up with my constant griping. Given my caseload and schedule for the rest of the year, there was no doubt that from a time perspective I would have to write the article over the Christmas holidays and submit it right after that in order to meet the deadline requirement for the spring issue. "Damn it, I just didn't need this added pressure," I complained. "I don't even know what title to call this thing," I quipped. "Well, what's it going to be about?" Marlene asked. "Economic development in poverty areas" I answered. "Well, why not make that the title?" she suggested. I nodded and agreed. As always Marlene had consoled me, and I was resolved that even as a reluctant author, I would write and submit this article.

As I began to research the matter, I became more interested in the subject, and I discovered that the idea of economic development in poverty areas stemmed from the riot years of the 1960s, which markedly illustrated the danger of allowing the problem of widespread poverty and urban deterioration to go unchecked. Old remedies weren't necessarily doing the trick. Slum clearance and urban renewal had too often meant the wholesale ouster of the poor from one poverty pocket to another. Income maintenance programs such as welfare, although absolutely necessary, had been little more than a stop-gap approach in fighting over-all poverty. Similarly, job training and vocational rehabilitation, although likewise essential, had proven to be a drop-in-the-bucket approach, allowing only a few of the entire poor community a chance to attain a better way of life. The conceptual approach of economic development was that in order to achieve any great degree of success in dealing with the poverty problems of the inner city, the method utilized needed to be one that aimed at uplifting the entire poor community, not only by attacking the causes of poverty, but by allowing the poor to be the primary beneficiaries of the attack itself. In many instances the business and commercial sector had fled the poverty areas of the inner city in order to establish themselves in the more affluent suburbs, thus setting in motion a downward spiral of less economic and commercial activity begetting more deterioration and decay, which in turn lead to even less commerce and so on. To reverse the cycle necessitated large scale re-establishment of business and commercial enterprises within the poverty area, thus revitalizing the poor community's economy. By involving the poor inhabitants as participant owners and operators of these new enterprises, one had the possibility of achieving a double-barrel effect of allowing the indigent poor inhabitants to benefit themselves, while at the same time uplifting the entire poor community, implanting the necessary attributes of hope and incentive, which could then grow and spread even further. When there was so much negative propaganda about how many of the poverty programs were "wasteful and ineffective," and how as a society we were losing the "war on poverty," I wanted to illustrate some of the success stories and show how Legal Aid lawyers performed an integral, interplaying roll between poor community groups, government programs, and private enterprise, knitting together the right combination of the essential ingredients of capital, credit, and skill in order to assist the poor communities in revitalizing the entire poverty neighborhoods.

For example, in the San Francisco Bay Area, which was one of the nation's notorious inner city poverty stricken areas, while working with a tenants' rights group, a neighborhood Legal Aid lawyer organized a small corporation for public housing tenants who wanted to establish and run their own coin-operated laundry. The business proved to be so successful that their little corporation morphed into the San Francisco Economic Development Corporation (SFEDC). The corporation successfully secured funds from various federal programs, such as the Small Business Administration (SBA), the Economic Development Administration (EDA), and the Research and Experiment Fund of the Office of Economic Opportunity (OEO). Skilled set people in the areas of law, accounting, marketing, and finance volunteered and came aboard. These were supplemented by business administration students from a nearby college who became interested in the project and decided to donate their time and effort. In no time the SFEDC had launched a whole host of a variety of businesses, which provided jobs for many of the poor inhabitants and had a significant impact in revitalizing the entire poverty ghetto area.

In New Mexico, Legal Aid lawyers assisted in forming the Home Education Livelihood Project (HELP). With about $250,000.00 in funding obtained primarily from a Ford Foundation grant, they assisted a poor community, consisting of mainly indigent Indians and Mexican-Americans, who were making blankets, ponchos, and leather crafts on a piecemeal basis, and aided them in forming the Del Sol Corporation, with the idea of mass producing these items and putting together a much wider distribution scheme for their sale. Later the corporation added jewelry and tourist clothing items and became hugely successful, with numerous outlets throughout the southwest. The entire community ended up prospering from this undertaking.

Many other examples existed, ranging from co-op grocery stores located in food desert areas that had been abandoned by large scale grocery chains, to maintenance and management companies of low income housing. In all of these instances, the businesses were owned and operated by the poor inhabitants themselves and provided employment opportunities for many members within the poverty community. Perhaps one of the most inspiring examples was where a Legal Aid lawyer worked with some social workers and convinced a neighborhood gang to re-channel their efforts in a more productive direction by forming a car wash business. The enterprise was so successful it expanded into a full-fledged automotive center, featuring auto maintenance and repairs. The entire business was owned and operated by youths who were once nothing more than a street gang. Some of the young men became excellent auto mechanics, and all learned that their present energies had been much more profitable than their past endeavors of petty crime ever was.

As planned I completed writing the article over the Christmas vacation, and shortly after New Year's I mailed it to *Case & Comment*. January, 1970, had started out good. My case involving representing the Concerned Tenants' Union, which was growing by leaps and bounds, saw some positive movement. John Daniels, the attorney representing the San Antonio Housing Authority (SAHA) had agreed to meet with me and negotiate some of the tenants' complaints, and I was excited about the prospects there. At any rate, I was finally finished with the article and relieved that my chore was over, and I wouldn't have to worry about it anymore. But before the end of the month, my secretary buzzed me and excitedly announced: "It's Sidney Bernstein with *Case & Comment*." "Okay, put him through," I directed. "Well Sid, what's the verdict? Am I in the book? I asked. "You're in the book," he replied, as he went on to inform me that *Case & Comment* had decided to publish my article and that it would appear in the March-April issue. We then went over some minor editorial corrections to which I readily agreed, and afterwards he related the second bit of news. "By the way you're in the contest for the cover," said Sid. When I asked him what that was all about, he explained that my article had been selected as one of the top three articles chosen for publication for that issue. "It's kind of like a horse race, with win, place, and show," as Sid went on to explain. The one that's picked to be the lead article is the winner and gets the cover. The *Case & Comment* artist crafts a rendition for the cover, which would be in accordance with the theme of the article, and the title of the article and the author's name would be prominently displayed in big print on the cover. The second place finisher or runner-up would get a corner banner on the cover bearing the title of his article and name, but in much smaller print of course. And the one who finishes third gets no special treatment or mention on the cover. "And that's how it works," said Sid. When I asked him who the other two contestants were, he advised me that they were Melvin Belli, who had written an article dealing with the liveliest cases of criminal law, and Father Robert Drinan, who had written a very thought provoking piece on the legal aspects as to public aid to parochial schools. When I asked him how the outcome would be determined, he stated that it was strictly up to their editorial board, and he wished me luck and said I would be notified at a later date.

That evening, I proudly announced to Marlene that my article had been selected for publication and that I was in the cover contest. When she asked who else was in it, I related: "Oh, it's only Melvin Belli, one of the most famous lawyers in all America." Marlene immediately recognized his name. He was a renowned trial lawyer, who was past president of the American Trial Lawyers Association and one of the founders of the International Academy of Trial Lawyers. He had written over thirty books and had been published countless times in various legal periodicals. "It's obvious, he's the one who is clearly going to be the winner," I predicted. I continued to explain that the other individual was Father Robert Drinan, who was the Dean of Boston College Law School, and how ironic it was that just three years ago, in 1967, he was a visiting law school professor and was my instructor in a Family Law class at UT. "And it's a good bet that he'll come in second," I added. Marlene and I both felt that coming in third wouldn't be all that bad and that it was an honor just having been selected for publication.

Within the next week or so I received a surprised telephone call from Massachusetts. It was Father Drinan, and I was absolutely floored that he had taken the trouble to look me up and contact me. It was rather flattering that he remembered me at all, and I felt even more gratified when he indicated that he recalled me as being one of his best students when he was at Texas. Our conversation was ingratiating, as we caught up on the happenings in each other's lives. We talked about the cover contest and of course wished each other good luck. We were pretty certain that Melvin Belli would be the winner, and so we made a gentlemen's bet on who would come in second. I naturally bet on him. That evening I told Marlene about the amazingly reminiscent chat that I had with my old professor, Father Drinan.

It was sometime in February, 1970, when I received the phone call from Sidney Bernstein. I was in an absolute state of shock when he informed me that the editorial board had picked my treatise as their leading article for the spring edition of *Case & Comment*. "Our artist is already at work designing an appropriate cover, and I think you'll be pleased," said Sid. "But we have to discuss colors, so what are your favorite two colors? He asked. I was too surprised to think. At that time my favorite two color combination was blue and green, but I couldn't fathom as to whether that would be suitable or look good on a cover, so I declined to render an opinion and simply said that I had no real favorites and asked him what he thought. "Well, let's see, you went to law school at Texas, didn't you? What are their school colors?" asked Sid. "Burnt orange and white," I answered.

{ 179

"Okay, what the hell is burnt orange?" he inquired. "Well, it's kind of a darkish orange," I explained. "Alright, dark orange and white it will be," said Sid, but the artist might have to add in some black for detail, would that be okay?" "Sure," I replied, and then curiosity finally got the best of me, and I asked: "by the way, who came in second?" "Oh, it was Father Drinan, and so he'll receive banner treatment on your cover," declared Sid, as he congratulated me. Of course, I was so pleased to hear that Father Drinan's name would appear along with mine on what was to be a burnt orange and white cover. How utterly appropriate, I thought, and so very reminiscent of the days when I was a student and he was my professor at Texas. That evening I told Marlene the wonderful news. Subsequently, I received one more phone call from father Drinan. Humorously, he wanted to congratulate me for winning our gentlemen's bet. "You were right," he said, "I did, indeed, come in second." It was a marvelous conversation, and we each saluted one another for having won out over Melvin Belli, and how unbelievably unexpected that was.

Later in the spring of 1970, the *Case & Comment* issue finally came out. I had received a call from Patsy Neyland, who advised me that Mr. Christian would like to see me. When I walked into the downtown office the place was a buzz. I was approached by a number of co-workers who congratulated me. I had not seen the issue yet, as mail received at the E. Houston Street office seemed to run a day or two behind that of the downtown office. One of the secretaries showed me a copy. In big, bold print the cover read: "Economic Development in Poverty Areas," by Melvin N. Eichelbaum. Sid was right. I was truly pleased with the cover's artwork. The artist's rendition depicted in a shadowy, dull background, a picture of dilapidated, slum buildings. Superimposed in front of them was a clearer and crisp portrait of a modern commercial center. In the foreground stood a distinguished looking businessman, dressed in a coat and tie, glancing at a file in one hand and with a telephone in the other, while standing behind a desk upon which sat a sign saying sales manager. It was as if the artist was trying to visually portray the message that the concept of revitalizing poverty areas through economic development would work if the idea could be sold. How brilliant, I thought, and of course the whole thing was dramatically done in burnt orange and white, just as Sid had promised. When I went in to see Christian, he was absolutely elated and reported that he had been receiving lots of phone calls. National was most pleased, and according to him, this was the topic of conversation at the Bexar County Courthouse. He informed me that he had spoken with Jimmy Allison, who was the Executive Director of the San Antonio Bar Association (SABA) and who pretty much ran the courthouse law library, and he had arranged with him to get me some extra copies of the magazine so I could give them to family members. I thought that was very considerate and thanked him.

Looking back, I still feel a sense of pride that my article was included in the Case & Comment, let alone to have it selected as the revered cover page story in that laudatory periodical. In retrospect, perhaps it was Mr. Christian's astute selection of the keen and timely importance of the subject matter that had a lot to do with them choosing this article for publication.

CHAPTER 12

So Why Can't Girls Wear Pants?

1971

The McCollum High School case

Hammonds v. Shannon, 323 F. Supp. 681 (1971)

It was just after the New Year's holiday in 1971, and young people were returning to school throughout the city. L. H. was a typical teenager, having typical teen concerns who lived in San Antonio's southeast side. The public school system in that part of town was run by the Harlandale Independent School Board, which was one of nineteen separate school boards that managed the different school districts within the greater San Antonio metroplex. Harlandale operated two traditional high schools, the older one, having the same name as the school district, was built in 1925, and the newer one, McCollum, was built in 1962. L. H. attended the latter and was in her senior year. She was a good student and had maintained nearly an "A" average. She was looking forward to completing high school and going onto college, and the idea of being able to get some scholarship assistance was a possibility.

In the 1960s the high schools throughout San Antonio had student dress codes, prescribing what the appropriate attire would be for students attending school. McCollum High School was no exception. Its student handbook provided that boys were not allowed to grow sideburns below mid-ear or to wear boxed haircuts, and girls were required to wear either dresses or skirts of appropriate specified length, but pants of any kind were strictly prohibited. These dress codes were enforced with varying degrees. Younger teachers, like Marlene, tended to adopt more of a relaxed attitude. While teaching at Edison High School, her idea was that she was there to teach the students math, rather than to waste her time measuring the length of girls' skirts or dresses to the nearest requisite millimeter. As long as the girl looked decent and the dress or skirt wasn't obviously too short, Marlene and most of the younger teachers would be apt to let the matter go. But some of the older teachers tended to be real sticklers for rigid enforcement. Marlene would often tell me of this one older teacher who roamed the school with a yardstick in hand, and who had an absolute penchant for going around measuring girls' dresses and skirts. Not only did she scout the hallways, but she would actually walk into other teachers' classrooms and disrupt class in order to accomplish her "important measuring." If a girl's skirt or dress fell short by just a fraction of an inch, she took great delight in escorting the girl down to the office.

It was somewhat of a bit of philosophical hypocrisy when social studies teachers extolled the United States as being a country that embraced the concepts of individual freedoms in contrast with certain other nations, which tended to take an opposite approach. And yet when it came to dress, particularly among the youth, there seemed to be somewhat of an anomaly, particularly when a dress code could be so zealously enforced with such rigidity so as to be disruptive of the educational process. I always felt Marlene was right in that it was more important that the girl learned to do the algebra problem rather than discover that her dress was a couple of millimeters too short of what was required. Like many of the students at McCollum High School, L. H. was aware of the student handbook dress code, and also like many of the students that was not exactly at the very top of their "thought list" as to what was of major importance.

During the night of January 7, 1971, a Texas norther blew through San Antonio. By the morning hours of Friday, January 8, 1971, temperatures had dropped below freezing and had registered at thirty degrees. With a constant, cold wind of ten miles per hour and a humidity of more than fifty percent, it made the wind chill factor feel like it was in the teens. Although in other parts of the country this wouldn't be considered severe winter weather, for San Antonio, it was downright frigid. When L. H. woke up that day, she decided to wear a very conservative looking pantsuit to school. What possessed her to do it? Clearly the icy, cold weather had something to do with it. Whether there was some sense of teenage rebelliousness mixed in as well, perhaps and possibly likely, but for whatever reasons, she donned her pantsuit and off to school she went. When she arrived at school things were pretty routine, until she was instructed to report to the office, where she was advised that she had violated the school dress code by wearing pants, and she was promptly removed from school and sent home. She was joined by two other girls, who had also decided to wear pantsuits to school that day, and who were likewise sent to the office and kicked out of school.

Following the weekend, on Monday, January 11th, L.H. returned to school with her mother, and they were ushered into the office of Pat Shannon, who was the Principal at McCollum. There L. H. received a stern rebuke about her disobedience of the school dress code. It was pointed out to her that she had never gotten cross-wise with school authorities in the past, and so she really didn't want to go down the road of becoming a disobedient and rebellious student. When she asked why girls couldn't wear pants, especially when it was so cold, Shannon double-downed and emphatically informed her on how trampy and un-lady like it was and how they didn't want McCollum girls to give the school that kind of negative impression to the community. The other two girls and their parents received similar treatment and heard the same lecture.

Teenagers talk, and during the next several days the topic of girls not being able to wear pants, even when the weather seemed to dictate the reasonableness of doing so, became part of the conversation amongst the students. The three girls had honestly felt that they had not done anything so despicably wrong. Many of their friends buoyed them up by indicating support for their position, while other members of the student body merely egged things on so as to keep the discussion bubbling along. What started as a reasoned and righteous inquiry with respect to an overly rigid and a rather authoritarian rule, surely but steadily built into a crescendo that something should be done in response to this ridiculous, arbitrary proposition that girls couldn't wear pants. It was like a volcano just boiling and waiting to erupt.

Finally, on Thursday, January 14, 1971, it happened. Approximately seventy students, including the three girls, walked out of McCollum and ringed the front of the school. Some of the students carried homemade signs saying: "Be fair to girls." A resounding protest chant rose forth from among a number of the girl members of the crowd as their voices cried in unison: "Give us a chance; let us wear pants." The demonstration was totally peaceful and remained so throughout.

Shannon was just beside himself. He evidently viewed this as a direct and embarrassing attack on his authority. His reaction was abrupt and immediate. Without any prior form of substantive notice or opportunity to be heard, all seventy students who were involved in the protest were automatically hit with three-day suspensions from school and were subsequently notified in order to gain re-entrance, they, along with a parent would have to undergo a personal interview with either Shannon or one of the two Vice-Principals, Earl E. Ott or Ernest Hoffman, Jr.

Timing was of critical concern to many of the parents of the suspended students in that the suspension period, at least in part, would be when important class time was scheduled for review in preparation for final exams that were to take place the following week, January 18th through January 22nd. So some parents were worried that the students' grades might be unduly jeopardized because of this. In the meantime following the Thursday of the walkout, the administration began to conduct an all-out mobilization against the walkout demonstration and the students involved with it. The idea was to categorize the protest as anti-McCollum and to demonize all those students who participated in it. On the following Friday, January 15th, students entering the school were faced with a large banner saying: "McCollum, love it or leave it." A letter writing campaign had been begun by some teachers and counselors in order to develop a wide showing of support for Principal Shannon. One school counselor even bragged about how by the following week she had collected over two hundred student letters indicating support for Shannon's policies. Rumors abounded about how the protesting students would be punished and perhaps even academically disadvantaged for their derisive conduct.

So was there any wonder that about eighty angry and upset parents flooded into the tightly packed room of the scheduled school board meeting of the Harlandale Independent School District on that Monday evening on January 18th. Numerous parents paraded to the microphone that had been set up and addressed the board, voicing their desire and expectation that their children be allowed to return to school tomorrow. It seemed to them that the requisite personal interview process was proceeding too slowly, and the parents of the suspended students felt that their children had already served their requisite three-day suspension, and they didn't want them to miss any more valuable class time, especially at this time of the year. Of course the elephant in the room was the "pantsuit issue," and many of the parents felt that Principal Shannon had over-reacted. One parent, Vernon Wier, finally had the courage to speak, saying that he objected to the dress code under which Shannon had refused to permit girls to wear pants at school. The Superintendent, Callie Smith, responded to the many speeches by the parents by giving a "law and order" talk, in which he defended Shannon's policies. He assured the audience that the personal interviews would be speeded up and that every effort would be made to get the students back in school just as soon as possible so that they could be placed in "study hall" and be able to prepare for their final exams, which for the suspended students would be given the following week, January

25th through January 29th. He urged all the parents to "follow the procedures" of the district and vouched that there would be "fair play" for the suspended students. One parent, who had already been through the interview process with Shannon, stated that she and her child were forced to sign a letter in which there was an admission of wrong doing on the part of the student in having participated in the walkout and that the student was being re-admitted to school on a "probationary status" and that any further violation of school rules would result in an "automatic and complete expulsion" for the remainder of the school year. Mrs. Joe Brown emphatically voiced her opinion that requiring such a letter to be signed was "wrong." Superintendent Smith said that he hadn't seen such a letter yet but that he would investigate it. As the meeting wore on, it morphed into complaints on the part of those in attendance about Shannon himself, and his policies at the school. There were some boisterous calls on the part of several parents to "get up a petition" to remove the Principal from the school. One angry parent even challenged Vice-Principal Hoffman "to go outside" and settle the matter. The stormy session finally broke up around 10:30 PM.

Within the next day or so L. H. and the other two girls who wore pantsuits were back at McCollum. They felt ostracized and uncomfortable. The declaratory "love it or leave it" banner still permeated the hallway. Their conferences with Shannon were scary and intimidating. He let them know that he was aware that they were "ring leaders in all this" and that he would be keeping an eye on them from here on out. They were all forced to sign the infamous Shannon letter, and they were informed that their final exams, since they would be after the regular ones, would likely be different and perhaps somewhat harder. The girls began to believe that what started as a protest against an arbitrary stance regarding their not being allowed to wear pants, simply because they were girls, had now grown into a situation where they feared disparate and unfair treatment. They felt this could result in their being harmed academically, and this possibly could have long-term consequences with respect to their getting into college, etc.

Angelo Parker was a young attorney who had recently been hired by the Bexar County Legal Aid Association (BCLA). He was undergoing his training period at the downtown office, when he first met L.H. and her mother. He began listening to them regarding their concerns about what was going on at McCollum. As the interview progressed, Angelo instinctively recognized the complexity and difficulty of the legal issues involved, and he briefly excused himself and went to Harry B. Adam's office to see if Harry could possibly join him in the interviewing process, which Harry did. Shortly afterwards, I received a phone call from Harry. "Hey Mel, I've got a young lady and her mom sitting here in my office, and they're telling me an interesting story about how she and a couple of other girls fear being targets of possible academic discrimination, all because of wearing pants to school one day." Harry continued and gave me a brief synopsis of what he had been told. "I'm asking them to come back tomorrow and to bring the other two girls with them, if they'll agree to come, I wanted to know if you'd be available to join us?" asked Harry. "The kids have school, and I don't want them missing any classes," said Harry, "so it will have to be later in the afternoon, say about 4:30 PM." I quickly glanced at my calendar and determined that I had no conflict, and said I would be there. And then suddenly the thought hit me. "Hey Harry, tell them I would like for the girls to wear the very same pantsuits that they wore on the occasion in question; wear the very same shoes, handbags, etc.; and to put on the same makeup and wear their hair the same way. I want them to look exactly as they looked on that day. I plan to bring my camera and take pictures," I explained. "Good idea," said Harry "It's a done deal, and I'll tell them."

It was late the following afternoon when I went to the downtown office to meet the three girls and their parents. Since the girls were full-time high school students with no or negligible income, there was no doubt that they would meet Legal Aid's eligibility test, but that wasn't good enough for Harry. He and Angelo pursued a detailed inquiry with the parents making sure that they qualified for Legal Aid as well, and they did. I photographed the three girls, and the pantsuits were conservatively colored and rather traditional. The outfits were comfortably fitted and weren't too tight, sexually explicit, or salacious in any way. Indeed, they were the type of clothing that women lawyers would wear to court today. With parental consent, Harry and Angelo took the girls off alone to interrogate them regarding their grades, any illicit drug usage, or previous disciplinary difficulties at the school while I sat with the parents and listened to their dissatisfactions with Principal Shannon. In the pit of my stomach, I got an eerie feeling as to whether this Shannon was the same person as the Coach Pat Shannon, who proved to be my nemesis at Jefferson High School and made me so anxious to get out of PE and into ROTC instead. Before too long I was able to connect the dots, and indeed, it was the very same person. Small world I thought. When Harry and Angelo returned from grilling the girls, they were satisfied. These girls were all good students, who were squeaky clean and had never gotten in any trouble at school before. We promised the girls and their parents that we would look into the matter further and would do some preliminary legal research. The girls promised us that they would study hard, take their finals, and do the very best they could.

The legal research proved not to be so kind. It seemed that the Texas courts were not very sensitive toward student rights nor seemed very keen on dress code litigation. Just within the last year a student had constitutionally challenged a school dress code in the case of *Wood v. Alamo Heights Independent School District*, 308 F. Supp. 551 (WD Tex. 1970) in which Judge Adrian Spears found the student dress code there to be valid and reasonable. Moreover, his decision was affirmed by the Fifth Circuit Court of Appeals on November 6, 1970 (308 F.2d 355). So it didn't appear as if the law was exactly in our favor.

After their final exams, Harry had heard from the girls again. Apparently their fears had been realized. Some of their final grades had come back, and they were definitely sub-par. The girls swore up and down that they didn't feel that they had done that bad. But how in the world were we going to be able to prove that they had been academically discriminated against in a way that resulted in adverse repercussions regarding their grades? Then as luck would have it, Harry received a call from a courageous teacher at McCollum, who kind of acted as a whistle blower. According to her a communication had been circulated from Principal Shannon to the teachers regarding the suspended students. It pointed out how "those students" were not to be given any considerations as to special circumstances or leniency. Rather teachers were instructed to "cut them no slack" for past classroom participation and performance, but rather to grade their exams with all strictness and severity, without applying any curve factor whatsoever, even if such a grading device had been utilized with respect to the other students. Fortunately, the teacher had kept a copy of the communication, and in no time Harry dispensed our ace investigator, Joe Padilla, who with his usual competence returned with a copy of the communication and with a signed affidavit from the teacher to boot. Affidavits as to Legal Aid eligibility and affidavits as to the pantsuits actually worn, which included the pictures I had taken, were quickly put together, as well. Harry felt that we needed to act fast before the girls' grades became part of their permanent school records. He and Angelo worked on the law suit draft, which would seek both declaratory and injunctive relief. The way we saw it, this was no longer just a typical lawsuit challenging a student dress code, but now it had become an action to salvage students' grades which may have been artificially manipulated lower as a device of punishment for their having participated in the protest demonstration. Harry and Angelo crafted a class action with ostensibly two overlapping classes: the first class being the entire student body adversely affected by an arbitrary, overly rigid, and unreasonable dress code, and the more important second class, which were those students who engaged in a peaceful protest over this, and as a result "were summarily suspended from school and further subjected to penalties, punishments, and sanctions of a cruel, degrading, and malicious nature." While Harry and Angelo worked on the pleading, I developed the initial discovery to be directed against Shannon, the two vice Principals, and the Superintendent. "I want to hit them hard, right after service," said

Harry, "and make those interrogatories tough—the kind of questions they really won't want to have to answer under oath."

By February 2nd, we had completed our work, and we had scheduled a pre-filing conference with our clients. By that time we had picked up an additional individual, who wanted to join our little cadre of class representative plaintiffs. He was a male student at McCollum who supported the girls' position regarding the "pantsuit issue" from the beginning. He had participated in the protest demonstration, drew a suspension from school, and suffered many of the same aftermath consequences. Once all our clients were gathered, we re-disclosed the attributes and exigencies of class litigation. Aside from themselves, we cautioned them with respect to talking to anyone else about the lawsuit. We warned them to gird themselves and get prepared for their being belittled and berated by some of their fellow students, teachers, school officials, and possibly even the press. After all, for some this would be viewed as an attack on the citadel of the public school system, and it could get ugly. Nevertheless, everyone was committed and resolved to move ahead.

On Thursday, February 4, 1971, the case of *Hammonds v. Shannon*, SA-71-CA-50, was formerly filed with the federal district court in San Antonio. We arranged for service upon the defendants, which obviously encompassed Principal Pat Shannon, but also included the two Vice-Principals, the Superintendent, and the entire school board. It wasn't long before we got the expected response to our complaint from the defendants, which for the most part denied all of our contentions and also contained a motion to dismiss our case as legally baseless. Immediately thereafter we served Shannon, the two Vice Principals, and the Superintendent with our discovery package in order to start the time clock running as to when they would be required to respond and answer the detailed questions we asked. By the very next day, Friday, February 5th, the press had picked up the story of our having filed the lawsuit, and Harry, Angelo, and I took a deep breath to prepare for the storm to come, and come it did. Shannon was screaming to the press and to any civic or political group that would listen about how Legal Aid was being misused and how government money that was meant to help poor people was being misdirected and being utilized to aid a bunch of malcontent and rebellious youths to attack a very solid, worthy, and reputable school district. His words were being echoed by various school teachers, school administrators, and of course by certain members of the local Bar Association who had never been friends or supporters of Legal Aid in the first place. It was like we had hit a hornets nest, and the angry insects were clearly on the attack. By the second week of February, Mr. Christian had received a call from Harry J. Burns, who was the president of the San Antonio Bar Association (SABA). Burns went on a rant about how he had received numerous angry and rancorous protest calls from SABA members and that something had to be done about this. He was offering his office as a "neutral site" for Shannon's and the school district's defense lawyers to meet with "Christian's lawyers" who filed this "trouble making" case in order to explore the possibility of a resolution. Christian went along with the idea of a meeting and had his secretary, Patsy Neyland, contact us and set things up.

Harry J. Burns was a member of the law firm of Kampmann, Kampmann, Church, and Burns, which was a rather Republican law firm with deep connections to Mayor Walter W. McAllister, the Good Government League (GGL), and the local Republican Party establishment. Their office was in the Alamo National Bank Building, which wasn't far from the Bexar County Courthouse or the downtown Legal Aid office. So on the day of the scheduled meeting, I met Harry Adams and Angelo Parker at the downtown office, and we all piled into my VW and proceeded together to make the short trip over to Burns' office. When we arrived there we were immediately ushered into a rather impressive conference room where Harry J. Burns sat at the head of a large table. On one side of the table sat the defense lawyers: Richard Harris, Oscar Gonzales, and North West, and we were motioned to sit at the opposite side of the table across from them, which we did. I had the distinct impression that they had been there for a while discussing the case amongst themselves before we ever arrived. Introductions were made, and you could just sense the tenseness in the room.

Mr. Burns began by addressing our side of the table by asking: "Do you all understand what barratry is?" And before anyone could respond, he went into a lecture about how it was the illicit solicitation of clients by an attorney seeking to pursue a questionable cause, and how sometimes a young lawyer could even end up losing his law license. I was shocked and could hardly believe what I was hearing. Was this guy implicitly threatening us? Well, it sure as hell felt that way, but I bit my tongue, kept quiet, and stoically listened, while I felt my temper steadily rising inside of myself. Then on came the attacks and accusations from the other side of the table on how questionable a role this was for Legal Aid to get involved and how this could be considered a misuse of Legal Aid's funding. Although Harry Adams did his best to respond by explaining that eligibility requirements had been checked "six ways from Sunday," and there wasn't any doubt that these students and their parents were indeed eligible under the Legal Aid guidelines; nevertheless the unwarranted allegations continued. "Neutral site" my ass, I thought. This was no more than a setup, designed to intimidate us, to convince us to drop the lawsuit, or at the very least to attempt to weaken our negotiating position. So when Mr. Burns again reiterated his barratry prattle, I had finally had it. I rose up, looked Burns straight in the eye, and said: "Mr. Burns, I've heard enough of your barratry lecture. I pride myself in being an ethical and conscientious lawyer, and this case here is anything but frivolous and legitimately deals with serious matters. We haven't done a damn thing wrong here, but if you think otherwise, then go ahead and bring your charges, and I'll see you in court." I grabbed my briefcase and abruptly departed, mumbling to Harry and Angelo that I would meet them back at the car.

After a while Harry and Angelo returned to the car. I immediately apologized for my having "lost my cool." They both said they understood and that it was okay. "Did you see the surprised look on their faces?" Harry commented. "It was like someone slapped them in the face," he added. He went on to say that after I left, things kind of simmered down and got serious and that a future negotiating session was to be scheduled, but this time without Burns' involvement. On the way back to the downtown Legal Aid office, I reminded Harry about the public housing action against the San Antonio Housing Authority (SAHA) and how he stayed in the background while I took the lead. Hear I thought it might be a good time to pull a reversal. I suggested that Harry and Angelo should take the lead, while I stayed in the background. "Besides," I jokingly remarked, "with Shannon on the other side, I'm not sure how objective I could really be." By the time we got back to the office we all agreed that my suggestion would probably be best.

At that time there were three judges who sat on the federal district court bench for the Western District of Texas, San Antonio Division. They were: Adrian Spears, D.W. Suttle, and John H. Wood, Jr. President Richard Nixon had appointed Judge Wood, and he had recently been sworn in just a couple of months ago on December 1, 1970. He was a Republican, of course, but he also had a reputation of harboring a rather right-wing leaning ideology, which would show little empathy toward poor people or minorities. Judge Wood would prove to be rather dogmatic against civil rights activists and Legal Aid lawyers, who he tended to dislike. Unfortunately, of the three judges, we ended up drawing Judge Wood for the *Hammonds* case. The defense counsels were gleeful with the selection, as he was most likely to summarily grant their motion to dismiss. Nevertheless, negotiations proceeded at a rapid pace. According to Harry, although the other side felt confident that Judge Wood would grant their motion to dismiss, they realized that should that happen, we would appeal the case to the Fifth Circuit Court of Appeals. We felt that there might very well be enough factual differences here, particularly concerning the possibility of students being academically harmed, so as to potentially merit a far different response from the Fifth Circuit as to what took place in the previous *Wood v. Alamo Heights Independent School District* case. "Besides, they simply do not want to have to answer your discovery," Harry reported.

Before too long, Harry and Angelo had successfully negotiated an agreement. The concocted deal entailed our not opposing their motion to dismiss, which we all believed Judge Wood would grant; and furthermore we would refrain from appealing that decision to the Fifth Circuit. In return we would get a very air-tight and enforceable letter agreement in which Shannon made major concessions that protected those students involved in the walkout. The suspended students would be allowed to make up all daily work and exams that were missed because of the suspension. Moreover, their papers and exams were to be fairly graded, using the same standard and parameters that were applicable to the non-protesting students. In short, the "fair play" promised by Superintendent Smith was to be placed in full force and effect. All prejudicial and negative notations concerning their participation in the protest would be eliminated from the students' records. The McCollum faculty would be asked to drop discussion of the walkout and further disparaging remarks and degrading comments would be definitely discouraged. Harry and Angelo were even able to put in a provision whereby for the remainder of the school year, Legal Aid lawyers would be able to monitor the grades and school records of the seventy students who had been suspended in order to ensure full compliance.

So when our clients were called to get together for a confab, we all settled into Legal Aid's conference room as Harry went over the settlement and letter agreement point by point. In essence, the other side were getting their dismissal and a technical court victory; whereas, we were getting an assured and complete protection against any academic retribution or unfair treatment as to the protesting students. Litigation would end, and the "pantsuit issue" that started all this would simply have to wait for another day. When one of the girls asked when we thought that girls would finally be allowed to wear pants at school, Harry honestly told them he didn't know. It was hard to explain that the courts just didn't seem to be with us on that issue yet, but for right now it was more important to protect them academically. Everyone agreed. It wasn't but a few days later that the settlement was approved and signed, sealed and delivered so to speak. The court was notified that resolution had been achieved, and on February 23, 1971, Judge Wood ended up dismissing the case of *Hammonds v. Shannon, 323 F. Supp. 681 (WD Tex. 1971)*, writing a somewhat vitriolic opinion, which he really didn't have to do, but evidently relished in doing so, while all the time knowing in advance that we weren't going to appeal. Although Harry felt somewhat backstabbed, he had the all-important letter agreement. And in the ensuing weeks he and Angelo were able to make sure that the called for corrective and protective measures had been accomplished—equitable grading systems were implemented, and where appropriate, students' grades were fairly adjusted. Also students' school records were cleansed of disparaging remarks relating to the protest.

As part of the deal and in order to provide Shannon with a "face saving" device, we agreed to remain silent about our letter agreement as long as the administration and school authorities continued to be co-operative and compliant. But Shannon couldn't keep his mouth shut and went about spewing untruthful statements and misinformation about Legal Aid. One day in speaking before a San Antonio civic club, he ranted that public dollars were used to aid dissenting students at McCollum and maliciously contended that a United Fund allocation of $32,332.00 to Legal Aid helped finance student lawsuits against the district. He further falsely claimed that an employee of the Wesley Community Center, posing as a student, was instrumental in provoking the walkout. Of course, from our personal perspective, we could fathom how Shannon's lack of administrative acumen and flexibility regarding the incident could be glossed over in favor of his personal preference to rationalize and believe that the happenstance was all the result of some grand conspiratorial scheme between Legal Aid, the United Way, and the Wesley Community Center. But this time Christian had had it. His tolerance level had finally been breached by Shannon's continued fallacious and unwarranted attacks. "That's it," he stated, as he directed Harry to get him a copy of the letter agreement. "We're going to issue a press release, and now we're going to make this public," he added. The next day the newspaper column headline read: "Legal Aid Group

Blasted Shannon's Statements." The news story not only contained Legal Aid's strong reply, but also went on to cite various provisions of the letter agreement, which made many of Shannon's statements appear to be wholly incredulous. The press column also included statements by officials of the United Way and the Wesley Community Center, who outright stated that Shannon's charges were false. And that was the last time that we ever heard from Pat Shannon, and after that he remained publicly silent regarding the matter.

Within the next two years, high school student dress codes within the Bexar County area slowly but surely began to change, becoming somewhat more flexible and relaxed. By the end of 1972, virtually all of the high schools in the greater San Antonio metroplex permitted girls to wear pants while at school. Would this have happened without our lawsuit? The answer was in all probability certainly "yes." But I'd like to think that it was the courage of L. H., the other two girls who wore pantsuits, and those that supported them that just might have sped the process along.

CHAPTER 13

The Amicus Curiae

1970–1971

Richardson v. Perales, **402 U.S. 389 (1971)**

Thursday, July 16, 1970, was a typical San Antonio hot summer day. It was late in the afternoon, and I was wrapping things up at the E. Houston Street office and getting set for my drive home in the sweltering heat when the phone rang. It was Patsy Neyland, Christian's secretary, stating that Christian wanted to meet with me and Harry Adams concerning an important matter first thing in the morning. When I quizzed her as to what this was about, she was clueless. After confirming I'd be there, I was curious as to what Christian wanted, and so I gave Harry a call. He was usually in tune with all the rumors and scuttlebutt circulating around Legal Aid, and so I figured he might know something. "Hey Harry, did Patsy call you about a meeting with Christian tomorrow?" I asked. "Yeah, I just got off the phone with her and was getting set to call you," he said. "Well, what's the low down? Have you heard anything?" I inquired. "No, not a damn thing," answered Harry. So neither one of us had the vaguest idea of what it might be about. Typical Christian, I thought—keep us in suspense until the next day. Except by now I was kind of used to this, and that evening, I matter-of-factly, barely made mention of it to Marlene.

That Friday morning, July 17th, I sat in Harry's office, sipping my coffee, while we anxiously awaited our conference with Christian, when Patsy finally paged us. As we proceeded to his office, I muttered: "Great, I guess we'll find out what the big surprise is." Harry smirked, as he nodded in agreement. As we entered Christian's office, he greeted us with a congenial smile, motioned us to be seated, and then in the usual Christian-like fashion got straight to the point. "Gentlemen, we have been invited to file an *Amicus Curiae* brief with the U.S. Supreme Court, and I believe we should do this." Harry and I momentarily glanced at one another and immediately understood that Christian's "we" reference meant "us," just as he said: "…and I want the two of you to take charge of this project." He went on to explain that this was a Social Security disability case being handled by Richard Tinsman, who had won the case in the federal district court here, and how that decision had even been affirmed by the 5th Circuit, but that the government had appealed the case to the U.S. Supreme Court. I knew that the term "*amicus curiae*" literally meant "friend of the court," and in this context our Legal Aid would be filing an advisory-type brief, which would offer important information bearing on the case that could aid the court in making its decision. "Mr. Eichelbaum, you've administratively handled some Social Security disability cases before, haven't you?" asked Christian. "Yes Sir," I replied, as I shook my head in confirmation. "Good, then you already have some understanding about how that agency's administrative process works," asserted Christian. "Besides, I know you two are experienced in writing a U.S. Supreme Court brief," he added. Of course, he was acutely aware of the fact that just the previous month (June 4, 1970) Harry and I had filed our Supreme Court brief in the *Gaytan v. Cassidy* case. "Wait a minute," cautioned Harry, "not just anyone can file an *Amicus Curiae* brief with the U.S. Supreme Court. I think you have to get permission first, don't you?" "That's correct Mr. Adams, and we've got it," said Christian as he passed two letters across his desk. Harry and I quickly glanced at them, and it appeared that each side concurred in granting permission. As Harry began to pass them back, I grabbed his arm and said: "Hold up, we'll probably need to include those in the appendix to our brief." I then asked Christian when the brief was due and was informed that it had to be filed by August 4th. "Wow, that's kind of short notice," I commented, as Harry chimed in saying: "Yeah, that's not really giving us very much time." "Well, I realize you'll have to totally familiarize yourselves with the case, do the legal research, and write the brief all within a very limited time period and that you might need some help here," Christian noted. He went on to say that, within reason, we were authorized to pull together a team for assistance. He also stated that he knew this entailed extra work and that he would be able to provide a little bonus money for those involved. "Just check with Ms. Neyland as to what you'll require, and gentlemen, I have every bit of confidence in you," Christian concluded.

We trooped back to Harry's office somewhat in shock. "What is this, the Supreme Court brief of the month club?" I sarcastically asked. "Yeah," Harry chuckled as he remarked, "we're going to be on a really tight time schedule." "You're right," I sighed, "we better get started." First we carefully examined the *Amicus* permission letters Christian gave us. One was from Richard Tinsman, the attorney representing the Social Security claimant. Tinsman was a prominent local trial lawyer, who kind of specialized in personal injury and workers compensation cases. He had also served as chairman of the board of directors of the Bexar County Legal Aid Association. His letter granting permission was dated July 8, 1970. "Okay, so what's the deal here?" I asked. From the body of Tinsman's letter it was clear that Christian's letter seeking permission was dated on July 7th, the day before. "You reckon they talked about this before?" I surmised. "I'll bet you dollars to donuts they did. It's likely Tinsman asked for the *Amicus*, and Christian agreed," suggested Harry. "Then on July 7th they put their plan into action," he concluded. "And if I know Christian," Harry stated, "that bonus money he talked about—that's not coming out of any Legal Aid funds; that's coming out of his own personal pocketbook, because this is something he's got a yen to do." "You're probably right," I concurred. The second permission letter was dated July 14th and was signed by Erwin N. Griswold, Solicitor

General. It was clear from that letter that Christian had sent out his *Amicus* permission request to the U.S. government on the same date, July 7th. "Damn it, if he knew two weeks ago that this was coming down the pike, you'd think he could have given us some more notice," I complained. "You would think," remarked Harry, as we completed our gripe session.

We got started. Harry, who knew Tinsman better than I did, called him to get the background details on the case. In the meantime, I logistically sprang into action. First, I spoke with Patsy and secured a duplicate set of keys to the downtown office building, which was typically closed on weekends. We would need access to the facility for the weekend work that this project would entail. Next, I called Jimmy Allison, the executive director of the San Antonio Bar Association (SABA) and who ran the Bexar County courthouse law library, which was also closed on weekends. Usually lawyers were not allowed to check out law book volumes, as then they wouldn't be available to other lawyers who might need them. I made arrangements with him to allow us to check out law books we might need as long as we did so late Friday afternoon, kept them at the Legal Aid office, and returned them first thing Monday morning. Finally, I called Dixie Printing and notified them that we would need them to print another U.S. Supreme Court brief for us and confirmed that they were up for the task. By lunch time we had cleared the boards. Harry had spoken with Tinsman and got a short background sketch concerning the case. Tinsman's office staff was busily copying appropriate documents we'd likely need, and they would be ready for us to pick up right after lunch.

During lunch Harry summarized his conversation with Tinsman, and I was beginning to get excited about the challenge of doing an *Amicus* for the U.S. Supreme Court. We needed to begin to pull together our team. One of the law clerks that worked with me at the E. Houston Street office was Barry Snell. While working there I had trained him in representing clients in administrative hearings at the Texas Department of Public Welfare (DPW). One didn't have to be a licensed lawyer to do these, and so it was a great experience for St. Mary's students who were clerking for us part-time while going to law school. There were some similarities between administrative hearings conducted by DPW and those by the Social Security Administration, and so I felt that Barry would have a good background for this. Besides he was an excellent researcher and no slouch when it came to writing. "I want Barry Snell on our team," I said, explaining my reasons to Harry. "Who would you like?" I asked. Harry momentarily pondered my question, and then declared: "Gus Wilcox." Gus was a law clerk who Harry had worked with at the downtown office. According to Harry he was sharp as a tack and one of the best law students at St Mary's. In fact subsequently, Barry and Gus would end up scoring the highest grade on successive Texas state bar exams. It was quite a tribute to St. Mary's that twice in a row two of their students would achieve that distinction. Later on Barry would become an outstanding lawyer in the areas of business and consumer law and would become a partner in the law firm of Bayne, Snell & Krause. Gus would end up as a solo-practitioner, having an accomplished criminal law practice. "Alright, it looks like we got our team," I said. "Not quite," Harry replied. "Let's pick up one more lawyer just as a back-up." "Okay, who do you have in mind?" I asked. "What about Fred Deyeso?" Harry suggested. "He's relatively new, but congenial and co-operative and should work well together with everyone else." I agreed. Fred would subsequently marry Jane, who was also a lawyer, and the two of them would establish a successful family law practice. Later on Fred would be shot in his office by a disgruntled client who pumped three bullets into him. Although he miraculously survived, he was never the same after that. Jane would eventually divorce him, and afterwards he somehow courageously managed to continue to practice on his own.

After lunch Harry took off to Tinsman's office to pick up our document copies, while I spoke to Patsy and advised her who we wanted on our *Amicus* team. Later that afternoon, our team settled into the conference room and began to pore over the papers that Harry brought back from Tinsman's office. I knew under Social Security law a disability claimant had to prove that he was unable to engage in any substantial gainful employment by reason of any physical or mental impairment(s) which can be expected to result in death or which had lasted or could be expected to last a year. It was not such an easy burden of proof, and at that time in San Antonio, the Social Security agency had the reputation of routinely denying initial disability claims nearly all the time.

As we continued our review we learned the history of this case. The claimant, Pedro Perales, was a Hispanic male of limited education. In 1965, he was thirty-five years old, was of average size and weight, and was a healthy, hard-working truck driver, who made a decent living. On September 29, 1965, while lifting an object at work, he experienced a severe pain in his lower back. Since the injury occurred at work, Texas workers compensation law came into play, and he was referred to his employer's workers comp insurance company's designated doctor, Dr. Ralph Munslow, a neurosurgeon, who initially recommended a conservative course of treatment. When the pain continued a myelography was performed, after which surgery was advised for a possible protruded disc at the L-5 area. At first Pedro hesitated regarding the back surgery, but when the pain persisted, he reluctantly consented and surgery was performed on November 23, 1965. However no disc protrusion or definite pathology was found and the post-operative diagnosis was: nerve root compression syndrome. By January 25, 1966, he had been discharged from Dr. Munslow's care, but when Pedro continued to complain, Dr. Munslow called in Dr. Lampert, a neurologist for consultation. Neither of them could find anything wrong and advised him to return to work. But his pain was unrelenting and on the advice of a friend, in April of 1966, he went to see Dr. Max Morales, a general practitioner, who ran a clinic on the Westside of town. After a thorough examination, Dr. Morales placed him in the hospital, where he remained from April 15th through May 2nd. His discharge diagnosis was: moderately severe back sprain of the lumbo-sacral spine, with ruptured disc not ruled out.

In May, 1966, Pedro applied for Social Security disability benefits. He was sent by the agency to one of its referring physicians, Dr. John Langston, an orthopedic surgeon, who examined him. Dr. Langston found no abnormalities and surmised that the "slight tenderness" of the muscles in the dorsal spine was due to poor posture and inactivity. And so as usual, the agency denied his initial claim. Pedro then requested reconsideration, and during that phase of the administrative process, Dr. Morales, who was still conservatively treating him, submitted an additional report. He concluded that Pedro had never really completely recovered from his back surgery, that he was not malingering, that he would not recommend any further surgery, that his injury was real and permanent, and that he was indeed totally and permanently disabled. Despite this the agency denied his reconsideration, and so a hearing was requested before an agency hearing officer. Before the scheduled hearing, the agency referred Pedro back to Dr. Langston, who brought in Dr. Richard Mattson to do an electromyography study. Although Dr. Mattson noted "some chronic or past disturbance in the nerve supply," he eventually sided with Dr. Langston's conclusion that Pedro was malingering.

The hearing took place on January 12, 1967, and a supplemental hearing was held on March 31, 1967. During the hearings Tinsman had Pedro, along with a fellow employee, and Dr. Max Morales appear in person and testify under oath. The agency's hearing officer, supposedly a "neutral," introduced into evidence the unsworn medical reports of Drs. Munslow, Lampert, Langston, and Mattson, over Tinsman's objection, as he asserted it was "hearsay" and that the claimant's right to confrontation and cross-examination was being denied. In addition the hearing officer brought in a "medical advisor," Dr. Lewis Leavitt, a teaching physician from Baylor University, who was board certified in physical medicine and rehabilitation. Without having ever talked to or examined Pedro, but merely based on his review of the medical records, Dr. Leavitt concluded Pedro was not permanently and totally disabled. The hearing officer also brought in a vocational expert who again, relying solely on the records and without any personal examination or testing of Pedro, testified that he could work as a salesman, a ticket-taker, a janitor, or watchman or guard. The hearing officer ruled against Pedro; whereupon a request for review by the agency's appeal council was made to no avail, and the hearing officer's decision was sustained.

As this was the last step in the agency's administrative process, Tinsman filed a lawsuit in the federal district court in San Antonio, seeking judicial review and asserting that the agency's decision was not supported by substantial evidence. The case of *Perales v. Secretary,* 288 F. Supp. 313 (WD Tex. 1968) was heard by Judge Adrian Spears, who was troubled by the way the hearing officer seemed to act more like an adversary to the claimant as opposed to a neutral adjudicator. Judge Spears indicated it produced "nausea" in him the way the hearing officer parroted "almost word for word" the conclusions of the "medical advisor." He felt that hearsay evidence in the nature of *ex parte* statements of doctors, particularly when you pyramid the hearsay from a so called "medical advisor" was not sufficient evidence, when contradicted by live and direct, competent testimony to the contrary. And so Judge Spears ruled in favor of Pedro, stating that the agency's decision was not supported by substantial evidence.

Rather than accept Judge Spears' decision, the government chose to appeal it to the Fifth Circuit Court of Appeals in New Orleans. At the 5th Circuit hearing, *Cohen v. Perales,* 412 F. 2d 44 (1969) and at the rehearing, *Cohen v. Perales,* 416 F. 2d 1250 (1969) the appellate court affirmed Judge Spears' ruling, holding that uncorroborated hearsay could not constitute substantial evidence when the claimant had objected, and the hearsay was directly contradicted by the testimony of live medical witnesses and by the claimant in person. Again rather than relent, the government chose to appeal the case to the U.S. Supreme Court, and *Certiorari* was granted, 397 U.S. 1035 (1970) and the High court agreed to hear the matter. [Note: In 1969, the Secretary of the U.S. Department of Health, Education, and Welfare (HEW), which governed the Social Security Administration, was Wilbur Cohen. By 1970, Elliott Richardson was Secretary of HEW.]

After our review session, everyone felt fairly familiar with the case. Harry, who was an ace at legal research, along with Barry and Gus were dispatched to the courthouse law library, while Fred and I began to work on a basic skeletal outline for the brief. It was late that afternoon when Harry and the guys returned, carrying volumes of law books that we would need. Fred and I had completed a rough outline, and we all agreed to meet early Saturday morning and get started. That evening I told Marlene not to make any social plans for us for that weekend and the next, as I explained that I would be tied up doing the *Amicus*.

It was early on July 18th, when we all met at the downtown office. Harry, who needed his traditional Saturday morning Tex-Mex fix, brought breakfast tacos for everyone. I had brought a coffee percolator from home and made sure there was plenty of coffee for all. As we consumed our breakfast, we discussed the parameters of the brief. We knew that a Supreme Court *Amicus* should not exceed 30 pages. Figuring roughly 250 words per page that translated to 7500 words, and so that was our set maximum limit. Brevity was key and the shorter the better. That meant our argument would have to be comprehensive and convincing, but yet concise, where every word would count. We considered our basic outline and decided to carve our brief into four portions: First, the requisite preliminary part would cover Legal Aid's interest in filing the *Amicus*, a statement of the issues and relevancy, and an overall summary of the argument. The other three parts would contain the argument proper. Point I would deal with Social Security benefits being a valuable right, which should be protected by fundamental concepts of due process. Point II would outline the history of hearsay and explain why courts have treated it as unreliable. And finally, Point III would emphasize the 5th Circuit ruling and advance a strong argument as to why it was correct and should be affirmed.

We broke up into two groups. Harry, Barry, and Gus continued the legal research, gathering supportive case law, taking notes, and copying pertinent quotes to be utilized in argument, while Fred and I worked on drafting the preliminary portion of the brief, which we were able to complete and put in final form. Meanwhile, Harry's group discovered that not only was our position supported by the 5th Circuit, whose ruling we were arguing should be upheld, but also, it appeared that two other Circuit Courts agreed with us, as well: the 4th Circuit in the case of *Hayes v. Gardner*, 376 F 2d 517 (1967) and the 6th Circuit in the case of *Mefford v. Gardner*, 383 F 2d 748 (1967). "Well," I declared, "this is a pleasant change. It looks like this time we have the majority of the case law going with us." "Yeah," Harry responded, "usually it's the other way around." By late afternoon we called it a day, but we were all prepared to meet the following weekend for the final push. During the week, we all had our regular work to do, and so there was little chance to work on the brief. Barry and Gus did manage to find a law journal article: *The Social Security Administration Versus the Lawyers… and Poor People too*, 39 Miss. L.J. 371 (Part I) and 40 Miss. L.J. 24 (Part II), which was rather explanative of the process and from which we purloined a powerful quote to use in our brief.

The week seemed to stream by and before I knew it, the weekend of July 25th was upon us. That Saturday morning we reconvened, beginning with our taco breakfast. These were the days before computers, and writing a brief, especially for the U.S. Supreme Court was a pressurized arduous, time-consuming task. It meant hand-writing the document on legal pads, while copying and scotch-taping in quotes from cases and other legal authorities. We decided to divide and conquer. I would work solo on Point I, while Fred and Barry handled Point II, and Harry and Gus tackled Point III. That afternoon we picked up sandwiches and chips for lunch and had a refreshing break before continuing. By early evening, Point I was complete and in final form. Points II and III still needed work. A discussion ensued whether we should stop and come back Sunday morning or continue and work round the clock until we were done. We took a vote, and the latter viewpoint prevailed. We would stick it out. Fred and Harry went out to pick up dinner and dessert. They returned with several large pizzas and two baker's dozen of donuts. I suggested a change of perspective might be helpful and so we switched writing teams. I would help Fred and Gus finish up Point II, while Barry worked with Harry on Point III. Shortly before midnight, my group had put the final wraps on Point II. We had woven together a scholarly classic, tracing the history of hearsay from 1696 forward and demonstrating how the judiciary traditionally treated it and why. We took a dessert break, and with my umpteenth cup of coffee, I scarfed down at least four donuts. Talk about a sugar high, I definitely grasped my second wind and felt like the Duracel Energizer Bunny. I often mused that the onset of my diabetes, which plagued me later on in life, was likely attributable to my donut gorging episode in the wee hours of that Sunday morning. We all came together and painstakingly squeezed the draft that Harry and Barry had written, revising it to fit into the requisite number of remaining pages that were designated for that portion, as we put the finishing touches on Point III. Finally, we were done. It was early Sunday morning on July 26th, when we left the building, and the sun was just coming up as I drove home.

On Monday, July 27th, Anita Herrera was busily typing our completed hand-written draft, and by Tuesday, July 28th, Harry and I delivered the final typed product to Dixie Printing so they could commence the type-setting process. By Friday, July 31st, their printing press had spit out a proof copy of our *Amicus* brief for our review and final corrections. We had managed to hold the entire brief, including the appendix, to just shy of the 30 page limit. On Sunday, August 2nd, Harry came over to our apartment, and he and I proof read the text several times, while Marlene carefully checked the table of cases and authorities. Early Monday morning, August 3rd, Harry and I took the final corrected version back to Dixie Printing, and by late that afternoon, we picked up the final printed copies of the *Amicus Curiae* brief. We packaged up the requisite number of copies for filing and got them to the downtown post office right before closing, and off to the U.S. Supreme Court they went. We got our copy of the transmittal letter date and time stamped so as to document our timely submission. By the time we got back to the office and wrapped things up it was after 6:00 PM. As I drove home I thought: what a way to spend my 28th birthday, but at least this was finally over with. I arrived late for the special birthday dinner that Marlene had prepared. Despite my tardiness, Marlene remained in good humor, and I knew that she understood. Later that evening, I took an extra copy of the *Amicus* brief, and on the inside cover, penned a note expressing my gratitude, stating: "To Marlene, my wonderful wife,…I can truly say without her help and understanding, this, my first *Amicus Curiae* brief for the U.S. Supreme Court could have never been completed." Afterwards I presented it to her to keep as a memento keepsake. Harry felt bad that my birthday had gotten messed up, and since his 27th birthday was coming up on August 12th, we decided that on Saturday, August 8th, he and Bev and Marlene and I would go to the Grey Moss Inn for a lovely combined birthday and celebratory "finishing the *Amicus*" dinner.

Subsequently, Harry let me know that Tinsman was elated with our brief. Later on Christian called us into his office to compliment us and to present us with our small, token bonus checks, for which we were nevertheless appreciative. Harry had guessed right, and it appeared that the money came from Christian's own personal funds. "Gentlemen," he announced, "it seems we're in good company," as he related that the American Bar Association and the Appalachan Research and Defense Fund had also filed *Amicus* briefs in this case. "But gentlemen, Mr. Tinsman thought our brief was the best, and I agree. Congratulations on a job well done," Christian added.

Everyone felt fairly confident that we were going to win this one, but I had a queasy feeling about it, which I kept to myself. Even though the case law seemed predominantly in our favor, and I personally believed that our argument was stronger than the government's; nevertheless I was fearful of what I dubbed as "Supreme Court politics." I was cognizant of the fact that four Justices: Burger, Blackman, Harlan, and Stewart had voted for *Certiorari*, and I viewed them as being dead set against us. So all they needed was just one more vote in order to prevail. Tinsman argued the case on January 13, 1971, and on May 3, 1971, the U.S. Supreme Court rendered its decision in *Richardson v. Perales*, 402 U.S. 389 (1971). By a 6-3 margin they over-ruled Judge Spears and the 5th Circuit, and held in favor of the government. The majority consisted of the four justices who had voted for *Certiorari*, who were joined by Justices White and Marshall. The government had argued that to allow claimant's the right of confrontation and cross-examination would "…threaten to disrupt the administration of the entire program…." Apparently that swayed the other two. Although White was no big surprise to me, Marshall was. My only conjecture as to him was that he served as a U.S. Solicitor General before he became a U.S. Supreme Court Justice, and so perhaps he was sympathetic to the government's position. Despite the loss, I felt gratified that Justice Douglas, who was joined by Justices Black and Brennan, wrote a strong dissent, and it was obvious that they had read and agreed with the arguments advanced in our *Amicus*.

The *Perales* case illustrated the friction in administrative law between an agency's tendencies, given an ever-increasing, mounting caseload, to become stridently over-reliant on paper processing versus the task of taking extra care to insure justice in each individual proceeding. Although Perales was not my client per se, I still felt sorry for him. Perhaps had he been my client initially, I might have sought to develop the case somewhat differently before the appellate process ever arose. I had learned a powerful lesson in 1969, while representing a client in a Social Security disability case that was similar to the facts in the *Perales* case. He too was a middle-aged man of limited education, whose work entailed hard, physical labor. He also sustained a back injury that never got better, and eventually he applied for Social Security disability benefits. His initial application and reconsideration were denied, and he came to Legal Aid for representation just days before his hearing. Prior to the hearing, the agency by utilizing their consulting doctors had developed ample "negative medical reports" regarding his condition. And of course, at the hearing all of that hearsay medical was admitted into evidence, over my objection. In addition and despite my constant objection, Mr. Buldain, the hearing officer, mercilessly bombarded my client with a barrage of questions concerning his sexual conduct with his wife. He wanted to know when, where, and how often they had sexual relations, and he insisted that those be described in rather explicit detail, including what sexual positions were being utilized. His excuse with respect to relevancy was that it bore on the client's flexibility and mobility. Naturally, Mr. Buldain denied his claim, and my client did not want to pursue the matter any further.

That case haunted me, and I complained to Marlene that the agency behaved more like an adversarial attorney rather than a neutral judge. "What's a man like that supposed to do?" I asked. The typical scenario seemed to be a man of limited education, who was a physical laborer, sustaining a persistent back injury. In all practicality, he finds himself unable to work, although from a strictly technical standpoint the physical injury itself is not considered severe enough to meet Social Security's rigid disability standards relating to that type of injury. So now he sees his wife going to work and becoming the sole breadwinner; while he hopelessly sits at home in pain and feeling utterly useless. My God, I thought, that's got to be depressing and emasculating. Add to that the stress of having to deal with the Social Security agency, and I felt that could very well be enough to send a person over the edge. Subsequently, I contacted Tommy Carr, who was an old Jefferson High School classmate of mine and who happened to work for Social Security at that time. He was able to get me a copy of the agency's handbook disability guidelines, particularly those dealing with psychiatric, psychological, and combinative mental impairments. Upon reviewing that information and further discussing it with Dr. Allen Chittendon, a psychiatrist, and Dr. Betty Lou Schroeder, a psychologist, I learned that my theory in such cases often rang true. And that the adverse effect on such individuals' psyches could result in psychiatric and/or psychological impairments that would be far more debilitating than the physical injury itself. So in appropriate cases from then on, I vowed never to let the Social Security agency develop that aspect of the case itself, but rather to do that on my own instead.

Richard (Dick) Haase was a young lawyer, who started working at Legal Aid in the early part of 1971. While there he developed an interest in handling Social Security disability cases, and he began shadowing me in several of my cases. In one instance I was representing a client with "tunnel vision" whose site had become severely impaired, and who had applied for Social Security disability benefits. Of course the agency had denied his initial application and reconsideration. Pre-hearing the agency sent him to one of their consulting doctors who "examined" him and administered a "pinhole" test and then issued an adverse medical report stating his site ability was okay. When the client came in for assistance there was ample time before the hearing, and I told Dick the key would be in developing the medical evidence. I sent the client to a reputable ophthalmologist who conducted a comprehensive eye exam, and who issued a report stating the client was all but "legally blind." I didn't stop there, and I had him tested and examined by a psychologist, who concluded he showed signs of severe depression. No wonder I thought. When Dick asked me if I was going to send the newly developed medical evidence to Social Security before the hearing, I answered: "Hell no, if they get it in advance, it will just give them a chance to attempt to counter it with their consulting doctors." I had drawn Mr. Buldain as the hearing officer again, but this time I was ready for him. He, of course, was ready to deny the claim based on his "pinhole" testing doctor's report. That is when we surprised him with our overwhelming contradictory and obviously more credible evidence. I forcefully argued that people don't go around living their lives and working while constantly looking through a pinhole, as I almost dared him to deny this claim. In the end we won, and the agency finally granted the client disability benefits. By the end of 1973, Dick Haase had left Legal Aid and set up his own private practice, specializing in handling Social Security disability cases. He was one of the first of a number of private practitioners in San Antonio who carved out that niche and successfully developed his practice accordingly.

In the 1960s and early 1970s, with economically eligible clients, Legal Aid lawyers took on Social Security disability cases and, in some respects, were responsible for developing the strategies and techniques for handling such cases. In those days, for the most part, private practitioners within the local bar association were unwilling to accept such cases on a contingent fee basis. And of course, that was the only way a poor client could have secured a non-Legal Aid private attorney. But by the mid-1970s that had all changed. There were plenty of private practitioners, like Dick Haase, who were willing to take on such cases on a contingent fee basis, and so Legal Aid lawyers quit handling such cases altogether, but rather referred them out to private attorneys through the San Antonio Bar Association (SABA) attorney referral program.

CHAPTER 14

A Grandparent's Dilemma

1971

Galindo v. Vowell (WD Tex. SA Div. 1971)

In 1969, Texas fully recognized the concept of a common law marriage. The requirements for legally establishing one were: First, the parties had to make a present agreement to be married. This could be a mere oral compact, and it was not necessary that it become a written memorandum, which had to be recorded at the county courthouse or anywhere else, for that matter. Second, the parties had to cohabitate and that meant living together and having had sexual intercourse with one another. And finally third, the parties had to hold themselves out to the public that they were husband and wife. But once these requirements had been satisfied and met, then in the words of my friend and colleague, Harry Adams: "The marriage was just as valid as if a wedding had been performed by twenty bishops."

Sometime in 1969, a poor, elderly couple, who were clearly eligible for Legal Aid, came to see me at my office at E. Houston Street. They were grandparents who had a twelve year old granddaughter, who they had raised practically from birth. Their daughter, who was the child's mother, lived with them before becoming pregnant and giving birth to the child. They had no idea who the child's father was. When the child was around two years of age, their daughter suddenly left home and never returned.

All attempts of filing missing person reports and trying to trace her whereabouts were to no avail. They never heard from their daughter again and had no idea as to her location or whether she was dead or alive. Now that over ten years had passed, they thought it might be a good idea to stabilize their family and to legally adopt their granddaughter, who was all in favor of the idea. Further inquiry revealed that there was no history of illicit drug use or criminality of any kind. They had an upstanding reputation within their community and attended church regularly. The idea of adoption had been recommended by their social welfare caseworker and was also supported by their parish priest. Their only concern was that they had never been "formally married" but considered themselves married under common law, and they were troubled as to how that might affect the adoption. Upon additional questioning, I was able to determine that all the integral components of a common law marriage had been adequately met some forty years ago when they first started living together, and they had continued to steadily remain with one another ever since. Using Harry's "twenty bishops" line, they were relieved to hear when I explained that their marriage was, indeed legal, under Texas law and was every bit as valid as mine was. I told them that their marital status should have no negative impact regarding the prospective adoption.

In the following weeks I prepared and filed the pleadings seeking the adoption of the child by the petitioning grandparents and the termination of parental rights of the defendants, i.e. the child's mother, who had disappeared and the unknown father. Service upon the defendants was accomplished by publication notice, and to insure due process, I arranged for two attorneys ad litem, one to represent each of the absent defendants. Finally, the case was ripe for hearing.

On the designated morning set for trial, I met the young girl, her grandparents, the social welfare caseworker, and the two attorneys ad litem at the Bexar County Courthouse, and we all piled into the Presiding District Judge's courtroom for the docket call. When the case was called, I announced "ready," and the Presiding Judge instructed me to get the court's file on the case and take it to the 150th, where Judge McKay would hear the matter. I secured the court's file from the clerk, and our entire cadre trooped over to the 150th.

James A. McKay had been elected as judge of the 150th district court in 1963. As of yet, I hadn't appeared before him, but I had been previously warned by both Harry Adams and John Sanders that he tended to be rather dogmatically rigid and that he wasn't exactly fond of Legal Aid lawyers, toward whom he seemed to have a somewhat crispy disposition.

As we entered the 150th district courtroom, I noticed the judge was not on the bench. I handed the court's file to the clerk who said: "Judge McKay is still in chambers, and I'll take this to him. He likes to review these in advance before coming out onto the bench. You all just have a seat." I directed the young girl, her grandparents, and the social welfare caseworker to be seated in the audience section, while the two attorneys ad litem and I took seats at the counsel table. We were there for a while, when I noticed the court clerk answer her pager and appeared to be listening attentively. When finished she motioned me forward, and I got up from the counsel table and went up to her desk. "Judge McKay would like to see you in his chambers," she announced. As I was about to get the two attorneys ad litem to join me, she indicated: "No, not them—just you for right now." I thought that was rather strange, and I shrugged at the other two lawyers, indicating I had no idea what was going on. Nevertheless, I grabbed my case file and a legal pad and proceeded into the inner sanctum of Judge McKay's chambers.

Judge McKay sat behind a large, wooden desk, the top of which was strewn with several case files and some law books. He was a somewhat short man, in his mid-fifty's, with thinning brownish hair. "Be seated," he sternly directed, as his head was buried in the court's file, while peering over the papers on our adoption case. "It's my understanding that this is an uncontested matter and that all of the service prerequisites have been met," he remarked. "That's correct, your Honor," I replied. Then looking up at me and with a scantly expressed grimace, he said: "Well Sir, I need to tell you that I have some real misgivings about this case." He continued stating that he considered the family's status to be potentially unstable because my clients weren't "really married." "Excuse me, your Honor, but they are married under common law," I asserted. With a slight nod in negativity, he went on to explain that their situation seemed to be too much of a manner of convenience and was just too transient for the fostering of a stable family relationship. And so under such circumstances, he would be very reluctant to grant the adoption. His suggestion instead was that I should seek a continuance, advise my clients to formally get married in church, and afterwards, for me to amend my pleadings reflecting that and come back to see him. Then, he would have no qualms about granting the adoption at that time.

I was in absolute shock and could hardly believe what I was hearing. What the hell was he talking about? I thought. The concept of "too transient" simply didn't compute. Although Texas legally recognized a common law marriage, there was no such thing as a common law divorce. And "unstable," good grief—give me a break, these folks had stuck out their marriage for forty years and had pretty much raised this kid from the beginning. In my opinion, not only was this judge misinterpreting the law, but he was also telling me how to represent my clients. With every ounce of control I could muster and carefully choosing my words, I responded: "With all due respect your Honor, it seems like we just disagree. I am not going to tell my clients they have to get married in church. As far as I'm concerned, they're already married. We are ready to proceed with trial today, and I'm hereby respectfully requesting a record. We need to have the clerk call and get a court reporter up here so we can make a complete record of this entire proceeding. After we present our case, of course as judge, you have every prerogative to rule however you want, and then we'll just have to take it from there." Judge McKay turned red in the face and reacted kind of angrily. "A record, a record—you legal aid guys are always wanting a record. I don't know what Frank Christian is doing with you all over there, but there seems to be a frequent propensity to cause trouble," he grumbled.

I was excused and went back to the counsel table in the courtroom. My heart was pounding. I'm sure the judge took my remarks as kind of a veiled threat that if he ruled against us we were going to appeal. Actually, in my mind it was more of a promise than a threat. But seriously, I was concerned about just getting through the trial without being held in contempt of court. When the two attorneys ad litem asked me what happened, I just shook it off and downplayed it, saying the judge merely had some minor questions concerning timing. Finally, the court reporter arrived and set up next to the clerk. Shortly after that the bailiff called out: "All rise," as Judge McKay entered the court, took his seat at the bench, and gaveled the courtroom to order. "May it please the court," and I began my presentation of our case. With each witness I painstakingly covered every aspect that indicated granting this adoption would clearly be in the child's best interest. When it came to proving up the common law marriage, I meticulously covered all of the component elements and made sure that the testimony reflected there could be no reasonable doubt that my clients were indeed married. When I was through I rested, and now it was up to the judge. I had no idea how he was going to rule, but I was satisfied that if he decided against us, we now had a record where we would obliterate him on appeal. Judge McKay announced that he would grant the adoption and curtly asked if I had an order. I presented him with the order that terminated the parental rights and granted the adoption by the grandparents, which I had previously prepared, dated, signed, and had gotten the two attorneys ad litem to sign, as well, signifying our approval of it. Judge McKay briefly scanned the document and signed it, making it official, and then promptly exited the courtroom. I secured permission from the clerk to take the court's file to the District Clerk's central office so I could get some certified copies of the order for adoption that the judge had just signed. I thanked the social welfare caseworker and the two attorneys ad litem, and my clients and the young girl trailed me to the District Clerk's office. There I got three certified copies. I retained one copy for our file, and gave the other two to my clients, advising them to keep one in a safe place, while they could carry the other one to show school officials, etc. "That does it," I said, and the grandparents thanked me. When the young girl asked me if this meant that "Mama" and "Papa" were now officially her parents, I said: "Yes, indeed," and I spotted a tear of joy roll down her cheek, as she gave me a hug. I watched, shaking my head in satisfaction, as the three of them walked out of the courthouse hand in hand.

It was July 1, 1971, and the old curmudgeon, Burton G. Hackney, had retired as the head of the Texas Department of Public Welfare (DPW). A younger and supposedly more dynamic individual had been chosen as the new top gun of DPW, and his name was Raymond W. Vowell. I had heard rumors coming down the pike about how there were going to be some changes made. There was nasty political talk about how the old administration had become too lax and soft, and how there needed to be a crackdown on "frivolous claims" and "undeserved benefits." The scuttlebutt was that there were going to be amendments to the DPW Financial Services Handbook, which I was not really looking forward to. The last thing we needed was a return to a "police state" type of situation at the welfare department. It had taken years and multiple lawsuits to finally mellow out Hackney and the DPW administration, and I was hoping that I wouldn't have to start all over again and see a return of the "Texas Welfare Wars," phase two.

In August, 1971, we had one of our periodic staff meetings. Not only was it an opportunity for Christian to talk to all of his troops, but also it was a chance for the lawyers of the various neighborhood offices to meet with one another, as well as with the downtown office lawyers in order to share experiences and exchange ideas. These meetings were usually held right before lunchtime so that afterwards groups of us could go out to lunch together. It was a great way to promote comradery and foster fellowship among all of us Legal Aid lawyers, and it was something I always looked forward to. On this occasion a large group of us ended up at Mi

Tiera, another one of Harry's favorite Mexican restaurants. Harry and I were seated across the table from Don McManus. Don had short crew-cut, sandy blond hair, and was a tall statuesque figure with a "Marlboro Man" type appearance. Once he began working for Legal Aid and having completed his initial training downtown, he was shipped out to run the Gen. McMullen Street office, which was situated on the Southside of town. Later on he would become a district judge. In fact he was one of about a dozen lawyers and law clerks who worked at Bexar County Legal Aid (BCLA) during the late 1960's and early 1970's, who would eventually take some judicial position within Bexar County.

During our lunch, while enjoying my enchiladas and casually talking with Fred Deyeso, my ears perked up when I heard Don tell Harry about a curious incident that had occurred at the Gen. McMullen Street office. Recently, an elderly woman had come in to inquire about the legality of her minor granddaughter's AFDC welfare benefits being terminated because she, as the grandparent, had failed to file criminal charges against her own son and daughter-in-law. I turned toward Don just as Harry said: "Hey, you ought to talk to Mel about that. Welfare cases are really his Bailiwick." "What's going on Don?" I asked, and he repeated the story. We agreed he would re-contact the woman and further verify the facts, while I would look into the legal aspect. We would then touch base with one another in the next few days.

Once back at my office on E. Houston Street, I pulled out my old seminar notebook that I received while attending a Legal Aid lawyer conference in New Orleans in the early part of 1969. Al Alonzo, Harry Adams, John Sanders, Lonnie Duke, and I all went. Christian in particular and Legal Aid organizations in general were big believers in the concept of Continuing Legal Education (CLE) way before the Texas State Bar Association ever became involved with the idea. The New Orleans conference was a major CLE seminar for Legal Aid attorneys throughout the South. While John and Al attended courses on juvenile justice and Harry on consumer law, Lonnie and I concentrated on programs dealing with welfare rights. During one of those presentations, I vaguely recalled the lecturer describing a situation that sounded familiar to what Don was talking about. As I thumbed through my notebook, there it was: a commentary and dissertation referencing the topic of "Notification of Law Enforcement Officials," a subject known in the welfare world as "NOLEO" requirements.

Over the next few days it was time to do some investigative research. First, I called one of my friendly contacts at DPW. My spy not only informed me that the NOLEO provisions were part of some relatively recent revisions of the DPW Financial Services Handbook, but also sent me a copy of section 2231, sub-sections 1, 2, and 3, which were the culprits that formulated the genesis of the onerous NOLEO requirements. Second, I contacted Henry Freedman with the national back-up Center on Social Welfare Policy and Law. He thanked me for calling, and said he would add Texas to the pervasive list of states that had instituted such a ploy. The idea of course was to force poor grandparent caretakers of children who would otherwise be entitled to receive AFDC welfare benefits to make a cruel choice. If they wanted their grandchild to receive the AFDC assistance grant, they would have to file criminal charges against their own son or daughter under the state's child abandonment statutes, or they could just forego the benefits and not receive them. Indeed, it was a grandparent's dilemma. Henry went on to explain that in the vast majority of these cases, state welfare officials knew that the law enforcement authorities wouldn't really do anything with respect to such charges, but they also knew that by automatically forcing such a choice, many potential recipients out of sense of fear, dignity, or loyalty simply would opt out and adopt a "forget about it" attitude. For state welfare departments looking to save money this made a lot of sense, and who cared if thousands of children who really deserved such benefits didn't receive them. He advised me that these rules, in his opinion, were clearly unconstitutional and violated the Social Security Act, and informed me that they had been aiding legal services organizations throughout the country in challenging these regulations. And according to Henry, they were having great success in winning in one state after another." I could send you some sample pleadings if you like," he said. I took him up on his offer and in a couple of days the sample pleadings arrived. Finally, I contacted Marvin Zimmerman, an attorney friend of mine, who at that time worked for the Bexar County District Attorney's office. Later on he and his wife, Gail, who was also an attorney, would venture into private practice, forming a husband and wife law firm. During a coffee date, I related the NOLEO situation to Marvin, and I wanted to know what the DA's office would really do with such cases. My suspicions were confirmed when he told me that they were far too busy handling the more critical cases of murder, rape, robbery, burglary, and grand theft than to mess around with that. They neither had the time nor manpower to waste on such nonsense.

Having completed my investigation on the NOLEO issue, I called Harry and let him know what I had found out. "It's time to contact Don and meet his client," I suggested. "Right, I'll set it up," he replied, and on the appointed day Harry and I drove to the Gen. McMullen Street location. Don McManus invited us into his office and that's where we met Petra Galindo. She was an elderly woman who was poor but proud. As the paternal grandparent she had raised her minor granddaughter, Patsy Galindo, almost from birth. The facts vis a vis grandparent to grandchild were strangely familiar and similarly akin to those in the adoption case that I had in Judge McKay's court back in 1969. Ms. Galindo verified her situation about how DPW had advised her that the small AFDC grant for Patsy would be terminated unless she filed criminal charges for child abandonment against her son and daughter-in-law. I explained to her that this was part and parcel of DPW's NOLEO rules and how I believed them to be illegal. Harry went on and advised her that we could file a federal class action lawsuit against DPW challenging their NOLEO regulations, if she would agree to be a named plaintiff in such a case. You could begin to see her mood change from a sense of despondency to one of hope. "Okay, Ms. Galindo, I need to tell you that I've actually spoken with a lawyer in the DA's office, and he told me that even if you were to file criminal charges with them against your son, odds are in all likelihood nothing would ever come of it. I thought you should know this before you decide," I disclosed. Ms. Galindo nodded her head indicating she understood. Then she raised her head, took a deep breath, and stared straight at us, and with a look of absolute resolution, adamantly proclaimed: "I am not filing any charges against my son, entiendes?" "Yes Mam, we understand. So I take it you are all in," I said. "Yes Sir, I'm definitely in," she asserted, "It's high time that we fight for our rights," she declared.

After she left, I commented to Harry: "Well, it looks like you and I will be gearing up to do another Law Reform case." At that time Don spoke up saying that he really would like to stay involved on this case. Harry and I had no objections, and so the three of us formed a triumvirate and agreed to work together on the case. I gave the sample pleadings that I had obtained from Henry Freedman's office to Harry, and in the following weeks he and Don re-crafted the papers to fit the Texas NOLEO scenario and Petra Galindo's particular factual situation. Meanwhile, I began working on our discovery package. These were the days of unlimited interrogatories, where a lawyer was allowed to propound as many questions as he wanted, as long as they were relevant, and not duplicitous or over burdensome. It was like peeling an onion, and by the time I was done, I had formulated over a hundred questions, which would have to be answered under oath, and were designed to bring out exactly what the NOLEO provisions were, the supposed policy consideration and reasoning behind them, that they would be wholly ineffective from an actual law enforcement standpoint, and what the real monetary motivation was behind their promulgation.

Shortly after Labor Day, Christian called me into his office. He questioned me how we were coming along on the NOLEO case matter. I reported that we were almost there and would probably be ready to file next week. He then asked me if I would feel comfortable letting Harry and Don take the lead on the NOLEO case. He had just been contacted by Bexar County Judge Blair Reeves concerning a problem with mandatory welfare guardianships that he wanted me to concentrate on looking into. I assured him that Harry and Don were more than adequate to finish up on the NOLEO case and that I could stay in the background providing direction there, while at the same time pushing into the new area of mandatory welfare guardianships of which he was speaking and that there would be no problem in doing so. Christian was satisfied, and so I obtained his blessing in moving forward in both areas.

By Monday, September 13, 1971, all was ready on the NOLEO matter and the case of *Galindo v. Vowell* was filed with the federal district court in San Antonio. The very next day the press picked up the story, and the newspaper column headline read: "Suit questions law on abandoned children," and stated that we had requested a three judge court to resolve the constitutional and statutory issues we raised. Later on I got a call from Harry. "Guess who we drew as judge on the *Galindo* case?" he teasingly asked. "Hm, let's see, it wouldn't be the infamous Judge Wood, would it?" I retorted. "Yep, you got it," said Harry. Just great, I thought—appeal here we come. Although I thought Harry would feel dejected because of our past experience with Judge Wood in the *Hammonds v. Shannon* case; instead, he was positively gleeful. According to Harry, if Judge Wood had the audacity to outright dismiss our case or deny us a three judge court, then we would wipe him out on procedural grounds in a 5th Circuit appeal. On the other hand, if he granted us the three judge court, then his anti-Legal Aid predisposition could be blunted by the other two judges, depending on who we drew. Worst case scenario was we could lose here at the district court level, but if we made a good record, he couldn't think of a stronger case to take up the appellate ladder. I knew he was right and agreed.

After our discovery had gone out and the week before Thanksgiving, we received a call from Pat Bailey, the Texas Assistant Attorney General assigned to our *Galindo* case. He had made major Thanksgiving holiday plans for him and his family, and the discovery responses to the *Galindo*, as well as on another major welfare case we were doing, were due on the Monday right after the Thanksgiving holiday weekend. He pleadingly asked if we would be willing to give him a one week extension, otherwise it was going to bust his Thanksgiving plans. Just because we were legally opposed to one another, there was no reason to be obstinate. Harry and I decided to be civil and comport ourselves as gentlemen. We readily agreed to Pat's request for an extension and wished him and his family a delightful Thanksgiving. He was most grateful, thanked us, and wished us enjoyable holidays as well.

After the Thanksgiving weekend, we received another call from Pat Bailey. After exchanging pleasantries, he completely surprised us by announcing that Raymond Vowell preferred not to have to answer our discovery questions but rather wanted to explore settlement instead, and Pat asked us if we could send him a proposal. We continued our conversation, covering the main points of contention, until Harry and I were thoroughly convinced that this wasn't just a stall, but they were really serious about settling this case. Harry and I immediately drafted a proposed agreed judgment that declared the offending NOLEO requirements as being illegal and in violation of the Social Security Act. We incorporated a permanent injunction whereby DPW would be completely prohibited from denying or terminating AFDC welfare benefits to any dependent child, who was living with a family relative, such as a grandparent, who refused to file criminal charges against the child's parents. To boot, we even put language in perpetually enjoining DPW officials from enforcing any unwritten policies which would require grandparents to legally adopt a grandchild as a prerequisite to AFDC eligibility. Finally, we provided for full retroactive benefits for Petra Galindo and her granddaughter, Patsy, as well as for the entire class. When we finished we shipped it off to Pat Bailey, while Don contacted Ms. Galindo to keep her aware as to what was happening.

A few days later, we heard from Pat, and they agreed to everything, except for only one hitch. Although they would agree to grant Ms. Galindo full retro-active benefits, they only wanted to do prospective relief for the class, as a whole. However, they did vow to widely publicize the rules change, to notify the class, and to expedite all applications from class members. I was torn. I wanted full retro-active relief for the entire class. But as Harry pointed out, if we canned the deal, the state could tie this case up on appeal and that could easily take two years. And these folks needed help now, not two years from now. The deal would even have broader implication than just affecting recipients in the jurisdictional limits of the Western District of Texas, but in essence our agreed judgment would be applicable to the entire state. Harry's points were too compelling. "Right," I said, "Let's take the deal." We called Pat back and notified him we had an agreement. We modified our proposed judgment in just that one respect and notified the court that we had achieved a complete settlement. Don informed Ms. Galindo of the good news.

On December 8, 1971, our agreed judgment in the *Galindo v. Vowell* case was approved by Judge Wood and formally entered by the court. The deplorable NOLEO provisions were gone for good. The very next day the story hit the press, and the newspaper column headlines read: "Welfare Judgment Entered" and "Court bans welfare's aid rules." That day I called Henry Freedman to let him know that he could check off Texas as another state where the NOLEO provisions had bitten the dust.

CHAPTER 15

Who Will Speak for the Disabled

1971

***Gomez v. Vowell*, SA-71-CA-280 (WD of Tex. SA Div. 1971)**

Strangely, in Texas things are not always what they appear to be. Indeed, an example of this phenomenon would be the state's system of county government. For instance at the county level, the legislative policy making branch of government is referred to as the "County Commissioners Court," which is not really a court at all, but is more like the county's version of a city council. Constitutionally, this legislative body is presided over by the county's chief executive officer, who is known as the "County Judge." Although bearing the title of judge, as being the head of the county's executive branch of government, his main duties are much more akin to that of a city's mayor. Now just to complicate the matter even further, despite the fact that the constitutional "County Judge" is not really considered as a member of the county's regular judiciary per se; nevertheless, he does possess some judicial functioning authority in the area of probate matters, such as cases dealing with decedents' estates and guardianships.

In 1971, the position of Bexar County Judge was held by Blair (Bruzzie) Reeves. He was a congenial, mild-mannered man in his mid-forty's, with a friendly smile, and who occupied a wheelchair, which he had learned to expertly maneuver. Coincidentally, he also had attended Thomas Jefferson High School, from where he graduated in 1942, the very year that I was born. At that time, World War II was raging, and so Bruzzie joined the U.S. Marine Corps. He served in the Pacific Theater and was involved in the U.S. Island-Hopping campaign against the Japanese Empire, where he personally participated in some of the nastiest jungle fighting of the war. During the battle of Okinawa, he was severely wounded, having been shot in the spine and receiving an injury that would have killed most men. Bruzzie, known as "the man with a will of iron," luckily managed to survive, although it meant two years in a naval hospital enduring an arduous routine of rehabilitation and recovery. He would never walk again and in his words: "He had to learn to live in a wheelchair." But Bruzzie never let that stop him, and under the GI Bill, he went to San Antonio College (SAC) where he picked up his first two years of college credit. It was there that he met and married his wife, Betty. After completing his undergraduate studies, he attended law school at St. Mary's, from where he graduated, receiving his law degree and becoming a lawyer. In 1966, with significant backing from the San Antonio Good Government League (GGL), he ran for the position of Bexar County Judge, and that November, he succeeded and was elected. Bruzzie served in that position for three consecutive terms, retiring from that post in 1979.

In the north side corner of the second floor of the old Bexar County Courthouse, sits an older and larger courtroom, which later would be utilized as the presiding civil district courtroom. But in 1971, it served as the probate courtroom for Bexar County. As you entered the courtroom, on the far left side, there was an alcove that led to the judge's chamber on the right and the clerk's office on the left. Inside the clerk's area was a hole-in-the-wall office, overlooking a small window balcony on the north side of the courthouse building. In that confined and cramped office space, behind his desk, sat David J. Garcia.

David also went to Thomas Jefferson High School, from where he graduated in 1957. While there he actually enlisted in the U.S. Army National Guard. Although not actually a member of Jefferson's ROTC, on occasion he worked with that program as a volunteer assistant. Indeed, during his senior year, he was the very one who had made the suggestion to me that I could select ROTC as an alternative to my hated PE gym class that I had been enduring under the dreaded coach, Pat Shannon—advice for which I was eternally grateful. After graduation, David enlisted full-time as a member of the U.S. Air Force. Upon completing his military service, at the end of 1961, he went to work as a temp clerk at the Bexar County Courthouse. His performance was beyond satisfactory, and by early 1962, he had earned a permanent position. While working there, he met his wife, Lucille (Bolie), and they were married in San Antonio in June of 1963. In 1966, shortly after he was elected Bexar County Judge, Blair Reeves designated David to be his administrative assistant, and in which capacity he also served as the county probate consultant, as well. In 1982, David ran for and was elected to the position of District Clerk for Bexar County. He continued to serve in that office and was re-elected for three consecutive times. Eventually, he retired from that post in 1997, after having served there a little more than fourteen years.

In the summer of 1971, pursuant to the Social Security Act, Texas still operated the four basic types of welfare programs aimed at providing public assistance to the poor. Aside from the often denigrated and politically demonized program of Aid to Families with Dependent Children (AFDC), the other programs to aid the aged (AA), the blind (AB), and the disabled (APTD), seemed more acceptable to a significant part of the Texas public. But even with these programs, the Texas Department of Public Welfare (DPW) wasn't above placing barriers in the way, which in effect, would deter or prevent people from receiving needed benefits. An example of this was with the APTD program where there were a number of persons, who were eighteen years of age or older and who had been deemed to be permanently and totally disabled by reason of having suffered a serious mental impairment. These poor individuals usually lived with a family member, such as a parent, grandparent, or sibling, who provided a caretaking function for the disabled person, who could not totally care for himself. In such cases, DPW automatically required a full-fledged legal guardianship be established and maintained as a prerequisite condition to receiving APTD assistance benefits. But this was a time consuming and costly undertaking, which discouraged many from attempting to initiate it in the first place, and for those who did decide to undergo the rigors of a formal guardianship, many of them found that they simply couldn't economically afford to maintain it. No one was more acutely aware of this conundrum than David J. Garcia. Although not a lawyer, when it came to the practical workings of the probate system he was rather well informed, and his knowledge in the area of probate law exceeded that of many attorneys in the San Antonio area, various numbers of whom would frequently seek out his advice.

It was Thursday, August 26, 1971, and the sky was an overcast, dreary grey. It had been misting all morning, and in the distance, the low rumbling of thunder could be heard as the storm front approached. His gloomy mood matched the weather outside, as David J. Garcia sat in his office, contemplating the pile of about twenty-five papers stacked on his desk. They were the probate court's warning letters, which were to be sent to guardians who had not yet filed their mandated annual accounting nor had renewed their required probate surety bond. The letters warned the guardians that if they failed to file their accountings and renew their bonds, their guardianships would be terminated. In ordinary guardianship cases, the guardian was required to file with the probate court a detailed annual accounting, which would be reviewed to insure that the ward's funds and property were appropriately being utilized for the ward's benefit, and not for the guardian's own selfish pleasures. In the law there is scarcely a higher sense of fiduciary responsibility that exists than that of a guardian's duties toward his ward. Likewise, it was required for the guardian to obtain from a licensed and reputable insurance company a surety bond, in a sufficient amount set by the court, which would afford the ward's protection against the malfeasance or misfeasance on the part of the guardian. Whereas David fully appreciated the valid need for such safeguards in normal guardianship proceedings, where there existed a large or even modest size estate, he began to wonder whether such extensive protective devices were all that necessary in what he termed as "welfare guardianships." Under the Texas APTD program, the typical adult mentally disabled recipient was cared for by a close family member, usually a parent or grandparent. The meager welfare grant of maybe about $85.00 per month likely wouldn't even cover the ward's most basic monthly needs, such as food, clothes, and toiletries. Realistically, there wouldn't be any money left over. Instead in most cases, the caretaker would usually have to dip into his own pocket book each month just to cover the deficiencies in order to meet the ward's actual basic needs. Obviously, these caretakers were acting out of a sense of love and duty and not out of some grand scheme to make a profit from the poultry $85.00 or so monthly APTD grant.

David continued to glare at the pile of warning letters. He knew most of them involved "welfare guardianships." He also realized that in many of these cases, often due to economic reasons, there would be a lack of compliance, and so those guardianships would be terminated. Once that happened the welfare grant would cease. And this was the same scenario, month after month, with about twenty "welfare guardianship" cases going through the same repetitive routine. To David this made no sense, and the more he thought about it, the more agitated he became. It just was flat unfair that poor mentally disabled adults, in order to receive their welfare assistance, were being forced into this guardianship fiasco. Moreover, this perpetual problem was unduly clogging up the probate court with far too many unnecessary and unmanageable guardianships, most of which were doomed to fail. There had to be another solution. As David pondered the matter further, he made up his mind that he had to do something about this welfare dilemma. After having discussed the matter with County Judge Blair Reeves, who was also most dissatisfied with the "welfare guardianship" situation, David obtained the go ahead to contact me in order to explore what possibly could be done to resolve the problem. And so that afternoon David called and spoke with Josie Reyna, who was then working as my secretary at the E. Houston Street office and scheduled an appointment to see me for the very next day.

That Friday, August 25, 1971, when I arrived at my office, Josie informed me that David J. Garcia, Judge Reeves' administrative assistant, had called and made an appointment to see me that morning. As I didn't have any cases pending before the probate court at that time, I was naturally curious as to why he wanted to see me. When David arrived I greeted him and after some reminiscent small talk about our days at Jefferson, he described the problem that the probate court was experiencing with "welfare guardianships," detailing some of the economic aspects involved. Clearly these folks wouldn't have to worry about paying attorney's fees, as they would be eligible to secure the services of a Legal Aid lawyer. However, they would have to come up with the court costs, which typically Legal Aid was prohibited from paying on their behalf. At that time the initial court cost for filing a guardianship case was $43.50. By the time one added service fees, the cost of guardianship letters, and the insurance premium for even the most minimum probate surety bond, that easily put the total price tag over $100.00. The entire monthly APTD grant was just maybe around only $85.00. So with people who were living on a day to day dollar survival existence, asking a poor family member, who was caring for a mentally disabled adult, to layout over $100.00 up front, which wouldn't even be returned by way of payment of a public assistance grant until a month or two later after the guardianship had been granted was a very big ask, indeed. And then in a year's period of time, when the annual accounting was due and had to be filed, more court costs would be involved. Also the probate surety bond would have to be renewed, and it was almost a certainty that the price for that would have increased. Was it any wonder why some poor families in that situation might choose to avoid the whole matter as being simply not worth it? And of course then those mentally disabled individuals wouldn't receive any welfare benefits whatsoever.

"There has to be a better way," exclaimed David. "What do the feds do where Social Security is paying disability benefits to mentally impaired individuals? We don't seem to have guardianship cases coming up in those situations," he commented. "You're right," I said and explained that in Social Security disability cases, the agency typically didn't require a formal legal guardianship. Rather all they demanded was that the adult caretaker be officially deemed as a "designated payee." Social Security figured the whole thing could be administratively handled by their agency. "So why can't the state do that?" asked David. "Well, I suppose they could if they wanted to," I replied, "but I think they would rather just dump it all on the probate court." I went on to point out for example that if DPW could curtail or eliminate twenty APTD cases a month, the welfare savings would be around $240,000.00 per year, and that's just for Bexar County. Now figure that for all of the other counties across Texas, on a state-wide basis. I think the state's monetary savings would be fairly significant. So by having this guardianship requirement, apparently DPW was kind of using the probate court in a complicit way to help limit APTD welfare benefit payouts. "Well, we've got to put a stop to this," declared David. "My friend, I think that would be a worthy goal," I said, "so let's see how we can plan to attack this."

Within the hour, we came up with the consensus of a plan. I would do the preliminary legal research, but my hunch was that we should be able to go into federal court with a class action, claiming that DPW's requirement of an automatic and mandatory legal guardianship as a condition precedent to receiving APTD benefits in cases where mental disability was involved would be in violation of the Social Security Act. David would pull together statistics, aid in developing discovery, and even act as an expert witness if necessary. He also believed that he'd be able to find a good class representative client. Of course, I would have to secure Mr. Christian's approval, and we would have to talk to Judge Reeves, whose political influence we thought might be helpful in that regard. Our plot was taking shape, and we parted with a resolve to move forward on this issue. In the next few days I did the research, and my hunch proved to be correct.

The culprit containing DPW's regulations was the agency's Administrative Procedures Handbook, a source akin to the genesis of the department's insidious NOLEO provisions, which we were already getting set to contest. In purpose and effect, I felt that DPW's guardianship rules were just as repugnant to the provisions of the Social Security Act, and likewise would be vulnerable to a federal court challenge. It was the following week and before the Labor Day weekend, when I received a call from David. He thought he had found a client for our prospective class action case. He had set up a meeting for the morning of Friday, September 3rd, with the idea of the two of us having a conference with Judge Reeves afterwards. He wanted to confirm if that was okay. Calendar wise I was clear and told him I would be there. I was rather surprised that he was able to find a potential client so rapidly; after all, it had only been a few days since we had talked.

With anxious anticipation, that Friday morning I proceeded to David's small office at the Bexar County Courthouse, where he introduced me to Pauline C. Gomez. She was a small, sixty-three year old Hispanic woman with a pleasant personality. She broke into a big broad smile when I told her that my mother's first name was also Pauline. It was like we became instant friends. As it turned out she was the caretaker for her mentally retarded daughter, Josefina, who was twenty-two years old and still lived with her. She had applied for APTD benefits for Josefina and after assessing her needs, DPW advised her that indeed Josefina would be entitled to receive a $70.00 per month APTD grant, but that she could not get it unless Pauline would take out a legal guardianship on her daughter, Josefina. When she went to the Bexar County Courthouse to inquire about it, she was sent to David's office. There she was chagrined to learn about the cost of such a proceeding and that the initial monetary outlay would be more than the monthly grant amount. Then David told her what his feelings were concerning the matter and about our recent conversation. When he asked her if she would like to meet me and be willing to talk to me about it, she responded affirmatively, and so David said he would set it up. Wow, could this be fate I thought, as I carefully outlined the risks and responsibilities of becoming involved in class action litigation. I went on to explain that although I would need to get Mr. Christian's final approval, I would be willing to file a class action case against DPW challenging their guardianship requirement, not only for her and Josefina, but for all others who found themselves in the same boat. Without any reservation, she consented in becoming our named plaintiff. I was glad she agreed because I didn't think I could have found a more congenial and co-operative client, nor one whose fact situation more clearly illustrated the problem. I thanked her and promised I would keep her informed as we moved forward.

Later that morning David and I reported to Judge Reeves' office. He made it pretty clear that he was exasperated about the "welfare guardianship" problem, and he felt the probate court was being swamped with these unnecessary cases. I informed him of the approach that we were planning to take and advised him that David had perhaps found the perfect client for our contemplated class action. He was pleased that we were going to attempt to do something and asked: "What are the chances of success on that kind of case?" "Judge, I believe they're good," I replied, "but I really could use your help in one respect." "How's that?" he asked. "Well Sir, if you could write Mr. Christian a letter kind of describing the problem from your perspective, explaining how it adversely impacts welfare recipients, and suggesting that Legal Aid might want to look into the matter, it might help in securing his approval," I stated. Judge Reeves smiled, and nodding his head said: "Well, I'll certainly be happy to do that." As we left his office, David and I felt satisfied that the morning had been successful. Later at lunch, David commented: "Of course, you know who is going to write that letter, don't you?" "Yeah, I know it's going to be you," I acknowledged, "but here's the deal. I'm already over-loaded with Law Reform matters, and I want Christian to approve this case and put me in charge of it, and I think that letter will help insure that happening." David grinned and affirmatively shook his head, indicating that he understood perfectly.

Apparently, the letter had its desired effect. Shortly after Labor Day, I was summoned to Christian's office. He informed me that he had received a letter from Judge Reeves, referencing how mandatory "welfare guardianships" were creating havoc in the probate court and that he felt it merited our looking into. I advised him that I was cognizant of the situation and believed it would be a worthwhile endeavor to take up a Law Reform case going after DPW regarding the matter. I explained that the *Galindo* NOLEO case had been fully prepared and was only days from being filed. I assured him that Harry Adams and Don McManus could adequately see that case through with me just remaining in the background. That would pretty much free me up to get onto this new matter full blast. Christian agreed, giving his approval to go forward on both cases. He even suggested that I could pick up Fred Deyeso for some additional assistance on the new matter. Later that day, I called David and Pauline and told them that we had been given the green light, and we were pushing forward.

During the following weeks, Fred and I were able to draft our initial pleading and brief. With considerable collaboration from David, we designed and crafted an extensive discovery package, consisting of numerous interrogatories directed squarely at Raymond W. Vowell, DPW's head man. "He's going to have a hard time answering these questions without effectively admitting our entire case," Fred observed. "That's the idea," I responded, "and we're going to co-ordinate the release of these with our discovery transmission in the *Galindo* case. In that way, Vowell and the AG's office will be under the maximum pressure and have to deal with both sets of discovery at the same time." "Now, that's downright diabolical," declared Fred, as I just grinned and winked in agreement.

By the end of the month we were all but ready to move. I called David and Pauline and advised that they could expect the filing to take place sometime early next month. On Friday, October 8, 1971, the case of *Gomez v. Vowell*, SA-71-CA-280 was officially filed in the federal district court for the Western District of Texas, San Antonio division. The suit challenged DPW's guardianship regulations, claiming that the agency was imposing legal guardianships in many instances where they weren't really necessary, and contending that the real purpose was to discourage applicants seeking welfare and to deny public assistance benefits. By the next day, Saturday, October 9th, the press had picked up the story, and the newspaper column headline trumpeted: "S.A. Suit Challenges Texas Guardianship Rule for Welfare." Later the following week, Christian called me to inform me that he had received a call from Bexar County Judge, Blair Reeves, who was elated that we were doing something about the matter. As it turned out, we drew D.W. Suttle on the case. Although I would have preferred judge Adrian Spears, at least it wasn't Judge John H. Wood, which would have definitely been my last choice, and so I was relatively pleased. As initially planned the discovery transmittals on the *Galindo* and *Gomez* cases went out in co-ordination with one another, so that the answers and responses would be due right about at the same time.

It was the week before Thanksgiving when we were contacted by Pat Bailey, who was the Texas Assistant Attorney General who had been assigned to both the *Galindo* and *Gomez* cases. He desperately needed a one week extension with respect to answering our discovery, and Harry and I, feeling that we had developed some personal rapport with him, agreed and consented to his having a one week delay. After the holiday weekend, he called and surprisingly informed us that Vowell wanted to settle both cases. Once we got over the shock, and we were convinced that they weren't just stalling but were serious, negotiations commenced in earnest. By December 8, 1971, an agreement had been finalized on the *Galindo* case, and an agreed judgment was entered, granting us nearly everything we wanted. We were very close on the *Gomez* case situation, and I notified David and Pauline of the likelihood of our being able to achieve a favorable settlement. Shortly afterwards we successfully concluded negotiations, and only five days after the entry of the *Galindo* case judgment, on December 13, 1971, Judge D.W. Suttle signed our agreed judgment and issued the court's order on the *Gomez v. Vowell* case. The automatic mandatory guardianship requirement in APTD cases where the adult recipient had been deemed disabled due to a mental impairment was declared illegal and was no more. DPW would be forced to amend their rules. From now

{ 237

on the need for a legal guardianship would have to be determined on an individual case basis, be factually based, and utilized only in cases where it was absolutely necessary. Pauline's daughter, Josefina, was to be awarded her APTD grant, and she was to receive full retro-active benefits, as well. For the rest of the eligible class, benefits were to commence no later than by December 15th. Since this involved rule changes, the benefits of the *Gomez* case exceeded the boundaries of the Western District of Texas, and for all practical purposes would be applicable state wide to all recipients in Texas. The press, of course, picked up the story, and the newspaper column headline heralded: "Judgment Overturns DPW Rule."

It had only been sixty-seven days from our original filing to the favorable conclusion of the *Gomez v. Vowell* case. This would end up being the record for the shortest time it took for all of the Law Reform cases in which I was involved. When I notified Pauline and told her she could forget about the guardianship fiasco and that Josefina would be getting her full APTD benefits and would be paid all back benefits too, she was unbelievably pleased and told me how this would be a special Christmas blessing. Of course, I called David and thanked him and let him know that this would have never happened without him. Bexar County Judge Blair Reeves was naturally happy with the outcome, and he let Mr. Christian know it, and Christian, of course, extended congratulations to me. But the most sentimental feeling of satisfaction I received was when I got a Christmas card from Pauline and Josefina wishing me a Merry Christmas.

CHAPTER 16

Sometimes a Loss Becomes a Win

1972 – 1973

Vasquez v. Vowel, SA-72-CA-166 (WD of Tex. SA Div. 1972); 486 F. 2d 1043 (5th Cir. 1973)

In 1970, in San Antonio, except perhaps for Legal Aid clients, who did have access to available neighborhood law offices, if you had to see a lawyer, likely you would be headed downtown, where the vast majority of lawyers' offices were located. At that time, hardly any lawyers had chosen to locate their offices in the suburbs. Harry and I fancifully dreamed and always envisioned that if and when we ever decided to leave Legal Aid and go into private practice that it would be a unique idea to apply the Legal Aid concept of neighborhood law offices to the private practice arena, with the vision of opening up a law office in a middle-class suburban area. Beginning in 1971, John Sanders, who was Legal Aid's top lawyer in handling juvenile cases, left Legal Aid and entered into the field of private practice. Acting upon our vision, which Harry and I frequently talked about, John opened a law office on Hillcrest Avenue, about a block from the Wonderland Mall, which was situated in the middle-class suburban community of Balcones Heights. A year later, early in 1972, my good friend and colleague, Harry Adams, had decided it was time to leave Legal Aid, and he joined John in private practice. In Harry's way of thinking, having handled the juvenile cases, John had the knowledge and capabilities in the criminal law area; whereas, he possessed fairly good experience and competency in the various areas of civil law. Between the two of them they pretty much could be able to cover all of the bases. Knowing that Harry was leaving right after New Year's, in the latter part of 1971, Christian tapped me as the sole chief attorney in charge of all Law Reform cases. He moved me to the downtown office and put a young African American attorney by the name of Albert McKnight in charge of the E. Houston Street office. Even though this was a promotion and it meant an increase in salary for me, I was sad to see Harry go.

In December, 1971, at Legal Aid's Christmas party, I made a wistful, goodbye and "we'll miss you" speech to Harry, while presenting him with an appropriate parting present. It was a belting leather briefcase, which he had long admired. Virtually everyone in the Legal Aid organization had chipped in to buy it for him, and so it was truly from all of the gang. Harry felt that he was leaving on a high. That December we had wrapped up and won the *Galindo* case on which technically he was the lead attorney, and the fact that the victory happened in Judge John Wood's court made the win even sweeter in Harry's point of view.

In 1972, New Year's Day came on a Saturday, so the Legal Aid offices closed early on Friday, December 31st, and we were officially closed on Monday, January 3, 1972, giving the entire staff just about a four day holiday, which we all appreciated. After that it was time to get back to work, and I found myself in a rather blue mood. I missed the comradery with Harry and just being able to discuss our cases, and every once in a while going out for a Tecate together after work. It took nearly the entire month of January to get over my "absent Harry" funk. But I guess when you work together with someone so closely and effectively over a period of years, you tend to miss your comrade.

It was February 2, 1972, when I got a call from David J. Garcia, which had the effect of finally snapping me out of my doldrums for good. "Hey

Mel, remember me, your favorite courthouse crusader," David stated. He announced that apparently there was still a situation concerning welfare and guardianships which he felt we needed to talk about. At that time, under state law, young people were considered to be minors until they reached the age of twenty-one, at which point Texas considered them to be legally adults. However, under federal law, particularly under the Social Security Act, an individual's minority status ended once he attained the age of eighteen. Hence, a poor person who suffered from a mental impairment, which rendered him totally and permanently disabled, would be qualified to receive an APTD public assistant grant. For those individuals who met that criteria and who were twenty-one years of age or older, they could receive their welfare benefits without a hitch, as their situation was fully covered and protected by our agreed judgment and court order in the *Gomez v. Vowell* case. But for those potential recipients between the ages of eighteen and twenty-one, the situation was unfortunately different. As these individuals were still considered to be minors under Texas law, DPW had decided to maintain their mandatory guardianship requirement with respect to them. In such cases, a full-fledged guardianship process would have to be instituted in the probate court and then maintained there until the recipient reached the age of twenty-one, at which time as an adult he would be free from such constraints as per the decision in the *Gomez V. Vowell* case. With regard to the potential minor recipient, DPW did recognize one alternative however, and that was to have a legal proceeding brought in the state district court, seeking to remove the minor's legal disabilities of minority, or in other words have the court declare the minor to be legally considered as an adult. Once an adult, of course, then the individual would fall under the provisions of the *Gomez v. Vowell* case, and a legal guardianship would not be required. And it was what David termed as this "legal age gap" issue that precipitated his call. We agreed to meet to further discuss the matter.

We met within the next few days and as we drank some coffee, David voiced his opinion. He felt that the poor mentally disabled between the ages of eighteen and twenty-one were being unduly discriminated against. If DPW could administratively handle welfare grants without a guardianship for mentally disabled APTD recipients who were twenty-one and older, then why couldn't they do likewise for those who were between the ages of eighteen and twenty-one? He couldn't see why the year or two differences in age should be factually that significant as to call for DPW's insistence on a guardianship with respect to the latter group. The same economic dynamics that were involved in the *Gomez* case would be equally applicable here. "Mel, it just doesn't seem right," claimed David. "Well, I agree," I said, "but playing the devil's advocate, we can anticipate DPW will argue that the fact they are still minors justifies a more protective status, ergo the continuation of the guardianship requirement wouldn't be unreasonable with respect to this age group." "Oh that's B.S. What a bunch of hypocrites," declared David. "If they were all that concerned about protecting minority rights, then why are they providing an option and telling families that it is okay to go onto district court and surrender their minority status and in essence have the court declare them to be legal adults ahead of time? How is that protecting their minority status? And that's another thing I strongly disagree with," David concluded. "Well my friend, those are some good questions, and you may have a point as to the formulation of a basis for argument against those practices. Give me a couple of weeks to look into it, and I'll get back to you," I replied.

During the following weeks, my preliminary research indicated that DPW was relying upon sections 2110(1) and (9), 2120, and 2130(1) of the Texas Administrative Procedures Handbook for the justification of their policies. I was able to knit together a credible argument outline challenging DPW's regulations and practices that required the judicial removal of a minor's disabilities of minority or the establishment of a legal guardianship as a condition precedent to receiving an APTD grant. My contentions were that these regulations and practices contravened and violated the purposes and provisions of Title XIV of the Social Security Act, 42 U.S.C. Sections 1351, et seq., and therefore, were invalid under the Supremacy

Clause of the U.S. Constitution. By the end of the month, I advised David of my progress. I asked him if he could talk to Judge Reeves about writing another letter to Christian concerning this subject, and of course, he agreed to take care of the matter. He also indicated that he would remain vigilant and keep his eye out for potential clients regarding this situation.

It was early in March, 1972, when Patsy Neyland called me to let me know that Christian wanted to see me. Of course, I already had a fairly good idea as to what it was about. At our conference, when Christian stated he had received another letter from Bexar County Judge Reeves and divulged its content, I responded by indicating that I was somewhat aware of the problem. During our discourse, I explained that although I felt a Law Reform case here might prove to be more difficult; nevertheless, I believed that we should pursue the matter, provided that we found the right clients, of course. Christian agreed and so blessed the project. He then suggested that I pick up Ron Flake as the attorney to work with me on this matter, should a case come to fruition.

Ron Flake was a fighter pilot in the U.S. Air Force. While serving in Vietnam, on August 3, 1967, his plane crashed on takeoff from the Cam Rahn Air Base. His fellow pilot died in the incident, and how Ron managed to get out from the flaming wreckage was nothing short of a miracle. He had sustained severe injuries with second and third degree burns covering 85% of his body. Much time had to be spent in military hospitals where he underwent extensive surgeries and skin grafts. A good part of this time, which included his recovery and rehabilitation, was spent at the famous Brook Army Burn Center in San Antonio. His left arm had been amputated at the elbow, his right hand had a reconstructed thumb and only two other remaining fingers, and despite all of the successive skin grafts there was rather visible scarring on his neck and a portion of his face. According to Ron, the military listed him as the worst burn victim to survive the Vietnam War in terms of overall percent of burns. Once released from the Air Force, he entered law school at St. Mary's, from where he graduated in 1971 with his law degree. By the end of that year, he had passed the Texas state bar exam and shortly afterwards went to work as a lawyer at Bexar County Legal Aid (BCLA), and so in 1972, as a young lawyer, Ron had expressed an interest to Christian on desiring to work on cases involving the rights of disabled individuals should any come up. I guess Christian remembered that when he suggested that I take Ron on as my teammate regarding this particular matter.

By the end of March, I received a call from David, and evidently he had come into contact with a couple of potential clients for the prospective Law Reform class action cases that we had been discussing. I asked him if he could set up a conference with them, which he did. On our scheduled meeting day, I met Ron and we headed over to David's office at the Bexar County Courthouse. As it wasn't being used at the time, we all met and sat around one of the large conference tables in the probate courtroom. There David introduced us to Jose Vasquez, a gentleman with a calm and simpatico demeanor, who was the caretaker for his eighteen year old daughter, Anna Marie. We also met Mary Rodriguez, a nice polite lady, who was the caretaker for her nineteen year old son, Albert. Regrettably, both Anna Marie and Albert suffered mental disabilities whereby under the guidelines they were considered to be totally and permanently disabled and so would be entitled to receive APTD assistance. Just as clear in both instances DPW had denied them the benefits because since Anna Marie and Albert were minors under state law, first they had to either have their disabilities of minority judicially removed and legally declared to be adults or a full-fledged legal guardianship would have to be set up. Both parents felt it wasn't right to force their child to give up their minority protective status in order to be able to receive needed welfare assistance; nor did they desire to embark upon a rather cumbersome and expensive guardianship proceeding. Ms. Rodriguez sounded in desperation as she tearfully looked at us and asked if there was anything we could do to help. After further discussion, Mr. Vasquez and Ms. Rodriguez readily consented to participate as named plaintiffs in our perspective class action case against DPW.

For the remainder of March and through the month of April, Ron and I investigated our clients' situations, leaving no stone unturned. We had to be sure that our fact situation was absolutely solid, and it was. Also considerable time was spent doing further legal research to sure up any loose ends. By the first part of May, we had completed our pleading, brief, and with David's help, our discovery documents, consisting of interrogatories and requests for admission designed to nail down every possible factual issue. Although both of our clients were deemed as named plaintiffs, we selected Mr. Vasquez to be listed first as he was clearly the calmer of the two.

By May 17, 1972, we were ready, and Ron and I took our papers to the federal courthouse in San Antonio, and the case of *Vasquez v. Vowell*, SA-72-CA-166, was officially filed in the U.S. district court. I called David to give him a heads up regarding the filing and contacted the clients, as well. By the next day, the press had gotten wind of the case, and the newspaper column headline read: "Suit charges welfare aid denied handicapped teens," as the news story related our clients' situations. Just on random coincidence our case was assigned to Judge D.W. Suttle. How fortuitous I thought, as he was the judge we had drawn in the *Gomez v. Vowell* case, where the issues were clearly similar. Out of the three federal judges in San Antonio, obviously he would be the most familiar with this matter. The fact that he was aware that DPW had consented and agreed to a favorable judgment in the *Gomez* case, and he was the judge who signed the court order putting our victory in the *Gomez* case into effect, made me feel rather upbeat and that perhaps the stars were lining up in our direction.

That summer was spent in completing the discovery process. As envisioned we accomplished exactly what we had designed to do. Every single factual issue had either been admitted to or resolved in our favor. It enabled us to draft a pre-trial order with very favorable stipulations of fact. Indeed there were no issues of factual contention that really remained. The whole case now boiled down to what was the appropriate and correct application of law. As DPW had settled in *Gomez*, I felt we would give them the opportunity to do so here, as well, and so that autumn we made a settlement overture to Pat Bailey, the Texas Assistant Attorney General representing the other side. Negotiations actually ensued, and after several fruitful communications, I felt we were making good progress, following along the lines of what we had accomplished in the *Gomez v. Vowell* case. Then all of a sudden I got a surprising phone call from Pat. "Mel, I'm afraid we can't settle this one," he stoically commented. "What's wrong, Pat," I asked; "I thought we had just about reached an accord here." "We had," Pat admitted, and disclosed that he had recommended settlement and that Raymond Vowell, DPW's Director, had also agreed, but that Crawford Martin, the Texas Attorney General, wouldn't let them do it. In fact, Pat divulged that even if they lost the case at the district court level, Crawford Martin was insisting that they would appeal it to the Fifth Circuit. "Well, Pat you know if we lose here, we will definitely be taking it up on appeal to the Fifth Circuit," I declared. So we agreed that apparently either way this case was going up to the Fifth Circuit for final decision. That being the situation, we both felt the sooner we got through the preliminary district court level the better. Hence, the case was submitted on summary judgment and briefs for Judge Suttle to decide. The day of the hearing, Ron and I split our side of the oral argument. I began with a brief summary of the facts and concluded with an introduction of the legal issues before the court. Ron had requested going last and undertaking the task of covering the main legal arguments of our issues. We had practiced this several times, and I felt he was both competent and enthusiastic with respect to doing it, so I agreed he could take it on. In my opinion, he did an excellent job, and at the conclusion, I was feeling fairly confident that we were going to win this, especially in the light of this court's previous ruling in *Gomez v. Vowell.*

    Life sometimes is full of surprises, and I was handed one of them when Judge Suttle decided against us. He noted that DPW was aware of the problem of whether a "natural guardian," such as a parent could receive assistance benefits on behalf of his or her mentally disabled needy child without the resort to judicial guardianship proceedings. He further noted that DPW had in 1970, previously asked for enabling legislation that would avoid the legal guardianship question, but that succeeding Texas Attorneys General had interpreted state law in such a way as to effectively block any changes in policy. And I suppose our argument was just a bridge too far for Judge Suttle, and he caved in to their state's rights contention, stating that without Congress having spoken very specifically to the contrary, the state would have great latitude with respect to making such decisions. The next day the newspaper column headline read: "Plaintiffs Lose Welfare Suit."

It was a bitter pill and a heartbreaking loss, and I hated having to make the aftermath phone calls to David, Mr. Vasquez, and Ms. Rodriguez. Although disappointed, I tried to engender hope by advising them that we intended to take the case up on appeal where we might be able to secure a better result. Our clients were very understanding and were in agreement with us taking the case up on appeal. Christian likewise gave his blessing, and so the case was appealed to the Fifth Circuit.

I have often heard the repeated refrain about how the Lord works in mysterious ways, and as a lawyer I've personally experienced instances where it appeared that fate took a hand in seeing that justice was ultimately accomplished. In 1970, the Vietnam War was going on full blast. Many youths between the ages of eighteen and twenty-one were dying or sustaining severe injuries, while serving in the U.S. Armed Forces and fighting overseas; and yet they didn't even have the right to vote. At that time, in the country, there was widespread support that that just wasn't right. And so on March 23, 1971, the XXVI Amendment to the U.S. Constitution was proposed, stating that: "The right of citizens of the United States, who are eighteen years of age or older, to vote shall not be denied or abridged by the United States or by any State on account of age." The Amendment was ratified effective July 1, 1971, and became part of the U.S. Constitution and the law of the United States.

Once that happened, then state after state began to change their laws, making the legal age of adult status to be conferred upon individuals to be the age of eighteen, as opposed to twenty-one. Texas followed suit, and the

63rd Legislature, which convened in January, 1973, passed a bill that the Governor signed, making the age of eighteen as the end of minority status. This became effective state law in September of 1973. So by then anyone eighteen or older was considered to be an adult. That included Anna Marie Vasquez, Jose Vasquez's daughter, and Albert Rodriguez, Mary Rodriguez's son. All of a sudden there was no longer any impediment to their receiving their APTD grants without their having to undergo a legal guardianship procedure or have their disabilities of minority judicially removed. They were no longer minors. Rather they were now adults, and as such their rights were fully insured and protected under our previous case of *Gomez v. Vowell*.

The Fifth Circuit recognized this, and on November 1, 1973, the case of *Vasquez v. Vowell*, 486 F. 2d 1043 (5th Cir. 1973) was dismissed per curiam on the grounds that the appellate issue was now moot, as Texas no longer had any "minor recipients." The welfare guardianship dilemma for mentally disabled individuals, who were eligible for APTD assistance and were between the ages of eighteen and twenty-one, was gone for good. In later years, David and I would reminisce about how the *Vasquez* case, which was originally a loss, in the end and for all practical purposes, eventually became a win.

CHAPTER 17

We're Going to New Orleans

1971 – 1973

Rodriguez V. Vowell, SA-71-CA-250 (WD Tex. SA Div. 1971)

No. 72-1663, 472 F. 2d 622 (5th Cir. 1973)

Cert. Denied, 406 U.S. 535 (1973)

Throughout history nations have struggled with how to handle the problem of poverty, and the United States proved to be no exception. During the colonial period, many of the British "Poor Laws" were imported and utilized, as they espoused concepts that early Americans were most familiar with. For the most part, these made a distinction between those who were unable to work due to their age or lack of physical health versus those who were able-bodied but lacked employment. With respect to the former group, minimal assistance was given by the government or by those acting in consort and cooperation in achieving the government's function, such as various religious and philanthropic organizations. As for the latter group, they were put to work, for bare subsistence, in almost a slave environment, doing assorted public service jobs or government subsidized labor tasks in a variety of workhouses or camps. During the latter 1800's there was a move to reform government's approach to poverty. This included everything from local communities, again often acting through religious and civic minded groups, who sent social workers to visit the

{ 249

poor so as to teach them "morals" and a "work ethic," to more direct federal government aid to certain targeted groups, such as injured and disabled veterans of the Civil War. Then in 1929, the country witnessed the stock market crash and the advent of the Great Depression, which had devastating economic consequences. All of a sudden vast numbers of middle and upper class Americans found themselves in the same valley of poverty in which many of their poor fellow citizens had been dwelling for some time. But this was the first time that such large numbers of the middle and upper class personally experienced poverty on a first hand basis, and they didn't like it one bit. A large roar arose from the populace demanding that government do something about it. Under the leadership of President Franklin D. Roosevelt, Congress got to work and passed a number of anti-poverty measures. Among them was the Social Security Act of 1935, which formed the backbone of the four basic welfare programs; whereby, in cooperation with the federal government, the states opted into in order to help alleviate the prevalent poverty situation. During World War II and in the post-war years, economic conditions stridently improved, and significant numbers of Americans were able to climb from the valley of poverty back up the ladder to the middle and upper class levels. After the Kennedy assassination, President Lyndon B. Johnson used his political capital to further advance anti-poverty legislative measures as part of his "War on Poverty," as he attempted to move America along the path toward the "Great Society" that he envisioned. Many of these programs did achieve a positive improvement and were successful. But welfare was never a perfect system, and there were enough instances of boondoggles and failures, as well. Perhaps spurred on initially from an attitude of racism, but steadily followed by respectable conservative thought that maybe the welfare system was developing far too much of an atmosphere of dependency, and by 1968, a mounting backlash against welfare was growing.

Meanwhile, 1971 turned out to be a momentous year with my engaging in several major welfare Law Reform cases against the Texas Department of Public welfare (DPW). That autumn not only saw the filing of the *Galindo* and *Gomez* cases, but yet a third case that was perhaps the most difficult and frustrating of them all. The *Rodriguez v. Vowell* case would end up taking me down a lengthy legal pathway, which would encompass a bitter battle in the U.S. district court in San Antonio and an intense but gratifying hearing before the Fifth Circuit Court of appeals in New Orleans, with the U.S. Supreme Court eventually weighing in on the matter in the finale.

Texas was running out of money again when it came to funding its welfare programs. It's not that the state wasn't doing well—indeed to the contrary, from an overall economic standpoint, Texas was doing just fine. But from within the realm of relative prosperity, there seemed to be an ever growing divide between those dwelling within the middle class and the upper ranges of society and those who inhabited what appeared to be a never ending cycle of poverty. On January 12, 1971, the 62nd Texas Legislature convened in Austin for its regular legislative session. And as usual, it was totally oblivious as to meeting its responsibilities concerning adequately funding the state's obligations with respect to the poor. From a budgetary standpoint, it certainly wasn't that there was a wholesale lack of funding sources. Apparently, there was ample consideration for special favorable treatment and largesse for big banks and insurance companies, wealthy ranchers, and lucrative oil company interests. In Texas, "welfare" for the rich never seemed to be a problem. On the other hand, welfare for the poor, who really needed the help, well that was a different story. There never appeared to be enough money left for that purpose. Legislatively, the attitude that seemed to permeate the body politic was that the problem of poverty would somehow magically disappear if it was just simply ignored. It was as if the Vietnam War had poisoned the American spirit, and a sickening malaise began to set in among far too many of our acquaintances among the middle class and nouveau riche, whereby the prevalent belief advocated was that the way to solve the problem of poverty was to devote less money and resources to it, and then the poor "would learn to lift themselves up by their own bootstraps;" and hence, poverty would dissipate. Of course the fact that the poor had no "bootstraps" or the money to buy them was missed entirely. It wasn't so much that America was losing the "War on Poverty," as it was that as a nation, we were losing the will to continue to fight it.

So with the welfare funds dwindling and with the Texas Legislature not having the political resolve to remedy the situation, it wasn't any wonder to see the DPW leadership invent and institute a series of conniving rules and regulations diabolically designed to throw as many people off of the welfare rolls as possible and to deny countless others access to needed assistance. And of course the group selected to be chiefly targeted to bare the biggest brunt of the economic deprivation was the politically demonized AFDC program.

In the past, typically an AFDC grant was calculated by first measuring a family's total needs, which were analyzed according to a certain minimum "standard of needs," which the Texas DPW had determined to represent the cost of the basic requisites essential for health and decency. Each adult caretaker was budgeted at $65.00 per month, and each child was allocated a $25.00 per month allowance. To the total of those amounts, a monthly shelter figure was budgeted at a maximum of $50.00 per month, and another $13.00 per month was allowed for all utilities. Second, the DPW applied a 25% reduction factor to the total sum in order to arrive at the family's recognizable needs, which was only 75% of the family's minimum "standard of needs." And third, if there was any outside income coming into the family it was subtracted, and the final sum was the amount of the AFDC grant to which the family was entitled to receive.

On January 1, 1971, the Texas DPW instituted their odious new provisions consisting of Paragraphs 15 and 16 of Section 3310 of the Texas Financial Services Handbook. From now on income and resources accruing to a child in his own right, such as child support, paid by a legal parent, would be considered in determining the child's eligibility and the amount of his grant. These resources accruing to a child in his own right could not be diverted to meet the needs of other members of the family in the household but had to be applied to meeting the child's own needs. The regulation specified: "If this income is sufficient or more than sufficient to meet the child's recognizable needs, the child would not be eligible to be certified or to be considered dependent. In instances where all potentially eligible children in the family have their individual needs met by benefits accruing in their own right, we have no needy children, therefore there is no basis for making an AFDC grant, regardless of whether or not there is sufficient income to meet group needs."

It was pretty clear to DPW officials that these new regulations were going to have a devastating effect on the Texas AFDC population, which was blindsided and caught completely off guard with respect to DPW's new rules. Many were hopeful that this would just be a temporary situation and that the Texas Legislature would act to save the situation by providing additional funding; thus, making the justification for such a radical regulation unnecessary. But by the end of May, 1971, when the 62nd Texas Legislature adjourned, having totally failed in doing anything helpful, a few held on to the slim hope that maybe Governor Preston Smith might call for a special session in January, 1972, to deal with the situation. In the meantime, the misery index began to increase exponentially. By the summer of 1971, the crescendo of complaints began to flood into the various Legal Aid offices. Seeing what was happening, I discussed the matter with Fred Deyeso, and we resolved to commence looking into the matter. By utilizing my spy network that I had developed over the years, I reached out to a friendly contact within the DPW agency. Before too long, I had obtained the history about how the DPW hierarchy came up with this scheme, and I had been sent a complete copy of the offending radical regulations.

After having concluded our preliminary investigation and research, Fred asked: "So what are we going to do about this?" "Well, we're going to have to fight this thing," I resolutely replied. "That will mean another welfare Law Reform case we'll be undertaking, and we'll need to get Christian's approval," commented Fred. "Yeah, I know—leave that to me," I stated, "and in the meantime why don't you get out a letter to the neighborhood offices, outlining the problem and setting forth the parameters of what we're looking for in potential named plaintiffs for a class action against DPW." I followed through with Christian and got his approval, and Fred completed and sent out our inquiry letter. Shortly afterwards, I received word that a possible candidate had been found, and a conference was set up for Fred and I to meet with her at our downtown office.

On the scheduled meeting day we introduced ourselves to Leonor Rodriguez. She was of average build and stature, with dark hair and dark eyes, and I guessed her age to be in her late twenty's or early thirty's. Leonor, who had been divorced, was now a single mother with two young children, who attended school full-time. She dispiritedly described how she and her family were thrown off the welfare rolls. Under the old rules as the parent caretaker, DPW had accessed her needs at $65.00 per month; whereas the children were each allocated $25.00 per month. To this $115.00 sum, DPW allowed the family $44.00 per month for housing and another $13.00 per month for utilities, for a grand total of $172.00 per month. To this they applied their 25% reduction factor, in order to arrive at the family's recognizable needs, which resulted in a figure of $129.00 per month, i.e. [$172.00 x .25=$43.00; $172.00-43.00 =129.00]. Ms. Rodriguez's ex-husband, the children's father, paid child support of $79.00 per month for the two children. This was subtracted from the $129.00 figure of the family's recognizable needs, and that left $50.00 per month, which DPW paid as an AFDC grant to the family. Hence under the old rules, between the child support of $79.00 per month and the AFDC grant of $50.00 per month, the Rodriguez family coped with living on a total of $129.00 per month, which was equivalent to DPW's standard of recognizable needs for a family of three. But now under the new rules, since each child received an amount of child support that exceeded DPW's allocated amount of $25.00 per month per child; therefore, neither child was any longer deemed to be "dependent," and that being the case, the entire family was no longer considered as eligible for an AFDC grant. So the Rodriguez family effectively went from a total of $129.00 monthly income to having to struggle to live on the $79.00

per month in child support alone. Not only was this a severe monetary loss, but by losing their AFDC grant, the family also lost their Medicaid benefits, as well. Ms. Rodriguez and her family perfectly represented the devastating effect that DPW's new regulations had on many AFDC families. After further interrogation and counseling, she made her decision to bravely step forward and willingly agreed to be a named plaintiff in our potential class action against DPW.

That evening at home after dinner, I was reviewing my notes on the Rodriguez matter, and Marlene sensed my feelings of frustration. "What's bothering you?" she asked. When I went over the arithmetic progressive steps pertaining to the Rodriguez family, Marlene, who was a Math teacher, referred to DPW's mathematical manipulations as "fuzzy math," a term I adopted and later even used in my oral argument.

In the following days, Fred and I concluded our research and began piecing together an outline for our pleading and brief. In the meantime, we picked up two additional clients: Ms. Oralia Serrato, a mother with two children, whose situation mirrored that of the Rodriguez family, and Ms. Delfina Rangel, a mother with one child. She was receiving a supplemental AFDC grant of $59.00 per month in addition to the $43.33 monthly child support that she was getting. But under DPW's new regulation given the amount of child support, she too was tossed from the rolls. Out of desperation, she tried to convince the child's father to make up the difference. However, all of her pressurized attempts were to no avail, and indeed they backfired, with child support payments being stopped completely, and this then allowed the Rangel family to recently get back on the welfare rolls. Her situation demonstrated the negative impact of DPW's new rules in that they actually discouraged some families from seeking or taking child support altogether.

By that autumn we were ready to file, and on September 14, 1971, the case of *Rodriguez v. Vowell*, SA-71-CA-250 (WD Tex. SA Div. 1971) was officially filed with the federal district court in San Antonio. The press picked up on the matter, and the newspaper headlines rang out: "Welfare

Suit Challenges ADC Regulations," which sat atop an excellent column article written by Wilson McKinney that vividly painted the plight of our clients. Unfortunately, we randomly drew Judge John H. Woods, Jr. on the case, and as far as I was concerned, we couldn't have ended up with a worse choice. Later that evening, I revealed my premonition to Marlene that this case would likely end up at the Fifth Circuit.

A few days later, I got a call from J.L. Covington, who was the chief attorney with the Texas Rio Grande Legal Aid program. It operated a legal services program covering the poor communities in what was known as the South Texas Valley, and included such towns as Brownsville, Harlingen, McAllen, San Benito, and Weslaco. "Hey Mel, I understand that you filed a class action case against DPW concerning their new AFDC budgetary regulations," inquired J.L. "Yeah man, we have. It's a deplorable situation, and we felt we had to do something about it," I stated. "Well, I agree," said J.L. "We've been working on that matter too, and we've gathered together some really good class representative clients." "Okay, do you all plan to file a class action case in the Southern District?" I asked. For federal jurisdictional purposes, Brownsville and the "Valley" were within the Southern District of Texas. "Well, we were headed in that direction, but when I saw you had already filed, I thought perhaps we could consolidate our effort and work together on this one. What would you think if we intervened in your case?" asked J.L. "Hey, I'd love to have you on board, but honestly I've got to warn you—we drew Judge John Wood on our case, and given this subject, I suspect he's going to be a bad hombre. Are you sure you wouldn't rather file a separate case in the Southern District?" I replied. "Yeah, I'm familiar with him," J.L. claimed, "but all in all, I believe it would be a good idea to show a united front, and I think we would rather take our chances and throw our lot in with you. Besides, it will be an opportunity to have our two programs work together," stated J.L.

We agreed to exchange client factual outlines and profiles. I realized that if we were going to merge our cases, then I wanted to vet J.L.'s clients. The last thing needed was to have the strong fact situation presented by our named plaintiffs muddled up by an unclear or questionable fact scenario by clients from the "Valley." And as a good lawyer, I realized J. L. would want to do likewise. But after our exchange, it appeared as if J.L. had done an excellent job on client selection. His group, headed up by Antonia A. Aguirre, consisted of sterling representative clients, who presented a factual picture as clear as our own group. After some discussion, we reached a decision to forge ahead together. J.L. filed his intervention petition, which in effect added his clients to ours and merged our two cases together. There was no opposition, and Judge Wood allowed the intervention. That evening I told Marlene about it, and how excited I was that the two Legal Aid programs would be working together. I felt that we had picked up a valuable ally.

At our preliminary hearing, Judge Wood surprised me when he ordered both sides to submit a report to the court outlining steps that the agency could take to eliminate any discrimination in the administration of the AFDC program. After the hearing the reporter, Wilson McKinney, wrote a follow-up news story entitled: "Aid Bias Elimination Plan Ordered by Federal Judge," and he even made reference to the other two suits which we had filed against DPW that autumn. Our press coverage had been pretty good, and I was relatively pleased. But whereas the *Galindo* and *Gomez* cases were destined for settlement and certainly were headed in that direction, there was no such light at the end of the tunnel with respect to the *Rodriguez* case. Here negotiations proved fruitless, as DPW and the AG's office stubbornly dug in their heels, and both sides moved forward in preparing for a fight to the finish. DPW's tact was that it was their way or no way, and if pushed, then they might have to cease having any AFDC recipients all together. Melvin E. Corley, the Assistant Attorney General in charge of the case echoed those sentiments and issued out a series of aggressive press releases, claiming that the AFDC program was running out of money. Ed Castillo, a local news reporter, picked up on Corley's comments and wrote an op-ed column entitled: "Welfare $s Said Dwindling," which stoked the fear campaign being pushed by DPW and the AG's office. One could sense public momentum beginning to change and solidify against the plaintiffs.

By February, 1972, we had completed discovery and all essential facts had been stipulated, and once again the whole thing would boil down to our legal argument as to what should be the correct application of the law. Prior to trial, as the plaintiffs' attorneys, we had a conference as to how we should split our presentation time and who should carry what part of the argument. After discussing the matter, J.L. and Fred felt it would be best if I just went ahead and did the entire argument. I was flattered for their confidence and resolved to do my very best so as not to disappoint them. Finally our trial date arrived, and on February 7, 1972, Fred and I met J.L. at Judge Wood's courtroom on the 5th floor of the old main post office and federal courthouse building, which was located on E. Houston Street, right across from Alamo Plaza. We seated ourselves at the counsel table on the left side. Across from us to the right at the other counsel table sat Melvin E. Corley, Assistant AG, accompanied by an attorney from DPW. Shortly afterwards, Judge Wood appeared and took his seat at the bench, and we began.

I wasn't even seven minutes into my argument, when a barrage of disruptive and highly slanted questions descended from the bench. It became rather evident that Judge Wood had chosen to ally himself with the AG's position and to join Mr. Corley in advancing his radical states' rights argument. It took every ounce of focus and concentration to hit the correct balance of standing strong in enunciating our points of our argument without being so belligerent with Judge Wood as to be subject to being held in contempt of court. If he was going to rule against us, my goal was to maneuver him into a corner and trap him into saying that certain key sections of the Social Security Act weren't applicable to the state of Texas.

At the conclusion of the trial, Judge Wood announced he would take the case under advisement and told us he planned to hand down a ruling within a week. I was under no illusion that his decision was going to be adverse, and by the following Monday, Judge Wood didn't disappoint me as he ruled against us. The newspaper headlines read: "Federal Court

Upholds DPW Regulation" and "Welfare Ruling for State," as the news stories documented our loss.

Judge Wood held that the challenged paragraphs of the state's Financial Services Handbook had not violated plaintiffs' due process and equal protection guarantees under the Fourteenth Amendment. He continued stating that the paragraphs were not arbitrary, capricious, and unreasonable, and that they had a real and substantial relationship to serve the purpose and administration of the AFDC program. He went on to say that the state did not discriminate against needy AFDC families where children have income in their own right and that plaintiffs' rights under the Social Security Act were not being violated. But as a jurist, who wholly bought into Corley's states' rights argument, he fell right into my trap by holding that Texas had the right to optionally pick and choose which sections of the federal act it needed to comply with. But at the district court level it was a complete loss and a total wipe out, and when Fred asked: "Well, where do we go from here?" my reply was direct and forthright: "We're going to New Orleans." And within a matter of days we had filed our notice of appeal and began our appellate process to the Fifth Circuit Court of Appeals, as the newspaper dutifully reported: "Benefits Cut Appeal Filed."

It was around mid-March, 1972, when my secretary, Anita Herrera, buzzed me and excitedly announced: "Mr. Eichelbaum, it's Henry Freedman from the Center on Social Welfare Policy and Law in New York on the line, and he wants to speak with you." "Okay Anita, I've got it," I replied as I picked up the phone. "Hi Mel, you guys are appealing the *Rodriguez* case, aren't you?" inquired Henry. "Yes Sir, we surely are," I acknowledged. Henry went on to say that they had been monitoring our case with great interest. They felt that it dealt with significant issues concerning the AFDC program. According to Henry, their statistical estimates were that the Texas regulations had thrown some 16,000 families off the rolls, while denying about another 24,000 families of needed assistance. He indicated that if we would be agreeable to it, they would like to file an amicus curiae brief on our behalf. After a courtesy call to J.L. seeking his agreement and advising

Fred on the matter, I called Henry back and welcomed him aboard, thanking him for joining in our effort. He informed me that Nancy Duff Levy, one of their attorneys who had expressed an interest in this case would be in contact with me. That evening, I enthusiastically told Marlene that we had picked up another important ally. Within the next couple of days Nancy called me and introduced herself, and over the next few days we had several conversations regarding our appellate brief and their amicus.

Before the end of March, Henry re-contacted me. He had come up with another idea. Rather than their filing an amicus in our favor, he suggested allowing them to become of counsel for plaintiffs in our case. Then in that way Nancy and I could work together and do one powerful combination brief. I liked his new idea, and after consulting with J.L. and Fred, let him know that we were all in agreement.

In putting together our brief, Nancy and I thought that the main thrust should be the statutory part of our argument, which was that the Texas regulations in question violated appellants' rights under the Social Security Act, in that they failed to consider the needs of the caretaker relative and thereby denied aid to "all eligible individuals" within the meaning of that federal statute. Nancy and I hit that head on and made that Point I of our brief. We carved that argument into two sub-points: Part A, which focused on the issue that the provisions of the Social Security Act are binding on the state of Texas, which I primarily undertook to write, and Part B, which argued that the Social Security Act required the inclusion of the needs of the adult caretaker relative in determining eligibility for AFDC and the amount of the assistance payment that Nancy chiefly wrote.

Although our writing styles were different, with mine being more formalistic and grammatical, and with hers being much more fluid and picturesque; nevertheless, like a good marriage we seemed to learn and benefitted from one another, and between the two of us, we were able to blend together a very formidable presentation of our primary argument.

For Point II of our brief, Nancy wanted to write a back-up statutory-regulatory argument, which contended that even if the needs of the adult caretaker relative are not included, appellee's assumption that the child who has income "accruing in his own right," is not needy would be in violation of 45 C.F.R. Section 233.20 and HEW state letter 1088. Meanwhile, I went ahead and put the finishing touches on our Point III, which dealt with the issue that even if the district court was correct in deciding that the Texas regulations did not violate appellants' statutory rights, that the court erred in determining that these provisions did not violate appellants' constitutional rights, as that question should have properly been referred to a three-judge court.

By the end of April we had finished our brief, and everyone seemed to be pleased with the final product. And on April 28, 1972, I signed our brief in Case No. 72-1663, *Rodriguez v.* Vowell and transmitted it for filing with the Fifth Circuit Court of appeals in New Orleans.

Finally, the case was scheduled for a hearing. It was a couple of days before our hearing at the Fifth Circuit when Fred and I drove to the San Antonio Municipal Airport to catch our flight to New Orleans. We wanted to get there earlier so we could have a day to reconnoiter the Fifth Circuit Court of Appeals and familiarize ourselves with the facility and the surrounding area. Although I had been to New Orleans previously, while attending a CLE seminar back in 1969, I had never visited the Fifth Circuit Court building before.

J.L. was flying in from Brownsville, and Nancy and Steven J. Cole, another lawyer from the Center on Social Welfare Policy and Law, were coming in from New York. We had all arranged to stay at a hotel that wasn't too far from where the Fifth Circuit was located. When we arrived in the "Crescent City" Fred and I grabbed a cab and shot over to our hotel. After checking into our room, we spent some time in the bar having a couple of drinks and just relaxing. By late afternoon J.L. had arrived and afterwards Nancy and Steven came in. We all hooked up together and went out for a pleasant New Orleans dinner.

The following morning after a hearty breakfast and several cups of the famously distinctive New Orleans coffee, we all met at the Fifth Circuit courthouse building. There we visited the actual courtroom where we would be doing our legal argument the following day. I had already seen the U.S. Supreme Court before, when back in 1963, I had visited Washington D.C. as the guest of Congressman Henry B. Gonzalez. I remembered how impressed I was in seeing the courtroom where the nine justices sat and heard cases. But I was amazed in that the Fifth Circuit courtroom where we were going to argue our case was equally austere and every bit as majestically impressive. We visited the Fifth Circuit Court library where we checked on some last minute authorities' updates. Afterwards everyone kind of did their own thing, with the idea that we would meet up later that evening in order to deal with the final preparations for our oral argument the next day.

Later that evening, dressed in casual lounge clothes, we all gathered in Nancy's suite, and amid plenty of pizza and beer, we discussed our oral argument presentation. Everyone agreed that the overwhelming emphasis should be on our statutory argument. Fred and J.L. thought we should split our presentation, with me beginning with Part A, and Nancy concluding with Part B. Having seen me perform in the hostile environment of Judge Wood's court, they had no doubt that I would make a strong start. On the other hand, Nancy and Steven felt that our presentation would appear to be less disruptive and more fluid if we picked one lawyer to undertake the entire oral argument, and Nancy truly wanted to do it. She entreatingly looked at me and said: "I can handle it—I really can." After giving it some thought, I broke the tie and voted for Nancy.

The following morning, I superstitiously wore the same charcoal grey suit that I had worn for the district court hearing on this case, and Fred ended up wearing the same navy pin-stripe suit that he had worn on that day. Perhaps it was part of a subconscious feeling of seeking complete vindication, down to our very clothes, from our previous experience before Judge Wood. We all met at the Fifth Circuit courtroom and sat together at the counsel table on the left side, and we all expressed cheering "go get them" words of encouragement to Nancy. Opposite us to the right,

I spied Melvin E. Corley from the Texas AG's office and a DPW attorney overlooking some notes. Suddenly, the three appellate court judges entered and took their seats at the bench, and our hearing began. "May it please the court," said Nancy, and off she went, delivering one of the most convincing and impassioned arguments I've ever witnessed. She was absolutely masterful, and totally demolished the other side. Of course, you never really know for sure how a court will ultimately rule, but after it was all over, I had a very comfortable feeling that we were going to win this one.

Once back in San Antonio, I told Marlene all about my New Orleans experience. "It sounds like things went pretty good," she commented. "Yeah," and with a confident voice predicted: "I think we're going to totally reverse Judge Wood." Later that week, I called Ms. Rodriguez and the other clients and gave them an update, stating that we had our appellate court hearing, that I felt we did fine, and that now we would have to wait for the appellate court to make its decision.

And on January 24, 1973, the decision in *Rodriguez v. Vowell*, 472 F.2d 622 (5th Cir. 1973) was handed down. That Wednesday, a reporter with the Associated Press in New Orleans was typing up a press release for dissemination entitled: "Woman wins welfare court appeal." The news article stated that the federal appeals court took a swipe at the Texas Welfare Department when it handed down its ruling today. The news story related how Leonor Rodriguez had objected to certain sections of the Texas Financial Services Handbook, and how she challenged the regulations that denied AFDC grants to families in which the child had income in his own right which was greater than his own state defined recognizable needs, even where such income was less than the recognizable needs of both the child and his caretaker relative. The reporter went on to detail how attorneys for Ms. Rodriguez contended that these provisions were inconsistent with the Social Security Act, but that the district court for the Western District of Texas ruled that the federal eligibility criteria was not binding on Texas and that the regulations were not in conflict with the federal act. However the story continued, announcing that the 5th Circuit agreed with

Ms. Rodriguez in her class action, stating: "Although each state may refuse to participate in the federal welfare program, once a state decides to participate, it must maintain a system consistent with the Social Security Act." The appellate court went on to say that eligibility for AFDC assistance is not to be determined by each state, but rather by reference to the federal eligibility standards. In short, federal criteria for AFDC are not optional as the district court concluded, they are mandatory. It is clear in the act that the needs of the caretaker relative, as well as those of the dependent child, are to be considered in deciding if a family is eligible for an AFDC grant. The appellate judges continued and declared: "Thus in measuring need, the need of the family unit is the question, not the need of the child alone; for the goal of strengthening the family entity can only be achieved if the needs of the caretaker relative are included in determining eligibility."

That Thursday afternoon I received a call from Henry Freedman, who gleefully informed me that we had won a complete and monumental victory. He advised me that they considered this to be one of their significant major cases and thanked me for all of my help and co-operation. I thanked him for all of their assistance, as well, and asked him to extend my regards to Nancy. Not fifteen minutes later, the phone rang, and it was a local news reporter. Evidently the Associated Press piece had been picked up by the local San Antonio newspapers and the story was going viral. The reporter asked me how I felt having helped win a landmark decision for welfare applicants. "I'm ecstatic," I exclaimed. Later on the way home, I picked up a copy of the newspaper, and there was a major news article entitled: "S.A. welfare mom wins—may shake state," which related the whole history and story of the *Rodriguez* case. Also there was a smaller op-ed piece which was entitled: "<u>Landmark Welfare Decision Victory</u>, 'Ecstatic,' says S.A. Lawyer," and I recognized my quoted words, which I shared with Marlene, once I got home, and that evening we ended up going out to celebrate. The reporter had asked me if I thought the state would appeal, and I answered that I honestly didn't think they would. My reasoning was based on the fact that it was a complete and embarrassing reversal of Judge Wood, and given the fact that it appeared to be such a strong Fifth Circuit opinion that simply blew apart Corley's states' rights balloon, while clearly rejecting the fallacy of DPW's convoluted reasoning, I thought it would be foolish for them to appeal, and that the state might want to leave well enough alone and not waste any more taxpayer money. I was wrong. I didn't' count on the out and out stubbornness of the Texas AG's office or the incorrigible attitude on the part of DPW. So appeal they did. But in the end our victory was made even more complete and sweeter when the U.S. Supreme Court refused to hear their appeal and denied certiorari, 406 U.S. 535 (1973).

The brave challenge pursued by Ms. Rodriguez and the other named plaintiffs were rewarded as their families' benefits were restored, and they received full retro-active relief. Moreover, their courageous stance had a tremendous positive effect on some 40,000 AFDC families throughout the state of Texas.

CHAPTER 18

⚖

Food for Thought

1972 – 1973

Murry v. USDA, 348 F. Supp. 242 (D.C. Cir. Ct. 1972)

USDA v. Murry, 413 U.S. 508 (1973)

The early 1970's witnessed a steady growing negative attitude on the part of a large segment of the public towards anti-poverty measures which were aimed at aiding the poor. Under this sentiment of backlash, the assaults against poor people continued with an ever increasing frequency and intensity. It wasn't only the consumer rip-off businesses, predatory lenders, and slum landlords who were preying upon the poor, but regrettably in many instances, it was the very governmental agencies who were charged with the duty to help those in poverty that were the ones who were perpetuating policies that exacerbated poor people and which made their lives even harder. As these unrelenting attacks multiplied, those groups providing legal services for the poor found themselves under constant pressure to ramp up their efforts to combat such never-ending onslaughts. At times that meant that various Legal Aid organizations would join together so as to pool their skills and resources in order to put forth a concerted determined attempt to fight back against these oppressors, and the Bexar County Legal Aid association was a real player participant in these combinative endeavors.

In many cases these collaborative approaches worked very effectively and indeed achieved meaningful, beneficial results for vast numbers of poor people. For example in 1972, the *Rodriguez v. Vowell* case was a perfect illustration of how such a combination of talents and tenacity were blended together to accomplish a significant win for the poverty community. However, not all such attempts were successful. In one instance for example, I teamed up with Jeff Skarda, a highly competent and dedicated attorney from Houston in a constitutional challenge to the Texas Vendor Drug Program. Jeff was born and raised in Clovis, New Mexico. He completed his undergraduate degree, graduating cum laude from Washington and Lee University at Lexington, Virginia in 1966. From there he went to law school at Columbia University where he obtained his law degree in 1969. Afterwards he moved to Houston, took and passed the Texas Bar Exam, and was licensed to practice law in the state of Texas on September 18, 1970. As a young lawyer Jeff chose to go to work for the Gulf Coast Legal Aid organization. In a relatively short period of time, he became the managing attorney for that entity and served in that capacity for some seventeen years (1973-1990), until he finally went into private practice in 1991. In the early 1970's (1972-1974) Jeff also was an assistant professor at the Texas Sothern University School of Law. During that time I had the distinct honor of being a guest lecturer at that law school. Later the school changed its name to the Thurgood Marshall School of Law, where to this day, a majority of the student body remains African-American and that educational institution is responsible for producing about 40% of the African-American attorneys practicing in the state of Texas.

In 1972, Jeff had contacted me about going after some of the provisions in the Texas Vendor Drug Program, which was created by Raymond Vowell and the DPW hierarchy and inaugurated on September 1st. Jeff felt the new regulations unduly curtailed the distribution of prescription drugs to the elderly poor, and particularly to those who tended to be more sickly. He was able to find two willing class representative plaintiffs in Houston, and I was able to locate two in San Antonio. Co-operating together, the class action case of *Vela v. Vowell* was filed in the federal district court for the Western District of Texas. The newspaper announced the happening with the headline: "<u>Filed in San Antonio</u> Suit Challenges Drug Plan." The case was eventually heard by a three-judge court, but despite our best and valiant efforts, the case was lost. Although I had already left Legal Aid in 1973, my understanding was that the case was appealed to the U.S. Supreme Court, but as far as I know the appeal languished and eventually died up there, *Vela v. Vowell*, 414 U.S. 1154; 415 U.S. 953 (1974). But perhaps the very height of such a conjunctive approach among various legal aid organizations dealt with the food stamp program and was embodied in the case of *Murry v. USDA*.

It is self-evident that a country's greatest asset is its people. So it shouldn't take a rocket scientist to figure out that those nations whose people maintain a level of relatively adequate nourishment, over-all and over a period of time, tend to be healthier; and therefore, more productive and economically more prosperous than those nations where the opposite is true. In short, starving societies just don't seem to do very well. Hence, it would seem that insuring that its population is receiving sufficient nourishment would naturally be of legitimate national concern. And therefore, both the adequacy and availability of food for the people should rightly be of a predominant public interest.

This was certainly true with the United States, although no major governmental significant action actually occurred until critical hunger issues were a problem for a massively large segment of the American public. During the Great Depression, under the leadership of President Franklin D. Roosevelt and his Secretary of Agriculture, Henry Wallace, a trial food stamp program was initiated. It allowed poor people in essence to purchase food at a discount by buying food stamps and then using the stamps as payment for the food. The ratio was roughly fifty cents to the dollar, and so by utilizing the food stamp method, a poor family could effectively buy their needed nourishment at about half price. The program began in the Rochester, New York area, and at its peak, participation had spread to four million in about eighty-eight municipalities throughout the United States. With the end of World War II and economic recovery taking place at a healthy pace, the program ended in 1945, because it was felt that the change in economic conditions rendered the program as no longer being really necessary.

During the 1950's, at the urging of several prominent U.S. Senators, including: Aiken, Humphrey, La Follette, Kefauver, and Symington there was a push to re-institute the food stamp program. These senatorial leaders, who came from states where agriculture played a significant role, felt it would be a win-win situation. Not only would the program make food more readily available and affordable for poor people, but also it would help solve the farm surplus problem, which was plaguing the agricultural industry, all at the same time. In 1959, under their leadership, together with the unceasing efforts of Congresswoman Leonor K. Sullivan, legislation was passed authorizing the Secretary of Agriculture to operate a trial food stamp program through 1962. However, the Eisenhower administration chose to never use that authority and so things sat dormant with respect to that issue.

Later on, in fulfillment of a promise he made while campaigning in West Virginia, President John F. Kennedy signed his first executive order on February 2, 1961, and announced that a pilot food stamp program would be initiated. By May 29, 1961, the food stamp program was operational and began in West Virginia. By early 1964, President Lyndon B. Johnson requested congress to end the program's pilot status and to make the food stamp program permanent. With widespread congressional support, and with the prevailing thought that it would strengthen the agricultural economy while improving the level of nutrition among low-income households, congress favorably acted, and the Food Stamp Act of 1964 was passed and signed into law. By 1970, the program had become one of the government's more successful undertakings and had spread to virtually all of the states, with participant levels reaching the ten million mark.

Of all the various assaults on the poor, many of which were done with dastardly design, perhaps one of the most devastating came about in a rather inadvertent manner. "Beware of unintended consequences," was an old adage popularized by Robert K. Merton, a 20th century American sociologist, and which, on occasion, was voiced by Stanley M. Johanson, one of my old law school professors. Well, this saying came squarely into play with the passage of legislation in 1971, which amended the Food Stamp Act.

During 1970, congress was interested in reforming the Food Stamp Act. The idea was to make the program even stronger by expanding it, developing better national nutritional guidelines, and improving the administrative processes. And so in January, 1971, the Food Stamp Act Amendments were enacted into law. Many of the provisions brought about beneficial reforms to the program. For example, the food stamp program was expanded to include the U.S. Territories, such as Guam, Puerto Rico, and the American Virgin Islands. In its effort to balance access with accountability, congress amended Section 5(b) of the Food Stamp Act of 1964. In doing so, congress was driven by a legitimate intent to prevent abuse of the program. They wanted to halt un-needy college students from relatively affluent households and other children of wealthy parents from unduly taking advantage and utilizing the program, which was meant for poor people. Hence, the new provisions specified that:

"Any household which includes a member who has reached his eighteenth birthday and who is claimed as a dependent child for Federal income tax purposes by a taxpayer who is not a member of an eligible household, shall be ineligible to participate in any food stamp program … during the tax period such dependency is claimed and for a period of one year after expiration of such period." This unfortunate over-broad language turned out to be the unintentional culprit that would have devastating consequences for vast numbers of poor families and would be the cause of my eventual involvement in a major Law Reform case against the United States Department of Agriculture (USDA).

It was in the springtime of 1972, and I was unaware of the troublesome problem that would be generated by the 1971 amendments to the Food Stamp Act, which went into effect that year. Initially I hadn't seen any significant increases in activity regarding people being denied food stamp assistance. In hindsight, part of the reason was obviously timing and that the application of the law had not filtered down to the local San Antonio poverty community, as of yet. And perhaps the remaining aspect for the lack of increased complaints was a feeling of docile acceptance, which seemed to be prevalent amongst large numbers within the ranks of the poor. Regrettably, in many instances when poor people were told by administrative officials, cloaked with the semblance of authority, that the reason for the adverse action being taken against them "was the law" and there "was nothing that could be done about it," all too often they would just blindly and submissively accept it. The idea of going to a lawyer to check it out wouldn't necessarily even cross their minds. Down through the years they were so used to being abused and victimized that they customarily recognized it as an unpleasant fact of life.

So that sometime in the spring, 1972, when I received that fateful call from New York City, it caught me somewhat by surprise. It was Henry Freedman with the Center on Social Welfare Policy and Law. "Hey Mel, have you heard anything about the fiasco that's happening with the food stamp program?" he asked. "No, not really, so what's going on?" I replied. Henry went on to brief me on the recent history of the 1971 amendments to the Food Stamp Act, and particularly the new income tax dependency provision of Section 5(b). "Wow, that's kind of over-broad," I commented. "Do you mean that in a case where say there was a mother and three kids, with one of them being eighteen; and then the father, who may live hundreds of miles away, claims that kid as a tax dependent, they're going to throw the whole household off of food stamps, regardless of over-all family need.?" I asked. "You've got it," answered Henry. "Well hell, that kind of sets up an irrebuttable presumption," I stated. "What if the father's claimed tax dependency is fraudulent altogether, or the amount contributed was inconsequential; the mother couldn't effectively contest that, and even if she could, is the family supposed to starve to death in the meantime?" I sarcastically asked. With a slight chuckle, Henry said; "You all but paraphrased our substantive due process contention. We intend to couple it with an equal protection argument and file a class action case in the D.C. Circuit Court that will constitutionally challenge this tax dependency crap." "Wait a minute, why are you filing there as opposed to New York?" I inquired. "Because our defendant will be the United States Department of Agriculture (USDA), and with its residence situs being in Washington D.C., if we file there, we won't have any jurisdictional venue problems. Besides that will give us our fastest ticket to the U.S. Supreme Court," explained Henry. What a clever strategy I thought, as he continued. "The key will be in presenting a picture of how gravely and widespread this affects the poor throughout the nation," Henry asserted. He advised me that ideally they were seeking to knit together six or so different legal aid organizations in different parts of the country, with each having a good class representative client with a clear and compelling fact situation. He informed me that they already had two plaintiffs from Alabama. One had lost $117.00 in monthly food stamp assistance for herself, two sons, and two grandsons, because her divorced husband living elsewhere for some eleven years, all of a sudden, claimed a couple of the children as tax dependents on his 1971 income tax return. The other Alabama plaintiff's household lost $134.00 per month in food stamp assistance due to her husband, who had since deserted the family, having claimed two of the children as "tax dependents" on his 1971 return. Henry went on to say that he also had a plaintiff in Iowa, another probable one in Colorado, and they were actively working with some west coast contacts. "But we want Texas to be included and be part of this, so I immediately thought of calling you," said Henry. "So what do you think? Would you guys like to join us in this?" he asked. I told him my initial reaction was: "hell yes," but that this would be considered a Law Reform case, and as such, I would need to get Mr. Christian's approval. I asked him to send me a brief synopsis of their case that could be used in getting Christian to agree, and he said he would. In the meantime, I told him we would engage in an appropriate search for potential class representative plaintiffs.

That evening I excitedly related the telephone conversation to Marlene. I was flattered in that out of all of the Legal Aid organizations in Texas, he chose to select us, and that he had sought to call me in particular. I was enthusiastically buoyant about having the opportunity to participate with them in what I surmised would be an important case that would have a significant impact on the lives of a large number of poor families throughout the nation. Within the next few days, I received Henry's synopsis letter. After doing some of my own legal research, I felt their constitutional challenge was solid, and I completely agreed with it, and so I contacted Patsy Neyland in order to arrange an appointment with Mr. Christian. In the meantime, I outlined a draft profile memorandum, detailing the parameters of what we'd be looking for in the way of a prospective class named plaintiff.

On the day I met with Christian, he examined Henry's correspondence and my research notations and commentary regarding the subject, and I could see that his interest was apparently piqued. "So Mr. Eichelbaum, what do you think our chances would be on this one, if we agreed to participate." he asked. "Excellent Sir, in my opinion we have a very good constitutional argument here. Besides it will give us a chance to co-operate and work with about half a dozen different Legal Aid organizations throughout the country. All in all, I think it would enhance our national reputation and status," I responded. Christian gently nodded, as a slight smile broke out on his face. "Of course, everything will hinge on our finding the right client," I added. Christian agreed, and I obtained his approval. Okay, that's step one—now to secure the perfect client, I thought.

In the next several days, I refined my profile memorandum and distributed it to all of our attorneys and law clerks too, as they were the ones who did a significant portion of the initial client intake work. I also had some signs made up, which read: "IF YOU HAVE HAD A PROBLEM WITH

FOOD STAMPS, PLEASE FEEL FREE TO DISCUSS THE MATTER WITH ONE OF OUR STAFF," and I arranged to have these posted in the reception area of our downtown office and in all the neighborhood offices, as well. Furthermore, I sent a "be on the lookout" informational notification to the various community welfare rights organizations and also to the tenants' union groups in the various public housing projects. We had cast a wide net, pro-actively searching for the right client, and now we'd have to wait and see what developed.

Charles A. Gonzalez, known as Charlie, was born on May 5, 1945, and was the younger son of Congressman Henry B. Gonzalez. He grew up in San Antonio and went to Thomas A. Edison High School. Subsequently, he obtained his undergraduate degree from UT in Austin, and then attended law school at St. Mary's where he received his law degree. Afterwards, he practiced law in San Antonio and began a steady rise in the judicial ranks within Bexar county, advancing from municipal court judge, to county court at law judge, and finally to district court judge. In 1998, when his father chose to retire, Charlie ran for his Dad's congressional seat in the 20th district and got elected. He proudly served as a U.S. Congressman for San Antonio for some fourteen years, from 1999 to 2013. But in 1972, during his senior year in law school at St. Mary's, Charlie was also working as a law clerk at Bexar County Legal Aid (BCLA).

It was late in April, 1972, and Charlie, in pursuit of his law clerk duties, was doing some routine client intake work, when he had the occasion to interview Leonila Nevarez. She was a short, petite woman, in her late thirty's, with short black hair, dark eyes, and a mild-mannered disposition. She was a single mother, who had five children: Larry, 18; Linda, 17; Marina, 16; Rocky, 5; and Daniel, who was barely 1 year old. The family had been receiving food stamp assistance, but recently she was advised by her caseworker that her family was no longer eligible for food stamps. Evidently, their office had been informed that her ex-husband had claimed the two older children as his income tax dependents on his 1971 return, and under their new rules that meant the family would no longer be entitled to receive food stamps. Although the caseworker was somewhat apologetic, she informed Ms. Nevarez that this was the result of a new law and that nothing could be done about it. Upon hearing her story and being aware of my profile memo, Charlie briefly excused himself, took the initiative, and gave me a call. He informed me that he was interviewing a client who appeared to have the kind of food stamp problem that I'd been looking for. With anxious anticipation, I instructed Charlie to make an appointment for her to come in and see me right away, which he did.

On the day of the scheduled appointment, I introduced myself to Ms. Nevarez, welcomed her to my office, and offered her some coffee. I had been given a copy of Charlie's intake sheets and notes, and so I carefully went over and verified the information that he originally obtained during the initial interviewing process. With further questioning, I learned that the family had been really struggling since being tossed from the food stamp rolls. Although the older children attended school as full-time students, all three of them held down part-time jobs in order to earn money so as to help out with family finances. Ms. Nevarez claimed that she also found a job, but when child care for the two younger children became more expensive and when little Daniel got sick and required her care, she had to quit. With an understanding nod, I asked: "Ms. Nevarez, out of curiosity, when your caseworker told you that you were no longer eligible for food stamps, did she make any effort to re-compute the rest of the family's needs, without taking into consideration the two children claimed as tax dependents?" "No Sir, they didn't do that," she responded. "I didn't think so, but I just wanted to be sure," I said. "Can I ask you what made you come to Legal Aid?" I inquired. "I was desperate," she replied. "Without some occasional help from the church, I don't know how we would have made it, and some people at the church suggested that I go to Legal Aid and maybe they could help." I told her that I was glad she came in, and empathetically stated that she wasn't the only one and that lots of other families throughout the nation found themselves in a similar situation. I explained that in my opinion, it was a "bad law" that caused this problem, and that I, together with a group of other Legal Aid lawyers from around the country planned to constitutionally challenge this "bad law." After going over the exigencies that class litigation would entail, I asked her if she would consider being a named plaintiff in our suit, and she willingly accepted. Afterwards, I called Charlie and thanked him.

Later on that evening, I enthusiastically told Marlene that likely we had found the perfect client for our food stamp case. That weekend we had a social event to attend. It was a house party where about twenty some odd couples, all around our age, had gathered for the evening. During the cocktails and hors d'oeuvres I overheard several individuals talking. One of them was ranting about how there were plenty of jobs available, and that a lot of these "welfare people" could work if they really wanted to, but they're all just too lazy. Another commented about how they didn't really need help and weren't starving at all, but were rather "too fat and needed to go on a diet." I was absolutely appalled by these remarks, yet I didn't speak up or challenge them, and to this day I regret it.

Unbelievably, as luck would have it, the following week I received a call from the Guadalupe Street neighborhood office. They had interviewed another woman, Victoria Alderete, whose fact situation closely mirrored that of the Nevarez family. After having conducted a follow-up interview, she also agreed to become a named plaintiff in our lawsuit. In the next few days, I drafted two detailed and well-documented affidavits, each one relating the fact situations pertaining to Ms. Nevarez and Ms. Alderete and their families. These documents were reviewed by the clients, who signed and swore to them, respectively.

Now that we had two strong, viable clients, it was time to contact Henry Freedman to let him know the good news and that Texas definitely would be on board. When I called him, he was most pleased. He asked if I could prepare sworn statements for the two clients and send them to him. I advised him I had already done so and that the statements would be forwarded to him post haste. He informed me that they had picked up the client in Colorado and another one in Washington, and they were working to get one in Hawaii, as well. He told me that I would be sent a draft for review of their initial pleading as soon as it was done.

In June, 1972, I received a copy of the initial pleading. Henry and the folks at the Center had done a masterful job. The petition painted a compelling portrait of how eight different low-income households in six different states: Alabama, Colorado, Hawaii, Iowa, Texas, and Washington, had all been denied food stamps due to the tax dependency provision of the 1971 amendments to the Food Stamp Act. The complaint stated that the plaintiffs, who were poor and who were otherwise clearly eligible for food stamps, like thousands of other indigents, were excluded from health-vital food aid solely because one or more of the people in the household were claimed as "tax dependents." And that under the statute the plaintiffs had no effective right to adduce evidence that the declaration was fraudulent, or that no support was actually paid by the taxpayer; or that the contribution given by the taxpayer was insubstantial.

That evening I mentioned the pleading to Marlene. It was a stunning example of how six different Legal Aid organizations throughout the nation had co-operated with the Center on Social Welfare Policy and Law to put together one hell of a powerful lawsuit, and I was damned proud of the fact that out of the eight named plaintiffs, two of them were our clients.

By July, 1972, all was ready, and the case of *Murry v. USDA* was filed in the D.C. Circuit Court. The local press picked up the story and ran a news column entitled: "Lawyers seek to halt 'Tax Dependent' Rule." Henry was right, and the case was, indeed, fast tracked, and within a relatively short period of time, it was argued before a three-judge court. And finally, on Monday, August 14, 1972, the court reached a unanimous decision in *Murry v. USDA*, 348 F. Supp. 242 (D.C. Cir. Ct. 1972). We had won an overwhelming victory, as the court held the offending statutory provision as being unconstitutional and issued out an injunction against the USDA and the six states prohibiting them from enforcing it.

When I got the word, I picked up a newspaper on the way home, as I had already been clued that the San Antonio press had picked up the story relating to the court's decision. The column headline read: "States Notified Of 'Tax Dependent' Ruling." According to the newspaper account, the court ruled that the statutory provision violated the equal protection clause in that it "creates a classification which denies similar treatment to all persons similarly situated and is … grossly unfair." Noting that Congress had passed the amendment to deny food stamps to young people with access to adequate income, the court said the amendment "wholly missed its target. By creating an irrebuttable presumption contrary to fact, the Amendment classifies households arbitrarily along lines that have no rational relationship to the statutory scheme or the Amendment's apparent purpose … Thus there is both a denial of due process and of equal protection." That evening I shared the news story with Marlene. I was obviously elated that we had won, and I felt gratified that it appeared that the court had picked up some of my verbiage and used it in its opinion.

The following Tuesday morning I verified the newspaper's account, and it was dead on accurate. I went ahead and notified both of our clients, and they were thrilled. I explained that official word would be forthcoming, but it was for sure we had won. Both clients asked if they could now apply for food stamps, and I advised them that since the court did, indeed, issue an injunction, I didn't see any reason why not. In the meantime I was contacted by Jim Dolan, a local news journalist, who was interested in the story and wanted to know if he could interview one of the named plaintiffs. Although we both knew he really didn't need my permission, I told him I appreciated the courtesy heads-up and thanked him, stating I felt that my clients would be happy to be cooperative. After talking with both ladies, I felt that Ms. Nevarez would be more adept at handling such an interview and seemed more willing to do so. Accordingly, I called Jim back and passed on the contact information so as to facilitate his getting in touch with her in order to arrange an interview.

It was Thursday, August 17th, when I got a phone call, from Ms. Alderete first, and then shortly thereafter from Ms. Nevarez. Both ladies informed me that they had been denied food stamps again, supposedly on the same old "tax dependency" grounds. "Oh really," I said in disbelief, as I promised them I would look into the matter further. I immediately began calling certain key food stamp and welfare officials, both at local and state levels, but all to no avail. I got the distinct impression that no one really wanted to talk to me and that I was being stone-walled. I was getting a little angry and rather frustrated, when Jim Dolan called. "What the heck is going on here?" he asked. He had been in touch with Ms. Nevarez, who informed him as to what had happened when she tried to get food stamps again. "I don't know, Jim," I replied. "I've been trying to find out, but so far I haven't had much luck." "Hey, let me give it a try," said Jim, "and maybe we can get to the bottom of it." "Go ahead and good luck," I exclaimed; "They may be more willing to talk to you, as a member of the press, than they are to me, as one of the lawyers who sued them." Meanwhile, after not having had any success in establishing contact, I went ahead and sent out "warning letters" to key local and state food stamp and welfare officials concerning the ramifications of engaging in conduct that would be in violation of the court's injunction. The next day I heard from Jim Dolan again. He related a tale of bureaucratic backlash and ineptitude that neither of us could hardly believe. "I'm doing a whole piece on this," said Jim, "and you'll be able to read all about it."

That Friday, Jim Dolan's news story appeared in the paper, with a huge headline that blared out: "**Red Tape keeps 2 S.A. families hungry**," together with a rather moving picture showing Ms. Nevarez holding one year old Daniel, while a pensive five year old Rocky stood nearby longingly looking up at his mother. In his column, Jim managed to capture the feeling of utter frustration and put into words the most scathing indictment of officialdom and the system that I had ever seen in a news story on the subject matter up to that time. After narrating the history of the food stamp amendment, relating the personal situations of the Alderete and Nevarez families, and reporting our favorable court decision, Jim quoted my sarcastic remark as having said: "This is a prime example of bureaucracy at its best," and then Jim went on to state:

So when the court decision came, things were all right. Or so Eichelbaum and the families thought.

THEY THOUGHT A permanent injunction issued against Texas and five other states would be enough to get the Alderetes and the Nevarez' back on food stamps. They were wrong.

They thought the state welfare officials would obey the court order. They were wrong.

And they even thought the federal government would take the trouble to notify concerned officials of the ruling. They were wrong.

The upshot of all this is the families still haven't been allowed on food stamp rolls. Mrs. Nevarez, for instance, was again turned away Thursday morning at the food stamp center at 214 S. Alamo St. and her family was still hungry.

LOCAL WELFARE WORKER Mrs. Judy Post referred the applicant to her superior because there was no authorization allowing Mrs. Nevarez back on food stamp rolls.

She went to Hector Saenz, regional food stamp director, who refused and pointed towards his superiors.

The next man up the ladder, Raymond Cheves, conferred with his bosses by telephone and again passed the buck upward.

William Herndon in Austin, chief of the commodities and distribution division, said he had learned of the court ruling by federal teletype Wednesday. Written instructions for field offices was being prepared and would be mailed in a few days, he said.

HE WAS TOLD the families in San Antonio were hungry at that time. Couldn't oral permission be given in this one case since written instructions would be issued next week?

'Absolutely not. Somebody higher might be able to do it. Not me,' he declared.

State Welfare Com. Raymond Vowell said the same thing. 'I'm sorry you think we're inhuman,' he told a newsman, 'but things have to be written. We don't enforce things by telephone.'

Gov. Preston Smith couldn't be reached but an aid promised to 'look into all this and call you back.'

So that's where things stood Friday. The five-month gap in food stamps was about to end for the Nevarez' and Alderetes.

But it wouldn't end until welfare officials had 'rewritten the manuals that spell out operations,' as Vowell put it. And neither official inquiry nor federal court order seemed able to speed up the process and avoid one last hungry weekend for the families.

That evening I shared Jim Dolan's newspaper story with Marlene. "Wow, that's quite an article. I can't believe they wouldn't do anything, even though there's a court injunction," she remarked. "Yeah, I agree," I said. "Well, what do you plan to do about it?" she asked. "I've already sent them a warning letter, and they better comply pronto. If they think I'm going to let another weekend slide by with those families being under the hunger

{ 281

gun, then they've got another thing coming. There is nothing I'd rather do than to haul Vowell and that whole gang into federal court on an enforcement action. But I bet it won't come to that and by next week they'll come to their senses and comply," I predicted. The following Monday I called Jim Dolan and complimented him on his hard-hitting news story. He thanked me and asked if I thought they would appeal, commenting that perhaps they believed they could get out from under the injunction by appealing. "They shouldn't bother appealing, but they're likely to do so," I surmised. "But I've got to tell you that even if they do, odds are that injunction will stay in place pending appeal. And Jim, if they do appeal, I'll bet you they're going to lose," I stated.

I was right on both bets. Before the end of the week, the food stamp and welfare officials relented, and both families received their food stamps and were put back on the rolls. The defendants did, indeed, waste the taxpayers' money and processed an appeal to the U.S. Supreme Court. The case of *USDA v. Murry*, No. 72-848, was argued on April 23, 1973, and by June 25, 1973, the U.S. Supreme Court reached a decision that upheld the lower court's opinion and injunction, *USDA v. Murry*, 413 U.S. 508 (1973). The defendants had, indeed, lost, and the families had won.

Unfortunately, the fight isn't over yet. Far too many poverty and hunger issues are still prevalent in America to this day. According to statistics of the San Antonio Food Bank, a valuable program that aids in fighting hunger in the city and fifteen surrounding counties, one out of every five adults go to bed each night not knowing whether or not they will be able to eat the next day. That's one-fifth of our area's adult population. It is even more drastic when it comes to children, where the ratio is one out of every four. In my later years when I retired from practicing law, Marlene and I taught religious school on Sundays at Temple Beth-El. As part of the concept of "Tikkun Olam" (making the world a better place) and with the cooperation and assistance of a representative from the San Antonio Food Bank, we taught our second graders about hunger issues. We wanted them to be aware that these issues were serious and real, and what we could do to help.

We wanted them to learn how there can be a connection between poverty and obesity, as poor people can't always get to grocery stores and markets where healthy fruits and vegetables are sold, because poverty communities are often located in what is known as "food deserts" – areas in which there is a drastic absence of the purveyors of healthy foods, who have chosen to locate their operations in the more opulent neighborhoods. And we wanted them to know how poor people often have no other choice but to satisfy themselves with high calorie processed foods, because nothing else is available or affordable to them. We didn't want our students growing up callous and uninformed like the adults who I overheard making inappropriate comments about "lazy fat poor people" at that house party I attended many years ago.

CHAPTER 19

A Child's a Child, No Matter How Born

1969 – 1973

***Gomez v. Perez*, Case No. 71-575, 409 U.S. 535 (1973)**

In 1967, I was in my senior year of law school. During the spring semester, I was enrolled in a Family Law class that was being taught by Father Robert Drinan. He was the Dean of the Boston College Law School and that year was a visiting professor teaching at the law school at UT in Austin. He was a masterful teacher, and I thoroughly enjoyed his energetic and up-beat teaching style, not to mention my getting a kick out of his Bostonian accent. One day in class while discussing marriage dissolution, a student asked about the extent of the responsibilities of the parties (both husband and wife) to support the children of the marriage, even after the marriage ended. We learned that Texas imposed a positive legal duty on the parents, requiring them to support the children of the marriage and that this could be enforced from both a civil and criminal law perspective. Then another student asked a follow-up question as to what would be the case if the man and the woman weren't married, and the child was born out of wedlock. "Oh a bastard situation, in other words the child is illegitimate," Father Drinan commented. "Well, in that case, under Texas law, the father would have absolutely no legal duty to support that child whatsoever; rather the duty to support would rest solely upon the mother," he added. When someone asked why this was so, he informed the class that this was only true in the states of Texas and Wyoming, and then quipped that it probably had something to do with the "cowboy culture" in those two states. As I had already completed my Constitutional Law class in my first year of law school, I felt that this was rather discriminatory and somewhat weird, and I made a mental note of this legal oddity.

In August, 1969, with the departure of Lonnie Duke that month, on August 8th Christian designated Harry Adams and me as his top two attorneys to be in charge of all of the law reform cases. He instructed us to come up with a list of the current cases of that nature already in process, as well as some prospective cases in which we felt we should be involved. The following Friday, August 15th, Harry and I agreed to meet after work at one of his familiar bars to discuss Christian's list while having a couple of drinks, relaxing and letting the traffic subside a bit before going home.

I got to the bar first, and as I entered the dimly lit, somewhat smoky atmosphere, I was immersed in the ambient sounds of western music coming from the jukebox intermingled with a mixture of laughter and occasionally vacuous voices coming from among the patrons. I spotted an empty table in the far corner and grabbed it. The air was a bit clearer there, and I knew Harry would appreciate it as his eyes tended to be rather sensitive to smoke. On the wall, above the table was a Lone Star Beer sign from which some light emanated making the area just a wee bit brighter. Placing my legal pad folder that I had brought on the table, I took off my coat and slung it across the back of the chair, then unbuttoned my shirt collar and stripped off my tie, folding it neatly and placing it into the right-hand side coat pocket. I sat down facing the doorway and waited for Harry to arrive.

A waitress came by and asked what I'd be having. I ordered a Tecate beer and explained that I was waiting for a friend to join me who would likely be ordering one too. She smiled, nodded, and whisked away. Within minutes she had brought me an ice cold Tecate with several slices of lime.

Just the way Harry likes it, I thought. "When your friend comes, just give me a high sign, and I'll be right over," she said. I thanked her, took a couple of sips of my drink, and began to relax. A few minutes later I spotted Harry coming through the doorway and motioned him over. We greeted each other, and he immediately ditched his coat and tie, as I signaled the waitress. "I see you started without me," said Harry. "Yeah, it's been quite a week, and besides I figured you'll catch up," I replied. The waitress appeared, Harry ordered his usual, and in moments he had his Tecate and lime slices.

After some small talk, I opened up my legal pad folder and suggested it was time to get down to Christian's list. We started with *Gaytan v. Cassidy* (the Texas driver's license case), as we were already working together on that one. To that Harry listed a pet consumer law prospect that he was pushing, and I easily added four welfare law matters, some of which we were presently doing and others getting set to do. "Okay, there's our list," I said pointing to my legal pad where I had noted the six items. Harry gazed at it and commented: "Yeah, but it's not very well balanced. We've got four in the welfare law group and only two in the non-welfare law category. We ought to add another one there so as to create more balance. And besides seven is a luckier number," he added. At times Harry could have a superstitious nature, and I decided to appease it, as we began to rack our brains as to what the last additional item should be.

Suddenly the light lit, as I remembered that day in Father Drinan's class, a couple of years ago. "I've got a wild hare," I exclaimed, what if we go after the Texas child support laws for the way they discriminate against illegitimate children?" As I further explained the idea, I could see a gleam in Harry's eyes. The more we talked about it, the more enthusiastic we became. "Alright, that's it," said Harry, as I penned that item as number seven on our list.

The following week Harry arranged for the list to be typed in final form and got it to Christian. In the meantime, I prepared a "be on the lookout" letter that outlined the type of client and fact scenario we'd be looking for concerning the illegitimate child situation, which I circulated to all of the field offices. Now we would have to patiently wait, and I thought it might be quite some time before we discovered just the right client. But fate proved the opposite to be true. It was shortly after Labor Day when I got a call from Royal Griffin, who was one of the attorneys working at the Gen. McMullen Street office. "Hey Mel, I think I found the client that you and Harry have been looking for," he declared, and after a brief discussion, it appeared that he might be right. An interview appointment was forthrightly made so that Harry and I could meet this individual.

On the morning of the scheduled appointment, I picked up Harry, and we drove to the Gen. McMullen Street office, where we were welcomed by the two attorneys there, Don McManus and Royal Griffin. An office was made available for our use, and Royal referred to us as Bexar County Legal Aid's top two attorneys who had come to speak with her, as he introduced us to Linda Gomez. She was a fairly attractive Latina woman in her mid-twenties, with a pleasant personality, who asked us to please call her Linda. She was single and had recently become a young mother, having just a few months ago, given birth to a little girl, Zoraida Gomez, on June 13, 1969. She had come to Legal Aid because she was searching for a way to get some child support from the father of the child. "Linda, we're going to have to ask you some questions, some of which might seem to be embarrassing, but we need to accurately ascertain the facts here in order to see if we can help you with your situation," I explained. "Is that okay?" I asked. She nodded in agreement and so the interrogation began.

"So who's the father?' asked Harry. "Francisco Perez," she answered. "And how can you be sure of that?" Harry pressed. Linda slightly flinched, then composed herself and explained that he would be the only possibility, as he was the only one she had any sexual relations with during that time. "So how did you meet this guy?" I asked, and she related that they had met at a party given by mutual friends back in June, 1968. She was single and unattached. And he told her that he was too. They became instantly attracted to one another, and shortly thereafter began an intimate relationship. "And I take it that the sexual relationship was mutually consensual?"

I asked. "Oh yes Sir," she replied. "Okay, Linda and you're absolutely certain that you weren't having sex with anyone else at that time?" I emphasized, as I intensely looked her in her eyes. "That's right Sir, he was the only one," she adamantly insisted. "Would you be willing to take a lie detector test regarding that?" Harry inquired, and without any hesitation she said she would. Harry and I both knew that lie detector test results were not admissible as evidence in a courtroom proceeding. But Harry asked the question just so we could gage her reaction. "Okay, was there ever any talk of marriage?" I asked. "No, not specifically," she said. "Of course, I had some hopes and aspirations, but although we talked in general terms as to how we felt about marriage, there was nothing specific," she added. "So, let me get this straight," I said. "He never promised to marry you or even intimated that he intended to do so. Am I right about that?" I asked. "Yes Sir, that's correct," she answered. "And so I take it, there was never any time where he introduced you or referred to you as his wife, or where you introduced him or referred to him as your husband, either seriously or even just in jest—is that correct?" Harry continued. "That's right Sir," she affirmed.

With further questioning we learned that the alleged father's full name was Francisco Ocasio Perez, and that he was in the military and stationed at Fort Hood in Killeen, Texas. "Hey Linda, you wouldn't happen to have a picture of this guy—would you?" I asked. "Yes Sir, I do," she answered, and quickly rummaging through her purse, she brought forth a photograph and handed it to me. "So this is the guy?" I inquired. "Yes Sir," she acknowledged. "Can I borrow this?" I asked. "We might need it later, and I promise I'll get it back to you," I assured her. "Yes Sir, of course," Linda agreed. She went on to relate that she had contacted the military and tried to get them to help her, but after having been given what she perceived to be a never ending run around, she finally gave up. She next went to the Bexar County District Attorney's office, but she was told by their Child Support Section that under her situation, there was nothing they could do for her. So then, as a last desperate hope, she came here. "So what's the deal? Can you help me?" Linda pleadingly asked. Then followed an explanatory conversation during which Harry and I advised her that it appeared it was fairly evident there was no common law marriage. That being the case, then the child was born out of wedlock, and so would be deemed to be an illegitimate child. Therefore, under current Texas law, the father would have no legal duty or obligation whatsoever to support that child. Seeing the look of disappointed acceptance on Linda's face, I said: "Look, there just might be an outside chance that we may be able to do something. So let's not give up hope just yet." We then explained that we'd like to do some additional research and look into the matter further, and we promised we would get back to her.

On the drive back to the downtown office, Harry and I discussed our meeting with Linda. "So what do you think? You think she's telling it straight?" I asked. "Oh hell yes, there's no doubt in my mind," replied Harry. "I agree," I said in affirmation. "I think Royal found us just about the perfect client," I commented. "So from what she says, what do you think of the father?" I inquired. "Oh he's no father: he's just a sperm donor," quipped Harry. "Yeah, that might be, but he helped make the kid, and I think he should help support it," I asserted. "Well, the first step is we're going to have to prove paternity, and that's not going to be easy. If he comes in and swears he never touched her, then we could end up with a classic "he said—she said," and it's liable to get a bit testy," Harry stated. This was in the days when DNA testing was not yet readily available for paternity testing, nor had it yet achieved wide-spread scientific reliability and judicial acceptance. So I realized Harry's observation was correct, and that our first major hurdle would be to establish that Perez was, indeed, the father of the child.

Once back downtown, Harry and I headed over to the Bexar County Courthouse law library to do some initial research in order to confirm the status of the Texas law. We discovered the Texas Supreme Court case of *Lane v. Phillips*, 6 S.W. 610 (1887), in which the court, citing the Common Law of England in construing the Texas family law statutory provisions, held that the father of an illegitimate child has no legal duty or obligation to support that child as he would if the child had been "begotten in wedlock."

As it turned out, this 1887 case was the leading civil law case on the matter, and its holding was still controlling and considered to be good law in the state of Texas. We also located the Texas Court of Criminal Appeals case of *Beaver v. State*, 256 S.W. 929 (1929), in which that court reversed a conviction of a father charged with deserting, neglecting, and refusing to provide for the support and maintenance of his illegitimate child, holding that the word "child" as referred to in the Articles of the Texas Penal Code pertaining to such matters refers to legitimate children only. Hence, it was pretty clear that both from a civil law and a criminal law standpoint, Texas outright discriminated against illegitimate children and had been engaging in this "legal discriminatory conduct" for some eighty years.

The rest of the week rolled by, as Harry and I caught up on other matters. But by late Friday afternoon, it was like déjà vu, as Harry and I returned to the very same bar and occupied the same table, and while downing some more Tecate beers, sat scheming away as we further discussed Linda's case. "Okay, let's assume we can successfully establish paternity and have Perez declared to be the father, the way I see it, the discriminatory dichotomy between legitimate and illegitimate children couldn't be clearer—it will be a straight head-on equal protection attack," I proposed. "Yeah, but I have a hunch this will be a tough one. We're not going to have the advantage of having a back-up statutory argument under the Social Security Act like we had in the welfare cases, and to add to it, I don't see much of a substantive due process argument either—do you?" Harry commented. "You're right, of course. As to a substantive due process argument, well maybe a little but not much, so like I said, it's going to be an equal protection argument all the way," I repeated.

"So how do you want to play this one—federal or state?" I inquired. Harry briefly pondered the point and said: "I'm afraid that if we go federal, seeking a three-judge court with a direct constitutional attack, and we neglect to give the state courts a chance to resolve the matter first, then we'd run the risk of the federal court invoking the abstention doctrine and dismissing our federal lawsuit and throwing it back to the state court. And then all that time would be wasted, and it would be like starting all over again," Harry postulated. "Yeah, and add to that we have to prove paternity and that will be viewed as a family law matter, which traditionally has always been within the province of the state courts. I agree, we have to go the state court route. I don't think we realistically have any other choice," I concluded.

Okay, so we start in state district court, and let's say we win on the paternity issue, we'll still lose the case on the child support issue—as a matter of law," predicted Harry. "That's right, and so from there we'll appeal to the Fourth Court of Civil Appeals on equal protection grounds, where we will lose again. And from there, we'll appeal to the Texas Supreme Court, with the same result," I asserted. "And so from there we appeal and take it to the U.S. Supreme Court," Harry added. "Yep, that's exactly where I think this baby will have to end up. I truly believe that's going to be the whole ballgame—getting the U.S. Supreme Court to accept and hear this case. Damn it Harry, if we can somehow convince them to take this case, I feel we can win this thing up there," I surmised. "Yeah, I agree, but the big battle will be getting them to hear it in the first place, and of course the odds will be against us," said Harry. We both were acutely aware that the U.S. Supreme Court accepted only a tiny percentage of appeals presented to it. "We need some kind of a hook—somehow we need to come up with a concept that would show a wider societal impact, going beyond just the adverse discriminatory effect against the group of illegitimate children, even though that really ought to be enough in itself," Harry hypothesized.

I momentarily puzzled with the thought, as I took another swig of my drink, and then it came to me. "Wait a minute, suppose, just suppose, we could use a welfare law argument here after all," I exclaimed. Harry looked at me rather quizzically; as I went on to explain. "How many kids on the AFDC rolls do you think are illegitimate?" I asked. "I have no idea," said Harry, as his eyes began to light up and a smile broke across his face. "Well, I'll bet it's over 20%," I predicted. "Let's say we could somehow develop statistics through the Texas Department of Public Welfare (DPW) that would show a significant number of children on the welfare rolls are illegitimate. We should be able to do an economic projection as to what it costs. To the extent that Texas fathers are not legally required to support these kids, then the Texas taxpayers have to pick up that tab instead through increased welfare expenditures. So if the law didn't discriminate against illegitimate kids, we could argue it would save a ton of money in welfare," I concluded. "Oh, I love it—talk about using a conservative argument to advance a liberal cause. That's exactly the hook we need," Harry stated. "Do you think you can work with DPW, and we'd have a realistic chance in doing this?" he asked. "I don't know, but I sure as hell would like to try," I replied. "So, for argument's sake, let's say we can do it, procedurally how would we get the welfare statistical info before the Supreme Court?" I inquired. "What if we did a "Brandeis brief" and included it as part of our Appendix in our Jurisdictional Statement?" propositioned Harry. "I like that," I pronounced. "So, we're all in on this one," I concluded, and we shook hands, as we wrapped up our plotting session. "We're all in," Harry echoed. As we parted, he mentioned: "I'll talk to Christian, and you talk to the client."

In the following week, Harry secured Christian's final blessing, and I spoke with Linda. I informed her that we had done the further research that we promised, and confirmed that the status of the law was virtually what we had previously indicated to her at our last meeting. I summarized my discussions with Harry and the conclusions we had reached. "So here is the deal, Linda. We are going to take your case, but you have to realize this will be a long shot. It's going to be a lengthy process that will take years. And I'm telling you we're going to lose in the trial court, and we'll likely continue to lose all the way up the Texas appellate court ladder. So you're going to have to be patient, not give up hope, and keep your eye on the prize. The object is to get this case before the U.S. Supreme Court. And once there, then I believe we've got a shot at hitting a home run. So what do you think?" I asked. Linda thankfully agreed, and when I explained that once we got started, she couldn't get discouraged, and I made her promise that she would stick it out to the end, and she swore that she would.

By mid-September, Harry and I had drafted a straight to the point and concise original petition. Aside from the introductory portion naming the parties and the concluding prayer for relief, the entire pleading consisted of only three short paragraphs and was just two pages long. In short, we sought to establish paternity and have Perez judicially declared as the father of the child. We claimed that the child was in need of support and contended that despite the fact she was illegitimate, as the father, Perez should be required to pay reasonable child support, which we alleged to be $50.00 per week. Harry arranged for the pleading to be typed in final form, signed it, and late in the afternoon of Thursday, September 18, 1969, case No. F-215903, *LINDA GOMEZ, individually and as next friend of ZORAIDA GOMEZ vs. FRANCISCO OCASIO PEREZ* was filed in the 150th District Court for Bexar County, Texas. It was just before closing time when the phone rang at the E. Houston Street office, and it was Harry, letting me know the case was filed. As I drove home, I felt a moment of excitement. From the beginning, I had a hunch that this was going to be a major case destined to go all the way, and I was glad we had finally gotten started. Once home, I informed Marlene that we had filed the case. "Looks like we're going to be pushing another case toward the U.S. Supreme Court," I announced.

The following Friday I notified Linda that we were filed and explained that the next hurdle would be getting the defendant served with process. At that time, I had no idea just what an obstacle that would turn out to be. Linda had told us that Perez, the defendant, was a sergeant and stationed at Fort Hood in Killeen, Texas, so that's what was alleged in the pleading. And when Harry filed the case, since the defendant wasn't living in Bexar County, he arranged for out-of-county process, and the citation, along with the service copy of the lawsuit papers, were sent to the sheriff's office in Belton, Texas, which was the county seat of Bell County, and approximately twenty miles from the town of Killeen and Fort Hood.

However, Fort Hood was a major training facility for the U.S. Army and is one of the largest military bases in the world. It spanned 218,000 acres and traversed the borders of two counties in Texas, with the southwestern portion being in Bell County, adjacent to the town of Killeen, and the predominant southeastern part being in Coryell County, which was where the U.S. Army HQ was located. We realized that since the defendant was in the military and on post that service of process might take longer. Add to it the phenomenon that sheriffs were elected, and when they served in more rural and less populated counties, sometimes there was a tendency to put the out-of-county citations coming from the "big city" at the bottom of the stack, giving a "home boy" preference to their in-county citations that needed to be served. So that being the situation, we adopted a rather patient attitude initially.

But with the passage of Halloween, we began to get concerned. It had been about a month and a half, and we hadn't heard a word. When Harry called the Bell County sheriff's office, they gave him some static about how they were having some difficulties with respect to getting on base to serve the defendant. In addition, they stated that maybe we should have sent the papers to the sheriff's office in Gatesville instead of them, as that was the county seat for Coryell County, which comprised the larger portion of the base and was the county in which the U.S. Army HQ was located. After some discussion they advised Harry they'd make another effort and to give them a couple of more weeks. I had been keeping Linda posted and could sense her feeling of frustration, which matched mine, as well.

So when the week of Thanksgiving arrived, and we still hadn't heard anything, I suggested that perhaps it was time to involve our private investigator, Joe Padilla. Any good lawyer knows the value of an experienced and reliable investigator, and Joe was one of the best. Harry and I met with him, giving him the low-down on the problems we were having in getting Perez served. During our conversation, Joe asked if, by chance, we had a picture of Perez. I pulled out my file and took out the photo I had clipped there and which I had secured from Linda at our initial interview. "I had a hunch this might come in handy," I stated, as I handed it over to Joe. It was decided that Joe would take a reconnaissance trip to the Fort Hood area and ascertain what was going on.

Once there and after doing some digging, Joe was able to confirm that Perez was indeed a sergeant stationed at Fort Hood. He informed us that the military authorities had not been exactly cooperative, but that the Bell County sheriff's office hadn't made that much of an effort either, as they thought we should have sent the papers to the Coryell County sheriff's office rather than to them. Harry feared that we might have to change and re-issue process, but Joe told him to hold up for a while and that he wanted to do a little more snooping around in the town of Killeen.

By now it was mid-December, and Joe had made another trip up there. In the latter part of the week Joe reported back. He had discovered that Perez was married to another woman. Indeed he had been married all along. He and his wife had a house in Killeen. Joe's idea was that rather than attempt to serve him on post, it would be better to try to catch him at home, and probably the best time to do that would be right around the Christmas holidays, which were coming up. Joe said he had established a rapport with a couple of the deputies at the Bell County sheriff's office and had coordinated this plan with them.

My Mom often repeated the saying of "the third time is a charm," and I felt that it just might be, as Joe was dispatched for the third time right after Christmas Day. And that weekend, accompanied by Joe, the Bell County sheriff's deputies successfully served Perez at his house in Killeen. Early the following week, right before New Year's Eve, I contacted Linda. "I've got a belated Christmas present for you," I announced. "We finally got Perez served," I reported, as I heard her break into a sigh and say: "thank God." It was going to be a Happy New Year's after all, I thought.

It was January, 1970, and Harry and I were waiting to see if Perez would file an answer in our lawsuit or just do nothing and allow the default time to simply expire. But toward the end of that January, Perez had, indeed, filed an answer, which consisted of a general denial and a plea in abatement, asserting "that no cause of action exists either by statutory or common law in Texas for the support of a minor child born out of wedlock." By answering, Perez had entered an appearance and locked himself into our lawsuit, and now we definitely had him in our case. And even though his plea of abatement correctly stated the Texas law, it clearly set up the exact constitutional confrontation at which our equal protection attack would be directed and that was just what we had wanted.

We scheduled a trial setting and notified the defendant by certified mail, return receipt requested so we could prove he received notice. The Friday before, as we prepped for trial, we agreed Harry would handle first chair in conducting the trial, while I would take second chair and serve as back-up. We debated whether Perez would actually show up and fight us on the paternity issue, or be a "no show" and merely rest on his laurels that under Texas law he would end up winning regardless. And we concluded the latter was more likely. For once the law that was so much against us might actually work in our favor. If Perez believed that there was really no need for him to bother to come and hassle on the paternity issue, because regardless he would win on the support issue, as a matter of law, and so then by failing to show up at all, it just might make proving our contention of paternity a bit less risky.

On Monday morning, March 23, 1970, the day of trial, Harry and I, together with Linda Gomez, were at the presiding district courtroom at the Bexar County Courthouse for docket call. When Judge Sol Caseb, who was presiding, called the case, Harry announced that plaintiffs were ready to proceed. There was no announcement from the defendant. As we predicted and hoped, Perez had not bothered to show up. We were instructed to pick up the court file and report to the 45th District Court where Judge Robert Murray sat. When we arrived there we handed the court file to the clerk who passed it over to the judge, who then reviewed it. Before we began, the judge called us to the bench for a preliminary discussion as to our proceeding. Harry gave him a brief synopsis of our case and that our presentation wouldn't take more than twenty minutes.

Linda Gomez was called to the witness stand, sworn under oath, and testified, telling her story and convincingly stating that Perez was for sure the father of the child, and how it couldn't possibly have been anyone else. With careful questioning Harry brought out that although there was an obvious need for support that factually there was no common law marriage, and that the child was, indeed, born out of wedlock. We were under no illusion, and we fully well expected that a trial court judge was not going to declare an eighty year old statutory scheme as being unconstitutional, and so Harry concluded with a very brief equal protection argument just so as to get it on the record. We anticipated we would lose, and we weren't wrong. Although Judge Murray gave us the factual findings that we were after, his legal conclusion and holding was in favor of the defendant. We gave notice of appeal of course, and the judge instructed us to bring him a judgment.

Contrary to belief on the part of most of the public, judges typically do not draft their own judgments that they sign. Rather, the lawyers do that. Harry and I were elated that we got positive findings of fact on the issues of paternity and the need for support. It was hard to explain to Linda why we were so happy, even though we had lost. I reminded her that I had told her that we would lose initially and how she would have to be patient and not give up hope while we ran this case up the appellate ladder. "You know Linda, sometimes you win, even when you lose. We got exactly what we needed to set up our appeal," I asserted. Linda said she understood and trusted us.

In the next couple of weeks Harry and I worked on drafting the judgment, carefully including the court's findings that Perez was the father of the child, that he wasn't married to Linda Gomez, not even by common law, and that the child, who was in need of support, was born out of wedlock. We concluded with: "The Court further finds there is no civil liability on the part of the father to support an illegitimate child." No one really blamed Judge Murray for his ruling, and in the future when by happenstance I encountered him in the courthouse, he always greeted me and asked how our appeal was going, stating that this was one case he wouldn't mind being overruled on.

All the time this was in process, I had called a couple of my friendly contacts within the Texas Department of Public Welfare (DPW) and sought their input on how it would be best to get word to Burton G. Hackney, the head of DPW, about a matter that might be of significant mutual benefit to both of our organizations. Accordingly, I put out feelers of my wanting to meet with Hackney to discuss that. Although no doubt initially my offers were viewed rather suspiciously and tenuously, I persisted in my entreaties, and finally I suppose their curiosity got the best of them, and a meeting was scheduled.

By April 23, 1970, we had completed our draft of the final judgment, and Harry took it to the judge and got it signed. I secured several conformed copies of the judgment, and along with my case file and a legal pad, threw them into my briefcase. Before the end of April, early in the morning of my meeting, I grabbed my briefcase, together with a thermos cup of coffee, and headed off to Austin. Having spent my law school years working part-time as a Legislative Assistant, I was fairly familiar with the various state offices, which were located in a number of the governmental structures that were situated on the north side of the Capitol Building, and so I had no trouble in finding the DPW offices. When I arrived I announced myself, and I was ushered into a conference room, and there, for the first time, I met person-to-person, Burton G. Hackney, DPW's head guy. Joining him were Raymond Cheves, a DPW higher-up, who I had previously dealt with on various occasions, and several others of the DPW hierarchy, who I had not met before. Also there was Pat Bailey, an Assistant Attorney General, with whom I was familiar due to my having handled a number of previous welfare law reform cases, where we opposed one another. I felt a little like Daniel going into the lions' den.

After introductions we sat down and I described our involvement in the *Gomez v. Perez* case. As I passed out and circulated copies of the judgment, I explained that although we had initially lost the case, that we had already given notice of appeal and intended to aggressively appeal the case on equal protection grounds. "Listen, I know you pretty much view me as the enemy because we've knocked heads against one another on a number of major welfare cases in the past," I stated. "But this time it's different. We are advocating for the illegitimate kids here, and for once our interests might be very much aligned and compatible. We might have a situation here where we could mutually benefit if we cooperated for a change," I continued. "Mr. Hackney, how many kids on the AFDC rolls are illegitimate?" I asked. Everyone kind of shockingly looked at each other, and then one of the DPW staff individuals stated that in November, 1967, an AFDC study had been made and it showed that 23.8% of the children on the rolls were illegitimate. "Okay, that's what I thought," I said. "Now since then do you think that figure has increased, decreased, or stayed the same?" I asked. No one really knew, but most guessed the number would have increased. "Is there any way we could document that for the year preceding this judgment—like say from May, 1969, through April, 1970?" I inquired. Again I saw puzzled looks, until another staff person stated that they should be able to statistically glean that information from the number of children with the code for an unmarried parent entered on their forms I-A and I-B. "Okay, for argument's sake, let's say that the figure turns out to be 25%, just how much money would DPW save if we were successful in changing the Texas law to where fathers had to support their illegitimate children?" I submitted. It was as if the lights lit up, and I saw the change of expression on Mr. Hackney's face. "Potentially, we'd be talking millions here," he declared. "Millions," he emphatically repeated, as he looked at the others in the room.

"So what do you think, Mr. Hackney? Can we cooperate in this instance?" I proposed. The response was universally positive, and one could feel the excitement in the room. The rest of the discussion involved how long it would take DPW to develop the statistics, and Mr. Hackney made it clear that he wanted it done expeditiously as a top priority. We talked about what would be the technical and procedurally appropriate way to make our official inquiry. I even suggested that perhaps Mr. Hackney might even want to consider asking the Texas Attorney General to write an amicus curiae brief in our favor, at which point Pat Bailey chirped in, stating that such a request needed to come from Mr. Adams, and not me. That if the Attorney General, Crawford Martin, saw my name attached to or connected with such a request, it would be like waving a red flag in front of a bull. Obviously, he wasn't a fan of mine due to my previous welfare cases. Understanding the politics of the matter, I agreed that Harry's name would be used on all communications while I stayed quietly in the background. Crawford Martin need not know of my involvement as of yet. It was a friendly atmosphere when we parted, and Hackney and I viewed our relationship differently from that day forward. It was like old enemies all of a sudden became allies.

When I returned from Austin, I informed Harry of my meeting and advised him that it appeared DPW might be cooperative with regard to providing us with statistics as to poor illegitimate children. We immediately followed-up by executing the plan developed at my meeting. Harry called Miss Lane, which was our official designated contact within DPW, and a formal request letter seeking the statistical information and even asking DPW to consider requesting an amicus was signed by Harry and sent out. In the meantime, Harry and I worked on our appellate brief on *Gomez v. Perez*, which now stood as case No. 14917 before the Court of Civil Appeals for the Fourth Supreme Judicial District of Texas.

It was Tuesday morning, May 26, 1970, and I was busily at work at the E. Houston Street office, playing a constant keep-up game with my routine cases, when Harry called. "Do you have any plans for lunch?" he asked. "No, not really," I said. "Fine, meet me at Mi Tiera at noon. There's something we've got to discuss, and I want to kick it around with you," he resolutely stated. When I tried to get him to give me a hint as to what it was all about, he said that he'd see me there and we'd talk then and that he had to go, as he abruptly hung up.

I arrived right around noon, and as usual Mi Tiera was crowded, but I managed to find Harry sitting at a table he had procured. "So what's going on? What's the big emergency?' I asked, as I sat down and joined him. "You better read this," he demanded with a serious scowl on his face, as he handed me a letter, which I spotted as having the official seal of the state of Texas on it. I apprehensively glanced at the letter and began reading it. The letter was dated May 21, 1970, was addressed to Harry, and was from Burton G. Hackney, Commissioner of the Texas Department of Public Welfare (DPW). It detailed that DPW had completed their statistical compilation and that since the major AFDC study which was done in November, 1967, which showed illegitimate children to be 23.8% of the AFDC rolls, effective as of March, 1970, the number of illegitimate children on AFDC had risen to 28.8%, an increase of 5%. In addition, an attached second page gave a monthly breakdown of those figures and their connected cost factors over a year's period of time, from May, 1969, through April, 1970, just as I had asked for at my meeting with Hackney. "Wow, this makes the illegitimate factor even larger than what I had originally supposed," I said, as I looked up and saw Harry smile. "This is exactly the statistical information we wanted and were hoping for, and it's all documented to boot," I commented. "I know," Harry chuckled. The practical joking nature of Harry had gotten me again. "Wait, it gets better," he said as he whipped out and handed me another paper. It was dated May 20, 1970, and was a copy of a letter from Commissioner Hackney directed to Crawford C. Martin, Attorney General for the State of Texas. The letter noted that illegitimate children were a significant part of the AFDC rolls and that our case could potentially have such a major impact on welfare expenditures; therefore, Hackney requested the Attorney General to write an amicus curiae brief on behalf of DPW and in our favor with respect to our appeal.

"Good grief, you got a state agency siding with us and asking the AG's office to write a brief in our favor—how in the hell did you ever manage to do that?" Harry exclaimed. I sheepishly grinned and said: "Well, you know they're not really going to do that. We're attacking the Texas statutory child support law, and if anything, the AG's office will be in opposition to us and filing a brief against us." "Yeah, I know that, and you know that, but by using our Brandeis brief method, we're still going to be able to get this letter before the appellate court, showing that the state welfare agency actually agrees with us and is on our side—good work, guy—damn good job," declared Harry.

After lunch we went back to Harry's office downtown and did some further work on our brief, we incorporated Hackney's letters and statistics into the Appendix section. I did some calculations and wrote a paragraph right before our brief's conclusion, which stated: "Taking Commissioner Hackney's figures to their logical conclusion, the taxpayers of the state of Texas spent $22,854,348.00 per year for the support of illegitimate children." "What do you think? Is that a big enough hook?" I asked Harry. "Hell yes!" he responded, affirmatively nodding his head. Having completed and filed our brief before the Fourth Court of Civil Appeals, we waited for the setting of oral argument, which came soon enough. In preparing for it, we decided that Harry would go first, presenting the summary of facts and legal history and then launch into a hard-hitting equal protection attack. I would conclude, winding up our equal protection argument and presenting the welfare implications of this case.

On the day of our oral argument before the 4th Court of Civil Appeals, I was unbelievably calm and relaxed. Perhaps it was because I already knew what the outcome would be. We were going to lose. As the three judges waltzed out and seated themselves at the bench, I was fully aware of their tendencies. When you're friendly with the court clerks and converse with the ordinary working people at the courthouse, you can learn a lot about the judges and what's happening in the courthouse world. I had already done my homework on our judicial panel and had a good feel for where their predispositions were. Seated in the middle and presiding was Justice Fred V. Klingeman, conservative to the core, and there was no way he was ever going to declare the Texas law as being unconstitutional. Seated to his right was a Justice whose name I have since forgotten, but I remember him as being a Klingeman clone, and so before we even got started, I knew for sure we had at least two out of three votes against us. To Klingeman's left sat Justice Carlos C. Cadena, who had the reputation of being an excellent judicial scholar, and who later would become a well noted professor in the law school at St. Mary's. I was familiar with him, having read and studied several of his past opinions. He was actually our only hope, and so our whole argument was really geared toward him. Our whole objective was to try to get a strong dissenting opinion from Justice Cadena.

Our oral argument went smooth and without a hitch. Afterwards we had our post mortem conference at Harry's office. We both felt we had performed well. "So, do you think we got Cadena?" asked Harry. "I was watching his face during oral argument, and it's my bet we got him, and we'll get a dissent from him," I predicted. "I don't know," commented Harry. "I'll guess we'll just have to wait and see," he posed. "Yeah, for sure, but I think we got it," I asserted. And thus began a long wait that spanned about nine months.

Finally, on March 10, 1971, the 4th Court of Civil Appeals came down with their decision, *Gomez v. Perez*, 466 S.W. 2d 41 (1971). Just as I predicted the vote was two to one. Judge Klingeman wrote the opinion for the majority, holding: "The trial court properly held that there was no cause of action in this State to impose civil liability on the part of appellee [the father] to support such illegitimate child. The judgment of the trial court is affirmed." On the other hand, it was worth the nine month wait for the blistering and well-reasoned, scholarly dissent by Justice Cadena in which he agreed with us. "The majority opinion notes appellant's [Gomez's] contention and then proceeds to ignore it by applying without effort to defend the very rule of laws which appellant assails as unconstitutional," wrote Cadena. He went on to state that even under the concept of maximum judicial self-restraint, "…the classification here under attack can be upheld only by freeing the judicial imagination to wander vagrant and unconfined, and indulging in the naïve assumption that relieving a man of his obligation to support his illegitimate children, the law encourages him to withhold his sexual favors from women who are not willing to marry him. This assumption has no basis in human experience. If this fantasy is dismissed, one must conclude that the discrimination against bastards with respect to paternal support has its basis in prejudice rather than reason." Cadena continued, pointing out that: "The classification here is characterized by a general illsuitedness to the advancement of any proper governmental interest. It is highly adaptable to uses which are oppressive in the sense of systematic and unfair devaluation of the claims of certain persons to substantial equality of treatment. It possesses a potency to injure and stigmatize the disadvantaged class by implying popular or official belief in their inherent inferiority or undeservedness. It penalizes a class of persons solely because of conditions which are wholly beyond their control and which result from the conduct of third parties occurring before the penalized persons came into existence. These are hallmarks of 'invidious' discrimination." "Hell, he wholly bought into our equal protection argument," I declared. "Look here, he even lifted some of our language from our brief and used it in his opinion," I exclaimed. Needless to say, Harry and I were extremely pleased.

I notified Linda of the decision of the 4th Court of Civil Appeals, and naturally she was disappointed. I cautioned her to stay the course and stated that we weren't near through yet. I explained we had gotten a very powerful dissent, which I felt would do us in good stead as we climbed up the appellate ladder. Harry and I dutifully went through the motions of procedurally seeking a rehearing, which, of course, was denied on April 7, 1971, as we knew it would be. And so now we would push the appeal to the Texas Supreme Court.

We commenced in preparing our Texas Supreme Court brief, which was technically called an Application for Writ of Error. In it we contended that the 4th Court of Civil appeals had erred in affirming the trial court's decision not to require respondent [Perez] to support his illegitimate daughter [Gomez] on the ground that there is no civil liability on the part of a father to support his illegitimate child. Point of Error No. 1 contended that it violated the equal protection clause of the Fourteenth Amendment to the U.S. Constitution, and Point of Error No. 2 stated it violated Article 1, Section 3 of the Texas Constitution. We wove together a powerful equal protection presentation, citing several of Justice Cadena's cogent points and incorporating the material we received from Hackney, while emphasizing the welfare aspect implications. I came up with a one sentence conclusion, which I inserted at the end of our argument and which stated: "There are no illegitimate children only illegitimate parents."

Our Application for Writ of Error before the Texas Supreme Court in the case of *Gomez v. Perez*, was officially filed as case No. B-2719 on May 5, 1971. "So what do you think? You think we'll actually get to argue this thing in Austin?" asked Harry. "Hell no, I doubt they'll ever grant us a hearing," I responded. I was thoroughly convinced that given the conservative composition of the Texas Supreme Court, with its entrenched orthodox ideology, I seriously did not think they would even bother to give us a hearing on a case constitutionally challenging their sacred eighty year old child support law despite the fact of its inherent invidious discriminatory characteristics. I ended up being right in my prediction again. On July 28, 1971, official word came down from Garson R. Jackson, Clerk for the Texas Supreme Court. "Dear Sir: You are hereby notified that the Application for Writ of Error in the case of GOMEZ v. PEREZ, No. B-2719 was this day refused. No reversible error," it said. By this action, the Texas Supreme Court in essence affirmed the ruling of the 4th Court of Civil Appeals, and so we had reached the juncture of having received an adverse ruling from the highest jurisdiction of the state court system, and so from here, there was only one direction we could go and that would be to appeal the decision to the U.S. Supreme Court.

Harry talked to Christian, obtaining his final approval on going forward, while I had the unfortunate task of letting Linda know we had lost again. Rather than sounding down and blue, I was positively gleeful. "Hey Linda, guess what. I've got great news. We finally lost at the Texas Supreme

Court. So we're finally through with the Texas court system, and now we can appeal this case to the U.S. Supreme Court which is where we wanted to be all along," I declared.

Our notice of appeal to the U.S. Supreme Court was officially filed on August 26, 1971, and Harry and I began working on our U.S. Supreme Court Jurisdictional Statement. In essence, this is the all-important preliminary brief, which is aimed at convincing the Supreme Court that it should grant jurisdiction and accept the appeal. As pointed out before, the U.S. Supreme Court only takes a very small percentage of all of the cases appealed to it. So this was a pressurized challenge—to put together a powerful and persuasive equal protection presentation, which would demonstrate an important constitutional matter of major significance that would convince the Supreme Court to take the case, and to do so within the confines of twenty pages or less.

We specified the Texas statutes in question as being Section 402, Chapter 4 of the Texas Family Code and Article 602 and 602a of the Texas penal Code. These were the culprits together with the Texas cases interpreting them, which resulted in a discriminatory child support scheme that was against illegitimate children. We managed to deal with the jurisdictional aspect, the factual summary, and the legal history of the case in the first five pages. That left only fifteen remaining pages in which to advance our argument that the constitutional question was substantial and that the Texas law was invalid under the equal protection clause of the Fourteenth Amendment to the Constitution of the United States. Harry and I managed to do it in ten, and concluded our argument stating: "Here the state of Texas has created an 'insurmountable barrier' to this illegitimate child because the State is denying the child the very sustenance necessary to pass without chaos and hardships from birth to adulthood. Nothing is more necessary for a child than support and maintenance by his father.

If the purpose of denying an illegitimate child the right to compel his natural father to support him when he is in need and want is to prevent moral decay or sin, then this is not an accomplishment of that purpose. For every man knows, that under the laws of the state of Texas, he may spawn through and seed the entire State but if he does so without the benefits of marriage, he is not responsible for the effects of his fecundity. It must fall to the burden of the State at large through its welfare agencies to take care of his responsibilities, for someone must care for a child in need.

How then is society protected if society must bear the burden of supporting the illegitimate child? We submit that the protection afforded by these laws is geared solely toward the individual malfactor and does not protect society at large. The law certainly does not protect the illegitimate child.

If the purpose and the ends of the law and decisions of the courts are to punish the illegitimate child, then this must be viewed as an intolerable situation. The illegitimate child is punished for an act over which he had no control, an act committed patently before his birth, and an act committed not by him but by two other people."

Following our argument proper, we added about a twenty-five page Appendix, which not only included Hackney's letter referencing the welfare statistics, which were already in the appellate record, but also Justice Cadena's well-written, analytical dissenting opinion. Our Jurisdictional Statement was completed and officially filed in case No. 71-575, *Gomez v. Perez*, in the U.S. Supreme Court for the October Term, 1971.

And so now began a long ten month wait to see if the Supreme Court would accept our case. At the end of the year (1971), Harry left Legal Aid to join John Sanders in private practice. So at the beginning of 1972, I was on my own with respect to the case. While we were waiting, there wasn't much more to do, save keeping Linda periodically posted and being on the lookout for any new cases that might have a bearing on ours. No rest for the weary, I managed to stay plenty busy with regard to all of the other cases I was handling at the time.

Then on Monday, June 26, 1972, I got word from the U.S. Supreme Court. They noted probable jurisdiction on our case and set it for oral argument. The first thing I did was to call Harry and let him know. Naturally, he

{ 307

was pleased. We felt that we had done it, as we both believed that the main obstacle was getting the Supreme Court to accept the case in the first place. Next, I notified Linda, and understandably she was unbelievably excited and overjoyed. I told her that I believed we had an excellent chance in winning the case, and I felt she would see her patience and perseverance come to fruition. And finally, I called Christian, who complimented and congratulated me.

On the way home, I picked up a newspaper, and sure enough the press had picked up the story, with the column headline reading: "Men who father illegitimate babies may pay." When I got home I told Marlene the news and showed her the newspaper. As she read the article, she pointed to the newspaper quotation: "the illegitimate is punished for an act over which he had no control, an act patently committed before his birth." "Isn't that your wording from your brief?" she asked. "Yeah, it sure is," I answered. It had become my routine habit to have Marlene to do the final review and proof on all of my major briefs, which she graciously agreed to do, and so she was familiar with the language I had used. "So does this mean you'll get to argue this case before the Supreme Court?" she asked. "It sure looks like it." I said.

Within the next several days, I got a call from Joseph Jaworsky. He was a very well-known and prominent attorney from the law firm of Bracewell and Patterson in Houston. It was a courtesy call to advise me that he had been appointed by the U.S. Supreme Court to represent Perez with respect to filing a brief on his behalf and arguing the case for him, *Gomez v. Perez*, 408 U.S. 942 (1972). At first I felt momentarily miffed, but I soon realized the Supreme Court was right in making sure that due process would be complied with and that Perez would be adequately represented before the High Court.

The powers were beginning to line up. Against us would be Jaworsky, who would be personally representing Perez. On his side, he would have the Texas Attorney General (AG), and his entire office staff, who would be ardently defending the Texas law. On our side would be the American

Civil liberties Union (ACLU), who had contacted me and sought my consent to file an amicus curiae brief in our favor. They thought this case had national implication and wanted to get involved. Of course I gratefully appreciated their gesture and welcomed them aboard as allies. And then there was us, Bexar County Legal Aid (BCLA) representing Linda Gomez and her child. The case was shaping up to be a battle royal, and yet I felt supremely confident.

Once jurisdiction was noted, Christian called me in, and since Harry was now gone, he asked me if I could use some assistance in drafting our final brief on the merits and in prepping for oral argument. Recently, a new young lawyer, about my age, had come aboard at Legal Aid. His name was Stanley Dalton Wright. He had a well-versed, wide range experience in both the federal and state court areas. After discussing the matter with Stan, I felt that he would be both knowledgeable and compatible, and so I chose him to assist me, and Christian agreed.

Stan had flaming red hair, the most charming smile, and possessed a pleasant, affable personality. He was born March 9, 1943, in Houston, Texas, where he was raised. He received his law degree from the University of Houston, Bates School of Law. After graduation he worked in Houston as an Assistant City Attorney, before going to work for the U.S. Department of Agriculture in Washington, D.C. As much as he loved the D.C. arena, Stan had a yearning to return to Texas and help poor people, and so he ended up at Bexar County Legal Aid (BCLA) in San Antonio. He intellectually was as sharp as a tack, and he had demonstrated a real dedicated passion for the cause presented by the *Gomez v. Perez* case.

Stan and I worked on the Appellant's Brief on the Merits, which was a slightly expanded and updated version of our original Jurisdictional Statement. It contained a hard-hitting equal protection argument, which incorporated the welfare aspect of the issue. We concluded with my previously patented phraseology: "To punish the illegitimate child for an act over which he had no control, an act committed patently before his birth, and an act committed not by him but by two other people can only be viewed as an intolerable situation under our Constitution and laws." Before the end of August, 1972, our Brief on the Merits was filed with the U.S. Supreme Court.

In September, 1972, I received a call from Sarah Weddington. She was a young attorney, who also had graduated from the law school at UT, but had done so a couple years after me. She was practicing in the Dallas area and advised me that she was representing a client by the name of Jane Roe, who in 1970 was an unmarried, pregnant Texas resident. Not wanting to carry her pregnancy through to fruition, Jane had an abortion. At that time, Texas made it a felony to abort a fetus, except for strictly the most severe medical reasons. On behalf of her client, Sarah challenged that on constitutional grounds. And so the case of *Roe v. Wade*, began in the federal Northern District of Texas, and had worked its way up to the U.S. Supreme Court, where it had already been argued on December 13, 1971. But the case was then set for a re-hearing, and Sarah was facing having to do a re-argument of the case on October 11, 1972. She had run across our case of *Gomez v. Perez*, which was scheduled for oral argument in December, 1972, two months after her. She noticed that our two cases had some issue similarities and decided to call to chat. Indeed, the two cases did have a mutual economic argument in that when it came to an illegitimate child, the state of Texas, had by law, chosen to place the entire economic burden of supporting and maintaining such a child, solely upon the woman alone. Of course our case was trying to change that, and Sarah correctly analyzed that if the Supreme Court agreed with us, then that would change the situation, and theoretically at least the economic burden would then become more shared between the woman and the man. In that respect Sarah felt that our case might impact her economic argument as to it being an influencing factor regarding a single woman seeking an abortion in that situation.

During our conversation, I agreed with her analysis but suggested that the economic argument was still worth mentioning, and I shared with her some of the welfare statistical information we had developed.

We concluded that we were both striving to improve the woman's position under Texas law, but we were coming at it from different directions. After further discussion, Sarah decided that although she would still include the economic argument, she would de-emphasize it, and instead concentrate more on the contention that a woman should have the right to control her own body. I wished her good luck, and she likewise wished us good fortune, as well.

By the end of September, 1972, I had arrived at the momentous decision to leave the Bexar County Legal Aid (BCLA) at the end of the year, and starting right after New Year's, 1973, to join Harry Adams and John Sanders in private practice. Given the importance of some of the matters that I had going on, including the *Gomez v. Perez* case, I felt it was only fair to give Christian more than the traditional thirty days' notice. So right before Halloween, I advised him that I'd be leaving. Although he stated he'd be sorry to lose me, he certainly understood my motivation and wished me well. A frank discussion ensued about my being able to wrap up the real important matters before I left, which I told him I felt I could do, save for the *Gomez v. Perez* case per chance. It was slated for oral argument before the U.S. Supreme Court on December 6, 1972, and so I would still be available for that. But then if there was to be any re-hearing, I would already be gone from Bexar County Legal Aid (BCLA) and wouldn't be around to re-argue the case as a Legal Aid lawyer. For that reason, Christian felt it would be best to switch to Stan for doing the oral argument before the U.S. Supreme Court rather than me. While disappointed, I could certainly understand his reasoning. He did ask for me to remain actively involved and to assist Stan with respect to preparing for oral argument, which I, of course, promised I would do.

That evening I gave Marlene the news that I would not be going to the Supreme Court to argue the *Gomez v. Perez* case. She could see that I felt somewhat let down, and she tried to console me, as she half-kiddingly but truthfully said with a smile: "Well, I guess you will be here for my birthday after all." I nodded and laughed. Although it took me that evening, I finally reconciled that even though my position was going to change from player to coach, I was still going to have an indispensable role in concluding this case.

In the month of November, 1972, Stan and I ran a couple of practice sessions, during which I cautioned him that several of the potentially adverse Justices might attempt to distract him and eat up his time with problematic procedural and evidentiary questions regarding the difficulty in factually proving paternity (Again this was in the days when DNA testing was not yet available for this purpose). I advised him that when this happened, as I thought it would, he needed to remind the Justices that in this case the factual issue of paternity was not contested, and that it was duly proven by credible evidence, so there isn't any unresolved factual issue of paternity here. And then I suggested that he follow-up by citing Cadena's argument in his dissent where he pointed out that the vagaries of local practice or the difficulties in ascertaining paternity cannot be utilized as an excuse to deny a constitutional right. Besides there are plenty of historical examples where science has caught up with evidentiary problems, such as photographs, fingerprints, etc. "Stan, don't let them tie you down. Point out there is no factual issue here, cite Cadena, and move on. You stay focused like a laser on our main point, which is: a child's a child, no matter how born," I asserted. "Oh, and don't forget to mention the welfare aspect regarding this issue," I added. Stan agreed, and by the end of our last practice, which I termed our "dress rehearsal," I knew he was ready. At the age of twenty-nine, he would end up being the youngest attorney to have ever argued a case before the U.S. Supreme Court up to that period of time. Later he would also leave Legal Aid and return to D.C., where he worked as a U.S. Attorney for the Department of Justice, Civil Division. After an extraordinary career, he died in January, 2012.

But on Marlene's birthday on December 6, 1972, Stan was in D.C. arguing the *Gomez v. Perez* case before the U.S. Supreme Court. That morning Christian called me in for a conference to assess my thoughts on the outlook of the case. "So, Mr. Eichelbaum, what do you think our prospects are?" he asked. "Oh, we're going to win it, Sir," I answered without hesitation. "You sound very confident," he remarked. "Yes Sir, I am," I replied. "You see the big battle was getting the Supreme Court to accept jurisdiction of the case and agree to hear it in the first place. Once that happened, I felt in all probability, we'd win," I added. I went on to point out to Mr. Christian that the composition of the U.S. Supreme Court had changed since our *Gaytan v. Cassidy* case (The Texas Driver's license case). Justices Black and Harlan had retired. They had been replaced by Justices Powell and Rehnquist. There was no question that Justices Rehnquist and Stewart would be flat out against us, no matter what. I viewed Chief Justice Burger as 50%-50%. He could go either way. And however he went, Justice Blackmun would follow suit. On the other hand, I counted on Justices Brennan, Douglas, Marshall, Powell, and White all going with us. "So you see Mr. Christian, at best we'll win this 7-2, but even at the very worst, we'll still take it 5-4," I surmised.

The very next day the press picked up the story about our case being argued before the U.S. Supreme Court, and the column headline read: "Unwed Mothers." The news reporter, Stryker McGuire, had apparently interviewed Christian after my conference with him, and reported that Christian had stated he was confident and said he based his optimism on the "simple fact the Supreme Court accepted the case in the first place." Richard Tinsman, president of Legal Aid's board of directors, also was reported on predicting a favorable decision. These two must have talked, I gathered, and evidently they chose to mimic my words. That evening when I shared the newspaper article with Marlene, she commented: "Isn't that exactly what you told Mr. Christian yesterday?" "Yeah, it sure is. It's kind of like being quoted incognito," I replied with a smile.

It was Wednesday, January 17, 1973, and I was working at my office on Hillcrest at the newly created law firm of Adams, Eichelbaum, and Sanders, when the phone rang. It was Stan Wright. He called to inform me that the U.S. Supreme Court came down with their decision in the case of *Gomez v. Perez*, 409 U.S. 535 (1973). He advised me that we had won it on a 7-2 vote. We congratulated one another, and he asked me to convey the message to Harry, which I, of course, did, and we were both obviously pleased. Within the next couple of hours, Christian called to extend his compliments and congratulations. After some cordial small talk, he asked if I would mind giving Linda Gomez a call. He indicated that she had already been informed about the decision but that she had expressed a desire to hear from me. I told him I'd be happy to oblige. When I called Linda, she said she wanted to personally thank me. I reminisced with her that we had begun this case way back in 1969, shortly after the birth of her daughter, and now some three and a half years later, thanks to her patience and persistence, we had changed the law for the whole state of Texas.

On the way home, I naturally picked up copies of the newspapers, and sure enough the column headlines blared: "Illegitimate fathers lose," and "Dad must feed illegitimate child." The news accounts related that the U.S. Supreme Court had ruled 7-2 that all children have an "essential right" to care from their parents regardless of whether there is a legal contract binding the parents into a marriage. The news report quoted the Supreme Court as stating: "A state may not invidiously discriminate against illegitimate children by denying them substantial benefits accorded to children generally." There it was our equal protection argument stated exactly in the words we had used. When I showed the news stories to Marlene, she immediately recognized the Court's quote as being directly lifted from our brief. "It says here that this case not only changed the law in the state of Texas, but in Wyoming, as well, she commented. "Yeah, isn't that amazing. We ended up changing the law in the state of Wyoming too—a state I've never even been to before," I replied.

The following day there was another newspaper story entitled: "Mother Lauds High Court Ruling on Child Support," in which the reporter interviewed Linda Gomez, who stated that she was happy and how she felt the decision would help many people. In the days to come, I was able to secure a copy of the Supreme Court's decision. Justices Rehnquist and Stewart filed a dissent—no big surprise, but it was evident from the majority opinion that our equal protection argument won out. And it was also clear that the welfare information we had developed had an impact on the majority's thinking. The national legal services community viewed *Gomez v. Perez*, 409 U.S. 585 (1973) as a "landmark case" decision, having a historical legal significance. Then on January 22, 1973, five days after having ruled on our case, the U.S. Supreme Court came down with its ruling on the case of *Roe v. Wade*, 410 U.S. 113 (1973), which was decided by the very same 7-2 margin.

Many years later, Marlene and I were attending a Family Law CLE seminar at the South Texas College of Law in Houston. During one of the sessions a Texas Assistant Attorney General was giving a presentation about how that agency had been actively involved in collecting child support from fathers and how millions of dollars had been collected, benefiting the lives of countless children. The speaker announced that it had all began many years ago when two young Legal Aid attorneys in San Antonio decided to challenge the Texas child support law. "How many of you have ever heard of the case of *Gomez v. Perez*?" he inquired. "That's your case," Marlene whispered, as she nudged me. A small smattering of hands went up, of which I was one of them. As we were seated within the first several rows, the speaker called on me.

"And how are you familiar with that case, Sir?" he asked. "I was one of the two Legal Aid attorneys you were talking about who started that case," I responded. There was a moment of silence, and then the speaker began to clap, as he was joined by nearly all of the entire audience, who rose and applauded, as well. It was an emotionally overwhelming experience.

CHAPTER 20

⚖

Transitions

September 4, 1972 – December 31, 2008

Sunday, September 3, 1972, was a beautiful, balmy end of summer day as I loaded Rob, our first son, who wasn't quite two years old yet, into his car seat in the back seat of my VW. Marlene packed all of the toddler take-along stuff on the back seat next to Rob, where she also carefully placed her famous Jell-O cake, which was a favorite with kids, but which adults liked, as well. "Okay, are we ready," I asked. "We're all set," she responded, as we climbed into my VW and took off for Harry's house, which was located in what was then the deep Northside, off of San Pedro Avenue and past the San Antonio Municipal Airport. Harry and his wife, Bev, had invited us to an old fashion Labor Day weekend holiday picnic at their new house. Of course, Harry and Bev's daughter, Tara, who was slightly older than Rob, would be present, and so the two of them could interact and play with one another. John Sanders, Harry's law partner, along with his wife, Mary, and his three children: Larry, Tommy, and Heidi, who were older, were all going to be there too. It had been a while since I had seen Harry, and even longer since I had seen John, and so I was looking forward to the get together and having an opportunity to catch up and reminisce about old times.

By the time we got there, John and his family had already arrived. Bev greeted us, parked Marlene's Jell-O cake on her kitchen table, which was loaded with other delicious foods, and then gave us the dime tour of their new house. We were then ushered onto their back patio, where the rest of the folks were gathered. It fronted an amply spacious back yard, which was perfect for kids to play in.

While the girls and kids congregated on one side of the patio, I joined John on the other side near the grill, as he watched Harry execute his barbecue mastery. Harry's prowess on the grill was widely renowned and his reputation as a grilling expert was well deserved. He was grilling enough hamburgers and hotdogs to feed a small army and was obviously enjoying himself. In the meantime the girls set out enticing portions of beans, coleslaw, macaroni salad, together with buns and all the fixings to go with the grilled fare. When Harry announced: "We're done—everyone dig in," we all grabbed plates and loaded them up with food and enjoyed partaking in all the delicacies of the feast.

When we were done eating, the kids went into the back yard and played, while the wives watched and socialized. In the meantime, at the opposite end of the patio, Harry, John, and I sat around a table, drinking beer and talking about lawyer stuff. I clued them in on the happenings at Legal Aid, and they related some of their private practice experiences.

According to Harry, their private practice undertaking at the Hillcrest office had grown great guns. Although it had been only two years, not only had they picked up some rather prominent clients, such as: Grady's BBQ, Montgomery Wards, and a good number of Red McCombs' various business enterprises, but also they had developed a caseload of regular clientele that was bursting at the seams. In a non-braggadocios manner, Harry informed me that they were already making considerably more than what their salaries had been at Legal Aid. It was a smooth operation, with John handling juvenile and criminal cases, plus covering a portion of the civil cases; while Harry dealt with the real estate and business law aspects, as well as the remainder of the civil law cases. But according to both of them, they had more work than they could handle.

Then came the bombshell—beginning at the first of the year (1973), they wanted me to come out and join them in private practice. Unbelievably, they were offering me a full partnership; whereby, everything would be equally split between the three of us. "Hell, we already know we're compatible and would make a great team, because we've worked together before at Legal Aid," said Harry. He then went on to point out that I would be a valuable addition, as I could more than adequately handle probate cases and administrative law matters, such as Social Security disability cases—areas of law where they weren't as strong as I was. "Besides Mel, with your accounting background and business management abilities, we feel you'd be a big help," added Harry. He continued stating that they knew that I was at the very top of the pay scale at Legal Aid and that if I wanted to make more money futuristically, then I really should consider going into private practice. Harry concluded that it would be great for me to join them, and John indicated his wholehearted concurrence. I was totally flattered and told them that naturally I wanted to talk with Marlene about it, but that I would seriously consider their proposal and think about it, and I'd get back to them and let them know.

The discussion between Marlene and me began on the way home and continued throughout the evening. Harry was one hundred percent right concerning the monetary aspect. Save and except for Mr. Christian, I was already the highest paid lawyer at Legal Aid, and I realized that I was at the very top of my salary range. Realistically, except for small, incremental annual cost of living increases, I couldn't expect any significant raises. Marlene wanted a house and another kid—goals which we shared in common. If I truly wanted us to be able to afford those things and to live a bit more comfortable life style, then strictly from an economic standpoint, private practice seemed to be the more lucrative avenue and the lure of Harry and John's offer appeared to be rather enticing. Hell, it was a golden opportunity.

On the other hand, I enjoyed practicing in the poverty law area and representing poor people who were in desperate need of legal services. But I would be kidding myself if I didn't realize that the pressure of trying to keep up a routine caseload of 150 cases or so, while at the same time handling a number of time consuming and work-intensified law reform cases wasn't beginning to take its toll on me. How much longer could I be able to continually endure 65 plus hour work weeks, week after week, with no letup in sight? And as Marlene pointed out, even in private practice, I could still engage in some pro-bono work, when I thought the client and subject were worthy of such treatment. Marlene said she would support my decision either way, but I could see the direction she was leaning, and I could certainly understand why.

Even after she went to sleep, I tossed and turned pretty much all night, wrestling with the decision. I thought that the concept of Legal Aid being likened to a "legal Camelot," which I had experienced, perhaps might be destined to come to a close and might be approaching its end anyhow. There had been rumors of program cutbacks and funding reductions. And for some time there had been scuttlebutt about restricting legal services attorneys from taking class actions, particularly if they would be against governmental agencies. The conservative political backlash was real, and at least in part, it manifested as a constant creeping assault upon the legal services programs, and politically had a distinctive anti-Legal Aid flavor to it. The War on Poverty was manipulatively being pushed to morph into a war against the poor. I had to be objective; I insisted and instructed my psyche. Just how much could one individual lawyer do to make a difference? Was I just rationalizing, or thinking realistically? Then I thought of all the law reform cases I had done thus far, and the significant differences they had made, and the ones still on tap like the *Gomez v. Perez* case. I really wanted to finish that one and to be able to argue it before the U.S. Supreme Court. Yet I knew that once I gave my notice, odds were Christian would not let me argue it. Don't be so damn proud and let that shape your opinion, I told myself. In all honesty, with proper preparation, I knew Stan Wright would be able to argue the case just as well as I could. Perhaps this was the right time to pass the baton on to the next runner and that I had already run my laps. After going back and forth for most of the night, by morning I had finally reached a decision. Over a nice Labor Day breakfast that she prepared, I told Marlene that I thought it would be best if I left Legal Aid and joined Harry and John in private practice. She smiled, congratulated me, and gave me a big hug. I could tell it was the direction she thought we should go. Later that day, I called Harry and John and let them know I was accepting their offer. So on January 1, 1973, the law firm of Adams, Eichelbaum, and Sanders was officially born. I had left Legal Aid, taking my trusted secretary, Anita Herrera, with me and moved into the Hillcrest office with the guys, and our practice thrived and prospered.

By February, 1974, Marlene and I moved into our first house, which we had built in Leon Valley (LV), a small bedroom suburban community located on the northwest side of San Antonio. Later that summer our second son, Mark, was born. That year with the encouragement of many of my neighbors, I ran for a Leon Valley (LV) city council position. Despite having two opponents, I ended up winning, receiving more votes than any other candidate, including the mayor. It turned out to be quite a good year for the law firm, as well. In 1974, Ron Flake left Legal Aid and joined our merry group, and we expanded by opening up a second office in Universal City, a suburban community on the northeast side of town.

But by the latter part of 1974, even though from an economic standpoint our law firm was flourishing, problems started developing on the horizon. A dissimilarity of interests was beginning to build and grow. Harry and Ron, who operated the Universal City office wanted to pour more and more resources into that office. They honestly believed that was where the greatest growth potential was. There was even some talk of considering not renewing the Hillcrest office lease for the ensuing year of 1975, and that we should all consolidate at the Universal City office and work out of there. John and I, on the other hand, felt that monies derived from the Hillcrest office operation were being overly spent and utilized to build up the Universal City enterprise. Neither one of us were comfortable with the idea of abandoning the client base we had built up on the northwest side. Finally, the polarities came to a head, and we all recognized that a business divorce would be necessary. It was a friendly procedure, but a split was accomplished. Harry and Ron stayed in Universal City, while John and I remained on Hillcrest.

However, little did I know that the legal career gremlin wasn't through with me yet, and a strange sequence of events were on stage and about to happen that would influence the course of my legal path. Earlier in 1974, Arch Adams (no relation to Harry) was a junior partner in the well-established law firm of LeLaurin & Adams. Their firm was situated in a posh suite of offices, located downtown in the Alamo National Bank Building on St. Mary's Street, within a couple blocks of the Bexar County Courthouse. Their practice was primarily known for commercial law, having a significant portion concerning bank and credit card debt collection. These were the days before San Antonio had a public defender system, or anything like one. Rather all of the practicing lawyers within the Bexar County area were subject to be drafted, so to speak, and ordered by the courts to serve in the position of being defense counsel in order to represent defendants, who had been legally charged with a crime and who were too poor to hire a private attorney to defend them.

Arch had been appointed to represent a juvenile, who was charged with the crime of murder, and who the DA's office was seeking to try as an adult. The juvenile had been the driver of an automobile, which transported three slightly older youths to an ice house. While the juvenile remained in the car, the other three youths went into the ice house, ostensibly to obtain some food and drinks. Once inside the premises, they attempted to rob the place, and in the process shot and killed the store clerk. Texas had changed its criminal law relating to principles and accessories, and when it came to the commission of a crime, under Texas law the driver of the vehicle would be just as guilty as the one who actually did the shooting, and so the juvenile was charged with murder.

Having been designated by the court as the juvenile's defense counsel, Arch had to defend the juvenile in the transfer trial proceeding. If he lost, the juvenile would be certified to be tried as an adult, and thus subject to the penalties of life imprisonment or possibly even the death penalty, should the DA's office decide to take that direction. But Arch ended up losing the case in the trial court, and so naturally sought to appeal. However, fearing his lack of experience in handling criminal cases, Arch honestly believed that in conducting the juvenile's defense, he may have unwittingly made some mistakes during the trial, which very well might give the juvenile the right to seek reversal on claims of ineffective counsel. Hence, he felt that there would be a potential conflict of interest for him to be forced to represent the juvenile on the appeal and that another disinterested attorney should be appointed to represent the juvenile for that purpose. Out of an abundance of caution, the judge agreed with Arch on the potentiality of a conflict of interest. Therefore, the judge gave him the names of three other attorneys and said on behalf of the juvenile, Arch could suggest the one he preferred. Of the three attorneys' names divulged, mine just so happened to be one of them. Having only in one instance served on a San Antonio Bar Association committee with Arch, my name was the only one with which he was familiar, and so Arch suggested it be me, and the judge agreed. Later I received an official notice from the court that I had been officially appointed to represent the juvenile on the appeal.

Naturally, I interviewed Arch in order to obtain background information regarding the case and that is how I met his senior partner, Louis LeLaurin. Both of them were rather worried that Arch unintentionally may have committed "malpractice" by being an ineffective counsel in the juvenile trial proceeding, and in fact they had put their malpractice insurance carrier on precautionary notice. Of course, I interviewed the juvenile, as well, in order to get a background perspective from his point of view. His story was that he got conned and duped. When he drove the other three youths to the ice house, he had no idea that they intended to rob the place, let alone kill anyone. After listening to him, I believed he was telling the truth, and I felt he really had been manipulated by the other youths and that he never had a clue as to what was going down. It was the classic case of a half-way decent kid hanging out with the wrong crowd.

Although factual inquiries would prove helpful in developing a background understanding of the case, it wouldn't make a flip as far as the actual appeal went. I wouldn't be able to just magically get a second bite of the apple and simply re-try the case in an attempt to secure a different factual outcome. Rather with the appeal, everything would be based on the record of the proceeding that had already occurred. In those records, somehow I would have to find some really basic grievous error in order to justify and get a reversal of the prior proceeding.

It took a while for the court reporter to prepare the trial court transcript, but finally that got done. I reviewed it, relentlessly going through it with a fine tooth comb, but nowhere could I find any serious egregious error. Although Arch was basically a commercial law attorney and inexperienced in criminal law, my assessment was that he, nevertheless, had done a relatively credible job in conducting the defense during the trial proceeding. I also examined the pertinent documents in the DA's file and reviewed the appropriate papers in the court's file, as well. At first blush, it appeared that everything was ordinary and regular. I was fast running out of any viable options.

Then by chance I seemed to recall that there was something in the juvenile law statutes that I had read which convinced me that I should take another look at them again. Reviewing the appropriate law book, I found that fairly recently Texas had up-dated its juvenile laws. The Texas Legislature had passed some new juvenile statutes and these had been duly signed into law by the governor. It was clear that these new changes were in place and fully applicable at the time of this case. And so there it was—under the new law the State had the obligation of and was required to serve due process notice of the charges and court proceeding, not only on the parent of the juvenile, but also on the juvenile, himself. Although there was a service return for the parent, there was none for the juvenile. Here it appeared that the DA's office had screwed up. They had served the parent, but evidently omitted serving the juvenile. I double checked with the District Clerk's office to make sure that maybe the missing juvenile's service return had just been misfiled, but that wasn't the case. There was none, because it had never been done. That meant that the juvenile's due process rights were violated and had not been complied with in accordance with the State's own prescribed standards. That would form the basis of my appeal before the 4th Court of Civil Appeals.

On the day of the hearing, I was fairly relaxed and felt rather confident. Basically I was going to use the State's own law against them. Arch had showed up as an interested onlooker and sat in the visitors' gallery. As the three judge panel entered, everyone rose, and I announced that I was ready to proceed. Although the assistant DA designated for the appeal half-heartedly but valiantly argued that it shouldn't make any difference, he knew that their office had goofed up. I gave a powerful due process argument, stating that once the State had set its own standard as to what due process should entail in these types of cases, then it couldn't be allowed to just willy-nilly go about and ignore its own standard. "Your Honors, our system operates as a government under the law, and not just of men, and accordingly even the great state of Texas must be held accountable and must obey its own law," I concluded. Although the appellate court took the case under advisement, eventually the decision did come down, and it was unanimous. We had won the appeal.

Arch was so ingratiated about the outcome that he constantly sung my praises to LeLaurin. By the latter part of 1975, they were seriously courting John and I to join their firm. LeLaurin, who was an older man but not quite ready to retire, became intrigued with the idea of merging our two law firms together. The concept of blending our general practice with their commercial law practice seemed to appeal to him. He felt such a combinative firm would have a much broader appeal, and so would have much more growth potential, and then there was the addition of the beneficial plus of upping and significantly increasing their legal talent.

As talks ensued, the idea is that we would shut down the Hillcrest office at the end of the year and not renew the lease there. Rather John and I would move downtown and join them in their ample spacious office suite, where we would each have our own separate offices. We would become full equal partners, and the starting contemplated draw-salary being offered was significantly more than we were currently making. I was dizzyingly becoming entranced with the idea of converting into a "big shot status downtown lawyer." After having talked it over with Marlene and being totally enchanted by the "big law firm dream," on January 1, 1976, John and I moved downtown, together with my faithful secretary, Anita Herrera, and the firm of LeLaurin, Adams, Eichelbaum & Sanders was formed. During the following four years, the firm grew to eight lawyers, with over a dozen support personnel, and with offices in both San Antonio and Corpus Christi.

But then in March of 1976, tragedy struck. Marlene had gone to Omaha to drop off our kids with her parents for a visit. Rob had recently turned five and Mark wasn't even two yet. Then she joined me in Chicago, where I was attending a Commercial Law league conference with Arch Adams, who was accompanied by his wife. The weather in Chicago was lousy—cold, damp, and windy, and unwisely Marlene had brought along only a spring coat. Together, as two couples, we had fun, going to several unique restaurants and seeing some entertaining shows. But unfortunately Marlene caught a rare strain of strep throat. After the conference, Marlene and I returned to Omaha to visit with her family and pick up our kids. While there she consulted with and visited her Uncle Jerry, who owned and was the doctor in charge of the same medical clinic she had worked for while attending college. He put her on some anti-biotic, which seemed to resolve her strep throat situation.

After we got home, Marlene mysteriously began to gain weight and her legs started swelling. Even after seeing her regular doctor, who put her on a diuretic, the situation didn't get better but got worse. Finally, she was referred to a Nephrologist, who placed her in the downtown Nix Hospital. After some testing, including a kidney biopsy, we learned the bad news. With the particular kind of strep that Marlene caught, in about 25% of the cases a kidney disease called Glomerulonephritis would develop. Of those who get this disease about 25% of them would end up with total renal failure. Regrettably, Marlene was one of the 25% of the 25%. After several weeks at the Nix Hospital, her kidneys were failing, and the uremic poisoning was getting to her heart. Meanwhile, I was trying my best to cope with being with Marlene as much as possible, taking care of two little kids, and keeping up with my law work at the firm. And so that dark day when two of her doctors approached me and told me there was little that could be done, and I should begin making preparations for her death, I just about crumbled.

That night, after enough tears and prayers, and in a state of a semi-trance, I had a long conversation with God, at least in my mind, which culminated in my resolute will to fervently do everything possible to change the predicted course of events which had been foretold to me by the two doctors on the previous day.

I was at the Nix Hospital very early in the morning and waited until her Nephrologist, Dr. Larry Dotin, arrived. After my having badgered him constantly, he revealed that there may be an outside chance if we could put Marlene on dialysis, but this would have to be done right away, and he cautioned me that it might be too late. "Well, let's give it a try," I insisted, and I signed some papers, and things began to happen pretty fast.

Dialysis is a complex medical procedure for artificially cleaning the blood. At that time, the only civilian dialysis unit in all of Bexar County was at the downtown Santa Rosa Hospital, and within the hour Marlene was being transferred there. Once at Santa Rosa, Marlene immediately underwent emergency surgery; whereby, a shunt was installed into her right wrist so she could be hooked up to a dialysis machine. While that was going on I consulted with Fred, a dialysis technician, and a Nun, by the name of Sister Ann, who was an elderly woman with a stern appearance, but who had very caring eyes. She acted like she ran the whole place and perhaps she did. At any rate, the two of them assured me that Marlene was now in the right place and that she was going to be okay. It was the first positive words I had heard since this whole episode began, and my heart filled with an encouraging hope.

At the completion of her surgery, Marlene was hooked up to a dialysis machine and given her first dialysis treatment. These continued at the regimen of three times a week. Sister Ann and Fred were right, and Marlene steadily improved, and within a couple of weeks, she was discharged and was able to go home. Of course, she would have to continue her dialysis treatments at the rate of three times a week, and ostensibly that would be for the rest of her life. Debbie Kempler, who was an ex-SAFTYite, a fellow LV resident, and a very good friend, took charge and arranged for a whole cadre of girls to cooperatively take part in forming and efficiently operating a whole transportation corps to convey Marlene back and forth to and from dialysis, week after week. Debbie controlled and managed the entire operation and made sure it ran smoothly without a hitch.

Then a miracle happened. Unimaginably, and for which the doctors had no medical explanation, Marlene's kidneys began to heal and function again. Her dialysis treatments were reduced from three times a week, to twice a week, to once a week, and then to none at all. Her kidneys had returned to about a 50% functioning capacity, which with periodic monitoring, allowed her to live a normal life without dialysis. According to Dr. Dotin, up until that period of time there were only two instances in the whole United States where that had happened, and Marlene was one of the two. Her case was written up in the John Hopkins Medical Journal.

Many years later, after we retired, and after having lasted for some forty years, Marlene's kidneys began to deteriorate again. She was too old to be put on the kidney transplant list, and given her age, it was unlikely that we could expect a second miracle of her kidneys reviving again. Neither I nor our two sons could be donors because of health reasons or we simply weren't a match. Several good friends looked into the possibility, but for age and health reasons they weren't good candidates either. It looked like Marlene would be destined to a life on dialysis once again. But then a second miracle occurred after all, when a young nurse-practitioner student by the name of Bari Eichelbaum, who is a third cousin of mine and who also happens to be our Goddaughter, popped up and called saying: "Aunt Marlene, I got an extra kidney that I don't really need, and I'd like to give it to you." Bari and Marlene turned out to be a perfect match, and on May 10, 2017, a kidney transplant operation was successfully done. At the time of this writing both donor and donee are doing exceptionally well.

In 1976, my political career came to an abrupt end. Having served one term as a LV city councilman, due to Marlene's illness there was no way I could afford to donate the time for a political campaign, so I chose not to run for re-election. However, subsequent to the election, the LV mayor appointed me, and I was unanimously approved by the LV city council, to the position of Chief Judge of the LV Municipal Court. This was a post I held and served in for nearly a decade.

Circa 1979 turned out to be a tumultuous year. I had to appear at the Bexar County Morgue in order to identify the body of Larry Sanders, John's eldest son, who was a murder victim. Meanwhile John's younger son suffered from some addiction problems, and subsequently John's wife would divorce him. John sank into a depressed state after all that, and who could blame him? He left the firm as he needed some time to recover, and unfortunately, the firm just wasn't a very conducive place for that. Arch Adams went through a bitter divorce and was never the same afterwards. By the latter part of 1979, I was the only lawyer at the firm who still had a working marriage. I felt like "The Last of the Mohicans."

By that time I had become disillusioned with the firm. The concept of meshing a general practice with a commercial law venture just wasn't working out. I wanted to handle more Social Security disability and consumer bankruptcy cases, but according to Arch these types of clients simply didn't fit the image of a commercial law firm. I suppose the last round up came about when I pulled Louis LeLaurin's irons out of the fire, and at his request took over a contested probate case in which he had become enmeshed. I managed to save a very large estate for the widowed wife, which her treacherous daughter, together with her scheming husband was trying to steal. Although they nearly got away with it, fortunately I was able to stop them in the nick of time, and we won the case for the widowed wife. Having done so, I generated the largest fee having ever been earned by the firm up to that period of time. Rather than a bonus, my reward was to have my draw-salary cut, supposedly because the commercial side of the firm wasn't doing well enough and needed some time to catch up. So accordingly Arch and another lawyer were sent on an all-expense paid trip to a ritzy ski resort to attend a fancy commercial law conference so as to try to drum up some additional commercial law business. I was getting sick of "big firm politics," and I felt it was time for me to leave.

Talking it over with Marlene, I expressed my yearning for just being a solo practitioner, with the idea of perhaps opening up my own office in Leon Valley (LV), where a significant number of my client base resided. Marlene agreed and thought that made sense. I became re-acquainted with an older lawyer, by the name of Tom Lee, who had served as a Representative in the Texas legislature during my law school years when I was working there as a Legislative Assistant. Tom had a law office, adjacent to his son's dental clinic, which was located on Bandera Road, which was the heart of the LV business district. The law office suite had enough room to accommodate a lawyer's office for me and with ample room for a reception area and my secretary. It was a storefront operation, and reminded me of my Legal Aid days at the E. Houston Street office. Tom actually liked the idea of me moving in. Not only would it add rental income for his son, but I'd be available for him to pick my brains and for him to get some help on some of his more challenging cases. A deal was cut, and in the latter part of 1979, I and my loyal secretary, Anita Herrera, left the firm, moved to LV, and opened up the Eichelbaum Law Office. It felt good to be finally disentangled from the old downtown firm, and to get away from the unpleasant "big firm politics" of the past. It was like breathing the fresh air of freedom. From now on out, I would be navigating my own ship and charting my own course.

At first it was rough going. Marlene had to go back to teaching school again just so as to bring some income into the family. Of course,

I had the monthly periodic payment that I was receiving from the firm as my buyout, but that was being paid over a five year period of time, and so the monthly amount wasn't all that much. However, that plus my LV Municipal Court Judge's stipend did help some. I realized it would take some time to rebuild, but in the meantime it was kind of scary. I had left the firm with an inventory of only five cases—ones that they didn't care to retain and didn't have the desire or legal ability to handle anyhow, and that was it. Truly, at the age of thirty-seven, I would literally be starting all over again, yet Marlene and I were willing to run the risk. We felt the price of freedom from the old firm was worth it.

The first month was a loss. The second month I had broken even. The third month I had generated a small profit, and I never looked back after that. In six months I was making equivalent to what I had been earning at the big firm. I kept my promise to Anita and set up a strong and what would be fully paid for and funded retirement program for her and me, as well. My practice was general in nature, including Social Security disability, consumer bankruptcy, probate and family law. The business steadily grew, and the practice thrived and prospered.

By the end of the school year of 1983-1984, Marlene was getting burned out on teaching. She was miffed at a new Texas law which had come up with some additional teacher certification and "competency testing" requirements for all Texas teachers. It was part of an all-out politically driven and publicity oriented public relations campaign to blame the teachers for all of the inadequacies of the Texas public education system. Forget about the fact that the Texas Legislature had failed to adequately fund public education for years, or the petty politics played by far too many school boards, or the number of inept school administrators, who ran schools for their own conveniences, rather than adequately assisting and supporting their faculties with respect to their educational efforts toward their students. No, instead "it was all the teachers' fault" was the mantra.

I was so empathetic with the feelings of the predominant number of teachers on the matter that in 1984, I wrote a guest editorial, entitled;

"Teacher Testing," for the local neighborhood newspaper, The LV Leader, which published it, and in which I lambasted the Texas approach of blaming the teachers. Unbeknownst to me the editor, Ron Lambert, submitted my editorial and entered it into a state-wide contest that was sponsored by the Texas State Teachers Association (TSTA), which at that time was the largest teachers' union in the state of Texas. Despite going up against other editorials by professional journalists from major newspapers in Dallas, Houston, and San Antonio, my editorial ended up winning first place, and in 1985, I received the prestigious TSTA School Bell award at a state-wide assembly in Austin where I was honored.

At the end of May, 1985, Marlene was seriously thinking of quitting teaching. Aside from her teaching degree, with a full-fledged degree in mathematics, she didn't feel she would have that much trouble in finding a decent paying job. The USAA Insurance Company, the Southwest Research Institute, and other large employer types were scrambling to find employees with math backgrounds. However, I begged her to come to work for me as my legal assistant. We were doing a lot more cases in probate and consumer bankruptcy, both of which involved math and numbers, and I thought she might enjoy the work. After my constant effort at trying to persuade her, she agreed to give it a trial period during the summer just to see if she might like it. I told her to be prepared because at times the work would be more pressurized, time consuming and work-intensified than what she was used to in teaching, and her answer was that for someone who taught middle school it would be a piece of cake. She found that she really enjoyed the work, and so a plan was set into motion. Marlene would teach the 1985-1986 school year, completing all of the requirements under the new law, including passing the teacher competency testing. She was absolutely determined to leave on a high note, and no one was going to be able to say that she was driven off from her teaching profession. Her choice would be hers and freely made.

So at the end of May, 1986, at the close of the school year, Marlene proudly marched into her principal's office, handed him her written resignation, and advised him that she would not be returning to teach. Thus ended her public school teaching career and began her new career as a legal assistant, and that summer she came to work for me. She received a full-time compensatory salary, together with all of the employee benefits, including being enrolled as a participant in our retirement program. After attending her first legal assistant educational seminar, I made her promise me that from that point on, she would not bother attending any of the educational programs designed for para-legal and legal assistants. Rather instead I would register her to attend the same advanced CLE seminars that I attended, and which were designed for the better lawyers. I explained that at first she might feel somewhat lost and not understand, but to be persistent and keep on going. My thoughts were that our being married, Marlene's legal assistant training would be so much more intensified than it would be in a normal employer-employee situation. Our conversations about the law, cases, procedures, and strategies wouldn't automatically stop at 5:30 PM, at the end of the work day. Rather it would likely continue far beyond that. So I felt her learning pace would be in a much faster lane, and she would be rapidly obtaining knowledge on a higher scale. Besides Marlene is a very quick learner, has lots of smarts, and her adaptive talent is amazing. My theory proved to be right. At first attending the advanced lawyer seminars was rather difficult for Marlene, but after a while, it was clear that she was getting it and understanding the material as well as most of the lawyers in the audience.

Since opening up my practice in Leon Valley (LV), my law business continued to grow at a steady rate. Indeed, while still staying within the confines of LV, eventually I had to move my office to the 4th floor of the bank building at the corner of Bandera and Wurzbach just so as to gain desperately needed additional space. But, when Marlene came out and joined me, the business absolutely mushroomed. It was as if our ability to handle cases doubled. Marlene tended to be a naturally curios person, and her learning did indeed expand at an exponential pace. She became a legal assistant extraordinaire, and hardly a week went by where some lawyer was calling her, seeking her advice on how to do certain procedures and accomplish certain tasks. In fact there were times when several of my competitors told her that if I should ever decide to quit practicing, she should contact them and apply for a position, and she would be hired.

Marlene was highly competent in all of the arenas of our thriving practice, but perhaps two of her favorite areas were probate and consumer bankruptcy, which happened to be two of my favorites, as well. Marlene jokingly referred to me as a lawyer who "specialized in death," either actual, as in the case of probate, or economic, as in the case of bankruptcy. In fact, in the bankruptcy area, she became well recognized for the quality of her work among the judges, trustees, and other lawyers. My secretary, Anita, once informed me that when a particular bankruptcy trustee called on one of our cases, she was instructed by him that he didn't need to speak with me, but to put Marlene on the phone, as she would know what would need to be done. Indeed, sometime during my presidency of the San Antonio Bankruptcy Bar Association (SABBA) in 1996-1998, Marlene was unanimously approved by that organization as its first non-lawyer full-fledged member.

In 1993, my oldest son, Rob, after having graduated from college at UTSA, decided to go to law school at St. Mary's, a decision that his wife, Jennifer, fully supported. During his attendance there he worked as a law clerk at our office. He often flatteringly stated that he learned as much law working with Marlene and me as he did in law school. Rob attained his law degree, graduating from St. Mary's in May, 1997. Later on he would become an associate professor of that law school, teaching mediation, bankruptcy, and family law. After taking and passing the Texas Bar Exam, he was licensed as a Texas lawyer on November 7, 1997. Although he obviously could have chosen to work elsewhere, I felt honored when he chose to come to work with us. He began as a staff attorney, and eventually worked his way up to becoming a full and equal partner with me in the Eichelbaum Law Office. There being only the two of us as partners, and with each of us having only one vote, Marlene who became the office manager, aside from carrying out her legal assistant duties, would end up being the tie breaking vote. Invariably, she usually sided with Rob, but on the really big major decisions, they both tended to go along with my preferences. The three of us together made rather a potent legal practice team for the next decade.

During my active practice years, I had two other outstanding law clerks, which in later years went on to become excellent lawyers. Oddly enough both came about through what I termed as the "Gerson family connection." My younger son, Mark, had married Jen Gerson. While going to college at UT in Austin, Jen had met Miriam Trubek, who was a sorority sister of hers. After college Miriam had decided to go to law school at St. Mary's. She needed to earn some money while going through law school, and in the meantime, she felt it would be a good idea to pick up some actual legal experience; and so therefore, she thought a job as a law clerk would be perfect. One day in a friendly chat, she divulged these thoughts to Jen, who then called me to see if we would be interested in interviewing her for a law clerk position. We did and Miriam was hired. And so circa 2000-2002, Miriam clerked for us. She was enthusiastic and a bundle of energy. Initially, she expressed a keen interest in family law cases, saying with conviction that that was the kind of lawyer she intended to be. According to her the one type of law she definitely was not interested in nor could ever see herself practicing was bankruptcy law. I suggested that she not make any snap judgments, and that she really wouldn't know what she liked and what she didn't until she tried it for at least six months. Although she did help out with family law cases, during her tenure as a law clerk I insisted she work on bankruptcy cases, as well. Dubbing them "her cases," I incorporated Miriam into the entire process in certain bankruptcy cases, from the initial client interview through the Section 341 hearing and final discharge. Under my auspices, watching her conduct an actual 341 hearing, it became apparent she was a natural, and she discovered she loved to practice bankruptcy law. During her latter year at St. Mary's she "was stolen" as our law clerk, when she was chosen to be a law clerk for Judge Leif Clark, who was the Chief Bankruptcy Judge for the Western District of Texas.

Actually we felt extremely honored, and we were very proud of Miriam in having been selected. After graduating law school and passing the Texas Bar Exam, she decided to move back to Houston, where her parents and other relatives resided. She went to work as a bankruptcy lawyer for the law firm of Walker & Patterson, P.C., where she still works to this day. Later on she met a special guy, fell in love, and married him. Today Miriam (Trubek) Goott is considered to be a prominent bankruptcy attorney, with a national reputation. On more than one occasion she was selected to be a speaker-presenter at the CLE conference of the National Association of Consumer Bankruptcy Attorneys (NACBA), a rather prestigious national organization of bankruptcy lawyers. Nationally, she was selected as one of the top 40 lawyers under 40 in bankruptcy by the American Bankruptcy Institute (ABI), and in 2017, Miriam was named as one of the top 50 lawyers in the state of Texas.

The other extraordinary law clerk was Kevin Robinowich, who served as our law clerk during the years of 2005-2007, while he was attending law school at St. Mary's. Kevin, who is Jen's cousin, and so "the Gerson family connection" was again instrumental in placing him with our office. Kevin was an excellent law clerk, who possessed a penchant for detail and was a superb legal researcher. He decided to go in a different direction and formulated a liking for the academic side of the legal profession. After graduating and passing the Texas Bar Exam, Kevin married a girl, who was an engineer by the name of Jennifer, and he continued to work at St. Mary's Law School. In 2016, he was selected to be the Assistant Dean of Student Affairs at the UNT Dallas College of Law, a position he holds to this day.

At the beginning of 2008, Marlene and I decided it was time, and that we would retire together at the end of the year. According to Marlene, commenting on my past, she often said: "Although you could take the lawyer out of Legal Aid; you could never take 'legal aid' out of the lawyer." And throughout my private practice years, I still had a sensibility for helping poor people, and we did more than our fair share of pro-bono work. Indeed, in 2004, I received a certificate from the Texas State Bar Association in recognition for having done more pro-bono cases in the area of bankruptcy than any other lawyer in the state of Texas. After forty-one years of actively practicing law, on December 31, 2008, the Eichelbaum Law Office was officially closed. But even so I wasn't quite done just yet.

CHAPTER 21

My Last Hurrah

2003 – 2011

In re R & I C., Case No. 03-50035-C & Adv. No. 03-5151-C,
U.S. Bankruptcy Court (W.D. TX.)

In re Ocwen Federal Bank FSB Mortgage Servicing Litigation,
MDL 1604

Case No. 04-C-02714, U.S. District Court (N.D. IL.)

Case No. 06-3132, U.S. Court of Appeals (7th Circ.)

Sometimes bad things happen to good people. The biblical story of Job graphically relates how a good and even a wealthy man can suffer ruinous financial reversal, resulting in devastating economic and health consequences. The vicissitudes of modern life can unkindly wield the unexpected loss of employment, the death or divorce of a spouse, or the illness or injury to oneself or a family member, all of which can lead to dire fiscal circumstances. On a wider scale, natural disasters can literally affect millions. Historically the 1930's "Dust Bowl" cut a wide swath through the states of Colorado, Kansas, Nebraska, New Mexico, and Texas, leaving many of their inhabitants financially destitute. On a more recent note in 2005, hurricane Katrina hit the city of New Orleans, nearly destroying it. And in 2017, hurricanes Harvey hammered Houston and Maria clobbered the island of Puerto Rico, and it is anticipated that recovery there will take at least a decade. So is it any wonder that society sought to develop a whole host of remedies in an attempt to deal with such severe economic catastrophes. Modern American bankruptcy law became one of the tools that came into play in blunting some of the adverse effects of harsh economic times.

One can find the evolution of such a concept going back to biblical times. In the ancient kingdom of Israel, an unfortunate individual who was hopelessly in debt could, by agreement, place himself in a slavery relationship with his foremost creditor, with the idea of laboring as a slave in order to work off his debts. But under Mosaic law, with the advent of the sabbatical year (the seventh year), the creditor had to grant the debtor slave his freedom; and moreover, if there was any part of the debt that still remained unpaid, the creditor had to forgive it. And so the idea of giving the debtor a second chance "fresh start" was born. However, down through the ages this theory got waylaid and wouldn't re-emerge until many centuries later.

The actual term "bankruptcy" can be traced back to Roman times. It is derived from the ancient Latin words of "bancus," meaning bench, and "ruptus," meaning broken. At that time the state-creditor course of action in handling a defaulting debtor situation was both rather dramatic and harshly resolute. In those days merchants typically sold their wares or plied their trade at benches that lined the market place. If an individual became hopelessly indebted, legionnaires would intervene and literally break his bench, which served as a visible warning to others that debts had to be repaid and was an unmistakable sign to all that the defaulting debtor was through and out of business. Meanwhile all of his goods, property, and other assets were seized, and these would be marshalled for liquidation for the benefit of his creditors. The poor debtor was left completely destitute and penniless and was driven off with the expectation he would either commit suicide or simply starve to death.

The harshness of bankruptcy didn't change much during the Middle Ages, and its first English reference was in 1542 during the reign of Henry VIII. For the next three centuries or so, the plight of the poor and those who had been economically devastated changed very little and was later dramatically depicted in such classics as *Oliver Twist* and *The Christmas Carol*, by Charles Dickens, and *The Hunchback of Notre Dame* and *Les Miserables*, by Victor Hugo.

Indeed, our forefathers understood tough economic times. Contrary to popular opinion, many of the settlers of the American colonies came in search of debt relief, and not because of religious reasons. These individuals fled Europe in order to avoid debtors' prison, which at that time was utilized as a device to punish people who could not afford to pay their debts. Prison conditions then were abominable. In many instances being thrown into prison was tantamount to a death sentence, where one was either worked to death or died from malnutrition and disease. Given a life or death choice, many Europeans decided to flee and take their chances by coming to the "New World."

After the United States won its independence from Great Britain, the American population was significantly comprised of the children and grandchildren of the original debtors who came here. The founding fathers who wrote the American constitution were sensitive to the concept of debt relief; and hence, they wanted to reserve the right to make bankruptcy laws to fall within the province of the federal government, and so accordingly specifically expressed that in the United States Constitution. Initially, for the most part, congress failed to act in this area. Being a young nation, they had more pressing problems to deal with, and so American bankruptcy remained a fairly creditor oriented device, retaining much of the flavor from its predecessor English common law heritage. However, with the financial panic of 1837, congress reacted and passed the Bankruptcy Act of 1841. For the first time the bankruptcy law permitted the debtor to initiate and file his own bankruptcy in order to seek protection of the court from the overly rapacious actions of creditors in seizing everything the debtor had, including the bare necessities warranted for his very survival. The idea of giving the debtor a second chance "fresh start," originally envisioned by Mosaic law, was beginning to see the light of day again after many centuries of darkness. The concept of not treating bankrupt debtors as complete throwaways and societal pariahs proved to be sociologically beneficial. Countless debtors who had gone bankrupt and who were given a "fresh start" proved their worth, making major contributions to the nation. Among these were: President Abraham Lincoln, H.J. Heinz, Henry Ford, Charles Goodyear, Walt Disney, and President Harry Truman, only to mention a few.

Down through the years American bankruptcy law continued to evolve and became an organized more balanced and even-handed approach to assist creditors in collection of their debts to the best extent possible; while at the same time, providing the honest debtor with a discharge of the remnant of uncollectable debt and a "fresh start" for the future. With the Bankruptcy Reform Act of 1978, modern American bankruptcy law had evolved to where it was the envy of the world and was frequently cited as a model, being taught at international insolvency law seminars by such notables as Leif Clark, who served as the Chief Bankruptcy Judge for the Western District of Texas.

Modern bankruptcy law set forth a wide range of programs to deal with insolvent situations. There was Chapter 9 which dealt with cities and governmental agencies who could not meet their debt burdens. Chapter 12 was a program for full-time farmers, ranchers, and commercial fishermen. Chapter 11, often called the "millionaires' bankruptcy," was a program for structured reorganization. However, the process tended to be rather work-intensified and costly, and so it was usually reserved for big corporations and extremely wealthy individuals. For normal consumers the best bet for debt relief was Chapter 7 or Chapter 13.

Chapter 7 was the oldest form of bankruptcy. Here the debtor sought to show the court that given his assets, income, and normal living expenses, there wasn't enough money left to pay the vast majority of debts which he had incurred. Therefore, the debtor asked the bankruptcy court to issue an order that in effect discharged or eliminated all of the debts that were legally dischargeable.

There were some debts which could not be legally discharged, even in a Chapter 7 proceeding. Among these were alimony and child support, criminal fines and penalties, taxes owed to the government, educational loans, and debts arising from drunken driving, willful or malicious injury to another, or fraud. Aside from these however, most debts were dischargeable in a Chapter 7.

While Chapter 7 was commonly referred to as a "liquidation bankruptcy," it did not mean that the debtor would be forced to give up or surrender all of his assets. Most normal assets in a typical consumer bankruptcy, either under Chapter 7 or Chapter 13, were exempted by the debtor's exemptions to which he was legally entitled. Even if the asset was pledged as security for a particular debt, such as an automobile for example, the debtor ordinarily could have the option of keeping the property by re-affirming that specific debt and paying it back, or conversely he could choose to surrender the property and have the debt discharged.

The other consumer program under the bankruptcy laws was Chapter 13. This program offered the debtor an opportunity to pay back all of his debts to the best extent possible, with the remaining debt being discharged in a similar fashion to Chapter 7. Chapter 13 plans varied greatly as to what percentage of debt the debtor was able to repay to the creditors depending on his income, living expenses, and the total amount of debt owed. One big advantage of a Chapter 13 was that a debtor could restructure the repayment of all debts, even those debts that were not dischargeable in a Chapter 7, such as taxes. In some instances because of the orderly controlled payments under a court approved plan, a debtor was able to do a full 100% payback plan. For those debtors willing to go the extra mile in doing this, the Chapter 13 Trustee's office offered an excellent program of credit rehabilitation.

The credit card industry started out rather modestly by offering a convenient way to pay for travel and related entertainment expenses. The Diner's Club card appeared in 1950, which was followed a number of years later by American Express in 1958. By that time some of the larger banks were getting itchy to get into the credit card market, and in 1958, Bank of America came out with its Visa card. Slowly but surely the other banks followed suit. The big oil companies, such as Mobil and Texaco, issued their own cards, as did virtually every major department store, such as Dillard's, Macy's, and Sears. It seemed like everyone and his brother was getting into the credit card business. By 1966, MasterCard came onto the scene as a competitor to Visa, but by the end of the decade, both cards pretty much dominated the market and were largely controlled by the banking industry.

When I began college in 1960, I remember applying for my very first Visa card. I recall having to fill out a rather detailed application disclosing my jobs, my income and expenses, and my other debts, etc. Then I went before a banker, who reviewed my application and gave me the third degree in order to determine if I was of a frugal nature and responsible enough to merit being issued a Visa card. Eventually, I was approved and felt so pleased to have received my very own Visa card with its whopping $200.00 limit, which I proudly slipped into my wallet.

And so it went throughout much of the 1960's with the steady growth of credit cards as American consumers became more accustomed to utilizing them. At the same time, like a swarm of locusts, credit card lobbyists descended on state legislatures throughout the nation. Many states, Texas included, had traditional usury laws that prohibited the charging of a rate in excess of 10% as interest. The aim was either to repeal those laws, or at least render them inapplicable as to credit card transactions. By the end of the decade the credit card industry had been largely successful in accomplishing their goal.

By the 1970's, and throughout the 1980's, the game was dramatically changing. Credit card companies no longer expected or even desired the consumer to pay off his monthly credit card charges when he received his monthly billing statement. Rather by increasing credit card limits, consumers were encouraged to charge more, and by allowing relatively low minimal monthly payments, consumers were enticed to accumulate debt balances that would tend to increase over time to higher levels. This would maximize profits with the credit card companies being allowed to charge above market interest rates, not to mention extra money coming in from additional fees assessed for over-limit charges and trap late payments. Rather than the cautious and reserved approach that was first used in the beginning with respect to issuing out credit cards, the industry then purposely switched and pursued a super aggressive and somewhat reckless campaign of flooding consumers with as many credit cards as possible. Nearly daily unsolicited credit card offers came willy-nilly via the telephone and poured through the mail. No longer was there careful checking. Rather it was just agree to accept, sign on the dotted line, and your brand new credit card would be on its way to you.

During the mid-1980's, my younger son, Mark, who was still in middle school at that time, received no less than three separate credit card offers in the very same week. And one of my neighbors humorously showed me how his dog, George, had received a credit card invite, which offered a higher credit card limit than what he, himself, had on the very same credit card. In just one decade, from 1980 to 1990, consumer debt had increased by a whopping 285%, and by the year 2000, the national consumer debt was approaching the majestic height of two trillion. The idea of getting Americans hooked on debt had been eminently successful.

But the credit card industry wasn't the only one to blame. A whole host of other financial outfits jumped into the profitable debt business and pushed even more outrageous predatory practices toward the consumer. Among these were the "credit repair" finance companies and payday lenders, who targeted the working poor and lower ranking military personnel, extending them small loans carrying exorbitant interest rates of up to near 1000%, and in some instances even more. Then there were the "debt consolidators," who would offer themselves as an alternative to bankruptcy. They would collect monthly payments from a debtor, and after taking a slice for themselves, they would supposedly pay the debtor's creditors on a negotiated pay-off scheme. However, what they failed to tell the debtor was that in many instances, these outfits received about 75% of their funding from the credit card industry. In truth they were credit collection entities in disguise. Typically, they also failed to advise the debtor that their negotiated schemes didn't truly bind any particular creditor, who was quite capable of pulling out of the deal at any time and once again engage in the pursuit of pressurized collection efforts, which the hapless debtor had thought he had avoided by going with the "debt consolidator," in the first place.

But perhaps the most heinous of all these were the "home equity lenders," who by using the devices of mortgage refinancing, or in some instances reverse mortgages, would somehow manage to convince debtors that it was in their best interest to utilize their home equity in order to gain funds to pay off their credit card debt; hence, exchanging what was once unsecured credit card debt and effectively converting it into secured debt instead, with the debtor's house being pledged as security. In many instances, debtors who had standard thirty year fixed rate mortgages, under the guise of lowering their monthly mortgage payments, would be alternatively conned into an "Adjustable Rate Mortgage" (ARM), not realizing that in a year or two, due to annual rate adjustments, their monthly mortgage payments would be higher than ever.

I never quite realized the grave depth of the relative connection between debt and health, until one day when I received a phone call from Dr. Betty Lou Schroeder. She was a clinical psychologist, who we had used as an expert witness in a Social Security disability case. Dr. Schroeder had called to refer a patient of hers to us for counseling on possible debt relief. Evidently, her patient had attempted to commit suicide by severely slashing her wrists. Dr. Schroeder said that she felt confident their office could adequately handle the depression and stress issues, but it would help immensely if somehow the debt issues could be alleviated.

Upon meeting her patient, I found the individual to be a young, relatively attractive female, who was a college student with a solid scholastic record. As a freshman and during registration, she was accosted by several credit card company representatives that enticed her with various gifts, as a reward for her to sign up for several different credit cards. With no prior experience or training, within a year or two she found herself inundated with debt. When she couldn't keep up with payments, the imposition of grotesque penalty interest charges and late payment fees just made the situation worse. When the accounts were turned over to collection, she was threatened that her parents and friends would be notified, as would the school administrative officials. The straw that broke the camel's back was when she was told that she could be criminally prosecuted and that an arrest warrant would be taken out against her. She tearfully told me that the pressure had become so overwhelming that she decided to end it all. After talking with her, it seemed that bankruptcy was a viable option and clearly warranted. At the Section 341 hearing, which in a bankruptcy case is the evidentiary proceeding where the debtor testifies under oath, the Chapter 7 Trustee, Pat Lowe, noticed her bandaged wrists and asked about them. When she responded and in her testimony told her story, the audience in the hearing room was definitely visibly moved to the core.

At a NACBA CLE conference, I had met James Scurlock, who directed a documentary film entitled *Maxed Out*, which dealt with the country's mushrooming consumer debt issue. In its investigative, hard-hitting 97 minute presentation, the film pulled no punches and showed how the credit card industry, acting in cahoots with other powerful business and political interests and in pursuit of absolute unrestrained greed, were putting far too many Americans at risk. The film culminated with its heart-wrenching stories of Sean and Mitzi, who were college students seduced by multiple credit card offers they couldn't pay for with their part-time jobs, and then racked up debt and guilt. Sean was a National Merit Scholar studying at the University of Texas at Dallas, who owed $12,000.00 on 10 different credit cards. He had driven home to Oklahoma to explore the possibility of bankruptcy, but before he could meet with the attorney and being overtaken with depression, he hung himself in his closet. Mitzi, a student at the University of Central Oklahoma, spread her credit card bills across her dorm bed before hanging herself with her bedsheet. Her credit card debt was $2,500.00. The film ended with the poignant interview with the mothers of the two deceased students. The mothers were unable to convince Oklahoma lawmakers to limit on-campus credit card solicitations. The Texas legislature was equally unresponsive. Mitzi's mother still received credit card mailings addressed to her dead daughter, proclaiming: "We want you back!" On various occasions, Sean's mother had picked up the phone only to hear debt collectors asking her to pay up in honor of her son's memory. I had already learned that debt could kill, but the moving impact the film had on the CLE audience was noticeable. I felt that the film should be required viewing for all individuals before getting their first credit card.

Our bankruptcy business became ever-increasing, as referrals steadily came in not only from psychiatrists and psychologists, but also from members of the clergy, as well as from former clients and a whole host of other attorneys, who did not practice bankruptcy law, but who recognized that bankruptcy relief might possibly be able to help out their debt distressed clients. There was a debt crises looming on the horizon, but the vast majority of the American public were oblivious to it, and for those who saw the danger signs, like Elizabeth Warren, their voices were a cry in the wilderness.

Instead of owning up to even an iota of responsibility regarding the debt tsunami that was coming and for which at least in good part, it was chiefly culpable in creating, the credit card industry malevolently decided to chart another course. Rather than attack the disease by curtailing the never-ending unwarranted credit card solicitations and ceasing the predatory lending and over aggressive collection practices, the credit card industry, along with its powerful allies, opted to go after one of the cure mechanisms instead. They chose to attempt to convince the press, the politicians, and the public that it was all the fault of the blatantly irresponsible debtors who, together with their bankruptcy lawyers, were abusing the system by recklessly shedding righteous debt. Forget the facts that in many instances the hapless debtor actually got hoodwinked into his over-indebtedness situation by the lending industry itself.

And so in the 1990's the battle for bankruptcy reform began. A well-funded publicity campaign was commenced carrying the message that a crackdown on bankruptcies was essential. A hoard of lobbyists were unleashed on congress to convince lawmakers that the bankruptcy laws were "too soft" and "too liberally in favor of debtors" and that corrective bankruptcy reform was necessary. I became so upset with this constant onslaught that I ended up writing my congressman, Henry B. Gonzalez, about the proposed bankruptcy reform legislation that was being pushed by the creditor community and was pending in congress. On March 5, 1998, Henry responded to my letter, stating in part: "While some complain about the rise in bankruptcies, consumer credit has also been pushed on the public in recent years. Consumer credit has doubled over the past decade to the point that the annual consumer debt now approaches $1 trillion in this country. Credit card companies send out almost three billion credit card solicitations a year. If we are going to address the increase in consumer bankruptcies, surely we must also address the massive amount of credit that is being pushed on consumers by financial interests these days as well." It was obvious from the balance of his letter that he was right up to snuff on the issue, and it was clearly evident that he hadn't been snowed by the financial industry's propaganda. I was so proud that he was my congressman.

Having not been successful the previous year, in 1999, the creditor community tried again, which prompted one of our Chapter 7 Trustees, Randy Osherow, to comment in the San Antonio Bankruptcy Bar Association (SABBA) newsletter of May, 1999, stating: "Congress continues to chug along passing the 1999 Visa/MasterCard Bankruptcy Welfare Act—sure to be vetoed by the President. You have to give the credit card lobbyists an "A" for persistence. While Visa and MasterCard post record profits one can only wonder is it really cheaper to buy the U.S. Congress or simply stop extending credit to those persons of high credit risk—say for example a widow receiving $600.00 a month from Social security?" Randy was right of course and his observation dead on. Even the credit community began to realize that even if they managed to push their legislation through congress, President Bill Clinton had gone on record that he would veto it. Hence, millions of dollars poured into Republican coffers prior to the next presidential election.

In 2000, with the election of George W. Bush as president, the credit card industry and their allies were heartened. Even a larger more intensified blitz campaign was waged to achieve the goal of passing a more restrictive bankruptcy reform bill which would clamp down on consumer filings under Chapters 7 and 13, while leaving the high-ended wealthy filers and corporate entities under chapter 11 pretty much unscathed.

In the four years from 2000--2004, consumer bankruptcy filings under Chapters 7 and 13 had reached a high of 1.56 million. But at the same time consumer debt had astronomically climbed from $1.7 trillion to $2.1 trillion. Despite the fact that credible and reputable studies had been done by Harvard and the Center for Law, Business & Economics at my alma mater, the University of Texas School of Law, both of which clearly indicated that abuse was neither a motivational factor nor did it play a role in the vast majority of consumer bankruptcies. Rather the studies showed that the traditional reasons for filing bankruptcy largely remained unchanged, but that even a greater number than originally thought—over 50% were due to medical bills. In our office, our own experience showed that number to be 62%--better than six out of every ten bankruptcies.

But after years of messaging, money, and pressure the powerful credit card industry had managed to procure the votes, and they weren't about to be dissuaded, nor were they in the mood for any compromise. Even the impassioned speech by Senator Ted Kennedy (D-MA), who was known as "the lion of the Senate," and in which he stated: "Americans are going to get thrown into bankruptcy and rather than let out so that they have a new chance and a new opportunity in life because they have done nothing wrong, they're going to be tied up and be paying credit card companies for the next five years. That's the way this bill works." But his words proved to be of no avail and failed to convince his fellow senators. On March 10, 2005, the bill was passed by the U.S. Senate, with Republican Texas Senators, Kay Bailey Hutchinson and John Cornyn, voting in favor of it. Tom DeLay, Republican House Majority Leader steered the bill through the House, which passed it on April 14, 2005. And on April 20, 2005, President George W. Bush signed the Bankruptcy Abuse Prevention Consumer Protection Act (BAPCPA) into law. Not even a scintilla of consideration was given to the credit card and lending industries' behavior in contributing, if not out and out manipulating the exploding consumer debt situation. Indeed, it was the excessive and never-ending greed of those industries, together with the narrow short-sightedness of congress in forthrightly dealing with the debt crises problem that would be a major contributing factor to the economic crises of 2008.

The new law placed an arbitrary means test on debtors, which pushed many potential Chapter 7 filers into long-term, 5 year Chapter 13 payment plans. The process was made more cumbersome, detailed, and costly. It was filled with a number of potential "gotcha" debtor pit traps, which would have to be skillfully navigated around and avoided. An attorney who represented debtors, in any public communications couldn't even refer to himself as an "attorney at law" anymore, but had to mandatorily add that he was a "debt relief agency." And so with congressional compliance and a stroke of his pen, President Bush magically supposedly transformed me from being a lawyer into being a debt relief agency.

Fresh from its victory in having successfully passed the BAPCPA the credit card and lending industries became further emboldened, which resulted in even more aggressive and irresponsible credit card solicitations and abusive collection tactics. A few months before the Christmas holidays, Visa and MasterCard were sending new credit card offers to debtors who were already involved in Chapter 13 bankruptcies where they were trying to pay off their indebtedness, among which were debts already owed to Visa and MasterCard. The implication was it would be okay to use the new cards to charge up Christmas shopping items. Most of our clients were aware of such trickery and avoided it, but a few succumbed to the temptation, essentially blowing up their Chapter 13 bankruptcies with disastrous consequences. When one couple, who ended up losing their house, announced to Marlene: "Oh well, at least we had a nice Christmas," it prompted Rob and me to take action and we drafted a warning letter, which would go out to our clients before the next Christmas holiday season, and which said:

> Dear Chapter 13 Clients:
>
> Well, can you believe another year has almost gone by, and we are fast approaching the holiday season. How time flies!
>
> Last year we experienced a more than normal amount of requests for Moratoriums and saw a number of dismissal actions filed by the Chapter 13 Trustee (for failure to make plan payments) and Lift-Stay actions by mortgage creditors (for failing to make post-petition house payments). Some of our clients we were able to still save, but not all. Some ended up losing their houses, cars, etc. Nearly all of our clients where this happened said it was due to overspending for Christmas.
>
> We realize that Christmas is a very important holiday, steeped with deep religious significance, and a time for family togetherness.
>
> We don't mean to sound like a Grinch! Indeed, we hope that each of you have a joyous and meaningful Christmas holiday, by all means we encourage you to contact family and friends and get together with them, if at all possible, do go to church and pray, and we sincerely hope that this Christmas be full of significant meaning to you.

However, as a caution and because we care, we are reminding you to please be careful with your spending. Love has no price tag, and all that is needed is merely to extend it to others. We believe that you can have a very meaningful and rememberable Christmas, without spending yourself into oblivion. So please be careful.

On behalf of our entire office staff, we wish you a wonderful Christmas and a New Year filled with hope.

Very truly yours,

Somehow the Chapter 13 Trustee got a hold of a copy of our letter (probably from one of our clients), and the bankruptcy judges were made aware of it as well. The letter became widely known as the "Grinch letter" and became all the rave at the next Western District of Texas Bankruptcy CLE seminar.

And so it was in this climate of a spiraling rise in consumer debt, which was the harbinger of the economic collapse to come, that I unexpectedly got involved in a marathon bankruptcy/consumer-advocacy case that would span eight years, taking me even beyond my official retirement date, and would end up being a "David and Goliath" story of how two humble and meek bankruptcy debtors helped vanquish a big powerful mortgage company.

Ocwen started in Orlando, Florida and meteorically rose in stature as a mortgage lending and servicing institution, spreading its tentacles into a multitude of different states, including Texas. In 2003, it seized a major and very lucrative contract with Freddie Mac to manage a large number of high risk mortgages through a loan modification process. By then Ocwen had vaulted into the position as the third largest mortgage creditor in the United States.

In the latter part of 2002, Mr. & Mrs. C., a senior Hispanic couple, came to see me regarding their debt problems. They had become over-extended and behind on their credit card debt. The imposition of late payment fees and penalty interest had exasperated the situation and made it even worse. At least in part, their credit card debt was due to charges related to medical expenses incurred because of Mr. C.'s prior health condition. Fortunately however, they had avoided some of the more abusive credit traps for debtors, and they had managed to stay current on their house payment, car payment, and taxes. After counseling with them, it appeared that given their monthly income and budgetary living expenses, there was a sufficient amount of remaining economic strength whereby the credit card debt could be paid over a period of time under a controlled repayment plan pursuant to the bankruptcy statutes. So on January 3, 2003, we filed a Chapter 13 bankruptcy for Mr. & Mrs. C., which included a 100% pay back plan. As verification of all of their debts, prior to filing we had obtained documentation by all of their creditors, including their mortgage creditor, who was Ocwen. Ocwen's statement to the debtors, dated December 31, 2002, indicated and showed that Mr. & Mrs. C. were absolutely current on their mortgage as of the end of the year. Likewise we monitored our clients' mortgage payment for January, 2003, and we knew it had been timely made. As per our instructions, Mr. & Mrs. C. continued to timely make their monthly post-petition payments to Ocwen.

So after filing, we were rather surprised when we received Ocwen's sworn-to claim, contending Mr. & .Mrs. C. hadn't made their monthly post-petition mortgage payment for January, 2003, and accordingly at the actual time of the bankruptcy filing, a mortgage arrearage existed and was due. And since the debtors' Chapter 13 plan didn't specify such arrearage, nor did it provide for the priority payment of it, Ocwen filed an objection to the confirmation of the debtors' Chapter 13 plan. Further investigation yielded evidence into the matter which showed that upon receiving notice of the debtors' bankruptcy, either by negligence or design, Ocwen chose to take the debtors' monthly post-petition payment it had received for the month of January, 2003, and place it into a suspense account, rather than credit it as a monthly payment against the debtors' mortgage; and hence, by doing so, manipulatively creating an artificial arrearage, whereas factually there was none.

At the court hearing before Judge Leif Clark, all of this came out, and we were able to prove that Ocwen's claim was erroneous and demonstrate that in truth there wasn't any mortgage arrearage. The Ocwen attorney embarrassingly argued that it was just all a mistake. Ocwen's arrearage claim was denied as was their objection to confirmation. They were instructed to take the monthly mortgage payments they had received and to transfer them out of their suspense account and properly apply them as credits to the debtors' mortgage. Ocwen was further cautioned not to assess any fees against Mr. & Mrs. C. due to this so called "misunderstanding" on their part. And so on May 5, 2003, the debtors' Chapter 13 plan was confirmed.

In talking to other debtors' attorneys, I learned that Ocwen was no stranger to these types of shenanigans. It was later on that summer when Mr. C. brought me a mortgage billing statement they received, and it appeared that Ocwen was attempting to charge them for bankruptcy related attorney's fees and to tack them on to their mortgage. First, there was a $150.00 charge for reviewing the debtors' Chapter 13 plan, which evidently they didn't review very well. Second, was another $150.00 charge for Ocwen's proof of claim, which was bogus and incorrect. Third, was a $300.00 charge for their objection to confirmation, which was erroneous and should have never been filed, and finally, there was a non-designated $75.00 charge, which appeared to be an arbitrary fee imposed upon the debtors for having filed a bankruptcy. These charges totaled $675.00, and this tab was added to the debtors' mortgage bill. Once we saw those flagrant fees, Rob and I decided that not only would we vigorously challenge those charges as legit, but also that it was time to go on offence and file an adversary case against Ocwen for having violated the bankruptcy law and various consumer laws, as well.

Earlier in 2003, Rob and I had attended a NACBA CLE conference in Las Vegas, where we had heard Gary Klein, a nationally prominent consumer lawyer, deliver a presentation on the topic of the nexus of bankruptcy and consumer law actions that could be taken against abusive and unscrupulous creditors. Given our situation in Mr. & Mrs. C.'s case, we decided to contact Gary. He was familiar with Ocwen and already had a consumer law class action against them that was ongoing in Massachusetts, and there were also some others pending in California and several other states. After several back and forth communications and upon obtaining the consent of our clients, Gary agreed to join us in utilizing Mr. & Mrs. C. as named plaintiffs in a class action case against Ocwen. And so on September 11, 2003, our class action adversary proceeding was filed in the bankruptcy court. On October 24, 2003, Ocwen filed their response, which included a motion to dismiss, asserting inter alia that plaintiffs lacked standing to bring this suit, that no cause of action existed, and that the case was moot.

In the spring of 2004, the NACBA CLE conference just so happened to be in Boston. That being rather fortuitous, Rob and I decided to go up there a couple of days earlier so we could meet with Gary in person at his law firm of Roddy, Klein & Ryan. During our conference we found out that the number of consumer class action cases against Ocwen had been expanding throughout the nation. Indeed, that April, Ocwen had managed to get a judicial panel to establish a multi-district litigation (MDL) court before Judge Charles Norgle in the federal district court for the Northern District of Illinois, which was located in Chicago. We learned that Judge Norgle was rather conservative and tended not to be pro-consumer in his orientation, which wasn't exactly good news for the thousands of class clients that Ocwen had been ripping off. So the game plan was to try to maintain our suit in San Antonio, proceeding with it in the bankruptcy court there and trying to utilize it as a forerunner to the MDL cases pending in Chicago. Ocwen's motion to dismiss was slated for argument that May, and they had hired Carrington, Coleman, Sloman & Blumenthal, LLP, a supposedly powerful creditors' law firm out of Dallas to represent them. Up to that point in time, Rob had not been involved in any class action litigation, and it had been quite some time since my Legal Aid days when I was very much engaged in such activity and so recognized that I was a wee bit rusty; therefore, Gary felt more comfortable in having a friend of his, Steve Gardner, who was an experienced class action attorney out of Dallas and who was also familiar with the Carrington firm, to join us so that he could handle the court argument on Ocwen's motion to dismiss. Rob and I agreed.

On the morning of May 10, 2004, we met Steve at Judge Leif Clark's bankruptcy courtroom. The Carrington firm's attorney argued Ocwen's motion to dismiss, and Steve countered him and did an excellent job in doing so. In the end we had won, and Ocwen's motion to dismiss was denied. Judge Clark had ruled that our case should go forward, and on June 21, 2004, we received a scheduling order from the bankruptcy court. It looked as if our game plan was working and that we'd be able to push our case ahead in San Antonio, which was just what we wanted. Then the very next day, June 22, 2004, the wind was taken out of our sails. We received notice from Ocwen that they had requested that our class action case be transferred to the MDL court in Chicago and consolidated with all of the other consumer class actions that were there. Although we valiantly tried to maintain the case in San Antonio, presenting what we felt were very good reasons, including the uniqueness of a bankruptcy law involvement in our particular case, as justification for our position, but it was to no avail. Rather the concepts of judicial economy prevailed, and on December 8, 2004, our client's class action case was officially transferred to the MDL court. By that time the number of consumer class action cases against Ocwen had mushroomed into suits emanating from sixteen different states, including: Alabama, California, Connecticut, Iowa, Illinois, Maryland, Massachusetts, Michigan, Minnesota, Mississippi, North Carolina, New Mexico, Pennsylvania, Washington, Wisconsin, and now Texas. The transfer order effectively split our case and would force us to have to fight a two front war. Our class action adversary case against Ocwen now sat before Judge Norgle in the MDL court in Chicago. Primarily, we'd have to rely on Gary to look out for our interests there. On the other hand, the administration of our clients' Chapter 13 plan remained with the San Antonio bankruptcy court. It would be the task of Rob and I to monitor that and to make sure that Ocwen couldn't maneuver things which could cause the debtors' plan to fail. Because if they did, then that could result in a dismissal of their Chapter 13 bankruptcy case, which could then in turn jeopardize their standing and status as named plaintiffs to be able to maintain their class action case against Ocwen pending in the MDL court in Chicago.

Meanwhile back on the home front in San Antonio, the Bexar County taxing authority sent out its real property tax bills in October of the tax year. Then traditionally the homeowner was expected to completely pay the taxed amount by the end of January of the following year. So for example, Mr. & Mrs. C. received their 2003 tax bill pertaining to their house in October, 2003. Customarily they would have had to pay that in full by no later than January 31, 2004. But a couple of years earlier, the county taxing authority came up with a new program for seniors. They could select the option to pay their taxes in four equal installments, for example, with ¼ being paid by December 31, 2003; ¼ being paid by March 31, 2004; ¼ being paid by June 30, 2004; and the final ¼ being paid by September 30, 2004. This program was designed and instituted by Bexar County to specifically help seniors, and there was no penalty or extra costs involved for seniors selecting this option. Accordingly, Mr. & Mrs. C. legitimately chose to pay their real property taxes in this manner. So in December, 2003, they paid their first ¼ portion and then in March, 2004, paid their second ¼ portion of their 2003 real property taxes.

Then in May of 2004, Ocwen decided to attack. Apparently they had verified that the debtors' real property taxes for 2003 had not yet been fully paid, but thoughtlessly failed to inquire further as to whether the debtors were current in their tax payments under the taxing authority's installment payment plan that had been adopted for seniors. So assuming the debtors were behind on their taxes, when in fact they were not, and without first checking with the debtors, or us as their attorneys, or the Chapter 13 Trustee, Ocwen hauled off and unilaterally intervened by advancing and paying the entire 2003 year taxes. Ocwen then assessed that against the debtors, together with penalties and fees, adding the entire sum to the debtors' mortgage and summarily increasing the debtors' monthly mortgage payment amount.

Later that month I received a panicked call from Mr. C. as to what he should do about the increased mortgage amount reflected on their billing statement for June, 2004, and whether or not he should make their 3rd installment payment on their 2003 real property taxes, which was scheduled to be paid that month. At about the same time, I received a call from an attorney representing the Bexar County taxing authority, advising me that an over-payment situation existed due to Ocwen's intervention in paying the entire amount of 2003 taxes, when Mr. & Mrs. C. had already paid half of that sum. Meanwhile, I also received a call from Marion "Al" Olson, the Chapter 13 Trustee, who exasperatingly expressed that he couldn't believe Ocwen's ill-conceived actions and how they managed to gum up the works regarding the 2003 taxes and to put an unnecessary risk on the debtors' over-all performance under their Chapter 13 plan, which had been working just fine up until now. Ocwen's attorney with the Carrington firm, Jennifer Salisbury, was notified of the mess that her client had managed to create. With some negotiations, and with the cooperation of the attorney representing the taxing authority as well as the facilitation of the Chapter 13 Trustee, an imaginative solution was devised by utilizing a plan modification/subrogation scheme, whereby Ocwen would be repaid the funds it had unwarrantedly advanced to pay Mr. & Mrs. C.'s 2003 taxes.

When the corrective remedy was approved by the bankruptcy court, Ocwen of course had to reverse all of the fees, penalties, and interest they had charged the debtors and had to put their mortgage payment back to what it was before. This tax fiasco caused by Ocwen ended up costing them attorneys' fees and costs, which they had to pay us for our work we did in straightening out the problem they caused. In his approval order, dated February 1, 2005, Judge Leif Clark, specifically cautioned Ocwen with respect to their future conduct, by stating: "The Respondent Ocwen Federal Savings Bank, FSB is hereby enjoined, without first seeking permission of this Court, from paying or attempting to pay the debtors' 2004 real property taxes. Rather the debtors should be allowed to pay their 2004 real property taxes on their own in accordance with the taxing authority's policy in that regard."

In May, 2005, a frustrated Mr. C. came to our office, complaining that Ocwen was trying to raise their monthly mortgage payment again. Sure enough the billing statement he brought in reflected that beginning on July 1, 2005, their monthly mortgage payment was being raised from $863.82 to $998.35, an increase of $134.53 per month. From the statement it was unclear as to just what justified this action. At Rob's suggestion, we drafted an inquiry letter under the Real Estate Settlement Procedures Act (RESPA), to which Ocwen would be obliged to respond. Mr. C. signed it, and we sent it certified mail—return receipt requested. We assured Mr. C. that we were determined to get to the bottom of this.

In June, 2005, Ocwen Federal Savings Bank, FSB in Orlando, Florida, either sold or transferred our clients' mortgage to Ocwen Loan Servicing, LLC in Chicago, Illinois. We still hadn't received a response to our RESPA letter, and I was a little concerned that the technical switch in "creditor entity" might be an attempt to avoid the injunctive effects of Judge Clark's order, or was I just becoming too conspiratorial in nature about the matter. Meanwhile Mr. C. was getting more agitated regarding the situation.

In July, 2005, Mr. C. was put into the hospital. I visited him there and learned that they feared it was heart related, but it was due to an anxiety attack instead. He was there for a couple of days and released as okay. Subsequently, Mr. C.'s doctor called me to discuss his concern with respect to the stress factor on Mr. C., and then even followed up by sending me a letter concerning the situation, which in pertinent part stated: "This patient is under my care. His condition can worsen under stress."

In the meantime, Mr. & Mrs. C. had been contacted by the county taxing authority, who informed them that they were entitled to a tax refund. Evidently, in June, 2005, when they paid their 3rd installment payment of their 2004 real property taxes, the whole amount of 2004 taxes had already been paid, as Ocwen had pulled the same stunt once again by advancing payment of the debtors' taxes, charging them fees and penalties, and then increasing their mortgage payment. Rob and I incredulously shook our heads, realizing that Ocwen had repeated its reprehensible conduct, even after having been told by the bankruptcy court not to do so. No wonder they hadn't responded to our RESPA letter—it seemed like they were trying to cover this up and slide it by. Watch, they'll try to use the technical switch in "creditor entity" as an excuse for their repeated "mistake," I thought. After checking with Gary to make sure it would not be disruptive of the MDL proceedings, Rob and I were determined to bring an enforcement action against Ocwen in the bankruptcy court. After all this was the second time, and we felt Judge Clark wouldn't look too kindly on his previous order being flaunted.

Prior to the court hearing, Ocwen's attorney, Jennifer Salisbury with the Carrington firm, contacted us. She conceded that it was Ocwen's error and offered to correct everything and make it right. In addition, by way of settlement she said Ocwen would be willing to pay Mr. & Mrs. C. $250.00 in damages and $500.00 to us to cover attorneys' fees. Our response was that we would see them in court. Rob and I were miffed that this was the second time they had done this, and yet they felt little or no regard as to the aggravation and trouble they caused and thought they should be able to walk away for peanuts.

At the court hearing, Rob handled the trial, as I ended up being a fact witness testifying about attorney's fees and expenses. About half way through my testimony, Jennifer and a more senior attorney from the Carrington firm, who had accompanied her to the hearing, asked Judge Clark if they could have a brief recess, which Judge Clark granted them. During the "time out," we went into a small conference room across the hall from the courtroom. After a very brief conversation, the more senior Carrington firm attorney excused himself so as to make a personal call to Ocwen. When he returned, we had a deal, and the case was settled. Ocwen's attorneys agreed on the record that everything would be corrected and straightened out. All charges of fees, penalties, and interest would be reversed, and that the debtors' mortgage would be put back to where it was as if this event hadn't happened. This time it cost Ocwen a significant amount more in attorneys' fees and expenses which they had to pay to us, as well as monetary damages, which were paid to Mr. & Mrs. C.

Meanwhile on the MDL front things were beginning to happen. After sitting on the cases in what seemed like forever and as anticipated, Judge Norgle had granted Ocwen's motion to dismiss the MDL cases. Since most of the MDL cases were based on various state law violations both in contract and in tort, the rationale was that plaintiffs' avenue of addressing these complaints should have been through the federal Office of Thrift Savings (OTS) pursuant to the Home Owners' Loan Act (HOLA). It was somewhat of a weak argument, and ironically it waxed even weaker in our case scenario, where Ocwen's infractions tended to transverse both federal bankruptcy law as well as various consumer laws. Now our case could very well prove to be a real nemeses with respect to Ocwen's choice in having had it moved into the MDL court, and wouldn't that be a piece of poetic justice. At any rate, Gary felt fairly confident and advised us that Judge Norgle's decision was going to be appealed to the 7th Circuit of the United States Court of Appeals. And indeed, in 2006 that appeal was filed.

Now various heavy hitters came into play, and a multitude of amicus curiae briefs were filed with the 7th Circuit Court in our favor by various noteworthy consumer advocate groups, such as: the AARP Foundation Litigation, the Center for Responsible Lending, the National Association of Consumer Advocates, the National Consumer Law Center, and the Trial lawyers for Public Justice. After a host of briefs, intensive hearings, and a lengthy consideration, finally on June 22, 2008, the justices at the 7th Circuit Court came down with their decision that essentially agreed with us. Judge Norgle's order granting Ocwen's motion to dismiss was overruled, and the MDL cases were remanded back to Judge Norgle's court with an order instructing him to move the MDL cases forward toward trial.

In the year 2008, with the 7th Circuit Court decision behind them, the combined plaintiffs' attorneys in the MDL cases began to progressively pursue discovery in earnest, probing into areas and practices, which Ocwen wasn't exactly anxious of being revealed. The year 2008 also saw the burst of the housing bubble. The scheme of foreclosing on properties and then reselling them at even a higher price, because of an ever increasing real estate value market, was no longer a viable option and came to a screeching halt. Many mortgage creditors and the holders of such securities now found themselves in a similar position likened to the one in which they had maneuvered many debtors into. The MDL cases, which had been ongoing for about five years, were beginning to have a sobering effect on Ocwen. Gary felt that after the 7th Circuit Court's opinion, and with facing the mounting pressure of discovery revelations and the realization of the risk that plaintiffs could ultimately win this litigation, plus the continuing legal expenses they were incurring, combined with the economy as a whole, that it just might bring Ocwen to the bargaining table to seriously engage in settlement negotiations.

Meanwhile back on the San Antonio scene, by the end of 2008, Mr. & Mrs. C. had successfully completed their Chapter 13 bankruptcy and received a discharge from the bankruptcy court. Of course, their MDL case against Ocwen was still pending. Marlene and I were scheduled to retire together at the end of 2008. Rob had decided not to continue practicing under the moniker of the "Eichelbaum Law Office," as a major San Antonio law firm had made him "an offer he couldn't refuse," and they were even going to hire our secretary, Alura Chavez, to go to work there with him. Rob and Alura left effectively the first of the year (2009). Although Marlene and I officially retired on December 31, 2008, it took us the better part of the first three months of 2009 to finally close the office.

Mr. & Mrs. C. were naturally concerned about the impact our office closure would have on their ongoing case, but they were consoled when Rob and I explained to them that we were going to continue to represent them in their MDL case against Ocwen. We had negotiated with the firm

{ 361 }

Rob was going to work with that their case would remain exclusively with us, and not become a part of Rob's new firm operation or subject to their auspices. In the meantime we notified Gary Klein of our new contact info, and he introduced us to Shennan Kavanaugh, an attorney with his firm who would be our point of contact with respect to MDL matters.

Once retired, I took up cooking, and toward the end of March, 2009, with Marlene's assistance, I had become proficient enough to make a scrumptious Greek shrimp dinner for Rob and his family. After the meal and during coffee, Rob informed me that recently he had engaged in discussions with an attorney with the U.S. Trustee's office, who was aware of our history with Ocwen. According to him their office was gathering evidence on what appeared to be Ocwen's new game plan scheme. Rather than using phony and questionable charges to try to torpedo and sink debtors' Chapter 13 bankruptcies during the administration of the plan (as they had attempted to do in Mr. & Mrs. C.'s case); their new strategy was wait and pounce after the Chapter 13 was over. During the Chapter 13 proceeding, they would surreptitiously accumulate bogus charges for non-essential reviews, un-called for drive by property inspections, unnecessary tax involvement, and the like. By the end of the Chapter 13 process these charges would end up totaling $2,500--$5,000, which would then be added to the debtors' mortgage amount. So that after the Chapter 13 bankruptcy was over, rather than a fresh start, the debtors would end up with an additional $2,500--$5,000 mortgage bill with a demand to pay up or lose their house. The frightened debtors would be referred to a different Ocwen division, who under the guise of "helping" would have the debtors sign a modification agreement, which would allow them to pay off the amount over a period of time, at a hefty interest rate of course. The modification agreement locked in all those fees and charges that Ocwen had piled up, and by signing it the debtors waived their right to challenge them. Rob advised me that evidently the U.S. Trustee's office was seriously looking into this matter and planned to get involved. Wow, this could even put more pressure on Ocwen, I thought. I sent Shennan a summary memo of the matter, as I thought that she and Gary should be aware of this. From time to time I would periodically correspond with Shennan so as to keep current on the MDL status, and then I would advise Mr. & Mrs. C. to keep them up to date. Of course, understandably they were becoming a wee bit impatient, after all their MDL case had been going on for seven years already. On April 16, 2010, I wrote them a letter stating:

"This is just a brief note to let you know that we have not forgotten about you. Recently, I have communicated with our head Counsel in Massachusetts, Gary Klein and Shennan Kavanaugh, in order to make inquiry as to where the MDL case was standing at this point in time.

Technically, the case has been remanded back to Judge Norgle (the District Judge of the United States District Court for the Northern District of Illinois). This was after the appeal dealing with pre-trial issues. Judge Norgle seems to be sitting on the case with a Motion to Dismiss that is being re-urged by the Defendants, however in the meantime Plaintiffs' discovery appears to be finally going forward. This should put some pressure on Ocwen, as well as some pressure in having to reveal facts and info that in my opinion Ocwen would prefer not to reveal. Do not hold your breath, but as discovery goes forward, it might reactivate settlement discussions.

I will of course keep you informed. Say a prayer and maybe we might have some news by the end of this year."

On May 28, 2010, I received a frantic call from Mr. C. He shockingly informed me that unbelievably Ocwen had pulled the same tax stunt for what was now the third time. They unnecessarily intruded and advanced and paid our clients' real property taxes so as to create a mortgage arrearage, which of course added unwarranted fees and charges, as well. I notified Rob and a RESPA letter was immediately prepared and sent out. My thoughts were "three strikes and you're out." Rob and I were ready to consider re-opening the bankruptcy case and going after Ocwen with a hard-hitting adversary and contempt action, this time seeking punitive damages. Rob's comment was he didn't think we'd have too much trouble in establishing a course of conduct, and I agreed.

It was a rainy July 1st when I met Mr. & Mrs. C. at the Bexar County taxing authority's office. We were able to verify that Ocwen had advanced payment of the real property taxes for 2009, despite the fact that Mr. & Mrs. C. had timely paid their 1st and 2nd installments, and had recently in June paid their 3rd installment. They were absolutely current in their tax payments when Ocwen intervened and sent in their payment for our clients' taxes. We went ahead and spoke to a counselor there, who was patient enough to allow us to go over the entire history of Ocwen's involvement in these matters. He just kept on shaking his head in disbelief and repeating: "what's wrong with these guys?" At the conclusion of our session, he promised that he would be writing up a report and that Mr. & Mrs. C. would be getting a letter from them shortly.

On July 6, 2010, our clients received a letter from the taxing authority, verifying the over payment and stating they were entitled to a refund. We informed Shennan of the situation and what our plans were concerning Ocwen, provided it wouldn't interfere with the MDL cases. In September, 2010, Mr. & Mrs. C. went ahead and made their 4th and final installment payment, so that the entire year's amount that had been intrusively paid by Ocwen now sat as a credit at the tax office capable of being refunded upon request.

On October 4, 2010, we filed our motion to re-open the bankruptcy case, and we were prepared to move forward on our new action against Ocwen. I actually relished the idea of taking them back to court. I thought Judge Clark might have a dim view with respect to their blatant cavalier attitude. Then, almost fatalistically, 48 hours later, on October 6, 2010, we received word from Shennan concerning a possible settlement regarding the MDL cases against Ocwen. She suggested we hold up for a couple of days and by then she should have some further news one way or the other. With anticipated excitement we agreed to hold our fire. Two days later, on October 8, 2010, we were on the telephone having a conference call with Gary and Shennan. Evidently, Ocwen had offered to settle, and although some small details and fine points still had to be hammered out, a deal was actually on the table. Roughly, the settlement was that in resolution of the matter, Ocwen would pay $8,000,000.00 as damages, which covered the stipulated sum of $7,500.00 for each named plaintiff, with the large remainder of the multi-million dollar sum being made available to cover the statutory and general claims of the represented class in the MDL cases. In addition, Ocwen would pay a total of $4,250,000.00 in attorneys' fees to cover the work of all the plaintiffs' attorneys. Gary felt it was a delicate balancing game, and he believed that they had pushed it about as far as they could realistically go. He and the other lead Plaintiffs' attorneys were concerned that if they pressed for any more, it could shove Ocwen into having to file for bankruptcy itself, which would be an unfortunate situation that no one really wanted. We reminded them of the recent problem we were having with Ocwen and advised them we would talk to our clients and then get back to them.

On October 14, 2010, Rob and I met with Mr. & Mrs. C. to discuss Ocwen's settlement offer with respect to the MDL cases, and also what the next steps should be in our contemplated new action against Ocwen concerning their latest intrusion into our clients' real property taxes and the resultant manufactured mortgage arrearage together with the unwarranted connected fees and charges. I could see on their faces how pleased and relieved they were regarding the settlement news on the MDL cases. As to the issue of embarking on a new proceeding against Ocwen, from a litigation standpoint, our clients were absolutely exhausted, and who could blame them. They just wanted this whole Ocwen matter over with once and for all, and why couldn't this all get done at one time? We told them we would try to handle it that way. In fact Mr. C. asked me that once this case was over, if I could help them get rid of Ocwen, which he referred to as the mortgage company from hell, and to assist them in re-financing their mortgage with a decent outfit. I could certainly understand his request and promised him that I would help them. We then called Shennan and notified her that we would accept the settlement offer, but with one caveat, which was that Mr. & Mrs. C. insisted that the latest tax fiasco caused by Ocwen be fixed and resolved first.

On November 5, 2010, we received Judge Clark's order re-opening the bankruptcy case, thus allowing us to proceed against Ocwen if we chose to do so. Even though we realized our clients really didn't want to litigate any further, we would hold this as an ace in the hole—kind of a back-up plan if Ocwen failed to remedy the mess they had caused.

After that things began to move fairly rapidly. On November 18, 2010, Shennan advised us that Ocwen was hastily moving to resolve the matter. According to her they did not want the settlement to be held up. Apparently, a significant portion of their mortgage ownership and involvement was going to be taken over by Chase; however, Chase was adamantly insisting that all of these current litigation issues concerning Ocwen had to be cleared up beforehand. By December 3, 2010, Mr. C. confirmed that they had gotten a refund from the county taxing authority, and those funds were turned over to Rob, who ran them through his trust account and forwarded them to Shennan to be transmitted and re-paid to Ocwen for the taxes it had paid. By December 8, 2010, Shennan confirmed that Ocwen had received and accepted the funds as repayment in full, and then immediately completely reversed all fees, charges, and interest in connection to the incident. All things were put back to normal and the matter was over with, just as our clients had wished.

On December 13, 2010, we received a copy of the entire settlement package, which was at least an inch thick, together with a note to review, make our corrective comments, and to send it back quickly, as it was scheduled to be presented at a hearing in Judge Norgle's court on December 21, 2010, which just so happened to be Rob's birthday—what a coincidentally appropriate birthday present. We reviewed it, making a few very minor corrections, and approved and returned the document. Mrs. C. said I was a prophet, as I had predicted that the MDL cases could be over by the end of the year. I cautioned her that even though the settlement was done, we'd still have to be a bit more patient; as the settlement would still have to be finally approved and then implemented and that this would obviously take some time. Subsequently we received a copy of the final settlement package, which except for a few minor typo-type changes, was virtually a carbon copy of the initial package we received. Included was a copy of Judge Norgle's order preliminarily approving it subject to a concluding fairness hearing that was set for April 15, 2011.

On Valentine's Day, February 14, 2011, our clients notified us that they had received their official claim form pursuant to the settlement. We met with them, helped them fill it out, and sent it back. Of course Mr. & Mrs. C. were naturally curious as to when they could expect their money, and we explained to them that things would be proceeding forward in a usual course, and from now on out it would just be the waiting time for the administration and processing of all the claims to be completed. I smiled and assured them that for all practical purposes it was all over but the shouting. And indeed, in April, 2011, the fairness hearing took place without a hitch and final approval was all but a foregone conclusion.

On May 10, 2011, Mr. C. asked me to make good on my promise and help them get rid of Ocwen and re-finance their mortgage with someone else. Having successfully completed their Chapter 13 plan, they were entitled to be recipients of the Chapter 13 Trustee's credit rehabilitation program, and so I knew finding a decent financial institution would not really be that difficult. Before too long our clients were meeting with Firstmark Credit Union, a very reputable San Antonio financial entity, who was more than willing to assist them. During the interim between the latter part of May, 2011, and the first part of June, 2011, the final moves of the endgame of the chess match against Ocwen were played out. Ocwen had to demonstrate their being a final pain in the butt. With respect to Mr. & Mrs. C.'s mortgage, Ocwen refused to cooperate and provide Firstmark with a mortgage payoff figure, stating that they could not provide that figure due to the fact there was pending litigation. This final hiccup was resolved with nearly simultaneous stern and rebuking communications from Rob and Shennan to the Ocwen attorneys, and the matter was fixed—checkmate!

Ocwen quickly gave Firstmark the requisite mortgage payoff figure, and by June 27, 2011, Mr. & Mrs. C. had a brand new mortgage with Firstmark. Ocwen had been fully paid off and was gone from the picture for good. Goodbye to the mortgage company from hell, and Ocwen was out of their hair forever. Our clients could not have been more pleased.

On July 1, 2011, Judge Norgle signed the final order approving and implementing the MDL settlement with Ocwen. Shortly afterwards, a discussion ensued among the various plaintiffs' attorneys involved in the MDL Ocwen cases. In order to make more funds available and to improve the ability of ordinary class members to better benefit from the settlement, it was proposed that the plaintiffs' attorneys agree to cut their attorneys' fees in half. After some discussion, I'm proud to say that in unanimity every single plaintiff's attorney involved agreed to this and signed off on it.

In July, 2011, and virtually every month thereafter, Mr. C. called me to inquire as to when they could anticipate getting their money. Mr. & Mrs. C. were becoming anxious, for which I couldn't really blame them. After all this year was the eighth anniversary from when this case first began. I advised him that we were keeping on top of the situation, but the administrative process did take some time, and I was hopeful that the money would come before Christmas of that year.

By September 3, 2011, we had finally received our clients' distribution checks for payment of their claims for having served as named plaintiffs in their class action MDL case against Ocwen. Rob and I received our check for attorneys' fees and reimbursement of expenses. A dinner engagement was set up at the Café Milano restaurant in Leon Valley. Rob, Marlene, and I met Mr. & Mrs. C. there and personally presented them with their checks. They were enthralled. We enjoyed a pleasant dinner, reminiscing about some of the happenings and moments we experienced during the course of our multi-year litigation against Ocwen. As we parted I had a good feeling and a sense that justice had been done. Later on that month, the Jewish New Year, Rosh Hashanah, would be upon us, and I recalled and was mindful of the biblical injunction: "Justice, justice shall you pursue." (Deuteronomy 16:18).

On March 2, 2012, I received word that as of that date there were a total of $304,539.62 in unclaimed class settlement checks. I fully understood that the MDL cases against Ocwen had drug on for eight years, and within such a time frame some plaintiffs could die, move away and disappear, or just simply lose interest. Fortunately in our stipulations in the settlement we had provided for such contingencies. Under the equitable doctrine of Cy Pres we had agreed that such unclaimed funds would be distributed to various Legal Aid organizations. After giving the remaining class members an additional 90 days in which to claim their funds, at the expiration of that time, a total in excess of $300,000.00 was paid over to various Legal Aid organizations so as to help them in their future battles on behalf of poor people. I felt a sense of satisfaction in that I guess I had come full circle. My very last case allowed me to participate as a small cog in a larger wheel, whereby the endeavor ended up with a significant contribution to Legal Aid. I guess I remained a "Legal Aid" lawyer after all.

Acknowledgements and Sources of Information

No one is an island, and in the broadest sense we are all connected to one another as members of humankind. Our attitudes and interactions mold and shape our very existence, defining who we are and what we want to be. Although we are powerless to go back in time and change the happenings of history, we can, indeed, change how we respond to history and its evolved status that exists today. How we resolve and act to meet that duty will go a long way in determining the kind of world the future will have in store for the generations yet to come.

In writing this book, I owe a deep debt of gratitude to a number of people to whom I wish to acknowledge and extend my sincere thanks.

First and foremost, to my wife, Marlene, for her continued manifold assistance throughout this undertaking. Her contributions were immeasurable.

To my sons, Rob and Mark, for their skillful editing assistance and for their excellent job in writing the "Forward" for this book.

To my daughter-in-laws, Jennifer and Jen, who are more like daughters; my grandchildren, Hannah, Hayden, Bailey, Maegan; and my God-daughter, Bari, for all of their consistent interest and support.

To all my teachers, but especially John D. Brantley, who solidly placed me on a steady path toward learning.

To all my colleagues, but especially Harry B. Adams III, a lawyer's lawyer, who I was privileged to have had the opportunity to work with.

To Marie A. Failinger, a professor at Hamline University School of Law, who with her book, *The Poverty Law Canon*, re-kindled my interest in my experiences at Legal Aid.

To Katharina Hering, past archivist at the National Equal Justice Library at the Georgetown University Law School, who implanted in me the idea of writing this book.

And to all those who co-operated by responding to inquiries and/or who participated in interviews, to wit: my wife, Marlene Eichelbaum; my son, Rob Eichelbaum; my sister, Sandy Schwartz; my brother-in-law, Leonard Schwartz; Anita Herrera; Harry B. Adams III; Michael Moriarty; Lonnie W. Duke; David J. Garcia; Jeff Skarda; Charles A. Gonzalez; Miriam Goott; and Kevin Robinowich.

Sources of information for this book came from:

1. Personal inquiries I made and/or interviews I had with the aforementioned individuals.

2. Originals and copies of briefs, court hearing transcripts, journals, letters, and notations, which I maintained in my possession.

3. Newspaper articles and press stories and editorials from my personal scrapbook.

4. *Case & Comment*, Volume 75, No. 2, March-April, 1970.

5. National Clearinghouse for Legal Services *Clearinghouse Review*, Vol. 4, No. 9, January 1971.

6. Various issues from *Consumer Bankruptcy News*, including Volume 16, Issue 11, May 11, 2006.

7. *The Poverty Law Canon*, by Marie A. Failinger and Ezra Rosser, University of Michigan Press Ann Arbor, 2016.

8. The documentary movie, *Maxed Out*, by James Scurlock, 2006.

9. Research derived from the Texas State Bar Association information and research site available to member lawyers.

10. Google

11. And last, but not least, my own memory.